THE DAWN OF DEVOTION:

A Sacrifice For Devotional Evolution

LINWOOD JACKSON, JR.

PUBLISHED BY BRILLIANT PUBLISHING, LLC

Contents

Introduction

1. The illustration of the living God's chief apostle suffering crucifixion is a central doctrine of the Bible's philosophy. This is a central doctrine not because it is an illustration to literally worship, but because it is an illustration to philosophically understand.

2. Philosophically, according to the mind inspiring the Bible's context, the living God "taketh not pleasure in the legs of a man."[1] To admit the illustration of this man's crucifixion as being the portrayal of a god-man purging and remanding sin from humanity is to assign to that illustration a context that the scriptures do not support. For while it says, "The Son of man came...to give his life a ransom for many,"[2] the author of the book of Luke, for example, omits this belief. This omission allows us to know that not all of the *gospel* writers believed in a "salvation" through a Jewish demigod, that belief, and many others, needing clarification through the scriptures.

3. The author of the book of Luke did not, according to their narrative, ultimately believe in the theory of salvation and redemption through a supposed Jewish god-man. The author of the book of Luke, despite the presence of their main character highlighting the "kingdom of God" as being an inward experience, believes in *salvation* through the law of Moses. We understand this because, while omitting their main character as sacrificing his life for the *salvation* of many, he is the only author citing the Jewish ceremony revolving around

---

1   Psalm 147:10
2   Mark 10:45

his main character. The author of the book of Luke, that it may be understood that there can be no apparent alleviation from sin without the law, and without honoring its code, promotes the parents of John, and also the parents of their main character, in order to drive home the belief that salvation is only through the law, as being faithful to the law of Moses.

4. What, then, ought we to believe? Are we to believe in a demigod who sacrificed himself so that human beings may be reconciled to his *Father*, or are we to believe that this man was, according to Luke, simply a martyred Jewish prophet, equal to Moses and Elijah, whose death brought no supernatural phenomenon to humanity but who, if following, gave the perfect example, through honoring the law of Moses, of how to honor *God* for "eternal life"? The authors of the *gospels* had specific agendas for their audiences, yet when observing the unfolding of their main character's life through the scriptures, not only will the point of that sacrifice surface, but also the fact of what was actually sacrificed.

5. When it comes to the living God's chief apostle, who is that Prophet prophesied by Moses, the scriptures do not mention him as a *divine* man or being, or as being the *divine Son* of *God*. The Bible does say, "Behold my servant, in whom my soul delighteth; I have put my spirit upon him,"[3] but what does this mean? Is the Bible saying, in mythological terms, that the supposed *immortal* essence of *God* is to fuse with a man? Is the Bible saying, in colorful terms, that *God* himself, through a special material and immaterial aspect of his self was to exist within a man? This is not what the Bible is saying. We understand that this is not what the Bible is saying due to how it says:

6. "And there shall come forth a rod out of the stem of Jesse, and a Branch shall grow out of his roots: and the spirit of the LORD shall rest upon him, the spirit of wisdom and understanding, the spirit of counsel and might, the spirit of knowledge and of the fear of the LORD; and shall make him of quick understanding in the fear of the LORD."[4]

7. When the Bible uses the term "spirit," it actually means "mind," even like as it says, "Be renewed in the spirit of your mind,"[5] or, "Stand fast in one spirit, with one mind striving together."[6]

---

3   Isaiah 42:1
4   Isaiah 11:1-3
5   Ephesians 4:23
6   Philippians 1:27

8. The prophet Isaiah lets us know that the Creator's "spirit" was to rest upon this man. The prophet doesn't leave us guessing as to what this means, letting us know that the knowledge, wisdom, and understanding of the Creator was to rest upon the spirit of this man's mind. That theorized mythological fusion of an aspect of *God* within an aspect of a man by popular theology is actually erroneous, the entrance of the science of the living God's devotional philosophy into this man's mind being the correct understanding.

9. The living God's chief apostle did have the Creator within him, but not in the traditional religious sense. According to the scriptures, the knowledge of the living God was within this man, and that knowledge appearing in no other form than as wisdom. This wisdom actually has an epithet. It says, "They shall call his name Emmanuel, which being interpreted is, God with us."[7]

10. Immanuel means, "God within us." The "with" in the saying, "God with us," actually means "within," in that the saying states, "God is within us." This name, Immanuel, is the "name" of the living God's chief apostle, and "name," to the Bible, means either "doctrine," "word," or concerning spiritual under-standing, "philosophy." This is understood from contrasting two verses: the first, "And hast kept my word, and hast not denied my name";[8] the second, "Thou holdest fast my name, and hast not denied my faith."[9]

11. The living God's present wisdom and knowledge is called "Immanuel." To hear that the Creator's mind was to rest upon this man's mind is to hear that Immanuel, the philosophy of the living God that is to also live within *us*, dwelt within this man's mind. This philosophy of the Creator existing within *us* is also the promise of the new covenant. That promise states: "I will put my law in their inward parts, and write it in their hearts; and will be their God, and they shall be my people. And they shall teach no more every man his neighbour, and every man his brother, saying, Know the LORD."[10]

12. The living God's present wisdom is a philosophy of a certain "law" existing within our inward person. This "law" is called "Immanuel," which wisdom is found prophesied in the saying, "A law shall proceed from me, and I will make my judgment to rest for a light of the people."[11] The living God's chief

---

7   Matthew 1:23
8   Revelation 3:8
9   Revelation 2:13
10   Jeremiah 31:33,34
11   Isaiah 52:4

apostle spoke a "law" or a "judgment" called "Immanuel." This is why it says, "For judgment I am come into this world."[12]

13. What is the "world" this man entered into? The "world" in reference is not the natural biological or ecological world. The definition of the "world," according to the scriptures, is understood from how it says, "I spake openly to the world; I ever taught in the synagogue, and in the temple, whither the Jews always resort; and in secret have I said nothing."[13] The "world" this man is referring to is the religious world, preferably that religious world most familiar to the Jews.

14. Because that "judgment" he spoke is for the religious world, we may know that the "us" the Creator is to exist within is not our literal or natural body. We must remember that "there is a natural body, and there is a spiritual body,"[14] and that if "God is a Spirit,"[15] then "that which is born of the Spirit is spirit."[16] The law of the living God's science is for the body of our faith's thoughts and feelings, or is for our devotional conversation. When it says that the Creator's mind rested upon this man's mind, we ought to therefore know that the scriptures are saying that the conscience of this man's devotional character had the present law or knowledge of the living God's wisdom within it.

15. This isn't, when rationalizing the scriptures, strange to think about. The Bible does not depict that prophesied Prophet as being a demigod, nor do the scriptures portray him as being strict to the law of Moses. The scriptures portray this man possessing a conversation both exercising and demonstrating the law of the living God's new covenant science. Is this not what was prophesied of him? Doesn't it say, "I will raise them up a Prophet from among their brethren, like unto thee, and will put my words in his mouth; and he shall speak unto them all that I shall command him"?[17]

16. This man did speak the living God's words. When he spoke, he taught "Immanuel." Whoever heard him, they heard salvation's new covenant philosophy. It was because of the inward devotional liberation that they heard when he spoke that another "name" found itself linked to him, even like as it says, "Thou shalt call his name Jesus: for he shall save his people from their sins."[18]

---

12   John 9:39
13   John 18:20
14   1 Corinthians 15:44
15   John 4:24
16   John 3:6
17   Deuteronomy 18:18
18   Matthew 1:21

17. This man has two "names," and both are one and the same. Being called "Jesus," which is but seen as being "Joshua," he was so referenced because his doctrine spoke of liberation, and of breaking down *barriers* preventing the living God's entrance. The liberation that "Jesus" taught was liberation from "sin." This liberation is mentioned in the second half of the new covenant's promise:

18. "And they shall teach no more every man his neighbour, and every man his brother, saying, Know the LORD: for they shall all know me, from the least of them unto the greatest of them, saith the LORD: for I will forgive their iniquity, and I will remember their sin no more."[19]

19. "Immanuel," because it is given to "purge your conscience from dead works to serve the living God,"[20] is a philosophy educating on the living God's labor within the conversation's conscience. This labor, because this philosophy is primarily for the conscience of the conversation, is for the eradication of "sin" from that *body* of devotional or spiritual understanding. If faithfully observing that philosophy, the conversation will comprehend the definition of "sin." Comprehending the definition of "sin," the conversation will learn that "Christ hath redeemed us from the curse of the law."[21]

20. From how the New Testament uses the terms "Jesus," or "Christ," it is evident that, this redemption and labor occurring within the conversation, both "Jesus" and "Christ," as terms, are no reference to a person or to a man. Four phrases, when contrasting their context, make this clear: the first, "The Lord Jesus Christ our Saviour";[22] the second, "The commandment of God our Saviour";[23] the third, "The doctrine of God our Saviour";[24] the fourth, "The kindness and love of God our Saviour."[25]

21. Observing these four phrases, and how they are used, it is seen that, while their endings do not change, their beginnings do. The author, by writing in this way, allows the reader to know that "the Lord Jesus Christ," "the doctrine of God," "the commandment of God," and "the kindness of God," are one and the same. "Jesus," "Christ," and "the Lord Jesus Christ," in right context, is not a reference to a man, but to the commandment or doctrine of the living

---

19   Jeremiah 31:34
20   Hebrews 9:14
21   Galatians 3:13
22   Titus 1:4
23   Titus 1:3
24   Titus 2:10
25   Titus 3:4

God's *kindness*. This kindness is for the conversation, to create it "perfect, as pertaining to the conscience."[26]

22. The living God's chief apostle was not literally called *Jesus* or *Jesus Christ*. The living God's chief apostle preached, taught, or lectured on "Jesus." "Jesus," being another *name* for the living God's philosophy, came out of this man's mouth. When this man spoke, the philosophy of Immanuel, which is also a philosophy called "Jesus Christ," came from out of his mouth and was heard and observed by them that heard him.

23. This is necessary to understand because what ought to be seen as being sacrificed was not a man, but rather a conversation. This fact is understood from how it says, "Christ hath redeemed us from the curse of the law, being made a curse for us: for it is written, Cursed is every one that hangeth on a tree,"[27] and, "Having abolished in his flesh the enmity, even the law of commandments contained in ordinances,"[28] and, "Father, into thy hands I commend my spirit."[29]

24. The illustration of the living God's chief apostle crucified is an illustration depicting an exchanging of devotional characters. The physical body of the man, according to the scriptures, is to represent a devotional conversation. Within this one conversation are two devotional philosophies: the first, which is his natural *wisdom*, "You are justified by the law";[30] the second, which is the foundation of the living God's wisdom, "The strength of sin is the law."[31]

25. When seeing that man's body crucified, we are seeing the crucifixion of an unjust and obsolete devotional philosophy. This is understood from how it says, "He that is hanged is accursed of God."[32]

26. To take this man's physical body to be the key to *salvation*, according to the scriptures, should we take the scriptures literally, is to take confidence in what is accursed. To the Bible, this man crucified is no revelation of salvation. To the Bible, the image of him crucified is an image of a man without respect. To take this image as being a literal image of salvation is therefore gross religious error, this image being an illustration of a conversation separated from that accursed religious philosophy governing the religious world.

---

26   Hebrews 9:9
27   Galatians 3:13
28   Ephesians 2:15
29   Luke 23:46
30   Galatians 5:4
31   1 Corinthians 15:56
32   Deuteronomy 21:23

27. The sight of this man crucified articulates the crucifixion of the belief and traditional religious doctrine that *righteousness* and *salvation* appear through the doing of handwritten religious laws. This is why it says, "If righteousness come by the law, then Christ is dead in vain."[33] This man's physical body, as we observe it crucified, is to rightly represent a conversation taking faith in doing a scripted religious routine. Hereafter it is to be understood that "the strength of sin is the law."[34]

28. To find this man's body revived is to find the man's devotional conversation revived. The man himself did not escape death to resurrect from it, but rather the conscience of his conversation resurfaced. This is why it says, "Father, into thy hands I commend my spirit."[35]

29. With the man's body representing his devotional conversation, with that conversation bearing within it two different devotional approaches, the death of that body means the death of a lame devotional conversation, but the regeneration of that body means the regeneration of that conversation kept safe and preserved by the living God's understanding. What we find in the illustration of this man's crucifixion is the exchanging of that philosophy of *righteousness* by what is handwritten for that philosophy of the experience of righteousness through learning of and doing the *law* of the new covenant's promise, or through learning of and doing "Immanuel."

30. What was sacrificed was not a man, but rather a conversation. The living God's chief apostle willingly sacrificed himself as a testimony of his conscience, to show what conversation ought to approach the living God. This was an offering exposing the fraudulence of the philosophy within the religious world and the kind benefit of applying self to the living God's new covenant science. When this man willingly gave himself up to death, it was not to be thought of as him killing himself for humanity's *salvation*, but for willing minds to understand the correct devotional character honoring the living God's science.

31. This fact concerning the ministry of the living God's chief apostle, because the welfare of our devotional character affects our human being, is the fact behind his crucifixion. The presently accursed devotional philosophy, by compelling the person to take *righteousness* through deeds and acts, builds up a certain level of pride within the heart, keeping it from observing no *thing* or no *one* else but self. But when consenting to experience this man's conversation,

---

33   Galatians 2:21
34   1 Corinthians 15:56
35   Luke 23:46

we are consenting to the construction of a devotional character that is able to instruct our human being.

32. Our human condition is on the Bible's mind, and by learning of and exercising self in "Immanuel," which is a philosophy also called "Jesus," just as the living God's chief apostle did, we will fulfill the saying, "God hath not given us the spirit of fear; but of power, and of love, and of a sound mind."[36] This man's death articulates the sharing of his devotional experience, philosophy, and conversation with us. When taking hold of the illustration of this man's crucifixion, we are to observe one dying for the belief that knowing and experiencing salvation's science is the right approach for our faith, and that to do otherwise, namely through handwritten religious laws, is false, leading the person to an erroneous devotional experience.

---

36   2 Timothy 1:7

1

A Doctrine Unfolded

1. Everything changed in the mind of the living God's minister when he left Nazareth. Nazareth is that city of Galilee his *parents* established themselves in.[37] "Jesus came from Nazareth of Galilee"[38] as a minister of a synagogue in Galilee under his *father*, where his understanding on the scriptures developed. After returning from his conflict with that spirit of error, "he came to Nazareth, where he had been brought up: and, as his custom was, he went into the synagogue on the Sabbath day, and stood up for to read."[39]

2. The language used by Luke, in saying, "The synagogue," singles out a peculiar synagogue familiar to the man. What synagogue did he enter? It was one that was not only dear to him, but one where he served a specific role over the people; only certain priests and ministers have rule over the church. Concerning "the Levites that taught the people,"[40] if "they that are of the sons

---

37   Matthew 2:23
38   Mark 1:9
39   Luke 4:16
40   Nehemiah 8:9

1

of Levi"[41] do "receive the office of the priesthood,"[42] and if they "caused the people to understand the law,"[43] it is that to observe this man standing in a synagogue and expounding the scriptures to the people, we are observing a minister of a specific Jewish church leading that assembly in prayerful meditation of that church's faith.

3. It is for this reason that we cannot take the *parents* of this man to be his literal kin, for it says, "Fathers, provoke not your children to anger, lest they be discouraged. Servants, obey in all things your masters according to the flesh."[44] In right context of language, a "father" is a *master*, even as a man once prayed, "O LORD God of my master Abraham."[45] This man was Abraham's chief priest, even "his eldest servant of his house, that ruled over all that he had."[46]

4. The relationship depicted is not natural or biological, but is spiritual, even as it is written, "As a son with the father, he hath served with me in the gospel."[47] Thus, like as Paul writes, "To Titus, mine own son after the common faith,"[48] so also when this man began his public ministry, "Jesus himself began to be about thirty years of age, being (as was supposed) the son of Joseph."[49] Again, this sonship is not typical or ordinary, as a legitimate son to his legitimate father, but is of a servant, a steward, or a scholar to his chief spiritual advisor, as it says, "The small as the great, the teacher as the scholar."[50]

5. Before his public ministry, he elevated the character of his conversation by a private ministry under the direction of *Joseph*, the father of them that were *servants* to his synagogue in Galilee. Thus, taking on one "found with child of the Holy Ghost,"[51] it is evident that this *child* was not Joseph's, but was inherited by him for the good of the *child's* training. Before his time with Joseph, as will be further discussed in other chapters, seeing as how "the love of God is shed abroad in our hearts by the Holy Ghost"[52] one, sharing the present law of the living God's wisdom with him, raised him.

---

41   Hebrews 7:5
42   Hebrews 7:5
43   Nehemiah 8:7
44   Colossians 3:21,22
45   Genesis 24:12
46   Genesis 24:2
47   Philippians 2:22
48   Titus 1:4
49   Luke 3:23
50   1 Chronicles 25:8
51   Matthew 1:18
52   Romans 5:5

6. The reception of the living God's influence is no accidental occurrence, which is why it says, "The Holy Ghost, whom God hath given to them that obey him,"[53] and, "To him that ordereth his conversation aright will I shew the salvation of God."[54] A personal devotional labor is required in order for the conversation to become the living God's creation. The character of one's personal devotional conversation must put off their traditional and superstitious upbringing if knowledge of the Bible's science should guide their heart into the living God's will, which is why it says, "Put off concerning the former conversation the old man, which is corrupt according to the deceitful lusts; and be renewed in the spirit of your mind."[55]

7. Conception occurs only by way of the spirit of the mind, for since "flesh and blood cannot inherit the kingdom of God,"[56] it is absolutely necessary to understand that "that which is born of the Spirit is spirit."[57] "There is a natural body, and there is a spiritual body,"[58] and because "God is a Spirit,"[59] must we lower the living God's person by sensually misinterpreting plain Bible speech? The living God is "the God of the spirits of all flesh,"[60] for even this man, who embraced creation's quickening,[61] is set forth as an example of "the kindness and love of God our Saviour toward man,"[62] seeing as how that "the last Adam was made a quickening spirit."[63] The living God can only conceive within that terrain after its own form, and this *birth* "with the washing of water by the word."[64]

8. Doesn't it say, "Except a man be born of water and of the Spirit, he cannot enter into the kingdom of God"?[65] Well, if "flesh and blood cannot inherit the kingdom of God,"[66] then it is that we must look for another prerequisite form to satisfy criteria for entrance into the decreed experience.

---

53   Acts 5:32
54   Psalm 50:23
55   Ephesians 4:22,23
56   1 Corinthians 15:50
57   John 3:6
58   1 Corinthians 15:44
59   John 4:24
60   Numbers 16:22
61   1 Peter 3:18
62   Titus 3:4
63   1 Corinthians 15:45
64   Ephesians 5:26
65   John 3:5
66   1 Corinthians 15:50

9. The *kingdom* of *God* is no future literal kingdom, for "the kingdom of God cometh not with observation: neither shall they say, Lo here! or, lo there! for, behold, the kingdom of God is within you."[67] The wisdom behind the living God's throne is the *kingdom* of *God*, and the will behind that wisdom is as Paul states: "If the Spirit of him that raised up Jesus from the dead dwell in you, he that raised up Christ from the dead shall also quicken your mortal bodies by his Spirit";[68] this is the *kingdom* and righteousness of *God*.

10. Because the *kingdom* of *God* is not literal, but is a will that must be fulfilled within the spirit of the mind, we also cannot expect the baptism of that will to be literal or physical, "for we know that the law is spiritual."[69] The *kingdom* of *God* is "the law of the Spirit of life,"[70] and the only way to become a creature of the *Spirit* is through mentally and spiritually discerning "the law of truth,"[71] seeing as how "of his own will begat he us with the word of truth, that we should be a kind of firstfruits of his creatures."[72] Thus, it is evident that any conception of the *Spirit* is not physical, but is to be understood as the instruction of the living God's wisdom concerning newness of mind for the organs of the heart.

11. A "child," then, of the *Spirit*, is consequently to be understood as no literal child, for no literal child can mentally discern the *Spirit's* tongue to become a minister of its law. We understand this fact by Samuel, of whom it says, "Samuel ministered before the LORD, being a child, girded with a linen e'phod."[73] No literal little boy is here referenced. Young and old males of fair age obtain passage into the ministry, as it says, "From thirty years old and upward even unto fifty years old, every one that entereth into the service, for the work in the tabernacle of the congregation."[74]

12. To be with child of the Spirit is to have, within the bowls of fellowship, one already trained in the living God's wisdom and experiencing "the mystery of his will, according to his good pleasure which he hath purposed in himself."[75] This minister, before inherited by *Joseph*, was conceived by an *angel* of the

---

67   Luke 17:20,21
68   Romans 8:11
69   Romans 7:14
70   Romans 8:2
71   Malachi 2:6
72   James 1:18
73   1 Samuel 2:18
74   Numbers 4:35
75   Ephesians 1:9

Spirit, for it is written, "The angel came in unto her,"[76] in the same sense that it is written, "And came in unto her, and she conceived by him."[77] Now, an angel is a human messenger of *heaven's* wisdom, as it says, "Who maketh his angels spirits; his ministers a flaming fire."[78] What entered in to *Mary* was, in reality, a spirit, and "a spirit hath not flesh and bones."[79] This is why it is well to understand that a spirit of the living God's *Spirit* is a mind having sober understanding of devotional science, even as it says, "I have filled him with the spirit of God, in wisdom, and in understanding, and in knowledge, and in all manner of workmanship."[80]

13. "A man of understanding is of an excellent spirit,"[81] and the likeness we may draw to such a man is Daniel, for "an excellent spirit, and knowledge, and understanding, interpreting of dreams, and shewing of hard sentences, and dissolving of doubts, were found in the same Daniel."[82] Concerning this man Daniel, one said of him, "O Daniel, servant of the living God,"[83] for this man, being the LORD's servant, was a minister and son of his *Mind*, even as it says, "He that delicately bringeth up his servant from a child shall have him become his son at the length."[84] Thus, a spirit such as Daniel's enlightened the womb of a woman who never had intercourse with a *man*, and a "man" is another term for an angel or a minister, as it says, "Though I speak with the tongues of men and of angels,"[85] and, "We are made a spectacle unto the world, and to angels, and to men."[86]

14. The spirit of a mind inclined to know and to do the living God's benevolent will filled up *Mary's* womb, and if one once said of Paul, "If a spirit or an angel hath spoken to him, let us not fight against God,"[87] it is that a spirit spoke to and consumed Mary's *womb*, and seeing as how "a spirit hath not flesh and bones,"[88] we cannot safely trust that the womb spoken of is not natural. Wisdom

76   Luke 1:28
77   Genesis 38:18
78   Psalm 194:4
79   Luke 24:39
80   Exodus 31:3
81   Proverbs 17:27
82   Daniel 5:12
83   Daniel 6:20
84   Proverbs 29:21
85   1 Corinthians 13:1
86   1 Corinthians 4:9
87   Acts 23:9
88   Luke 24:39

and understanding is not tangible, wherefore it is well to understand that a train of thought was transferred to *Mary*, to the end she "might be filled with the knowledge of his will in all wisdom and spiritual understanding."[89]

15. Now, if it says, "The evil spirit from God came upon Saul, and he prophesied in the midst of the house,"[90] should not Mary prophesy if the angel said, "The Holy Ghost shall come upon thee"?[91] These rules concerning the movement of the spirit remain in tact for her as they did for Saul, meaning that like as Saul prophesied in the midst of the house when moved by a spirit sent from *God*, so also Mary, filled with the living God's *Spirit*, should also utter the knowledge of that Spirit. Herein we understand that "Mary," that "woman" filled with the *spirit* of the *angel*, is in reality a "house," and a house is another name for a church, as it says, "The house of God, which is the church of the living God."[92]

16. If Saul, filled with *God's* spirit, did prophesy in the house, we should also receive word of others prophesying when filled with *God's Spirit*, wherefore Luke records that "when Elisabeth heard the salutation of Mary... Elisabeth was filled with the Holy Ghost: and she spake out with a loud voice."[93] The angel of the spirit says, concerning his manner of erudition, "I shall speak to you either by revelation, or by knowledge, or by prophesying, or by doctrine,"[94] and to hear of a virgin *woman* with *child* of the *Holy Ghost*, it is to hear of a church solely devoted to "the knowledge of the Son of God,"[95] which is the full "law of Christ,"[96] without any traditional or superstitious taint "after the commandments and doctrines of men."[97]

17. Our *Father* appeared to this Jewish *woman* to bear and to prepare "the desire of all nations,"[98] and in the midst of rehearsing to us the history of this man's origin, Luke has disclosed to us a fact of spiritual renewing that cannot be ignored. Conception's process is revealed to us by Mary and Elisabeth's encounter, for Elizabeth was only filled with the Holy Ghost when she heard Mary's salutation. Whatever address Elisabeth heard to have the LORD's Spirit

---

89   Colossians 1:9
90   1 Samuel 18:10
91   Luke 1:35
92   1 Timothy 3:15
93   Luke 1:41,42
94   1 Corinthians 14:6
95   Ephesians 4:13
96   Galatians 6:2
97   Colossians 2:22
98   Haggai 2:7

come upon her, it is the same pleasure that Mary heard to experience the same event. The Spirit does not, cannot, and will not reach into man's natural flesh to accomplish its end, for a line is set: "That which is born of the flesh is flesh; and that which is born of the Spirit is spirit."[99] What filled Elisabeth with the *Spirit* was the knowledge of a doctrine; the wisdom of a saying; and this saying is what the angel first told Mary: "The Lord is with thee."[100]

18. To hear, "The Lord is with thee," it is to hear, "They shall call his name Emman'uel, which being interpreted is, God with us."[101] That spirit entered into Mary's *womb* was a *name*, and "name," in right context, means faith or word, as it says, "Thou holdest fast my name, and hast not denied my faith,"[102] and, "And hast kept my word, and hast not denied my name."[103] The Faith of this salutation is called "Jesus Christ," which is why "the Lord Jesus Christ our Saviour"[104] is, in proper context, "the doctrine of God our Saviour."[105]

19. This is a "doctrine which is according to godliness,"[106] which is why the *angel* told her, "The Lord is with you," for the science of this knowledge within man's inward parts was revealed to her. This doctrine is that *kingdom* where, according to this law of inward creative redemption, we are "to be strengthened with might by his Spirit in the inner man."[107] The might or the power of our conversation's *spirit* is to be "Jesus Christ," and "Jesus Christ" is, again, the *name* of the living God's benevolent wisdom, which is why it says, "Christ the power of God, and the wisdom of God,"[108] and, "Let the word of Christ dwell in you richly in all wisdom."[109]

20. And the law of the *Spirit's* wisdom and instruction is no new understanding, for one man from this minister's line once saluted his men by saying, "The LORD be with you. And they answered him, The LORD bless thee."[110] It is that, at the right time, the living God's wisdom appeared on the earth that "he might gather together in one all things in Christ, both which are in heaven,

---

99   John 3:6
100   Luke 1:28
101   Matthew 1:23
102   Revelation 2:13
103   Revelation 3:8
104   Titus 1:4
105   Titus 2:10
106   1 Timothy 6:3
107   Ephesians 3:16
108   1 Corinthians 1:24
109   Colossians 3:16
110   Ruth 2:4

and which are on earth."¹¹¹ This knowledge of the *Spirit's* will and intention filled *Mary's* bowels, and by her unfermented understanding of this saying, one minister conceived from her *womb* was born, and this man took the saying delivered to her and thoroughly proved it to become the first to experience the full end of its promise, which is why he says, "I know him, and keep his saying."¹¹²

21. Thus, a young steward of the living God's *name*, and the *mother* of his upbringing, were adopted by one called *Joseph*.¹¹³ The man, while joined to this young priest and his *mother*, founded a synagogue in Nazareth of Galilee, where he brought up the young minister as his own son after the common faith. Joined to this man, the youth in training would have the opportunity to understand the religion of David's house in light of the living God's wisdom. Such a house was governed by the law and religion of Moses, and finding himself joined to a man of the Jews' religion, it did not take long for him to realize the depth of the Hebrew religion, wherefore he taught in the synagogue at Nazareth, "Before faith came, we were kept under the law, shut up unto the faith which should afterwards be revealed. Wherefore the law was our schoolmaster to bring us unto Christ, that we might be justified by faith."¹¹⁴

22. With a perspective enlightened on "the time of reformation,"¹¹⁵ He spoke a doctrine that appeared to be at odds with the carnal and flesh-based religion of Moses, preaching, "Are ye so foolish? having begun in the Spirit, are ye now made perfect by the flesh?"¹¹⁶ But not every synagogue could entertain his philosophy. He found, on many occasions, great conflict.¹¹⁷

23. At Nazareth, conversations were unwilling to open up to a higher comprehension of *God's* voice, but when he left the church of Nazareth and entered in to others, his understanding rejuvenated his heart; "from that time Jesus began to preach, and to say, Repent: for the kingdom of heaven is at hand."¹¹⁸ The Jews of Nazareth had crucified the *body* of *God's* knowledge, but in Caper'naum, he found conversations that "begged the body of Jesus,"¹¹⁹ "in that they received the word with all readiness of mind, and searched the scrip-

---

111   Ephesians 1:10
112   John 8:55
113   Luke 1:27
114   Galatians 3:23,24
115   Hebrews 9:10
116   Galatians 3:3
117   Luke 4:28-32
118   Matthew 4:17
119   Matthew 27:58

tures daily, whether those things were so."[120] "Ye received the word of God...
not as the word of men, but as it is in truth, the word of God, which effectually
worketh also in you that believe,"[121] he said to them.

24. "Caper'naum, which is upon the sea coast, in the borders of Zab'ulon
and Neph'thalim,"[122] is located "by the way of the sea, beyond Jordan, Galilee of
the Gentiles."[123] This area is particularly famous for housing Gentile or pagan
converts to the Jews' religion. The living God's chief apostle, after experiencing
their hardheartedness, left those natural Jews of Nazareth and stumbled upon
a synagogue filled with Jewish converts ready to hear, accept, and do, the living
God's will.

25. It is prophesied, "A law shall proceed from me, and I will make my
judgment to rest for a light of the people,"[124] wherefore "leaving Nazareth, he
came and dwelt in Caper'naum, which is upon the sea coast, in the borders
of Zab'ulon and Neph'thalim: that it might be fulfilled which was spoken by
Esa'ias the prophet, saying, The land of Zab'ulon, and the land of Neph'thalim,
by the way of the sea, beyond Jordan, Galilee of the Gentiles; the people which
sat in darkness saw great light; and to them which sat in the region and shadow
of death light is sprung up."[125]

26. In Nazareth, he taught the law of the Creator's benevolence, and there
it was fulfilled, "They crucify to themselves the Son of God afresh, and put him
to an open shame,"[126] but in Caper'naum, Jews, and especially their converts,
received his doctrine. This experience influenced and perfected his speech, for
with Galilee being a location for Gentile converts to Judaism, even though the
elders of the Jews' religion rejected him, "there followed him great multitudes
of people from Galilee, and from Decap'olis, and from Jerusalem, and from
Judae'a, and from beyond Jordan."[127] This Prophet did many great works in
Galilee,[128] for the light of salvation's law shined upon a land perverted by the
Jewish religious world, but there "the power of the Lord was present to heal
them."[129]

---

120   Acts 17:11
121   1 Thessalonians 2:13
122   Matthew 4:13
123   Matthew 4:15
124   Isaiah 51:4
125   Matthew 4:13-16
126   Hebrews 6:6
127   Matthew 4:25
128   Matthew 4:23
129   Luke 5:17

27. Galilee, due to Jewish ignorance, was greatly spoken against, which is why one man, when hearing that one out of Nazareth was thought to be that Christ, said, "Can there any good thing come out of Nazareth?"[130] Because of Galilee's reputation for being an unsavory location, it was hard for Jews to accept the speech and person of any minister from there. "Out of Galilee ariseth no prophet,"[131] believed the Jews, for they had no idea of this man's history, and if they did, they ignored it for whatever prejudice they held against him. For, that little church of Nazareth, it is headed by one who is a son and minister of *David's* devotional character, who is a son of *Abraham's* devotional mind, who is a steward of *Shem's* doctrine, who was *Noah's* understudy, who received his understanding from *E'noch*, who received his knowledge from *Seth*, who was trained by *Adam*, who received his wisdom from the *Mind* of the living Creator.

28. The living God, in the midst of Galilee, cast forth a light "as the stones of a crown, lifted up as an ensign upon his land."[132] "The law is light,"[133] and in the land of Zab'ulon and Neph'thalim, "the law of the Spirit of life"[134] won many synagogues to the living God's new covenant will. It is therefore our responsibility to pass through the same course of this same law to know, for the welfare of those nearest to us, the end of its *kingdom*.

---

130 John 1:46
131 John 7:52
132 Zechariah 9:16
133 Proverbs 6:23
134 Romans 8:2

2

The God Of Our Confidence

1. It is a custom to call *the LORD's Christ, God*, which is why it is well to understand scripture's tongue, to the end we might better know the matter behind reverencing the living God. We understand that our devotion is to the living God not simply because it says, "True worshippers shall worship the Father,"[135] but it is also counseled, "Unto us a child is born, unto us a son is given: and the government shall be upon his shoulder: and his name shall be called Wonderful, Counsellor, The mighty God, The everlasting Father, The Prince of Peace."[136]

2. This child and son, it is his "name" that is to be called *God*, and not the son in and of himself. It is the *name* that makes the person worthy of applause, and not the physical person of that name, for from that *name* the inward person witnesses to the conscience, moving that mind to respect the act of the body above the actor of the body. Right reverence towards the living God's minister is therefore to his *name*; there is no thing more or less than this.

---

135 John 4:23
136 Isaiah 9:6

3. The Bible counsels us that a child is born, and that this child is a son that is given; it is well for us to understand, in right context of language, what a "child" and "son" is, and in what manner he is given, and why. It is then that, after such examination, the prophecy will make sense.

4. It is true that there is only one living God. Isaiah plainly reiterates this fact to us. A "child" is no reference to a literal little child, but rather to a priest, for it says of Samuel, "Samuel ministered before the LORD, being a child, girded with a linen e'phod."[137] For a "child" to be given, it is for a priest to stand before the living God for the good of the assembly, even as Aaron, of whom it says, "Aaron was separated...he and his sons for ever, to burn incense before the LORD, to minister unto him, and to bless in his name for ever."[138] Herein we understand that the vocation of a "child" is that of a "son," and that both are references to being a priest, even as it says, "The children of Aaron, the priests,"[139] and, "The priests, Aaron's sons."[140]

5. To hear of a son or a child given to us, it is to observe the fulfilling of the saying, "I will raise me up a faithful priest, that shall do according to that which is in mine heart and in my mind,"[141] for it is promised, "I will raise them up a Prophet...and he shall speak unto them all that I shall command him."[142] This prophesied son and child, he is that Prophet, and as that Prophet, he is "a merciful and faithful high priest in things pertaining to God,"[143] ministering on the wisdom flowing from out of the living God's direct presence.[144]

6. Thus, as one that "hath an unchangeable priesthood,"[145] "seeing he ever liveth to make intercession,"[146] we can understand the error in taking him to be that *God*, especially since it says of him, "He shall stand and feed in the strength of the LORD, in the majesty of the name of the LORD his God."[147] Again, the *name* of *God's child* is to be that *God*, or a sovereign doctrinal authority, over the worship and service of the assembly, and since this same child educates his host on the Creator's majesty, both the *name* of the *child* and the *name* of its

---

137   1 Samuel 2:18
138   1 Chronicles 23:13
139   Joshua 21:19
140   Leviticus 1:5
141   1 Samuel 2:35
142   Deuteronomy 18:18
143   Hebrews 2:17
144   Hebrews 9:24
145   Hebrews 7:24
146   Hebrews 7:24
147   Micah 5:4

Father are one. The Bible's wisdom perfectly speaks through the pen of Micah, that it is this *child's God* that is to be magnified. He is to draw his flock nearer to the living God, and the only way he can do so is through his *name*, which is why it says of him, "There is none other name under heaven given among men, whereby we must be saved."[148]

7. If our conversation is not lawfully calling on this minister's *name*, it will be impossible to experience that *name's* intended benevolence. Should we execute this *name*, as opposed to sensually worshipping an image of the one that presented this *name*, we would know "the kindness and love of God our Saviour toward man."[149] This good kindness is in the man's *name*, and "name" means "faith," as it says, "Thou holdest fast my name, and hast not denied my faith."[150] If we know the science of the Bible's "faith, and of the knowledge of the Son of God,"[151] we understand that the living God's *name* is preserved by this Prophet's philosophy.

8. How negligent would it be for Aaron to preach, "I am a God, I sit in the seat of God"?[152] "Aaron was separated...to burn incense before the LORD, to minister unto him, and to bless in his name for ever,"[153] wherefore "no man taketh this honour unto himself, but he that is called of God, as was Aaron. So also Christ glorified not himself to be made an high priest; but he that said unto him, Thou art my Son, to day have I begotten thee."[154]

9. Paul rightly connects that Prophet with Aaron because his *name* today, like Aaron of old, blesses the living God's congregation, which is why it is said of him, "Blessed be the King that cometh in the name of the Lord,"[155] and, "Blessed be he that cometh in the name of the LORD: we have blessed you out of the house of the LORD."[156] There is a reason why the psalmist blesses the one appearing in *God's name* from out of *God's* church, and it is because a "king" is an appellation for a priest, as it says, "And hast made us unto our God

---

148   Acts 4:12
149   Titus 3:4
150   Revelation 2:13
151   Ephesians 4:13
152   Ezekiel 28:2
153   1 Chronicles 23:13
154   Hebrews 5:4,5
155   Luke 19:38
156   Psalm 118:26

kings and priests,"[157] and, "The kings of the earth set themselves, and the rulers take counsel together."[158]

10. "The ruler of the house of God"[159] is "also chief governor in the house of the LORD,"[160] which is why it says, "Out of thee shall come a Governor, that shall rule my people Israel,"[161] and, "A child is born, unto us a son is given."[162] As that *child*, he is in no way above the living God in *name*, for "when he saith all things are put under him, it is manifest that he is excepted, which did put all things under him."[163]

11. The office of the living God's chief apostle is strictly ecclesiastical, for the LORD, concerning Aaron's room, once counseled Moses, "Make holy garments for Aaron...that he may minister unto me in the priest's office."[164] Now, what right priest of the LORD would enjoy his congregation worshipping him as *God*? There is a negligent priest "who opposeth and exalteth himself above all that is called God, or that is worshipped; so that he as God sitteth in the temple of God, shewing himself that he is God."[165] Is this character the LORD's minister?

12. There is a profound difference in the two mentioned priests: one will deliver all that come unto *him* by *him*; the other will rescue all that approach the living God by his *name*. Herein we understand that we call the living God a liar, *His* Spirit corrupt, and that chief apostle of no value, when calling that *Man* that *God*, and when refusing to acknowledge the divine right of his *name* over the regeneration and reformation of the spirit of our mind, which is why it says, "The Lord Jesus Christ be with thy spirit."[166] Because "a spirit hath not flesh and bones,"[167] we cannot expect any tangible or carnal thing to suffice. But "the law is spiritual,"[168] and when hopeful to understand what must please our spirit, it is well to remember that "there is a natural body, and there is a spiritual body."[169]

---

157   Revelation 5:10
158   Psalm 2:2
159   1 Chronicles 9:11
160   Jeremiah 20:1
161   Matthew 2:6
162   Isaiah 9:6
163   1 Corinthians 15:27
164   Exodus 28:4
165   2 Thessalonians 2:4
166   2 Timothy 4:22
167   Luke 24:39
168   Romans 7:14
169   1 Corinthians 15:44

13. Because "that which is born of the Spirit is spirit,"[170] and because "a spirit hath not flesh and bones,"[171] for "the Lord Jesus Christ" to be with our spirit, it must be that "the Lord Jesus Christ" is presented in a manner easily accepted by, and in a form similar to, the spirit of our mind. It is for this reason that we are counseled, "Though we have known Christ after the flesh, yet now henceforth know we him no more,"[172] for with *Jesus Christ* being the subject of all *things*,[173] and with creation being no longer physical but inward, "the Lord Jesus Christ our Saviour"[174] is in reality "the commandment of God our Saviour,"[175] which commandment is "the kindness and love of God our Saviour toward man."[176]

14. "Christ" is to be with our spirit, or with the character of our conversation, which fellowship is expressed by the saying, "Unto us a son is given,"[177] for by exercising faith on this man's *name*, which *name* is "the law of truth,"[178] the conversation praying, "Create in me a clean heart, O God; and renew a right spirit within me,"[179] will soon confess, "The law of the Spirit of life in Christ Jesus hath made me free from the law of sin and death."[180] The "name" of this minister is "Jesus Christ," and the living God has given that *name* this appellation because it "shall save his people from their sins,"[181] this is why that *name*, "being interpreted is, God with us."[182]

15. The *name* of the living God's minister is salvation's law working within the inward parts of the person to resurrect the mind for purifying the members of the heart. This is why Paul highlights the resurrection as figuratively illustrating the regeneration of the conversation's mind;[183] this act is the *name* and praise of *God*. The *name* is called "God" because the mediation of this *name's* counsel is terrible against the constitution of our faith's frame. Thus, like as it

---

170   John 3:6
171   Luke 24:39
172   2 Corinthians 5:16
173   Ephesians 3:9
174   Titus 1:4
175   Titus 1:3
176   Titus 3:4
177   Isaiah 9:6
178   Malachi 2:6
179   Psalm 51:10
180   Romans 8:2
181   Matthew 1:21
182   Matthew 1:23
183   Romans 8:11

says, "He is mighty in strength and wisdom,"[184] so it is says, "Christ the power of God, and the wisdom of God";[185] the living God's commandment is to enter into the heart and mind to refresh the natural personal and devotional understanding to better care for the living experience.

16. It is true that the *God* of salvation's assembly is "Jesus Christ." Seeing as how "Jesus Christ" is but the *name* of the living God's wisdom, it is that this wisdom is ordained to reign over the personal devotional conversation. The wisdom makes the living God the focus of the conversation; "God is the LORD";[186] but the *God* regulating the conversation, the *Guide* of the practice, the *Spirit* of the conscience, the *Lord* of the conversation's wellbeing, it is the law of the Bible's *Mind*, which is the *name* of the living God's chief apostle, even as Paul admits, "With the mind I myself serve the law of God,"[187] and, "God is my witness, whom I serve with my spirit in the gospel of his Son."[188]

17. Herein is witnessed the worshipping of "the LORD God of the Hebrews"[189] through the law of this Prophet, and that reverence occurring through the mind and not the body, which is why it says, "Live according to God in the spirit,"[190] and, "Worship God in the spirit."[191] If we honor the living God by the spirit of our mind, we confess to owning a "spirit that confesseth that Jesus Christ is come in the flesh,"[192] but then there are conversations "who confess not that Jesus Christ is come in the flesh. This is a deceiver and an an'tichrist."[193] It is our responsibility to confess that "Christ" is come in to our conversation, and to do so involves risking belief that the *name* of the Creator's Prophet is a personal savior consecrated to forward salvation's science, even like as it says, "Ye have purified your souls in obeying the truth through the Spirit."[194]

18. Seeing as how it is written, "Thy law is the truth,"[195] and, "Thy word is truth,"[196] the reformer's assignment is to firstly obey the law of the living

---

184 Job 36:5
185 1 Corinthians 1:24
186 Psalm 118:27
187 Romans 7:25
188 Romans 1:9
189 Exodus 9:1
190 1 Peter 4:6
191 Philippians 3:3
192 1 John 4:2
193 2 John 1:7
194 1 Peter 1:22
195 Psalm 119:142
196 John 17:17

God's *name* by their mind and then through the body, for the mind must have knowledge to experiment with in order to develop a "faith which worketh by love."[197] He or she learning of and executing the wisdom maintained within the scriptures will have defined to their mind the Creator's *name*, which is why it says, "To him that ordereth his conversation aright will I shew the salvation of God."[198] It is "the spirit of wisdom and revelation in the knowledge of him"[199] that allows the conversation to obtain "his Father's name written in their foreheads."[200]

19. Conversations confessing the living God's benevolence will experiment with faith on the mediation of that will for knowledge, but that mind of an'tichrist will not learn of salvation's commandment, refusing to bring into their heart any sober thing. There is then a major difference between the conversation honoring the *name* of the living God's chief apostle and the conversation inordinately affectionate towards the man, for while one, being filled with the Creator's wisdom is experiencing the newness attached to its *name*, the other "feedeth on ashes: a deceived heart hath turned him aside, that he cannot deliver his soul, nor say, Is there not a lie in my right hand?"[201]

20. "We have received a commandment from the Father"[202] concerning a *name*, which *name* is not of ashes, that is, of perpetual *death*, but is a *name* escaped from *death* and consecrated with a ministry over death, whose mediation is blessed for newness of mind and character, seeing as how, concerning this *name*, "it pleased the Father that in him should all fulness dwell."[203] If we lawfully call on this *name*, rightly examining and doing the law of its intercession, we will understand that it is only a vehicle to lead us in to the living God's *name*. This is that *name* praying, "Holy Father, keep through thine own name those whom thou hast given me,"[204] for we are, through this man's *name*, to know and love the living *Mind* within the Bible, "and this is love, that we walk after his commandments."[205]

---

197 Galatians 5:6
198 Psalm 50:23
199 Ephesians 1:17
200 Revelation 14:1
201 Isaiah 44:20
202 2 John 1:4
203 Colossians 1:19
204 John 17:11
205 2 John 1:6

21. The *name* of the living God's Prophet should be *God* leading us to "the LORD, the most high God, the possessor of heaven and earth."[206] The conversation passing through their faith's higher learning will know that there is only one Creator, and that "Jesus Christ" regulates this living experience.[207] Conversations passing through this experience will understand why it says, "Put off concerning the former conversation the old man, which is corrupt according to the deceitful lusts; and be renewed in the spirit of your mind."[208]

22. As we allow our mind to understand the Bible's wisdom, faithfulness to the living God will be the delight of our conversation, even as one after the same ambition once prayed, "I will meditate in thy precepts, and have respect unto thy ways."[209] If we patiently and temperately learn to call the *name* of the living God's chief apostle that mighty *God* over the organs of our heart and mind, we will demonstrate our love for the Creator of this wisdom by keeping His commandments, and "we do know that we know him, if we keep his commandments."[210]

23. We therefore demonstrate that we do not know the living God when sensually honoring *His Son*. Our flesh-based conversation reveals blatant offense against the mind at the core of the scriptures, wherefore it is written, "Great peace have they which love thy law: and nothing shall offend them."[211]

24. No thing within the scriptures will offend the doer of salvation's law because they are passed through an education refreshing and reforming their mind on its character. Examining self through this assignment creates a device within the mind where the knowledge retained by faith's exercise is weighed against self-cultivated and inherited tradition. Liberty of conscience from the weight of self's irrational heart and the religious world's policies is the end of "Jesus Christ," for by a mind renewed in knowledge through this *name*, a clearer perception of the living God's intention will soberly draw the heart nearer to the throne of its origin, causing the person to fulfill the vision, "Therefore are they before the throne of God, and serve him day and night in his temple: and he that sitteth on the throne shall dwell among them."[212]

---

206   Genesis 14:22
207   1 Corinthians 8:6
208   Ephesians 4:22,23
209   Psalm 119:15
210   1 John 2:3
211   Psalm 119:165
212   Revelation 7:15

25. By allowing the *name* of this man to wonderfully counsel the heart and inward person, the *God* and Supreme Instructor of the character's illness is revealed, moving it to pray, "I bow my knees unto the Father of our Lord Jesus Christ,"[213] and, "The LORD he is God: it is he that hath made us, and not we ourselves."[214] This knowledge allows us to discern the wisdom of our upbringing, that it does not lie when saying, "Beside me there is no God."[215]

213   Ephesians 3:14
214   Psalm 100:3
215   Isaiah 44:6

3

I Am

1. There appears to be a bit of confusion surrounding how that "Jesus said unto them, Verily, verily, I say unto you, Before Abraham was, I am."[216] This verse, taken alone, will draw the mind to cast upon the canvas of the imagination a sketch that is bright and colorful.

2. All things in the Bible "are spiritually discerned,"[217] meaning that when hopeful to comprehend any *thing* within it, "comparing spiritual things with spiritual"[218] is the best route. If we would investigate the language preceding this quoted statement, we would find that the context is not in reference to any supposed days of existence, but that these words are rather based upon a saying, showing that Abraham can be seen.

3. To the Jews, when once age has reached a certain season; fifty years old; Abraham can be observed, which is why they said, "Thou art not yet fifty years old, and hast thou seen Abraham?"[219] We may read the Jews as sarcastically

---

216   John 8:58
217   1 Corinthians 2:14
218   1 Corinthians 2:13
219   John 8:57

20

insulting this man over his claim of seeing Abraham, for Abraham had not been dead for fifty years, but rather for over one thousand. "How can such a young man, not even fifty years old, see one that has long since been dead?" they thought, but the issue at hand was not over literal years of existence. The living God's chief apostle made no claim of literal years, but said, "If a man keep my saying, he shall never see death."[220]

4. We, when hearing him speak, must always remember how it says, "He whom God hath sent speaketh the words of God."[221] Because "God is a Spirit,"[222] it is well to remember that for him to speak the living God's words, it is for him to speak the character of the mind within those words. The Jews misunderstood his speech because he spoke the living God's mind, and we must remember that "the natural man receiveth not the things of the Spirit of God: for they are foolishness unto him: neither can he know them, because they are spiritually discerned."[223]

5. The Jews did not perceive his words and had no thought for the context in which he spoke because they were yet natural or sensual in their spiritual understanding. All throughout this discourse in the final verses of the eighth division of the book of John, he says such things as, "Why do ye not understand my speech? even because ye cannot hear my word,"[224] and, "If I say the truth, why do ye not believe me?"[225] and, "Ye therefore hear them not, because ye are not of God."[226] Again, to be of "God" is to be of the "Spirit," to be conceived of and educated by the living God's mind, and this birth, because "that which is born of the Spirit is spirit,"[227] is not physical or fleshly. To be of the *Spirit* of *God* means to own a mind according to the *Mind* at the core of the scriptures, and this man possessed that mind. This "mind" is a "saying," and he kept and dressed his conversation by it, which is why he says, "I know him, and keep his saying."[228]

6. It is a greater mystery that he should know the LORD; of whom it says, "Art thou not from everlasting, O LORD my God";[229] than that he should have

220 John 8:51
221 John 3:34
222 John 4:24
223 1 Corinthians 2:14
224 John 8:43
225 John 8:46
226 John 8:47
227 John 4:6
228 John 8:55
229 Habakkuk 1:12

seen and known Abraham, yet the Jews fail to pick up this thought. They passed over this incredible statement because their heart was insulted over the claim that he had made about the supposed *father* of their tradition. They missed the wisdom pouring forth from his mouth because their pioneer had supposedly come under attack. He did not speak any bad thing against Abraham, for if they actually maintained Abraham's mind, they would have accomplished Abraham's labor to know his speech through "the faith of Abraham; who is the father of us all."[230]

7. Language is terribly important when hopeful to understand just what the scriptures are saying, wherefore when we hear such things as, "Your father Abraham rejoiced to see my day,"[231] and, "If I honour myself, my honour is nothing,"[232] and, "Art thou greater than our father Abraham, which is dead? and the prophets are dead: whom makest thou thyself?"[233] as students of the Bible, we must pick up its pattern language if we should know what is said. The controversy between this man and the Jews is over doctrine. We understand this from how he says, "If a man keep my saying, he shall never taste of death."[234]

8. While the Jews took this speech to be literal he, having kept the saying of the living Creator, and having full knowledge of the will within that saying, spoke of an ever-during life-current to appear within the inward parts by the execution of that will. Now, Abraham, being *God's* man, spoke a doctrine through circumcision, and this doctrine could not do what it ultimately foreshadowed, for by this physical act, it was preached that "circumcision is that of the heart, in the spirit."[235] What the LORD physically gave Abraham was a spiritual doctrine to appear at a later date and under a better covenant functioning under a better ministry and *Mediator*.

9. This baptism by circumcision was the chain believed to link the seed of Abraham to *heaven's* throne, but circumcision was only the means whereby every minister should remember how it was said of their father, "Abraham obeyed my voice."[236] Abraham received the sign of circumcision because he was a partaker of the LORD's righteousness by faith on the LORD's *voice* of

---

230 Romans 4:16
231 John 8:56
232 John 8:54
233 John 8:53
234 John 8:52
235 Romans 2:29
236 Genesis 26:5

promise. It is well to remember that Abraham wasn't born into the knowledge of circumcision.[237]

10. If the living God's chief minister is saying, "I know him, and keep his saying,"[238] and if he tells us of himself by saying, "Him hath God the Father sealed,"[239] then it is an indisputable fact that this man was *circumcised* to the living Father. Bearing in mind that "circumcision is that of the heart, in the spirit,"[240] he fully obeyed Abraham's doctrine and perfected his conversation through the faith of Abraham, and this he did by cooperating with the Creator's commandment through the spirit of his mind, which is why it says, "Be ye transformed by the renewing of your mind, that ye may prove what is that good, and acceptable, and perfect, will of God."[241]

11. Circumcision is today mental and inward.[242] For this cause, we cannot ignore the fact that "whosoever believeth that Jesus is the Christ is born of God,"[243] for if he says, "I proceeded forth and came from God,"[244] then he openly admits birth to *God*, and if born of the *Spirit*, then he openly admits his devotion to actively believing on "Jesus Christ."

12. The saying that he kept is called "Jesus Christ." If he says of himself, "A man that hath told you the truth,"[245] if "the truth is in Jesus"[246] and it says, "Thy word is truth,"[247] and, "Thy law is the truth,"[248] then the "truth," preached by this minister, which saying he also kept, is a commandment and "law of truth."[249] This is why he says, "I speak that which I have seen with my Father,"[250] and, "He gave me a commandment, what I should say, and what I should speak."[251]

13. Like as he was given a commandment to keep for him to know the living God's *name*, so too through his ministry "we have received a commandment

---

237   Romans 4:9,10
238   John 8:55
239   John 6:27
240   Romans 2:29
241   Romans 12:2
242   Galatians 6:15
243   1 John 5:1
244   John 8:42
245   John 8:40
246   Ephesians 4:21
247   John 17:17
248   Psalm 119:142
249   Malachi 2:6
250   John 8:38
251   John 12:49

from the Father"[252] concerning the manner of conversation we ought to adopt.[253] In order to be born of the *Spirit*, it is necessary to keep the saying of the *Spirit's* commandment, which saying is "the law of the Spirit of life."[254] Every right mind is conceived by this law "according to the promise of life which is in Christ Jesus,"[255] making Paul's language, and the context in which he speaks of "Christ Jesus," crucial to our understanding of what promise of life exists through "Christ."

14. Seeing as how "the Spirit is life because of righteousness,"[256] the promise to be received through the Spirit is the Spirit's righteousness, which is why it says, "The blessing of Abraham might come on the Gentiles through Jesus Christ; that we might receive the promise of the Spirit through faith."[257] Abraham's blessing was circumcision, and the means he obtained that circumcision was through active faith on his LORD's promise. Our circumcision; which is within the inward parts of the conversation; is by the same means, for like as how Abraham exercised faith on a saying to receive the praise of that saying, so we today have received a commandment to receive the end of that saying, which saying is called, "Jesus Christ."

15. We receive blessing only through doing "Jesus Christ," and seeing as how this blessing is not fleshly, as was Abraham's, "Jesus Christ" should not be thought of any fleshly thing, and this is why Paul teaches, "Henceforth know we no man after the flesh: yea, though we have known Christ after the flesh, yet now henceforth know we him no more. Therefore if any man be in Christ, he is a new creature."[258]

16. Newness of devotional thought and feeling is the end of "Jesus Christ," wherefore if the saying and commandment of the living God's minister preaches this newness, then it is well to understand that "the Lord Jesus Christ our Saviour"[259] is, in reality, "the commandment of God our Saviour,"[260] which is "the doctrine of God our Saviour."[261] Because "there is a natural body, and

---

252   2 John 1:4
253   2 Peter 1:3
254   Romans 8:2
255   2 Timothy 1:1
256   Romans 8:10
257   Galatians 3:14
258   2 Corinthians 5:16,17
259   Titus 1:4
260   Titus 1:3
261   Titus 2:10

there is a spiritual body,"[262] and because "that which is born of the Spirit is spirit,"[263] the doctrine of the living God's saying is not, nor can it ever be, firstly for the natural body, but for the organs of the mind. Him saying, "The words that I speak unto you, they are spirit,"[264] witness to this fact.

17. Conception, because it is wholly mental; as it says of this creation, "To be strengthened with might by his Spirit in the inner man";[265] must occur by exercising faith on a commandment. If our aim is for this *baptism*, the spirit of our faith's mind must find itself immersed within the living God's saying, to the end "he might sanctify and cleanse it with the washing of water by the word."[266] Therefore, because the will of our Father is the resurrection of the inward person, the "eternal life" spoken of and promised to the doer of this commandment must not find itself outside of the context in which it is spoken. This is why he says, "If a man keep my saying, he shall never see death."[267]

18. The "death" spoken of is not literal, as in a passing away of the person from physical life and mental consciousness. This "death" is philosophical in context of language, and being so, it is defined according to the saying, "Without understanding; which have eyes, and see not; which have ears, and hear not,"[268] and, "They have not known nor understood: for he hath shut their eyes, that they cannot see; and their hearts, that they cannot understand."[269]

19. The "death" spoken of is to "the eyes of your understanding,"[270] which is why the recovering conversation, that it "might be filled with the knowledge of his will in all wisdom and spiritual understanding,"[271] prays, "Lighten mine eyes, lest I sleep the sleep of death."[272] Because it is the living God's will to "purge your conscience from dead works to serve the living God,"[273] he says, "If a man keep my saying, he shall never see death."[274] If "the spirit giveth life,"[275] then it is that the living God's will is in administering perpetual *life* for the good of the

---

262   1 Corinthians 15:44
263   John 3:6
264   John 6:63
265   Ephesians 3:16
266   Ephesians 5:26
267   John 8:51
268   Jeremiah 5:21
269   Isaiah 44:18
270   Ephesians 1:18
271   Colossians 1:9
272   Psalm 13:3
273   Hebrews 9:14
274   John 8:51
275   2 Corinthians 3:6

conversation's members, which is why it says, "This is the will of God, even your sanctification...that every one of you should know how to possess his vessel in sanctification and honour."[276]

20. Abraham's circumcision could not do this for anyone, and proof is in the rationale of the Jews who said, upon hearing this doctrine of the conversation's course for everlasting care, "Now we know that thou hast a devil. Abraham is dead, and the prophets; and thou sayest, If a man keep my saying, he shall never taste of death."[277] Why didn't these priests, upon hearing, "Your father Abraham rejoiced to see my day,"[278] say, "He could not have seen you, for he was before us"? Why was it more of a wonder to hear of one drawn from the past, and not of one observing the future from the past? Abraham saw this man's *day*, and again, the language isn't literal.

21. The "day of Christ" is "the acceptable year of the Lord";[279] neither the "day" or the "Christ" mentioned are literal terms. "The acceptable year of the LORD, and the day of vengeance of our God,"[280] is one dispensation "to bind up the brokenhearted, to proclaim liberty to the captives, and the opening of the prison to them that are bound."[281] This work is not a physical work, for the year of "Christ" is no literal year, but is a doctrinal reign or appointment. Abraham saw the service of "Jesus Christ" through his devotional conversation.[282] To have seen "Jesus Christ" means to have experienced a peculiar type of learning for a peculiar type of benefit, and by his faith, Abraham saw and experienced "the Lord Jesus Christ our Saviour,"[283] which is, in all actuality, the experience of "the kindness and love of God our Saviour toward man."[284]

22. The entire point of the living God's present commandment is for our conversation to possess a new and personal devotional character.[285] When we hear how it is said of Abraham, "Abraham obeyed my voice, and kept my charge, my commandments, my statutes, and my laws,"[286] we may know that "Jesus Christ" labored within the spirit of his mind. Circumcision of his flesh

---

276   1 Thessalonians 4:3,4
277   John 8:52
278   John 8:56
279   Luke 4:19
280   Isaiah 61:2
281   Isaiah 61:1
282   James 2:23
283   Titus 1:4
284   Titus 3:4
285   Ezekiel 36:26,27
286   Genesis 26:5

did not do this, but rather consistent and unswerving obedience to the living God's *voice*.[287]

23. This man honored this promise with his entire mind, "and being not weak in faith...he staggered not at the promise of God through unbelief; but was strong in faith, giving glory to God."[288] By exercising faith on this promise, Abraham's heart was made to go through a process of pruning and purging, whereby at the end of this training his conversation may sincerely celebrate the *God* of that promise. Abraham only received the sign of the LORD's praise because of the inward baptism he had long since experienced. When we observe the fact that Abraham honored every word of *God*, we may know that it was due to no fleshly labor, but rather "the work of faith with power."[289]

24. If the Jews had correctly heard the living God's minister, they would have understood that the temporal doctrine of Abraham, when spiritually executed as he first executed it, should never have let any conversation fail of the intended edification, but because they indulged only in the act of a tradition, the effect of that blessing could find no place in their heart. Foolishly, then, they took his speech as a reference to his physical body. "Obey my doctrine and receive eternal life in some plane of existence beyond this one," they heard, yet by their response, although "they understood not this saying, and it was hid from them, that they perceived it not,"[290] their belief about what occurs after death is revealed, which belief Peter also shares.

25. "Abraham is dead and not even circumcision could halt this in him," they thought, for Abraham was nowhere but in the ground. Peter also, when discussing his argument on the resurrection, cancelled out any thought for any sphere of action for man after death.[291] Peter leaves no room for the thoughtful mind to believe that David, in his prophecy, spoke of himself somehow found at *God's* right hand. This is why he says, "Therefore being a prophet...he seeing this before spake of the resurrection of Christ."[292] Thus, like as Abraham saw the *day* of the living God's minister, and he saw Abraham's, this vision is not of literal sight, but of mentally discerning the revelation of the *name* "Jesus Christ."

---

287   Romans 4:18
288   Romans 4:19,20
289   Romans 4:19,20
290   Luke 9:45
291   Acts 2:29
292   Acts 2:30,31

26. Abraham did see this man's *day*, for his *day* is the fulfillment of the charge, "Worship him that made heaven, and earth, and the sea, and the fountains of waters."[293] Hearing that Abraham obeyed every word given by the *Mind* within the scriptures, we are but observing one experiencing the end of salvation's commandment to know "the mystery of his will, according to his good pleasure which he hath purposed in himself."[294] Thus, when the Jews, now inwardly disturbed because of their inability to rightly hear that voice, heard this man's philosophy, "then took they up stones to cast at him."[295]

27. The discussion between him and the Jews is not over the physical estate of man, but when they said, "Whom makest thou thyself?"[296] it is a reference to speech or *name*. One's "name" does not point to one's literal name, but "name" means doctrine, as it says, "And hast kept my word, and hast not denied my name,"[297] and, "Thou holdest fast my name, and hast not denied my faith."[298] The Jews' examination is concerned with his *name*, or with the doctrine that he taught. For them to say, "Whom makest thou thyself?"[299] it is for them to question the *name* that he stood by, for it appeared to them that he had insulted the *name* of Abraham. To this end he says, "It is my Father that honoureth me,"[300] which is why he then says, after the Jews took the weight of Abraham's religion to be greater than that of the living God's, "Before Abraham was, I am."[301]

28. These words are a confession of devotional philosophy. "Abraham," as it is here used, is no reference to a literal man, but to "the steps of that faith of our father Abraham,"[302] which are "the works of Abraham."[303] The entire discussion between this man and the Jews hinges upon the application of a saying; "If a man keep my saying, he shall never see death,"[304] he says; therefore when discerning just what he means by saying, "Before Abraham was, I am,"[305]

---

293   Revelation 14:7
294   Ephesians 1:9
295   John 8:59
296   John 8:53
297   Revelation 3:8
298   Revelation 2:13
299   John 8:53
300   John 8:54
301   John 8:58
302   Romans 4:12
303   John 8:39
304   John 8:51
305   John 8:58

it is well to take into account the context in which he speaks, and of what direction his words point to.

29. Before "Abraham" existed, "I Am" existed, that is, before the manners of Abraham were picked up by the man Abraham for others after him to follow, the manners of him that claimed to be that "I Am" transcend whatever man or father should ever concoct. When we hear "Abraham" and "I Am," we should not think sensually, but rather philosophically, in terms of *name* or faith, and this we should do because it is written, "God said unto Moses, I AM THAT I AM..."[306]

30. Herein we observe "the LORD God of the Hebrews"[307] stating his *name*, for when Moses said to the people, "I AM hath sent me unto you,"[308] it is that he said, "The LORD God of the Hebrews hath met with us."[309] Our responsibility, then, is towards the *name* of the LORD, for his *name* is "I Am," and when this man says that before Abraham existed there was nothing but "I Am," we must come up higher in our thinking. Thus, to hear, "I Am," is to hear, "He is the living God, and stedfast for ever, and his kingdom that which shall not be destroyed, and his dominion shall be even unto the end."[310]

31. The *name* of the LORD, which is, "I Am," signifies his claim to his throne's steadfastness, and to the perpetuity of his reign on earth and in heaven. We cannot know this fact of his *name* but through another *name*, which is why it says, "They shall call his name Emman'uel, which being interpreted is, God with us."[311]

32. The *name* of the living God's chief apostle is, "God with us," and because "God is a Spirit,"[312] his *name* or philosophy is, "The Spirit is with us." To discern the living God's *name*, that his words and mind is of imperishable power and understanding, the *name* of his *Spirit* or understanding must find itself examined and executed, which is why it says, "He that doeth the will of God abideth for ever."[313] That "I Am" is the living God's doctrine placing within the doer of that philosophy an unceasing *substance* to grant uninterrupted power to resurrect and reform the inward parts. This is the Creator, *name*, *kingdom*, and

---

306   Exodus 3:14,15
307   Exodus 3:18
308   Exodus 3:14
309   Exodus 3:18
310   Daniel 6:26
311   Matthew 1:23
312   John 4:24
313   1 John 2:17

praise, which is why it says, "Blessed be the name of the LORD from this time forth and for evermore."[314]

33. The will of this *name* can only be discerned through the *name* of his chief messenger, which is why it says, "There is none other name under heaven given among men, whereby we must be saved."[315] His *name* is the living God's law "of the faith, and of the knowledge of the Son of God,"[316] which is why it says, "He that hath the Son hath life,"[317] and, "He that believeth on the Son of God hath the witness in himself,"[318] and, "It is the Spirit that beareth witness, because the Spirit is truth."[319]

34. Again, if it says, "Thy word is truth,"[320] and, "Thy law is the truth,"[321] if the Spirit is truth, then the Spirit is law, and if the Spirit's law bears witness to our *circumcision*, and if that circumcision is within the spirit of the mind, then because "the Spirit is life,"[322] our consent to do this man's knowledge is the means whereby we may know that "to us there is but one God, the Father, of whom are all things, and we in him; and one Lord Jesus Christ, by whom are all things, and we by him."[323]

35. Creation is by "Jesus Christ"; the living God has "created all things by Jesus Christ."[324] Seeing as how this manner of creation is not natural; as it says, "Create in me a clean heart, O God; and renew a right spirit within me";[325] "Jesus Christ" can only administer life to the mind, rendering, again, "the Lord Jesus Christ our Saviour"[326] as "the commandment of God our Saviour,"[327] and our executing this commandment the means to receive the intention constrained to it, which is knowledge that "before Abraham was, I am."[328]

36. The reason he could say that the keeping of his saying meant liberty from *death* was because his saying was the living God's *name*, which is why

---

314   Psalm 113:2
315   Acts 4:12
316   Ephesians 4:13
317   1 John 5:12
318   1 John 5:10
319   1 John 5:6
320   John 17:17
321   Psalm 119:142
322   Romans 8:10
323   1 Corinthians 8:6
324   Ephesians 3:9
325   Psalm 51:10
326   Titus 1:4
327   Titus 1:3
328   John 8:58

he says, "I know that his commandment is life everlasting."[329] His obedience to this commandment; as it says, "The commandment of the everlasting God, made known to all nations for the obedience of faith";[330] is what allowed him to understand the promise given to every doer of it. Thus, his own experience with salvation's will confessed to him, "Of his own will begat he us with the word of truth, that we should be a kind of firstfruits of his creatures."[331]

37. There is no other wisdom in existence than that "I Am," and we can only know this fact by passing through its science to sincerely pray, "Thy righteousness is an everlasting righteousness, and thy law is the truth."[332] The living God's *name* is a law of the everlasting devotional wellbeing, which is why every student-patient of this knowledge knows, "Ye have purified your souls in obeying the truth through the Spirit."[333] The controversy within the eighth division of the book of John is between the limited doctrine of *men* and the unbounded wisdom of creation.[334] Therefore before Abraham's *name*, and before "every name that is named, not only in this world, but also in that which is to come,"[335] only one *name* is permanently fixed, which *name* the living God's chief apostle pronounces for us as, "I Am."

38. If the Jews would have carefully accomplished the wisdom of Abraham, they would have heard him say, "If God were your Father, ye would love me: for I proceeded forth and came from God."[336] The "me" referenced is not the man, but he says, "He that rejecteth me, and receiveth not my words."[337] The subject of his speech is the instruction or counsel that came out of his mouth. "He that hath received his testimony hath set to his seal that God is true,"[338] and the testimony to be received is not physical or tangible, "for he whom God hath sent speaketh the words of God."[339]

39. To receive and believe on "Jesus Christ" is to learn of and do a *name*, which is why it says, "As many as received him...even to them that believe on

---

329   John 12:50
330   Romans 16:26
331   James 1:18
332   Psalm 119:142
333   1 Peter 1:22
334   2 Timothy 2:9
335   Ephesians 1:21
336   John 8:42
337   John 12;48
338   John 3:33
339   John 3:34

his name,"[340] and, "That believing ye might have life through his name."[341] "I Am" is to be the *name* that we are all to know through "the excellency of the knowledge of Christ,"[342] which is why he prayed, "Holy Father, keep through thine own name those whom thou hast given me."[343] The Word made flesh is the will of the Father for us all, which is why "we have received a commandment from the Father"[344] to own a "spirit that confesseth that Jesus Christ is come in the flesh."[345] The Word in flesh is "Jesus Christ" appearing to the conversation's members, and again, neither the "Word" nor "Jesus Christ" is a literal reference to any *thing* but to salvation's law.[346]

40. The point of "Jesus Christ" is a course of learning "through sanctification of the Spirit and belief of the truth."[347] Such learning places into the conversation "the grace of life,"[348] for it is "the grace of God that bringeth salvation."[349]

41. The intended salvation, being strictly for the conversation's inward parts, is perfected by *grace* within the spirit of the mind, which is why it says, "The grace of our Lord Jesus Christ be with your spirit."[350] Seeing, then, as how justification is through knowledge,[351] we are rightly counseled, "Grow in grace, and in the knowledge of our Lord and Saviour Jesus Christ."[352] If the Jews had properly developed their conversation, they would have received Abraham's blessing to discern the Prophet's mind. So too we, if we fail to know the living God's *name*, it will be very difficult for us to not only receive the *name* of his chief witness, but to also experience the point of that *name*.

---

340   John 1:12
341   John 20:31
342   Philippians 3:8
343   John 17:11
344   2 John 1:4
345   1 John 4:2
346   Romans 7:14
347   2 Thessalonians 2:13
348   1 Peter 3:7
349   Titus 2:11
350   Philemon 1:25
351   Proverbs 11:9
352   2 Peter 3:18

4

A Name To Wait On

1. From what has thus far been reviewed, it is fair to conclude that there is no such thing as the living God's *Spirit* naturally impregnating human flesh; "this wisdom descendeth not from above, but is earthly, sensual, devilish."[353] We understand that it is wholly erroneous to think such a thing because if this were the case, the living God would have somehow told us so. Proof of this fact is found in the saying, "The Spirit like a dove descending upon him,"[354] and, "I saw the Spirit descending from heaven like a dove,"[355] and, "The Holy Ghost descended in a bodily shape like a dove upon him."[356]

2. In every one of these quotes, the *Spirit* of *God* is spoken of as picking up a physical nature. To be in a bodily shape is to be in the corporeal, actual, tangible, fleshly form, for the body mentioned is unspiritual. This plain language is not the same language used in reference to the birth of the living God's man,

353   James 3:15
354   Mark 1:10
355   John 1:32
356   Luke 3:22

for it was said to Mary, "The power of the Highest shall overshadow thee."[357] Nowhere, from Genesis to Malachi, is there any written record of the *Holy Ghost* descending from *heaven* in the bodily form of a man, or as any *thing* mixed with flesh, for such a record, being nowhere mentioned or even hinted at, is but an invention.[358] If the Bible would have us think a certain way about this man, it would have plainly directed our mind into that manner.

3. Now, seeing as how there is "one Spirit,"[359] even "one Spirit unto the Father,"[360] if "the Holy Ghost descended in a bodily shape like a dove upon him,"[361] should the Spirit of *God* now take up two fleshly forms? There is only one Spirit,[362] so if this man is sensually become the fleshly embodiment of the *Holy Ghost*, and the same *Holy Ghost*, falling upon him in the bodily shape of an animal is become another fleshly embodiment at the same time, then there is more than one Spirit. Again, there is only one *Spirit* because there is only one *Father* of that Spirit.[363] If this man is carnally that Spirit in human flesh, and that dove is the same Spirit in that flesh, then there is clearly an issue.

4. The *Holy Ghost* not only descending in the bodily shape of a dove, but found resting on this man, witnesses to the fact that this Spirit, if ever desiring to physically interact with flesh, must become flesh, therefore to impregnate flesh it must become flesh, and secondly, that if found without and physically upon the man, it is that *it* is not literally or actually within the man in any lewd or pagan fashion. This is true, and it is true because it says, "That which is born of the flesh is flesh; and that which is born of the Spirit is spirit."[364] Thus, when thinking on the manner of this man's *birth*, it is not that the *Spirit* descended in a bodily form, but that the *Holy Ghost* conceived him within the spirit of his mind.

5. "As the children are partakers of flesh and blood, he also himself likewise took part of the same,"[365] for this man, being the first creature of the *kingdom* or dispensation of the living God's *name*, it is well for us to remember "that flesh and blood cannot inherit the kingdom of God."[366] Why is it that flesh and blood cannot inherit this *circumcision*? It says, "The kingdom of God cometh

---

357   Luke 1:35
358   Jeremiah 23:26,27
359   Ephesians 4:4
360   Ephesians 2:18
361   Luke 3:22
362   John 15:26
363   1 John 1:2
364   John 3:6
365   Hebrews 2:14
366   1 Corinthians 15:50

not with observation: neither shall they say, Lo here! or, lo there! for, behold, the kingdom of God is within you."[367]

6. The *kingdom* of *God* is no literal kingdom. Seeing as how "God is a Spirit,"[368] the kingdom of God is the kingdom of the Spirit, and a "kingdom" is a figurative illustration of a "throne," as it says, "The throne of thy kingdom,"[369] and, "The throne of his kingdom."[370] The kingdom of the Spirit is the throne of the Spirit, and because "a spirit hath not flesh and bones,"[371] it is well to realize that the Spirit's throne or sovereignty is over and within the inward parts of the devotional conversation, which is why it says, "To be strengthened with might by his Spirit in the inner man,"[372] and, "That which is born of the Spirit is spirit."[373]

7. For the living God's chief apostle to say that the *kingdom* is not with observation; meaning that it is no physical reality; is for him to introduce a philosophical dispensation for the conversation's organs, seeing as how "there is a natural body, and there is a spiritual body."[374] What is for the *Spirit* is and always will be spirit, and because the spirit is not fleshly, the *Spirit* must inhabit that *body* similar to it. This is why, not a physically descending body of the *Holy Ghost* was to fill up Mary's *womb*, but rather the "power" of the *Holy Ghost*.

8. The conversation's inwards, because they are to be conquered by the *Holy Ghost*, need a special material for the desired end of that fellowship, which is why it says, "I delight in the law of God after the inward man,"[375] and, "Thou desirest truth in the inward parts: and in the hidden part thou shalt make me to know wisdom."[376] The power of the *Holy Ghost* is the law and wisdom of the *Holy Ghost*, which is why it says, "Christ the power of God, and the wisdom of God,"[377] and, "The law of the Spirit of life."[378] In right context, "Christ" should be understood or thought of as a reference to the living God's law of creation.[379]

---

367   Luke 17:20
368   John 4:24
369   2 Chronicles 7:18
370   2 Samuel 7:13
371   Luke 24:39
372   Ephesians 3:16
373   John 3:6
374   1 Corinthians 15:44
375   Romans 7:22
376   Psalm 51:6
377   1 Corinthians 1:24
378   Romans 8:2
379   2 Corinthians 5:16,17

9. Creation is the end of the Bible's science, wherefore it is well to understand that "the Lord Jesus Christ our Saviour"[380] is, in proper context, "the commandment of God our Saviour."[381] This commandment is "the kindness and love of God our Saviour toward man,"[382] that kindness being the resurrection of the personal and the devotional character.[383] The end of "Jesus Christ" is creation, and this creation beginning when once the *name* of the living God's wisdom or commandment is examined and executed.

10. When we hear of a "child of the Holy Ghost,"[384] creation within the mind by the living God's instruction is the illustration that is conveyed. Again, "that which is born of the Spirit is spirit,"[385] and creation of the Spirit appears only through "the Lord Jesus Christ our Saviour,"[386] which is, in reality, "the doctrine of God our Saviour,"[387] seeing as how the living God "created all things by Jesus Christ."[388] It says that creation is through "Jesus Christ," and again, "Jesus Christ" is observed to be an appellation of salvation's science according to the saying, "Of his own will begat he us with the word of truth, that we should be a kind of firstfruits of his creatures."[389]

11. "Jesus Christ" is the "word of truth," and seeing as how it says, "Thy law is the truth,"[390] because "the law is spiritual,"[391] it is that creation's science is through "the law of Christ,"[392] that is, "through the knowledge of God, and of Jesus our Lord."[393] "Through knowledge shall the just be delivered,"[394] wherefore it is counseled, "Let the word of Christ dwell in you richly in all wisdom,"[395] for by taxing the mental faculties on salvation's law, the creature of that wisdom will obtain the promised conception, which is why it says, "In his law doth he

380   Titus 1:4
381   Titus 1:3
382   Titus 3:4
383   Romans 8:11
384   Matthew 1:18
385   John 3:6
386   Titus 1:4
387   Titus 2:10
388   Ephesians 3:9
389   James 1:18
390   Psalm 119:142
391   Romans 7:14
392   Galatians 6:2
393   2 Peter 1:2
394   Proverbs 11:9
395   Colossians 3:16

meditate day and night."[396] Brainpower must be spent "rightly dividing the word of truth"[397] or else we fail of receiving its benefit. The actual record of the living God's man is no Greek tragedy; the birth of his mind is ours to experience, which is why it says, "Be renewed in the spirit of your mind."[398]

12. There is a great difference in hearing the Holy Ghost descending in bodily form and hearing the Holy Ghost descending in power. The fact that we are made to observe the Spirit in a bodily form and without the man, even resting upon him in that bodily form, is enough to witness to the fact that this man was conceived by the *Spirit* within the character of his conscience, even as we are "to be strengthened with might by his Spirit in the inner man; that Christ may dwell in your hearts by faith."[399] Paul is here rehearsing salvation's science, highlighting how that the conception spoken of is within. Because this manner of creation is only through active and experimental faith on the *name* "Jesus Christ," the living God's chief apostle, in order for his conversation to partake of the intended kindness, had to examine and do "Jesus Christ" in order to know the benevolence constrained within "Jesus Christ," which is why he says, "I know him, and keep his saying."[400]

13. The saying that he kept, it is the same commandment that he preached, and he conquered his personal and devotional constitution by this law resting within the heart of his conversation; this is why he could say, "I know that his commandment is life everlasting."[401] This man so diligently studied the mind within the scriptures that his character, along with his conversation's disposition, was transformed by it, and this is why we are counseled, "Be ye transformed by the renewing of your mind, that ye may prove what is that good, and acceptable, and perfect, will of God."[402]

14. To say that "Jesus Christ" is come in the flesh is to say, "The Word was made flesh,"[403] or, "The life was manifested."[404] Now, "Jesus Christ," "the Word," and "the life," these are all one and the selfsame thing, and because "the Spirit is life,"[405] it is that in every one of these instances, the Spirit of the

---

396   Psalm 1:2
397   2 Timothy 2:15
398   Ephesians 4:23
399   Ephesians 3:16,17
400   John 8:55
401   John 12:50
402   Romans 12:2
403   John 1:14
404   1 John 1:2
405   Romans 8:10

LORD was manifested and continued in *flesh*. This manifestation is through the limbs of the body and is recognized by the conscience of another, even as it says, "We are made manifest unto God; and I trust also are made manifest in your consciences."[406]

15. The *Spirit*, because it is the living God's wisdom, operates only through the spirit of the conversation's mind. This operation begins when once the mind chews and digests its saying. The demonstration of this saying within our conscience is witnessed by how we carry our conversation.[407] Thus, the Word made flesh is the wisdom of the knowledge of salvation's law living within and proceeding from the person, even as how "God anointed Jesus of Nazareth with the Holy Ghost and with power..."[408]

16. Herein is revealed to us the end of the living God's benevolent intention, for it says, "My name shall be great among the heathen,"[409] and, "Wait for his law."[410] Our conversation is to have faith in the law of the living God's *name*.[411] If our confidence is not on this *name*, then we are deserving of the rebuke, "Ye worship ye know not what."[412] And why? Isn't it written, "That the name of our Lord Jesus Christ may be glorified in you"?[413] and, "Ye might have life through his name"?[414] and, "We should believe on the name of his Son Jesus Christ"?[415] and, "Ye are justified in the name of the Lord Jesus"?[416]

17. While there is no sensual record of any *divine thing* resting within the physical nature of that man, every record points to the fact that the Creator conferred upon this man's *name* a most fitting appointment for the doer of that *name*. Therefore when hearing "name," it is well to know that "name" means knowledge or doctrine, as it says, "Thou holdest fast my name, and hast not denied my faith,"[417] and, "Hast kept my word, and hast not denied my name."[418] For this cause, when hearing that we must exercise faith on the *name* of "Jesus

---

406   2 Corinthians 5:11
407   Romans 6:13
408   Acts 10:38
409   Malachi 1:11
410   Isaiah 42:4
411   Matthew 12:21
412   John 4:22
413   2 Thessalonians 1:12
414   John 20:31
415   1 John 3:23
416   1 Corinthians 6:11
417   Revelation 2:13
418   Revelation 3:8

Christ," it is that, in right context of language, salvation's student must exercise and experiment with faith on the law of the knowledge and instruction at the core of the scriptures. This knowledge is the living God's *name* for us to know the character of its wisdom, which is why our example says, "I know him, and keep his saying."[419]

18. It is our responsibility to wait on this law for the reception of the living God's righteousness, which is why it says, "Through the Spirit wait for the hope of righteousness by faith."[420] What is it that Paul counsels us to wait on? He says, "the Spirit," but in another place he says, "We might be justified by the faith of Christ,"[421] which is but saying, "The law of the Spirit of life in Christ Jesus hath made me free from the law of sin and death."[422] It is our responsibility to do exactly what the Bible instructs through Isaiah, that is, to wait on the law of the knowledge given by the living God's chief apostle.

19. This "waiting" is not inactive or lethargic. To wait on any thing is actually very hard labor, which is why it says, "Let thine heart retain my words: keep my commandments, and live,"[423] and, "Keep my commandments, and live; and my law as the apple of thine eye."[424] We "wait" for wisdom,[425] making it that much more important to have the instruction of "Jesus Christ" within our faith's character. We get wisdom only by personally experimenting with this *voice*, and it is in this manner that our mind is sealed to its Creator, which is why it says, "Ye are clean through the word which I have spoken."[426] For this cause, our main concern should not be over some inordinate and base infatuation with the flesh of a man, but with his *name*, which *name* is the living Creator's *name*, seeing as how through him "we have received a commandment from the Father."[427]

20. The *name* of the LORD is decreed to be great among the *heathen*.[428] To understand who these *heathen* are, we observe the warning given to John: "What thou seest, write in a book, and send it unto the seven churches which are in Asia."[429] The churches of Asia are the subjects of this discourse, and we

---

419   John 8:55
420   Galatians 5:5
421   Galatians 2:16
422   Romans 8:2
423   Proverbs 4:4
424   Proverbs 7:2
425   Proverbs 4:7
426   John 15:3
427   2 John 1:4
428   Ephesians 2:11,12
429   Revelation 1:11

begin with Eph'esus because every church of Asia draws its heritage from this ancient church of Asia. "Asia," in context, should not be thought of as a literal location, but as a spiritual *place* where an erroneous religion should find itself.

21. The history of this Asia was given to Daniel, who was told, "By him the daily sacrifice was taken away, and the place of his sanctuary was cast down."[430] We begin this vision of the eighth division of the book of Daniel with the Medes and the Persians, and then find ourselves observing Greece under Alexander the Great until we are brought to view Rome, that empire which "magnified himself even to the prince of the host."[431] That prince is the living God's chief witness, for Rome said, "Knowest thou not that I have power to crucify thee, and have power to release thee?"[432] The power that accomplished this act is also the same power that should exchange its pagan sacrificial system for an abominable practice crucifying this man afresh, putting down that former pagan sanctuary to cast down or establish another.

22. Rome did fulfill this vision, and John recorded it for our learning, for the revelation says, "Thou hast there them that hold the doctrine of Ba'laam, who taught Ba'lac to cast a stumblingblock before the children of Israel..."[433] This language is not literal. Ba'laam, a symbol of a false prophet or religious institution, is observed having unlawful intercourse with Ba'lac, who is a symbol representing a pagan government or kingdom. The history of the Christian church; who Ba'laam represents; and of Constantine; who Ba'lac represents; fulfills the vision.

23. Upon receiving the already apostate Christian religion, Constantine cemented this religion with a new name, "Christianity," and relocated it to Asia Minor, calling the place of its palace, "Constantinople." The Revelation begins its discourse with Eph'esus because the religion of Asia, or of Constantine, is that practice confessing "the temple of the great goddess Diana...whom all Asia and the world worshippeth."[434] The heathen, or the Gentiles that should come to trust in and honor the *name* of the LORD, would be them of the temple of *Diana*, who say, "The city of the Ephe'sians is a worshipper of the great goddess Diana, and of the image which fell down from Jupiter."[435] Thus, the Gentile

---

430   Daniel 8:11
431   Daniel 8:11
432   John 19:10
433   Revelation 2:14
434   Acts 19:27
435   Acts 19:35

religious world is understood as them that honor Diana, or "the queen of heaven,"[436] and her son fallen down to them from Jupiter.

24. To be Gentile or heathen is to be without "the Lord Jesus Christ our Saviour,"[437] or rather, without "the commandment of God our Saviour."[438] This commandment educates on the *name* of the living God through the *name* and wisdom of his chief apostle's ministry, and the Revealtion begins at Eph'esus because the religious heritage of this church of Asia is contrary to salvation's spiritual understanding. The religion of Asia worships Diana and that "image of jealousy, which provoketh to jealousy,"[439] who before this time was called Isis and Horus, and who today is called *Mary* and *Jesus*. This Roman religion celebrating the sun's day and that is followed by "them which say they are Jews, and are not, but are the synagogue of Satan,"[440] is who the Revelation's message is directed to.

25. The *name* of the living God's chief apostle is to become our diet. The living God's wisdom is one that is born to "purge your conscience from dead works to serve the living God,"[441] and the conscience is not physical. Asia's counterfeit religion is one that would remove the heart and mind from thoughtful exercise to lame policies that ruin the character for "fulfilling the desires of the flesh and of the mind."[442] In this state, "philosophy and vain deceit, after the tradition of men, after the rudiments of the world,"[443] suffice to direct the conversation. A low perception of the Bible removes the mind from its intention, keeping the heart from fully comprehending its *name* to obtain understanding. The elders within the early Christian church suffered this tragedy, their dormant spirit causing them to miss the new covenant's promise, opening them up to religious error.

26. This wrath that they experienced upon their understanding is the reason an erroneous religion came about, which practice moved the author to write, "They went out, that they might be made manifest that they were not all of us."[444] If their mind was on the *name* of salvation's science, if their thoughts

---

436   Jeremiah 44:18
437   Titus 1:4
438   Titus 1:3
439   Ezekiel 8:3
440   Revelation 2:9
441   Hebrews 9:14
442   Ephesians 2:3
443   Colossians 2:8
444   1 John 2:19

were on the law of its wisdom, these priests would not have consented to plain religious error.[445] This religion that came about from them[446] found itself in direct opposition to creation's philosophy. The religion of Asia is that practice the living God would bring our conversation out of, which is why it still says, "I am the LORD thy God, which have brought thee out of the land of Egypt, out of the house of bondage."[447]

27. The *name* of the living God's chief apostle is understood as that "Savior" because it is the Captain of our exodus from Asia, which religion is wholly *Egyptian*. But although it has opened up the door of that promised *Place* to us; as it says, "Ye are come unto...the heavenly Jerusalem...";[448] this *name* has not fulfilled the goodness of this *Place* within any conversation. It only opened up the door of this Temple to our faith, making it our responsibility to enter this Building for learning of and doing our example's *name*, to the end we receive the promise that our Father has hidden within the knowledge of its intercession.

445   1 Timothy 6:20,21
446   Revelation 2:2
447   Exodus 20:2
448   Hebrews 12:22,23

5

David's Child

1. It is written, "Jesus...being (as was supposed) the son of Joseph."[449] The author's pen pronounced a certain uncertainty surrounding the relation of this man to Joseph because he is not the son of Joseph, and we may know this from how it says, "His father David."[450] The *father* of the new covenant's ambassador is David. Because this is so, our understanding on the words "son" and "father" are crucial to our discerning just what the author of the book of Luke is saying.

2. A "son," to the Bible's mind, is no literal reference, neither is a "father" any reference to any legitimate biological bond to a "son." Because the Bible is firstly a book that "is profitable for doctrine, for reproof, for correction, for instruction in righteousness,"[451] our understanding of its language should never escape its context. To hear of a "son" and a "father" is to hear of a stewardship or apprenticeship between a religious teacher and his pupil, as it says, "My own son in the faith,"[452] and, "Mine own son after the common faith,"[453] and, "As a son with the father, he hath served with me in the gospel."[454] To hear of one as the son of Joseph, or as the son of Shem, or as the son Job, is not to hear of any blood relation among human beings; the bond is philosophical. We understand

---

449   Luke 3:23
450   Luke 1:32
451   2 Timothy 3:16
452   1 Timothy 1:2
453   Titus 1:4
454   Philippians 2:22

this because the record of sons and fathers given by the author of the book of Luke ends with Adam, who was not the legitimate child of *God*, but was a creature of *breath*.

3. The first son of *God* was of the earth but received the LORD's breath within his body.[455] This first *man* received *breath* into his *body* for activation, and this experiment, failing as it did, only proved to the LORD that a more potent manner to help aid *man's* natural mind was necessary, wherefore it was decreed that *God's* breath should hereafter find place within man's inward parts to properly heal his conscience, which is why it says, "To be strengthened with might by his Spirit in the inner man,"[456] and, "In the hidden part thou shalt make me to know wisdom."[457]

4. The first main *son* of *God* received *breath* into his *body* and failed, but the most notable *son*, the living God's chief apostle, received *breath* into his mind and never saw *death*, which is why he preaches, "If a man keep my saying, he shall never see death."[458] Therefore like as how Adam became that son; that is, through *breath*; so we find ourselves observing the living God's chief minister as a "child of the Holy Ghost."[459] The birth or conception spoken of is not natural or literal, seeing as how "that which is born of the Spirit is spirit."[460] The *Holy Ghost* can only reach and serve the spirit of the mind, for "God is a Spirit."[461] As a Spirit, should the Spirit unlawfully or perversely interact with flesh?

5. If we believe that the LORD's Spirit should unlawfully commune with flesh for any reason then we "blaspheme his name, and his tabernacle, and them that dwell in heaven."[462] "The spirits of just men made perfect"[463] make up "the general assembly and church of the firstborn, which are written in heaven,"[464] for this is the location of that *Spirit*. If it says, "I saw the Spirit descending from heaven,"[465] then where that Spirit ascends to, and remains, is in *heaven*. "Heaven," in right language, is the Building of the LORD's heavenly Temple, as it says, "He hath looked down from the height of his sanctuary; from heaven

---

455 1 Corinthians 15:45
456 Ephesians 3:16
457 Psalm 51:6
458 John 8:51
459 Matthew 1:18
460 John 3:6
461 John 4:24
462 Revelation 13:6
463 Hebrews 12:23
464 Hebrews 12:23
465 John 1:32

did the LORD behold the earth,"[466] and, "The LORD is in his holy temple, the LORD'S throne is in heaven."[467]

6. The *name* of the living God is found within the heavenly Sanctuary, and the mind of every member within this assembly witnesses to that *name's* praise, for they have prayed, "Create in me a clean heart, O God; and renew a right spirit within me,"[468] and upon having their prayers answered, "The law of the Spirit of life in Christ Jesus hath made me free from the law of sin and death,"[469] they confess. Creation is the end of this *name*, and this law of creation, which is that "commandment from the Father,"[470] is the means whereby our conversation may possess a "spirit that confesseth that Jesus Christ is come in the flesh."[471] "That which is born of the Spirit is spirit,"[472] therefore we should not, if hopeful to not simply comprehend it, but to also know its benefit, remain so sensual when thinking on any facet of the Bible.

7. Thus, we may read of one conceived of the Spirit, but no spirit receives consciousness without a father, and concerning this man's father, we read, "His father David."[473] Now, David did have sons in his own generation, but of the age in which the living God's chief apostle lived, a great many of generations have passed since David. The relationship between this man and David cannot be literal or physical, but rather spiritual or philosophical. Therefore "David," in proper context of language, is a reference to a particular doctrine "of the house of David."[474]

8. A "house" is figurative language denoting a church, as it says, "The house of God, which is the church of the living God."[475] What gave rise to Mary's *womb* was the seed of David, and "the seed is the word of God."[476] Whatever saying David kept, it is the same saying that added strength to the bones of *Mary's child* as the development of his structure commenced within her *belly*. This saying she actually received from the *angel*, for the salutation that impregnated her said,

---

466   Psalm 102:19
467   Psalm 11:4
468   Psalm 51:10
469   Romans 8:2
470   2 John 1:4
471   1 John 4:2
472   John 3:6
473   Luke 1:32
474   Luke 1:27
475   1 Timothy 3:15
476   Luke 8:11

"The Lord is with thee."[477] This salutation, it did not begin at this point, but we find it clearly mentioned by Bo'az; who is the father of O'bed, who is the father of Jesse, who is the father of David. This "Bo'az came from Beth'-lehem, and said unto the reapers, The LORD be with you. And they answered him, The LORD bless thee."[478]

9. The law and doctrine of the LORD's peculiar blessing had been passed down from the LORD's *Spirit* to *Adam*, from Adam to Seth, and then from Seth to Noah, and then from Noah to Shem, from Shem to Abraham, from Abraham to Israel, from Israel to Judah, from Judah to Pha'rez, from Pha'rez to Bo'az, and then from Bo'az to David, but it never found itself fully explained until that Prophet perfected the mystery of that wisdom.[479] This preist, having received the forgotten commandment of David's church from his *mother*, examined that doctrine with David's *spirit* in mind, for "the spirits of the prophets are subject to the prophets."[480]

10. This man learned what it meant to have the living God with him, and in what context, for when he heard how it was written, "I will meditate in thy precepts, and have respect unto thy ways,"[481] and, "The LORD said unto my Lord, Sit thou at my right hand,"[482] and, "Thou wilt not leave my soul in hell; neither wilt thou suffer thine Holy One to see corruption,"[483] and, "Renew a right spirit within me,"[484] and, "Blessed be he that cometh in the name of the LORD: we have blessed you out of the house of the LORD,"[485] then he "came into Galilee, preaching the gospel of the kingdom of God."[486] He, having passed through creation's course of learning, understood why it said, "Blessed are the undefiled in the way, who walk in the law of the LORD."[487] By doing this law of creation, he could reasonably teach, "I am the way, the truth, and the life."[488] Now, it says, "Thy law is the truth,"[489] and, "The Spirit is life,"[490] and, "The way

---

477   Luke 1:28
478   Ruth 2:4
479   Ephesians 1:9
480   1 Corinthians 14:32
481   Psalm 119:15
482   Psalm 110:1
483   Psalm 16:10
484   Psalm 51:10
485   Psalm 118:26
486   Mark 1:14
487   Psalm 119:1
488   John 14:6
489   Psalm 119:142
490   Romans 8:10

of truth,"[491] and, "The Spirit is truth."[492] Herein that way, truth, and life leading to the living God, it is his "law of the Spirit of life,"[493] and without doing this commandment, we cannot know the living God to receive the end of his *name*.

11. It is well to understand that although, in the *narratives* of the living God's chief messenger, he says "I" and "me" in certain instances, he by no means references himself, and we may understand this by how it says, "He that rejecteth me, and receiveth not my words,"[494] and, "If ye abide in me, and my words abide in you,"[495] and, "Whosoever shall be ashamed of me and of my words."[496] Rightly discerning scripture's language and context is crucial to the development of our faith. When we hear, "I am the way," the reference is to the words that he spoke. Our confidence in him is not in whatever superstition is held to his *flesh*, but it is wholly in his *name*. *Name* is not flesh; *name*, being mental, transcends flesh, which is why, after retaining the wisdom of David's conversation, he taught, "It is the spirit that quickeneth; the flesh profiteth nothing: the words that I speak unto you, they are spirit, and they are life."[497]

12. Our responsibility is to the conscience of our faith's character or spirit, which is why it says, "Worship God in the spirit,"[498] and, "Be renewed in the spirit of your mind."[499] Our assignment is to observe the *name* of the living God's chief apostle, for he says, "This is the will of him that sent me, that every one which seeth the Son, and believeth on him, may have everlasting life."[500] Is this man to be literally seen? Where on earth can you see him? What institution has him? What man is him? We discern his *form* mentally, within the spirit of our conversation's mind, which revelation, seeing as how "that which is born of the Spirit is spirit,"[501] is the beginning of our conception.

13. This is what it means for the living God to be with us, for if "God is a Spirit,"[502] and if "that which is born of the Spirit is spirit,"[503] then it is that the

---

491   Psalm 119:30
492   1 John 5:6
493   Romans 8:2
494   John 12:48
495   John 15:7
496   Luke 9:26
497   John 6:63
498   Philippians 3:3
499   Ephesians 4:23
500   John 6:40
501   John 3:6
502   John 4:24
503   John 3:6

living God's Spirit is to rest within the organs of our conversation for a certain resurrection. This is the science of the living God's righteousness, which knowledge is explained in the saying, "If the Spirit of him that raised up Jesus from the dead dwell in you, he that raised up Christ from the dead shall also quicken your mortal bodies by his Spirit that dwelleth in you."[504]

14. The wisdom of David is one exercising and experimenting with faith on the living God's ability to revive and reform, which law is "the kindness and love of God our Saviour toward man."[505] Wherefore David, having philosophically experienced this newness within his conversation, inevitably sought to act it out, saying, upon one occasion, "Is there not yet any of the house of Saul, that I may shew the kindness of God unto him?"[506] David physically demonstrated this goodness by not only bringing one that was born lame to perpetually eat at his table, but he also, for the memory he had of this man's father, restored to him the land that had been lost to him. Herein is the end of salvation's doctrine, that we, for the sake of that Prophet's *name*, should be found at *creation's* table within *creation's* Building[507] to have restored to us, by the perpetual renewal of our understanding, the lost portions of our heart.

15. We do have a heart to amend, and "he that hath no rule over his own spirit is like a city that is broken down, and without walls,"[508] wherefore our Father thought it to devise a law specifically for our faith's development. Our heart cannot find itself healed without a strong mind or spirit, for "the spirit giveth life."[509] The spirit of the mind is to be the instructor of every thought and feeling, "casting down imaginations, and every high thing that exalteth itself against the knowledge of God, and bringing into captivity every thought to the obedience of Christ."[510]

16. It is for this reason that the *name* of this Prophet blesses our spirit, and seeing as spiritual blessings come from the living God,[511] it is that every shower of blessing is given that we "might be filled with the knowledge of his will in all wisdom and spiritual understanding."[512] Thus, the everlasting life promised to

---

504   Romans 8:11
505   Titus 3:4
506   2 Samuel 9:3
507   Hebrews 12:23
508   Proverbs 25:28
509   2 Corinthians 3:6
510   2 Corinthians 10:5
511   Ephesians 1:3
512   Colossians 1:9

the one that discerns the *body* of salvation's knowledge, and actively believes on it, it is even "the grace of life,"[513] and is ordained only for the mind when learning creation's law to become a new creature of it, which is why it says, "The grace of our Lord Jesus Christ be with your spirit."[514] "Grace" is creative power pouring out from the living God every time brainpower is spent "rightly dividing the word of truth,"[515] which is why it says, "Grow in grace, and in the knowledge of our Lord."[516]

17. If we should have a strong conversation that is confidently proficient in "the mystery of Christ,"[517] grace is necessary, but grace is not given without mentally chewing and digesting the Bible's *voice*. "Comparing spiritual things with spiritual"[518] is the means whereby the mind may become strong enough to properly instruct the members of the heart, wherefore, since "the excellency of knowledge is, that wisdom giveth life to them that have it,"[519] it is well to know that "wisdom strengtheneth."[520]

18. The spirit gives life to the conversation because of the wisdom it retains when examining the law of "the excellency of the knowledge of Christ."[521] In order to receive the intended conception, diligent obedience to this knowledge is demanded, for it says, "The Holy Ghost, whom God hath given to them that obey him."[522] "The commandment of the everlasting God, made known to all nations for the obedience of faith,"[523] is that charge requiring the use of our inward faculties to know the praise of its *name*. As our example patiently and temperately studied and applied himself to David's doctrine, he began to understand why it says, "To him that ordereth his conversation aright will I shew the salvation of God."[524] Because it is "the grace of God that bringeth salvation,"[525] the conversation embracing reform will know the regeneration born from exercising their faith on the Creator's *name*.

---

513 1 Peter 3:7
514 Galatians 6:18
515 2 Timothy 2:15
516 2 Peter 3:18
517 Colossians 4:3
518 1 Corinthians 2:13
519 Ecclesiastes 7:12
520 Ecclesiastes 7:19
521 Philippians 3:8
522 Acts 5:32
523 Romans 16:26
524 Psalm 50:23
525 Titus 2:11

19. The saying, "Have faith in God,"[526] is similar to the saying, "The LORD be with you,"[527] which means, "God is with us."[528] Now, if he said of old, "Let them make me a sanctuary; that I may dwell among them,"[529] must we expect this charge to suddenly fail today? Because we are to be built as "an habitation of God through the Spirit,"[530] we are "to be strengthened with might by his Spirit in the inner man";[531] how do we suppose this inward temple is to be constructed? Our counselor says, "Whosoever heareth these sayings of mine, and doeth them, I will liken him unto a wise man, which built his house upon a rock."[532]

20. That rock, it is the combined sayings of the living God's mind forming one sound foundation to construct the *house* of our temple on. This temple that we are building must be of the same *material* of the living God's heavenly Temple, which is why it says, "It was in the heart of David my father to build an house for the name of the LORD God of Israel."[533] If David is this man's father, then we must find this man establishing a Temple for the *name* of this same LORD, and we do, for it says of him, "He shall build the temple of the LORD."[534] This is why it says of him, "He shall be great, and shall be called the Son of the Highest,"[535] and, "He shall be a priest upon his throne."[536] Wherefore like as how his *name* is "a merciful and faithful high priest in things pertaining to God,"[537] it is our duty, through that *name*, to build a similar temple in devotion to the same *Mind*.

21. Again, Solomon says, "It was in the heart of David my father to build an house for the name of the LORD God of Israel,"[538] for the *name* of the LORD is this Prophet's *name* and knowledge. The entire point of the living God's doctrine is to have Spirit to spirit communion, and like as how he anciently communed with Israel about their worldly sanctuary, so too our communion

---

526   Mark 11:22
527   Ruth 2:4
528   Isaiah 8:10
529   Exodus 25:8
530   Ephesians 2:22
531   Ephesians 3:16
532   Matthew 7:24
533   1 Kings 8:17
534   Zechariah 6:12
535   Luke 1:32
536   Zechariah 6:13
537   Hebrews 2:17
538   1 Kings 8:17

with him cannot be as perfect as it should be without a temple within the heart of our conversation's conscience.

22. To have builders for this temple, and then to keep this temple in good shape, the organs of our conversation must have within it "the spirit of God, in wisdom, and in understanding, and in knowledge, and in all manner of workmanship."[539] This temple for the *body* of our faith, because it is constructed by the power and wisdom of the living God's *Wisdom* or *Spirit*, cannot fail of any commandment or principle of that wisdom's heavenly Temple. This is why "we have such an high priest, who is set on the right hand of the throne of the Majesty in the heavens,"[540] for this man's *name* is the means whereby our regeneration and reform to *heaven's* conversation is sealed and finished. He himself had to pass through this course of learning, saying, "I know him, and keep his saying."[541] If he did not keep the *Spirit's* commandment, he could not say of himself or his doctrine, "Him hath God the Father sealed,"[542] and if he failed in this manner of learning, no conversation under his guidance would ever have "his Father's name written in their foreheads."[543]

23. The *name* of this man's Creator is crucial for our faith's development, even so crucial that he prays, "Holy Father, keep through thine own name those whom thou hast given me."[544] Again, we cannot get to the living God's *name* without passing through his *name*. Thus, when Joseph found this *Spirit's* young minister, he found him in the *name* of the living God's knowledge as a child of its wisdom.

24. Again, a "child" is no reference to a literal minor. We read of Samuel, concerning his appointment next to the then high priest: "The child was young."[545] This "Samuel ministered before the LORD, being a child, girded with a linen e'phod."[546]

25. No literal child was given this special position, but only a young man of a certain amount of years in faith, as it says, "Thirty years old and upward even unto fifty years old, every one that came to do the service of the ministry."[547]

---

539   Exodus 31:3
540   Hebrews 8:1
541   John 8:55
542   John 6:27
543   Revelation 14:1
544   John 17:11
545   1 Samuel 1:24
546   1 Samuel 2:18
547   Numbers 4:47

Every "child" was reckoned from their mid twenties to their thirties, and upward to their fifties. Because "that which is born of the Spirit is spirit,"[548] the Spirit must have a mind that is ready and willing to function, as it demands, for the reception of the conception it decrees.

26. The Spirit's young minister, when Joseph found him and brought him in to his fold, was no son or priest of his, but was a steward of the living God's wisdom and knowledge. This man, having the character of David's faith as his instructor, had no fellowship with *men*, but diligently, "beginning at Moses and all the prophets,"[549] trained his mind. In this manner he learned the *name* that he should assume, and in picking it up, he never put it down.

---

548   John 3:6
549   Luke 24:27

6

His Name's Sake

1. Because "that which is born of the Spirit is spirit,"[550] when thinking on how it says, "She was found with child of the Holy Ghost,"[551] our understanding of how the *Holy Ghost* operates is essential to rightly comprehending the vision, "A virgin shall be with child."[552]

2. A virgin, properly understood, is some *thing* kept out of sight, some *thing* kept veiled or private, and in this instance, from *men*. The *Spirit* of *God* can only conceive by way of the spirit of the mind,[553] and if "a spirit hath not flesh and bones,"[554] then it cannot physically interact with any natural body, leaving the spiritual *body* to be the primary subject of the Spirit.

3. "God is a Spirit,"[555] and "God is the LORD,"[556] so must the LORD, who is wholly Spirit, think to unlawfully possess flesh to accomplish a spiritual will?

---

550   John 3:6
551   Matthew 1:18
552   Matthew 1:23
553   1 Corinthians 15:44
554   Luke 24:39
555   John 4:24
556   Psalm 118:27

Isn't he "the LORD, the God of the spirits of all flesh"?[557] Isn't he "the Father of spirits"?[558] Must the LORD's Spirit sensually give birth to flesh, creating a fable, or must the LORD's Spirit not rather baptize the spirit of the mind, seeing as how he possesses that Spirit for every spirit existing in *flesh*? The LORD chose the latter, exempting that prophesied minister from no human qualities and deficiencies, for he was born "in the likeness of sinful flesh";[559] there is no thing more or less than this.

4. The living God's chief apostle is not the first *child* prophesied to be born. In language familiar to his revelation, a man of *God* once said to a king of Israel, "A child shall be born unto the house of David, Josi'ah by name; and upon thee shall he offer the priests of the high places that burn incense upon thee, and men's bones shall be burnt upon thee."[560]

5. This child, as a child, should execute great religious reforms in the LORD's church, and we find that when he should do this, he should be no literal child. We are told that these great movements by this *child* occurred in the eighteenth year of his reign, and since he began his reign in Jerusalem at eight years old, this child should be twenty-six years old when the prophecy should be fulfilled.

6. No "child" prophesied by the Spirit accomplishes any thing as a literal infant. For like as Josi'ah was born to and by wholly human parents, we cannot, and should not think any less or any more for that Prophet. There is no doubt that this man, like Josi'ah, was only human, but what made him special, above every minister in his age, was the fact that his mind was not conceived by a flesh-based religious experience, but by the living God's mind of wisdom. With the devotional conversation already owning a negligent spirit upon conception, a greater work of conception wrought is herein pronounced, which is why it says, "Be renewed in the spirit of your mind."[561]

7. In order for the Spirit to conceive, it must renew or regenerate the spirit of the mind, allowing us to understand that the word "conception," in relation to the spirit, is no reference to physical or natural birth, but rather to mental realization, impression, perception, cognition, thought, or meditation, which is why it says, "In his law doth he meditate day and night."[562] Again, "there is a

---

557   Numbers 27:16
558   Hebrews 12:9
559   Romans 8:3
560   1 Kings 13:2
561   Ephesians 4:23
562   Psalm 1:2

natural body, and there is a spiritual body,"[563] and since "that was not first which is spiritual, but that which is natural; and afterward that which is spiritual";[564] when hearing of a *child* of the *Holy Ghost*, we are hearing of an already formed human being that is already passing through the Spirit's higher learning.

8. Our conversation is first born naturally, within the religious world. What is after this birth, according to the living God's will, is a philosophical conception occurring from considering and discerning that will's knowledge. This second birth, is according to how "it is written, The first man Adam was made a living soul; the last Adam was made a quickening spirit."[565] The Bible does not speak of a literal "child" of the *Holy Ghost*, for that "child" is actually a young minister in years of faith. When we observe Matthew's opening record of this man, it is then well for us to understand that we are receiving the vision of a young priest trained in the new covenant promise.

9. A "child" is a "son," as it says, "Unto us a child is born, unto us a son is given,"[566] and, "He that delicately bringeth up his servant from a child shall have him become his son at the length."[567] The child, being a son, is therefore of no blood relation to any legitimate male or female, but is a servant or pupil to a religious minister or priest, as it says, "Mine own son after the common faith,"[568] and, "As a son with the father, he hath served with me in the gospel."[569] Thus, when Paul says, "We have had fathers of our flesh which corrected us, and we gave them reverence,"[570] he makes no reference to any literal familial relationship, but to the instruction one receives from priests on spiritual things.

10. A "man," in scripture, is not speech delineating a male human being. That Prophet once said, "The Son of man shall be delivered into the hands of men,"[571] and to explain what he meant, he said, "The Son of man must suffer many things, and be rejected of the elders and chief priests and scribes, and be slain."[572] A "man," in right context, is an elder or priest, and the "child" is typically a young man in years of faith under an experienced minister, and this is the testimony of Samuel, of whom it says, "Samuel ministered before the

---

563   1 Corinthians 15:44
564   1 Corinthians 15:46
565   1 Corinthians 15:45
566   Isaiah 9:6
567   Proverbs 29:21
568   Titus 1:4
569   Philippians 2:22
570   Hebrews 12:9
571   Luke 9:44
572   Luke 9:22

LORD, being a child, girded with a linen e'phod."[573] This *child* of the Spirit is a young minister of the Spirit, even of Samuel's age, whose age is according to the saying, "From twenty years old and above, shall give an offering unto the LORD."[574]

11. No son of the Spirit is naturally conceived by the Spirit in any lewd manner, for there is an order to the LORD's mind; to break that order is for to announce the LORD as carnal, base, and fleshly. A human child was born, but this birth, being wholly mental and spiritual deserves, in order to discern the *name* that quickened his spirit, more careful attention. Thus, to hear of a "virgin" conceiving of the *Holy Ghost* should move the mind to understand that, as this birth occurs by way of "the knowledge of his will in all wisdom and spiritual understanding,"[575] the "virgin" carrying this child is no literal woman with a literal womb.

12. If "that which is born of the Spirit is spirit,"[576] what literal womb fits into this equation? Our natural understanding would have us think, "Can he enter the second time into his mother's womb, and be born?"[577] but there is a higher concept here at work. This devotional birth occurs as the human is in a state of consciousness and as the flesh is in a state degeneration, and hearing this, we are again moved, and frustratingly, to ask, "How can a man be born when he is old?"[578] This man is explaining the mental baptism to occur by *God's Spirit*, but this priest couldn't understand it. The spirit of the mind is to be given to the living God's wisdom "that he might sanctify and cleanse it with the washing of water by the word,"[579] for its will is to "purge your conscience from dead works to serve the living God."[580]

13. This manner of learning involves no literal womb, and it cannot, because "that which is born of the Spirit is spirit."[581] No literal womb can suffice for this spiritual labor, for "that was not first which is spiritual, but that which is natural; and afterward that which is spiritual."[582] Thus, when hearing, in the Bible, of a virgin set to conceive a son, it is well to remember how it is said, "These are they

573   1 Samuel 2:18
574   Exodus 30:14
575   Colossians 1:9
576   John 3:6
577   John 3:4
578   John 3:4
579   Ephesians 5:26
580   Hebrews 9:13
581   John 3:6
582   1 Corinthians 15:46

which were not defiled with women; for they are virgins...These were redeemed from among men."[583]

14. The virgin is one that is not defiled by *women*, and in this verse, the Bible links "women" to "men," for the two are one and the same. A "woman," in proper context, is figurative language denoting a church.[584] "Men," being elders and ministers of religion, are the women spoken of, for they are the head of the church. The "virgin" is a woman that is not defiled by other *women*, or is not debased or polluted "after the commandments and doctrines of men."[585] The virgin that *conceived* that Prophet, she had no interaction with priests of religion, wherefore when hearing that *she* should produce a priest of her own, she said, "How shall this be, seeing I know not a man?"[586] "Every high priest taken from among men is ordained for men in things pertaining to God,"[587] yet to this woman was given the charge to raise up a seed of the *Spirit* without any *man*, and "not in the words which man's wisdom teacheth, but which the Holy Ghost teacheth,"[588] which is why it was told her, "The power of the Highest shall overshadow thee."[589]

15. No thing but the power of the Spirit should fill her *womb*, wherefore seeing as how we are "to be strengthened with might by his Spirit in the inner man,"[590] the power of the Spirit should bless the inward parts of the woman to aid her in her mission. Again, "that which is born of the Spirit is spirit,"[591] and if the spirit should consent to creation, then the spirit needs a certain material to uplift its organs for transformation. This is why it says, "Let the word of Christ dwell in you richly in all wisdom,"[592] and, "Thou desirest truth in the inward parts: and in the hidden part thou shalt make me to know wisdom."[593]

16. The power of the Spirit is the living God's wisdom. Creation's present science is based upon the spirit of the mind examining, digesting, and doing the living God's knowledge, which is why it says, "Of his own will begat he us

---

583   Revelation 14:4
584   Ephesians 5:23
585   Colossians 2:22
586   Luke 1:34
587   Hebrews 5:1
588   1 Corinthians 2:13
589   Luke 1:35
590   Ephesians 3:16
591   John 3:6
592   Colossians 3:16
593   Psalm 51:6

with the word of truth."[594] There is no such birth of the Spirit without bringing the Creator's present understanding within the inward parts. The *Holy Ghost* cannot work if there is no mental energy diligently spent on its *voice*. Thus, for the Spirit's power to overshadow *Mary*, it is that her spirit was filled with the work and the effect of salvation's science, which is why she says, "My spirit hath rejoiced in God my Saviour."[595]

17. In order for this woman to fulfill her labor, she must refrain from the tradition and the superstitions of *men* to wholeheartedly examine the living God's will. By the impression that she should receive, a blessed *son* should pass out of her *bowels*, which is why, when Joseph found her, "she was found with child of the Holy Ghost."[596]

18. This *child* within the book of Matthew is of Samuel and Josi'ah's age in years of faith when found. Having refrained from *men*, this virgin heard and obeyed the charge of the *angel*, "Go unto my father's house, and to my kindred,"[597] and in so doing, gave birth to a *son* of *David*, which is why it says, "His father David."[598] The sonship mentioned is not literal because the conception is not natural. This *woman* learned David's doctrine to have her mind blessed and created by the wisdom of that understanding, and in time, a *son* of her conversation, seeing as how "God giveth not the Spirit by measure unto him,"[599] proceeded out of *her* to more perfectly do and experience the living God's will and power.

19. This immeasurable goodness, this everlasting *power*, this limitless abundance, was poured into his faith's intellect, allowing him to overcome personal and devotional error to better serve that will, exemplifying that it is this will's intention to "purge your conscience from dead works to serve the living God."[600] This man's resurrection only served to witness for the Bible's desire for our inward parts, which is why this experience is not only held to his conversation.[601] This young minister, when we are introduced to him, is already in creation's

---

594   James 1:18
595   Luke 1:47
596   Matthew 1:18
597   Genesis 24:38
598   Luke 1:32
599   John 3:34
600   Hebrews 9:14
601   Romans 8:11

new covenant course by "the law of the Spirit of life,"[602] and his record is for our learning and reproducing.

20. Our celebration of this minister should not be "through philosophy and vain deceit, after the tradition of men,"[603] but after the fact that his mind suffered creation.[604] The sacrificed conversation of this man is the means whereby we today may hold fellowship with the same wisdom of the same creation. Because he, having "in the days of his flesh, when he had offered up prayers and supplications with strong crying and tears unto him that was able to save him from death, and was heard in that he feared,"[605] faithfully observed creation's commandment, suffering his experience links us to the same victory.

21. Because of his exercised confidence in the new covenant promise, every conversation of every age is positioned to freely receive the end of that promise, the only issue is in accepting that new covenant's course of learning to receive the end of its hope. He may have sealed the experience to that wisdom's will, but he by no means fulfills this promise within any conversation. Just because we are linked to the living God by his experience does not mean that his efforts substitute for the end of that communion, or for our own personal labor to obtain that end, because they do not. For every conversation joined to the living God's will, it is written, "Those that have made a covenant with me by sacrifice."[606] Just because he offered his conversation a sacrifice for our course in devotional newness doesn't mean that his sacrifice alleviates our own necessary offering. The oblation of his devotional character was a general sacrifice for the assembly. All it did was open up the doors of an experience so that we might know the mediation of his *name*.

22. No conversation is freely given the blessing contained within that experience. No conversation is lethargically connected to the living God for the reception of the Spirit's promise, as if by that offering we are entirely "ok"; this is not Bible philosophy. A sacrifice is demanded in order to solidify our consensual acceptance of the new covenant's will, and that sacrifice must be an offering like the one given by that Prophet. This is why it says, "Thou shalt make his soul an offering for sin."[607]

---

602   Romans 8:2
603   Colossians 2:8
604   1 Corinthians 15:45
605   Hebrews 5:7
606   Psalm 50:5
607   Isaiah 53:10

23. The offering up of our faith's *soul* and mind is the means whereby it may find itself joined to the wisdom within the scriptures for sanctification. There is no such thing as reconciliation without sanctification, for it says, "And sanctified it, to make reconciliation upon it."[608] We are reconciled to the living God through the *name* of his chief apostle, but in order to receive it, the conversation must pass "through sanctification of the Spirit and belief of the truth."[609] This higher education is the sacrifice that we must make, for without it, we stand divided from salvation's science.

24. Our thoughts on the record and upbringing of the living God's chief witness must exceed a flesh-based understanding. What the Bible, through the pen of its writers, is pronouncing to us, is "the mystery of his will, according to his good pleasure which he hath purposed in himself."[610] Because *men* of old did not personally know this mystery, religious tragedy occurred through "profane and vain babblings, and oppositions of science falsely so called."[611]

25. Suddenly the science of salvation found itself blotted out by unfamiliar clouds, for the ministers of the early Christian church "changed the truth of God into a lie."[612] Instead of understanding that the *name* of the Prophet is what holds the living God's power and glory, "behold, there sat women weeping for Tam'muz."[613] The end of "Jesus Christ" is creation within the conversation's inward parts, and because this is plainly a mental and spiritual ordeal, it is well to understand that, in right context, "the Lord Jesus Christ our Saviour"[614] is "the commandment of God our Saviour."[615] Thus, when we hear them say, "My Lord and my God,"[616] and hear him say, "All power is given unto me,"[617] the reference is not literally to the man, but he says, "If a man love me, he will keep my words,"[618] and, "Whosoever therefore shall be ashamed of me and of my words."[619]

608　Leviticus 8:15
609　2 Thessalonians 2:13
610　Ephesians 1:9
611　1 Timothy 6:20,21
612　Romans 1:25
613　Ezekiel 8:14
614　Titus 1:4
615　Titus 1:3
616　John 20:28
617　Matthew 28:18
618　John 14:23
619　Mark 8:38

26. The words of this man are the Lord and the God of every conversation, the Sovereign Ruler and Counselor of ever mind, magnifying the fact that "there is one God, and one mediator between God and men, the man Christ Jesus."[620] Language and context is important, which is why all things within the Bible "are spiritually discerned."[621] There is absolutely no doubt that "Jesus Christ"; the name of the living God's commandment; is the God and Governor of the conversation, but in the context in which scripture speaks, it is wrong to take any thing of this man as abolishing or replacing or subduing the Creator of his ministry.

27. Because "when he saith all things are put under him, it is manifest that he is excepted, which did put all things under him."[622] Thus, being above him, the living God is, and always will be, "the most high God, the possessor of heaven and earth."[623] But concerning the *name* of his chief messenger, that every conversation may find harmony with the living God's will and wisdom, the promised edification was confined to his *name*.[624]

28. This is why his *name* matters.[625] His conversation is figuratively positioned next to the living God so that we might never fulfill the errors that were accomplished under the first covenant, and because that covenant gave only ten laws that one may violate, our duty is still to those same ten precepts, albeit through a more acceptable *name* to honor them.

29. The living God instituted this course of devotional learning so that we might have a clear revelation of the value behind those precepts.[626] If we find ourselves at odds with any one of those ten precepts, we may know that we are without knowledge of that wisdom's consecration.[627] We cannot keep those commandments because we fail to do the commandment of that wisdom's will.[628] This commandment is the means whereby we receive entrance into the new covenant's promise, wherefore we know that we fail to have a right knowledge of that science's character when we have no understanding of the effect or definition of its righteousness.

---

620   1 Timothy 2:5
621   1 Corinthians 2:14
622   1 Corinthians 15:27
623   Genesis 14:22
624   Colossians 1:19
625   Hebrews 9:15
626   2 John 1:6
627   1 John 2:3,4
628   2 John 1:4

30. Our conversation is to be reconciled to the *name* at the core of the scriptures "for the redemption of the transgressions that were under the first testament,"[629] meaning that our faith is to be cleansed to find our person in harmony or in agreement with the living God's devotional character. Now, if it says, "I ascend unto my Father, and your Father; and to my God, and your God,"[630] then our duty is plainly to this living understanding, which is why he says, "True worshippers shall worship the Father."[631] This care will not find itself impressed upon our conversation if we are not executing "Jesus Christ."

31. The only way he could say, "I have kept my Father's commandments, and abide in his love,"[632] is if he kept the saying of living God's *Wisdom*, and he did, for he says, "I know him, and keep his saying."[633] His example is for our learning.

32. To hear of a *child* of the *Holy Ghost*, it is that we are hearing of a converted minster to the living God's will and wisdom. This man has set the example for our conversation, that it is our responsibility to learn of and do salvation's commandment for the end of that promise, which end is according to the saying, "The Word was made flesh,"[634] and, "The life was manifested."[635]

33. "The Word of life"[636] is so pronounced as such because "the Spirit is life,"[637] and the only way for the Spirit to pass in to the *flesh*, or the conversation, is through "the Lord Jesus Christ our Saviour,"[638] which is, in all actually, "the doctrine of God our Saviour."[639] A "spirit that confesseth that Jesus Christ is come in the flesh"[640] is the end of "Jesus Christ," and the manifestation of this science is according to the saying, "God anointed Jesus of Nazareth with the Holy Ghost and with power..."[641]

34. The Spirit, finding place only by the spirit of the mind, is represented as being the Creator of the devotional conversation's mind. The *name* "Jesus

629 Hebrews 9:15
630 John 20:17
631 John 4:23
632 John 15:10
633 John 8:55
634 John 1:14
635 1 John 1:2
636 1 John 1:1
637 Romans 8:10
638 Titus 1:4
639 Titus 2:10
640 1 John 4:2
641 Acts 10:38

Christ" means, "God is with us,"[642] wherefore the *Word* made flesh is "the law of the Spirit of life"[643] conquering "the body of the sins of the flesh"[644] to "fulfil the law of Christ."[645] For this cause, "the end of the commandment is charity out of a pure heart, and of a good conscience, and of faith unfeigned."[646]

642   Isaiah 8:10
643   Romans 8:2
644   Colossians 2:11
645   Galatians 6:2
646   1 Timothy 1:5

7

Creation's Continuing Office

1. What are we to make of the saying, "Father, glorify thou me with thine own self with the glory which I had with thee before the world was"?[647]

2. Is this minister confessing to a peculiar state of his existence? Are his words directing us to observe his "nature" in a special way? What is it that he is actually saying? Bearing in mind that "he whom God hath sent speaketh the words of God,"[648] when we hear him saying, "Glorify me," the "me" that is referenced is in no direct connection to the man. We understand this from how he says, "If ye abide in me, and my words abide in you,"[649] and, "He that rejecteth me, and receiveth not my words,"[650] and, "I have given unto them the words which thou gavest me."[651]

3. If he says, "If I bear witness of myself, my witness is not true,"[652] to believe that he is asking the LORD for any thing concerning himself is for him

647   John 17:5
648   John 3:34
649   John 15:7
650   John 12:48
651   John 17:7
652   John 5:31

to contradict himself; "The Father himself, which hath sent me, hath borne witness of me,"[653] he says. This "me" is a subject of its own, for this "me" is his words. These words, they equate to one commandment, even as he says, "The Father which sent me, he gave me a commandment, what I should say, and what I should speak."[654] We cannot ignore the fact that this *Commandment* is that *Word*, and because "the Word was made flesh,"[655] it is this *Word* that is uttering the prayer. This prayer, then, when rightly understood, is the Creator's Wisdom asking its permission to assume the same stature that it; the Word or that Wisdom; had before it took on *earth's* present assignment.

4. The "Word" is, in reality, "the Word of life."[656] When it says, "The Word was made flesh,"[657] it is that "the life was manifested...that eternal life, which was with the Father."[658] Because "that which is born of the flesh is flesh; and that which is born of the Spirit is spirit";[659] and because "there is a natural body, and there is a spiritual body";[660] the Word cannot enter in to the flesh by the flesh, but only by the spirit. It must be remembered that this Word of life is "the Spirit of life from God,"[661] and seeing as how "God is a Spirit,"[662] and that "a spirit hath not flesh and bones,"[663] the Spirit, in order to find itself readily accessible to the human being, must find itself confirmed to that *body* similar to it, which is why "that which is born of the Spirit is spirit."[664] The Spirit, then, must find itself, because it can only commune with the spirit of the mind, in a form digestible to the mind, and the mind is not a physical or natural *thing*.

5. The "Word" is, according to the mind and the context of the scriptures, a commandment from the living God, which is why it says, concerning the relationship between the Spirit and the living God's words or counsels, "My spirit that is upon thee, and my words which I have put in thy mouth,"[665] and, "The Spirit of the LORD spake by me, and his word was in my tongue."[666] The Word

---

653   John 5:37
654   John 12:49
655   John 1:14
656   1 John 1:1
657   John 1:14
658   1 John 1:2
659   John 3:6
660   1 Corinthians 15:44
661   Revelation 11:11
662   John 4:24
663   Luke 24:39
664   John 3:6
665   Isaiah 59:21
666   2 Samuel 23:2

made flesh is the Spirit made flesh, and the Spirit made flesh is a Command-ment made flesh, wherefore it is well to know how it is said, "The command-ment is a lamp; and the law is light."[667]

6. The *Word* of *God* is the Law, Intention, or Commandment of the living God's *Mind*. In order for this law to be made flesh, it is that the spirit of the mind must absorb "the law of the Spirit of life,"[668] for this law is not to trans-form the physical body, but it says, "The body of the sins of the flesh."[669] This Commandment is ordained to conquer that irrational and intemperate *mind* within the natural devotional conversation's constitution, which is why it says, "God sending his own Son in the likeness of sinful flesh, and for sin, condemned sin in the flesh."[670]

7. The Bible's science is for the revival and reform of the devotional conver-sation for right control over the limbs and members of the body, which is why it says, "If Christ be in you, the body is dead."[671] "Christ" in you is the "Word" in you, and what must be in "you," that is, in "the body of this death,"[672] is "Christ"; this is that "mystery among the Gentiles; which is Christ in you, the hope of glory."[673] Therefore, by the manner in which "Christ" is mentioned, it is well to understand that "Christ" is spoken of as a reference to the knowledge of a commandment, even that same commandment that made the author confess, "The life was manifested, and we have seen it."[674] For this cause, we must know that, in right context, "the Lord Jesus Christ our Saviour"[675] is "the command-ment of God our Saviour,"[676] which commandment is "the doctrine of God our Saviour."[677] "Christ" is the name of the Spirit's law, which name is the faith that the Prophet preached, which is why it says of him, "They shall call his name Emman'uel, which being interpreted is, God with us."[678]

---

667   Proverbs 6:23
668   Romans 8:2
669   Colossians 2:11
670   Romans 8:3
671   Romans 8:10
672   Romans 7:24
673   Colossians 1:27
674   1 John 1:2
675   Titus 1:4
676   Titus 1:3
677   Titus 2:10
678   Matthew 1:23

8. Seeing as how "God is a Spirit,"[679] for *God* to be with us, it is for "the Spirit of truth, which proceedeth from the Father,"[680] to be within our inward parts, which is why it says, "To be strengthened with might by his Spirit in the inner man; that Christ may dwell in your hearts by faith."[681] There is no other way for salvation's science to find its accomplishment within the human being unless through the spirit of the conversation's heart and conscience, which is why it says, "Be renewed in the spirit of your mind,"[682] and, "That which is born of the Spirit is spirit."[683]

9. Renewal of the devotional mind cannot occur by any other means than by mentally discerning and mediating on *God's voice*, which is why it says, "Let the word of Christ dwell in you richly in all wisdom,"[684] and, "In his law doth he meditate day and night,"[685] and, "I delight in the law of God after the inward man."[686] Brainpower must be spent in order to fall in to the benefit of the Bible's present ministry, which is why "we have received a commandment from the Father."[687] It is our responsibility to personally examine and do the commandment for the end of its will, for "the end of the commandment is charity out of a pure heart, and of a good conscience, and of faith unfeigned."[688] The *Word* and the *Life* manifested in the *flesh* is the end of the living God's commandment, and demonstrated by the limbs and organs of the conversation, which is why it says, "All men know that ye are my disciples, if ye have love one to another."[689]

10. The organs of the *flesh* or conversation, the *Word* being within them, are become instruments for the Creator through the law and knowledge of his chief apostle. The aim of creation's present science is for us "to be conformed to the image of his Son."[690] In order to possess this man's likeness, it is first necessary to possess self, and self cannot be possessed unless the conversation's mind is reformed, and that reformation cannot occur until the spirit of its mind is

679   John 4:24
680   John 15:26
681   Ephesians 3:16,17
682   Ephesians 4:23
683   John 3:6
684   Colossians 3:16
685   Psalm 1:2
686   Romans 7:22
687   2 John 1:4
688   1 Timothy 1:5
689   John 13:35
690   Romans 8:29

regenerated; "the spirit giveth life"[691] for the good of the *body*. This is the living God's righteousness, which praise is "the kindness and love of God our Saviour toward man."[692]

11. The natural religious conversation is, both personally and devotionally, injurious to its self. To help it overcome its self-centered and self-righteous disposition, the living God decreed a law for it to keep and exercise, saying, "A law shall proceed from me, and I will make my judgment to rest for a light of the people."[693] A philosophy of newness of mind for the conversation was to proceed from the living God's *Mind*, the goal being for the conversation to regain its lost mental and moral faculties."[694] Such a course should be bitter against its character, "nevertheless afterward it yieldeth the peaceable fruit of righteousness unto them which are exercised thereby."[695] Hereafter it should love every mind encountering it.[696]

12. To "love" means, in reality, to edify, for where it says, "Love one another,"[697] it means, "Comfort yourselves together, and edify one another."[698] The "comfort" spoken of is not physical, but is mental and concerns learning, seeing as how it says, "All may learn, and all may be comforted."[699] If he says, "As I have loved you, that ye also love one another,"[700] and if this manner of love is not physical but mental, then as our heart has come to "serve in newness of spirit,"[701] it is that we must move other souls to say, "They have refreshed my spirit."[702]

13. Salvation's commandment is so strict against the mind because of the vocation its student should pick up afterwards.[703] The Word made flesh is no vision of a sensual interaction between some lewd superstitious understanding and a traditional pagan lore, but is rather the revelation of the living God's educational course finished within, and demonstrated by, the character of the

---

691   2 Corinthians 3:6
692   Titus 3:4
693   Isaiah 51:4
694   Hebrews 12:22
695   Hebrews 12:11
696   Romans 15:2
697   1 Thessalonians 4:9
698   1 Thessalonians 5:11
699   1 Corinthians 14:31
700   John 13:34
701   Romans 7:6
702   1 Corinthians 16:18
703   1 Timothy 4:16

devotional conversation. The living God's will is that "we should be holy and without blame before him in love,"[704] and this cannot commence but "through sanctification of the Spirit and belief of the truth."[705] This creation begins only as the *name* of the knowledge of the living God's chief witness is exercised within the inward parts.[706]

14. When we hear him praying, "Father, glorify thou me with thine own self with the glory which I had with thee before the world was,"[707] our main concern should be with what the *Father's* "self" is, for then we may understand what glory *he* is again asking to possess. When we can understand the Father's "glory" and "self," then we may correctly understand just what this prayer is for, but if without inquiring after just what that "self" and "glory" is, we open up ourselves "to fables and endless genealogies, which minister questions, rather than godly edifying which is in faith."[708]

15. There is no such thing as flesh existing in a time other than when it presently exists, and then until it ceases existence in death. What dwelt with the *Father* in the beginning was not the man, but the *Word*, the *Father's* own *Mind*, *Devotional Spirit*, or *Wisdom*.[709] If, at this point in the end of his ministry, he is praying for the glory with the *Father* that *he* had before the *world* was, then his prayer is for that same *Wisdom* to do within conversations just what it was doing before the then philosophy within religious world existed, and before all *things* pertaining to it were conscious.

16. "Christ was raised up from the dead by the glory of the Father,"[710] for it was "the Spirit of him that raised up Jesus from the dead."[711] The "glory" of the *Father* is his "Spirit," and through the act of raising *him* up, the "self" of the Father is revealed according to the saying, "God, who quickeneth all things,"[712] and, "God, who quickeneth the dead, and calleth those things which be not as though they were."[713]

17. The glory of the living God is the righteousness of the living God, and the righteousness of the living God, as exemplified by the *resurrection*, is

---

704   Ephesians 1:4
705   2 Thessalonians 2:13
706   Ephesians 3:9
707   John 17:5
708   1 Timothy 1:4
709   John 1:1-3
710   Romans 6:4
711   Romans 8:11
712   1 Timothy 6:13
713   Romans 4:17

in regenerating and reforming the conversation to find harmony with salvation's present science.[714] The *resurrection* was only an illustration of the living God's will, that we, through the commandment of his *Wisdom*, should fulfill the charge, "Put off concerning the former conversation the old man...and be renewed in the spirit of your mind...that ye put on the new man, which after God is created."[715] This faith is a law of creation conforming the conversation doing that law to the conversation once held by its chief witness, which is why the doer of this law says, "The law of the Spirit of life in Christ Jesus hath made me free from the law of sin and death."[716]

18. The "me" that should be glorified with the same glory as the *Father* is the *Spirit* of the *Father*, for, the Word fell upon this man's spirit in such a special way that, after he should finish his work, sealing to the character of conversations his communion for renewal, *he*; the Word; should return to the *LORD* that *he* came out from, which is why he says, "I leave the world, and go to the Father."[717]

19. It is written of this Prophet, "I have put my spirit upon him."[718] To have any thing "put upon" is to array, or to clothe, or to enter in to for the purpose of carrying, and the commencement of this communion between this man's spirit and the *Spirit* of the *LORD* is by him discerning the words of the scriptures, which is why it says, "I will pour out my spirit unto you, I will make known my words unto you."[719] This is why it says of this Prophet, "The spirit of the LORD shall rest upon him, the spirit of wisdom and understanding..."[720] The spirit of his conversation's conscience knew only communion with the living God's wisdom for knowledge of its will, which interaction formed his doctrine. It is due to this fellowship that he preached, "Whosoever believeth in him (that *Wisdom*) should not perish, but have everlasting life."[721]

20. There is only one force granting everlasting life, and this same minister counsels, "I know that his commandment is life everlasting,"[722] and, "The words that I speak unto you, they are spirit, and they are life."[723] Only "the words of

---

714   Romans 6:5,6
715   Ephesians 4:22-24
716   Romans 8:2
717   John 16:28
718   Isaiah 42:1
719   Proverbs 1:23
720   Isaiah 11:2,3
721   John 3:16
722   John 12:50
723   John 6:63

eternal life"[724] procure eternal *life*, and seeing as how "the Spirit is life because of righteousness,"[725] the eternal life spoken of is for the purpose of creation within the mind. Everlasting life is everlasting Spirit, that is, everlasting power for making us "of quick understanding in the fear of the LORD."[726] When he says, "It is the spirit that quickeneth,"[727] it is that the spirit of the mind makes the conversation's organs quick in understanding how to rightly live by the counsel at the heart of the scriptures.

21. This man didn't just overcome his naturally injurious conversation, but also the mind within the religious world, for he says, "I have overcome the world."[728] The words of eternal life are for quitting self's *spiritual* notions and the religious world's heresy to own the right fear and philosophy within the Bible, for we are to "be dead with Christ from the rudiments of the world."[729] Again, with "Christ" being an appellation for salvation's wisdom, to be "dead" with "Christ" means to have our conversation sanctified by the knowledge of the *name* of the living God's chief apostle for "casting down imaginations, and every high thing that exalteth itself against the knowledge of God."[730] He or she subscribing to this *name* will receive "everlasting consolation and good hope through grace"[731] "to be conformed to the image of his Son."[732]

22. Everlasting life is, in right context, everlasting consolation for the conversation's creation. This consolation is that good hope of the living God's *name*, for it says, "The commandment of God our Saviour...which is our hope."[733] The hope of the conversation should be on the good intention contained within salvation's commandment, which is why it says, "He that believeth on me hath everlasting life,"[734] and, "Whosoever believeth in him should not perish, but have eternal life."[735] The "me" and the "him" is no reference to the literal man, but to the commandment that came out of his mouth, which is why he says, "Ye

---

724   John 6:68
725   Romans 8:10
726   Isaiah 11:3
727   John 6:63
728   John 16:33
729   Colossians 2:20
730   2 Corinthians 10:5
731   2 Thessalonians 2:16
732   Romans 8:29
733   1 Timothy 1:1
734   John 6:47
735   John 3:15

are clean through the word which I have spoken unto you,"[736] and, "If a man love me, he will keep my words."[737]

23. There is no such thing as lethargically or inactively believing on the *name* of the living God's chief apostle. The mind must be "renewed in knowledge,"[738] for by "rightly dividing the word of truth,"[739] everlasting *life* will be given to forward creation's science within the inward parts, even a never ending supply of "the grace of life"[740] for the conversation. Grace assists righteousness, which is why it says, "They which receive abundance of grace and of the gift of righteousness shall reign in life by one, Jesus Christ."[741] Thus, knowing that the conversation could not embrace salvation's science without "Jesus Christ"; which "Jesus Christ" is creation's present law and commandment; the Prophet prayed for the glorification of the living God's wisdom for every willing and hopeful mind.

24. Creation is only by "Jesus Christ." The prayer, "Glorify thou me with thine own self with the glory which I had with thee before the world was,"[742] is a prayer for "Jesus Christ" to be the means whereby the mystery of creation's science is accomplished. For this cause, we cannot, because the creation spoken of is not literal, take "Jesus Christ" as signifying a literal man.[743] Herein it is well to remember that "the Lord Jesus Christ our Saviour"[744] is "the commandment of God our Saviour,"[745] which commandment is the *Word* or *Wisdom* of regeneration, which *Word* is "the kindness and love of God our Saviour toward man,"[746] or "the law of the Spirit of life."[747]

25. The Prophet's conversation is actually the one uttering the prayer. The glory that the living God's wisdom had before the *world* existed was an office for creation, and with the words of eternal life; which words are called, "Jesus Christ"; returned *home*, this wisdom should have every positive resource to create conversations after the likeness of its first *creature*, which is why it says,

736   John 15:3
737   John 14:23
738   Colossians 3:10
739   2 Timothy 2:15
740   1 Peter 3:7
741   Romans 5:17
742   John 17:5
743   2 Corinthians 5:16
744   Titus 1:4
745   Titus 1:3
746   Titus 3:4
747   Romans 8:2

"Of his own will begat he us with the word of truth, that we should be a kind of firstfruits of his creatures."[748] Thus, the ascension and high priestly mediation of this man's conversation means that conversations have an advocate to receive this wisdom's righteousness within their self.[749]

---

748   James 1:18
749   2 Corinthians 7:1

8

Distinct Bodies

1. If it is written, "All these things happened unto them for ensamples: and they are written for our admonition,"[750] when thinking on any acceptable *body* to sacrifice to the living God, our attention should find itself drawn to what did "serve unto the example and shadow of heavenly things."[751] When we think about this Prophet, and the *government* that existed within him, we should consider what government filled up the lamb or the beast that was offered.

2. Did the LORD accept an offering that was corrupt? He did not, which is why when they did bring flesh that was *sick*, they were told, "Cursed be the deceiver, which hath in his flock a male, and voweth, and sacrificeth unto the Lord a corrupt thing."[752] Every offering had to be without fault, for if it was with any fault, then that priest offering that error was considered a deceiver. Thus, if the *LORD* should offer any *thing* that is corrupt, then it is lawful for us to call him no *God* at all.

---

750   1 Corinthians 10:11
751   Hebrews 8:5
752   Malachi 1:14

3. If it says, "Neither doth corruption inherit incorruption,"[753] if we find "the eternal Spirit"[754] carnally inheriting flesh and blood, seeing as how "man is like to vanity,"[755] then we may know that the *LORD* of this transaction is a liar. The Spirit is eternal and without corruption because it is "the Spirit of truth, which proceedeth from the Father,"[756] and this *Father* is that "LORD God of Israel from everlasting, and to everlasting."[757] An error, then, should be made, if any offered male of his hand should have any blemish within him, and the eternal Spirit sensually mixed with the erroneous human being is a tragic flaw, which is why it says, "Either make the tree good...or else make the tree corrupt."[758]

4. Now, the LORD did once make a tree that contained both good and evil, that is, that had within its flesh the knowledge of the flesh's appetite and the knowledge of *heaven's spirit*. But what was the advice concerning this tree? He said, "Of the tree of the knowledge of good and evil, thou shalt not eat of it."[759] Herein it is well to understand the definition of a "tree," "for the tree of the field is man's life."[760]

5. When we hear of a "tree," our mind should not think on the tree that is in our backyard or in a forest, but it says, "He looked up, and said, I see men as trees, walking."[761] This tree of good and evil is a *man* owning the combined *nature* of *earth* and *heaven*; a "man" is representative of a priest, even as it says, "Then pleased it the apostles and elders, with the whole church, to send chosen men of their own company,"[762] and, "Seventy men of the elders of Israel."[763] Now, the "men" in company with the apostles were such figures as "James, Ce'phas, and John, who seemed to be pillars,"[764] wherefore when observing a *tree* of good and evil, it is that we are observing the conversation of a priest crafted after the a dark understanding and housing within itself an aspect supposedly of *heaven*. The instruction given to Adam was to not eat from this

---

753   1 Corinthians 15:50
754   Hebrews 9:14;
755   Psalm 144:4
756   John 15:26
757   Psalm 41:13
758   Mathew 12:33
759   Genesis 2:17
760   Deuteronomy 20:19
761   Mark 8:23,24
762   Acts 15:22
763   Numbers 11:16
764   Galatians 2:9

confused *tree*, but when pointing to that wholesome tree, they wee told, "Eat, and live for ever."[765]

6. Adam did not take knowledge of his *LORD's* charge, ignoring the counsel.[766] Adam failed to personally discern "the kindness and love of God our Saviour toward man"[767] through that *tree* of life, making it well to remember that "the Spirit is life."[768] This *tree* that bestowed *eternal life* on the eater was of only one shape, even the build of its *God*, and "God is a Spirit."[769] "The Spirit is life because of righteousness,"[770] and because it is the Spirit's righteousness to regenerate the inward parts; as it says, "To be strengthened with might by his Spirit in the inner man";[771] the consumption of this *tree* would provide the spirit of its eater with an abundant supply of newness in thought and feeling, which is why it says, "Be renewed in the spirit of your mind,"[772] and, "That which is born of the Spirit is spirit."[773]

7. If the Spirit is life for the good of righteousness, and if this righteousness occurs only in the spirit of the mind, then it is that "the spirit giveth life,"[774] and if the mind is the means whereby newness is received, then it is "that wisdom giveth life,"[775] which is why it says, "Let the word of Christ dwell in you richly in all wisdom."[776] This tree of life is a minister created by the knowledge of the living God's righteousness within the spirit of his mind, and for Adam to eat from this tree; that is, to obey the counsel, "If a man love me, he will keep my words";[777] then they too would assume the likeness of this *tree* to know and love the *name* of that tree's Creator.

8. But Adam disregarded the *LORD's* commandment and did not study the mind of *life's tree*. Instead, Adam fastened his attention on that corrupt minister owning a perverted devotional *form*, for they "saw that the tree was good for food, and that it was pleasant to the eyes, and a tree to be desired to make one

---

765 Genesis 3:22
766 Genesis 2:17
767 Titus 3:4
768 Romans 8:10
769 John 4:24
770 Romans 8:10
771 Ephesians 3:16
772 Ephesians 4:23
773 John 3:6
774 2 Corinthians 3:6
775 Ecclesiastes 7:12
776 Colossians 3:16
777 John 14:23

wise."[778] Now, isn't it written of that Prophet, "He hath no form nor comeliness; and when we shall see him, there is no beauty that we should desire him"?[779]

9. When we hear of the songs and psalms devoted to this cursed tree, knowing that if it was the *LORD's* it should not be desired, to whom do we suppose praise is towards? When the applause for a tree of good and evil becomes the universal creed of *earth*, knowing that if the earth did honor life's tree that the *earth* should find no pleasure in the tree, but in the words of the tree's fruit, when hearing the *earth*, and our own self, laud what is *pleasurable*, must we not wonder why the *earth* is so idolatrous and inordinately affectionate towards the *tree* of its adoration? Why was the tree of good and evil pleasant to the eyes, but not that Prophet who is a figure of that tree of life? The "eyes" mentioned are not literal, but are "the eyes of your understanding."[780]

10. Because conversations are naturally sensual, they would have a lazy and flesh-based religion that conforms to their natural understanding. This cursed tree was easily understood because it involved no thought: simply *eat* its *fruit* and retain its wealth without taxing the heart and mind. Chant its *name*, crave its *flesh*, believe its imagination, and own the fantasy of its perception, for then "a dispensation of the gospel is committed."[781]

11. When Eve saw this tree, a supposed shortcut to understanding the *LORD's* will presented itself to her, and she would have it. We understand that Eve chose a religion that was flesh-based because she rejected the right mental labor of the correct tree.[782] All things learned of *God* are through firstly mentally taxing the mind, which is why the conversation created by the Bible's wisdom says, "I will meditate in thy precepts, and have respect unto thy ways."[783] Without thoughtfully meditating on the law and commandment of the mind at the core of the scriptures, no knowledge of that mind's *name*, or of the knowledge of its chief apostle's *name*, will be given to the conversation.

12. Eve was supposed to learn her *LORD's name* by examining creation's right tree. By studying creation, and by comparing creation with the fruit of creation's tree, Adam was to know that their *LORD* is that *God* "who quickeneth the dead, and calleth those things which be not as though they were."[784]

---

778   Genesis 3:6
779   Isaiah 53:2
780   Ephesians 1:18
781   1 Corinthians 9:17
782   1 Corinthians 2:14
783   Psalm 119:15
784   Romans 4:17

Having this knowledge, they would have understood that creation's *voice* has within it a substance for regeneration, and when hearing any doctrine contrary to its *name*, they would have confessed, "He hath blessed; and I cannot reverse it."[785] Yet, because they failed to know the creating wisdom, and had failed to pass through that course of learning to make their lower nature better, the uncultivated members of their conversation guided their heart to a tree established upon a tragic fable.

13. For their negligence, because they "saw that the tree was good for food, and that it was pleasant to the eyes, and a tree to be desired to make one wise,"[786] they suffered a plague in that part of their being that led them astray, even their *eyes*. Herein the saying is fulfilled, "They have not known nor understood: for he hath shut their eyes, that they cannot see; and their hearts, that they cannot understand,"[787] and, "The LORD hath poured out upon you the spirit of deep sleep, and hath closed your eyes: the prophets and your rulers, the seers hath he covered."[788] Because their ambition fulfilled the saying, "Your eyes shall be opened, and ye shall be as gods, knowing good and evil,"[789] "if he called them gods, unto whom the word of God came,"[790] and if the word of God is born for priest and ministers, then it is that Adam should be cursed from understanding the plain doctrine of the *LORD's Spirit*. Hereafter Adam should share the heritage of *gods*, that is, of priests outside of their *garden's* mind.

14. This religious heritage is knowledge of a craft founded on the good and evil *form* of a tree, that is, of the corruptible and incorruptible shape of a *priest*. This foreign knowledge, it not only became the *death* of *Adam*, but every minister of Adam hopeful to honor the *Mind* of that *garden* would now suffer a slumber in their understanding, which slumber should redirect them to principles of *good* and *evil*. This "death passed upon all men"[791] inclined to honor that *Mind*, wherefore the *LORD*, understanding the plight of priests and minister, invented a means whereby they should escape this *death*.

15. Today, we have opened up to us the opportunity to quit this slumber for rightly refreshing our conversation on "the knowledge of his will in all wisdom

---

785   Numbers 23:20
786   Genesis 3:6
787   Isaiah 44:18
788   Isaiah 29:10
789   Genesis 3:5
790   John 10:35
791   Romans 5:12

and spiritual understanding."[792] The living God anciently promised, concerning this curse and our reconciliation to that promise's throne, "I will put enmity,"[793] which is why it says, "A law shall proceed from me, and I will make my judgment to rest for a light of the people."[794] By this law, *Adam* should obtain a new *birth* to the living God for perpetual communion, and this judgment is what the living God's chief apostle taught, which is why he said, "For judgment I am come into this world."[795]

16. His mission was to seal this law within the religious world. His mission was to establish a law for annihilating "sin" against the living God's *name* and the conversation's conscience.[796] He could not, in any other devotional form, have linked the spirit of the conversation to the character of the living God's conversation. Adam, possessing a flesh-based spiritual understanding, erred in judgment, therefore this Prophet, to amend that error, must also find his conversation in the same condition for its creative redemption. If the living God gave us a minister whose conversation possessed the *form* of good and evil, and if that conversation was sacrificed as an offering, then the *Mind* at the core of the scriptures would be a liar, for it cannot accept such a perverted oblation, meaning that conversations, by this defiled offering, would be without hope.

17. Seeing as how "in me (that is, in my flesh,) dwelleth no good thing,"[797] can what is in the form of good and evil suffice for what emptiness exists within our flesh? The reason why Adam chose a fable was because, like us, they also had no good thing within their flesh. Conversations are born from the *earth*, and the original nature of the *earth* is without any form of regenerative and benevolent understanding. Our conversation, being from the *earth*, owns a spirit after the *earth's* personality.

18. The natural estate of the human and of the devotional being is the natural mind of the animal, which is a build fulfilling the saying, "Thine eyes and thine heart are not but for thy covetousness, and for to shed innocent blood, and for oppression, and for violence, to do it."[798] So then what good can a *tree* born of a *good* and *evil* condition do for the naturally lame human and devotional character? It can do no good thing, for it will only lower that being to

---

792   Colossians 1:9
793   Genesis 3:15
794   Isaiah 51:4
795   John 9:39
796   Romans 8:3
797   Romans 7:18
798   Jeremiah 22:17

death, which is exactly what occurred in the beginning. Any perverse offering of the *LORD* would continue to confuse the mind and character of *Adam*, which is why it says of that Prophet, "As the children are partakers of flesh and blood, he also himself likewise took part of the same."[799]

19. The religious world, because of Adam's error, has within it a *tree* formed by *good* and *evil*. This tree is contrary to the work and labor of righteousness, fulfilling the saying, "O full of all subtilty and all mischief, thou child of the devil, thou enemy of all righteousness, wilt thou not cease to pervert the right ways of the Lord?"[800] Being a product of "that old serpent, called the Devil, and Satan, which deceiveth the whole world,"[801] we can no longer trust what is on the face of the *earth*, which is why it says, "I leave the world, and go to the Father."[802]

20. There still exists a *tree* of life and a *tree* of the knowledge of good and evil; what took place of old is for our learning today. The offering of the living God's chief witness removed the living God's wisdom from the religious world to rest above the *earth*, separating it from what is on *earth* by bringing it up in to the living God's direct presence. This act has left in the *earth* "a famine in the land, not a famine of bread, nor a thirst for water, but of hearing the words of the LORD,"[803] which is why the *eyes* of our faith are to be on "those things which are above."[804] That famine is caused by that same perverted *tree*, and if we are not where the *name* of this Prophet is, then we are become servant to the religious world's *lord* and *savior*. This is why it says, "Through knowledge shall the just be delivered."[805]

21. The entire point of this man's offering was to rescue our devotional understanding from the religious world's spiritual error, which is why it says, "To open their eyes, and to turn them from darkness to light, and from the power of Satan unto God, that they may receive forgiveness of sins, and inheritance among them which are sanctified by faith that is in me,"[806] and, "He shall redeem their soul from deceit and violence."[807] The power of error is deceitful

---

799　Hebrews 2:14
800　Acts 13:10
801　Revelation 12:9
802　John 16:28
803　Amos 8:11
804　Colossians 3:1,2
805　Proverbs 11:9
806　Acts 26:18
807　Psalm 72:14

violence against the living God's *name*, and this heresy takes place through a counterfeit *wisdom*, as it says, "Her priests have polluted the sanctuary, they have done violence to the law,"[808] and, "Shall the enemy blaspheme thy name for ever?"[809]

22. That tree of foreign knowledge is a perversion of truth, for where it says, "Thy law is the truth,"[810] and, "Thy word is truth,"[811] it is that a spurious craft mishandling "the law of truth"[812] should "cast down the truth to the ground."[813] The living God's chief apostle offered his conversation and its conscience for our consolation away from the religious world's demeaning practice to know the law of the Creator's *name*, that "the law is light."[814] This is why "that which is born of the Spirit is spirit,"[815] and why "the Spirit is life because of righteousness,"[816] because "every one that doeth righteousness is born of him."[817]

23. Birth to the living God is not by any belief without right action. His wisdom's righteousness is an active and experimental learning by faith on the hope of the knowledge of that Prophet's *name*. This righteousness or kindness must be done because the spirit of the mind can retain no thing without exercise. It is by the exercising of our faith on this *name* that redemption will occur, which is why it says, "Be ye transformed by the renewing of your mind, that ye may prove what is that good, and acceptable, and perfect, will of God."[818] This man must then own a conversation with no other spurious form because his offering is to benefit empty conversations. Therefore with his spirit; which are his *eyes*; having passed through salvation's course; for he says, "I know him, and keep his saying";[819] he, by one offering, has linked the *eyes* of conversations to the *Mind* at the core of the scriptures for the finishing of salvation's will within them.

24. With any other type of *form*, this man's experience is perverted and his act of no weight, but by his suffering, conversations are joined to the living God

---

808   Zephaniah 3:14
809   Psalm 74:10
810   Psalm 119:142
811   John 17:17
812   Malachi 2:6
813   Daniel 8:12
814   Proverbs 6:23
815   John 3:6
816   Romans 8:10
817   1 John 2:29
818   Romans 12:2
819   John 8:55

for justification to ensure reconciliation to the wisdom of such an intention. For if the *LORD* anciently accepted any polluted offering then we might have a license to believe whatever we might, but when it says that Moses "took the blood of calves and of goats...and sprinkled both the book, and all the people,"[820] seeing as how no animal has within it any other form than that of flesh, it is that the new covenant's will must be sealed with *blood*, for what else can and would suffice?

25. Moses used a beast to bless the people under the first covenant, and because "man hath no preeminence above a beast,"[821] the pattern of flesh for flesh must continue. But this new offering is of much greater value than that of old, for what sacrificed beast can account for the human being? With conversation sacrificed for conversation, and with the mind of a conversation perfected by the living God's wisdom and offered for the perfecting of other conversations, the example devotional experience is witnessed.

26. The goal is to have placed within the conversation the *name* of salvation's knowledge for a "spirit that confesseth that Jesus Christ is come in the flesh."[822] The Word made *flesh* and then sacrificed for *flesh* means a right conversation offered to enter into the mind of other willing conversations. This creation, being wholly inward, and by the living God's law of creation, should not move us to forget that "the law is spiritual."[823] Therefore, when hearing that "the Lord Jesus Christ our Saviour"[824] is come in the flesh, it is well to know that "the commandment of God our Saviour"[825] is come in to "the body of the sins of the flesh."[826] Because a *human* devotional conversation was offered with a mind confessing "Jesus Christ," it is that every natural conversation should also possess a mind created by "the kindness and love of God our Saviour toward man."[827] This "kindness" is "the doctrine of God our Saviour,"[828] "the doctrine

820   Hebrews 9:19
821   Ecclesiastes 3:19
822   1 John 4:24
823   Romans 7:14
824   Titus 1:4
825   Titus 1:3
826   Colossians 2:11
827   Titus 3:4
828   Titus 2:10

of Christ,"[829] or is "the law of the Spirit of life."[830] This is why praise is attributed the *name* "Jesus Christ."[831]

27. Because the living God has done right by our conversation, it is well to do right by the living God, for "we have received a commandment from the Father."[832] Our conversation should rest on this commandment for "understanding what the will of the Lord is."[833] If it is that we subscribe to the *earth's tree*, and not to the living God's *tree*, *earth's tree* will say, "It is too much for you to go up to Jerusalem."[834] It would not have us know about this *Place* because within it is "the general assembly and church of the firstborn, which are written in heaven,"[835] which is why it says, "But Jerusalem which is above is free, which is the mother of us all."[836]

28. This *heavenly Church* is that Mother Church for our understanding in justification's science. In order to receive any benefit from the mediating wisdom within this *Building*, it is demanded that we follow it into the place where it is at, seeing as how it "is gone into heaven, and is on the right hand of God."[837] The living God's chief apostle did finish his mission to the Mind at the core of the scriptures.[838] This mission is only half the task, for now we must see this man's conversation and take knowledge of its *name*. This *name* is no instrument of torture, nor is it in a grave, nor is it on *earth*, but the living God "raised him (his *name*) from the dead, and set him (his *name*) at his own right hand in the heavenly places."[839] Our personal vision of that *name* must therefore reveal it as our faith's intercessor.[840]

29. There is a reason why the living God's minister is called that *Son* of *man*. He is called this due to his philosophy being the chief minister and counselor of conversations. The word, "son," in this context, means a minister, steward, priest, or servant after Aaron's calling, as it says, "The sons of Aaron

---

829　2 John 1:9
830　Romans 8:2
831　Philippians 2:10,11
832　2 John 1:4
833　Ephesians 5:17
834　1 Kings 12:28
835　Hebrews 12:23
836　Galatians 4:26
837　1 Peter 3:22
838　Genesis 14:22
839　Ephesians 1:20
840　Revelation 1:13

the priests,"[841] and, "Aaron the priest, and the garments of his sons, to minister in the priest's office."[842] As a priest or minister, what good could a priest or minister not after the full likeness of priests and minister do? Again, such a minister of a perverted form would only minister to *death*, wherefore "we have not an high priest which cannot be touched with the feeling of our infirmities.[843]

30. Now, for example, if this man was carnally *God*, he should not be tempted, "for God cannot be tempted with evil, neither tempteth he any man."[844] But, being tempted, we understand that within him was no sensual establishment, but that he, possessing a natural *human* conversation, quit error against the living God, and this he did by the *name* "Jesus Christ," for it says, "Thou shalt call his name JESUS: for he shall save his people from their sins."[845] This man kept "Jesus Christ" to obtain a conversation that would not only violate the living God's charge, but serve as an example for conversation to do the same.

31. For this cause, our celebration of this man should quit all flesh-based "profane and vain babblings, and oppositions of science falsely so called,"[846] to reverently cast our *eyes* upon one "that, though he was rich, yet for your sakes he became poor, that ye through his poverty might be rich."[847] He could have taken the *wealth* of his knowledge to adopt the pride of the *trained*, but he refused status and embraced a ministry bringing the living God's words to life.[848] He lived out the mind at the center of Abraham's conversation. We learn this man's *nature* through the scriptures, that he carried his conversation according to Abraham's *form*, settling the dispute over his *nature*.

32. Seeing as how "the seed is the word of God,"[849] the seed of Abraham is the faith and doctrine of Abraham, which faith says, "To him that worketh not, but believeth on him that justifieth the ungodly, his faith is counted for righteousness."[850] The *nature* of the living God's chief messenger is that of Abraham and of his *offspring*, which is a mind obeying creation's commandment for the promise of its *voice*. Abraham faithfully obeyed and received the

---

841 2 Chronicles 31:19
842 Exodus 31:10
843 Hebrews 4:15
844 James 1:13
845 Matthew 1:21
846 1 Timothy 6:20
847 2 Corinthians 8:9
848 Hebrews 2:16,17
849 Luke 8:11
850 Romans 4:5

LORD's righteousness in the form of circumcision, wherefore this man obeyed and received the like *circumcision*, albeit within the heart of his conversation.[851] The conversation of the living God's chief apostle is our advocate for creation's great baptism, which is why our praise should wholly rest on his *name's* understanding.

---

851 Romans 2:29

9

Life's Nature

1. When thinking on the *nature* of the living God's chief apostle, not only must our thoughts rise higher than the human constitution, it is also necessary to define language according to what is written. When it says, "He took not on him the nature of angels; but he took on him the seed of Abraham,"[852] we have revealed to us a more important perspective than an understanding that depends upon the sensual form of a man. "Nature" is here defined as "seed." If we would like to know the "nature" of this man, it is not that our thoughts should run away with any lewd conjecture, but that this man took on the shape of a *seed*, and by that *seed* found himself classed with a specific assembly.

2. There are two natures to choose from: the first is of *angels*; the second is of *Abraham*. This means that one nature is better than the other, for if he chose Abraham's form then any other form is lame; if "the good seed are the children of the kingdom,"[853] then the bad seed, the *angels*, "are the children of

---

852   Hebrews 2:16
853   Matthew 13:38

the wicked one."[854] Thus, knowing that "the seed is the word of God,"[855] it is that the nature of angels and that nature of Abraham educate on a doctrine to whoever would find themselves with their *shape*. Now, if "the scripture, foreseeing that God would justify the heathen through faith, preached before the gospel unto Abraham,"[856] then it is well to be created after Abraham's *likeness*, because "if ye be Christ's, then are ye Abraham's seed, and heirs according to the promise,"[857] meaning that any other *nature* falls short of creation's present experience.

3. For the living God's chief apostle to find himself made after Abraham's seed, it is for him to be "Christ's" offspring for the reception of the promise through "Christ." Herein we are made to understand that "Christ" is but a reference to a philosophy, which is why it says, "We might be justified by the faith of Christ,"[858] and, "As many of you as have been baptized into Christ have put on Christ."[859] When hearing the use of the word "Christ," in proper context, it is well to remember that we are not hearing of a man, but of a doctrine.[860] "Christ" is a title or a term used for denoting the living God's new covenant law.

4. In order to be made after Abraham's seed, it is that "Christ" must work and accomplish a great labor within the person, which is why "the blessing of Abraham might come on the Gentiles through Jesus Christ; that we might receive the promise of the Spirit through faith."[861] The "seed" of Abraham is the "blessing" of Abraham, and this blessing must follow after the like reward given to him by faith, which is circumcision. This circumcision, because he received it by exercising faith on a promise, must occur in the same fashion, which is why we are to commit our conversation to what resurrects.[862] Therefore this circumcision, because it is performed by the living God's *Wisdom*, is greater than that circumcision of old, for since "God is a Spirit,"[863] that promise of the Spirit should only take place in the spirit of the mind, making this baptism a permanent consecration to the living God.

---

854   Matthew 13:38
855   Luke 8:11
856   Galatians 3:8
857   Galatians 3:29
858   Galatians 2:16
859   Galatians 3:27
860   2 Corinthians 5:16,17
861   Galatians 3:14
862   Romans 4:24
863   John 4:24

5. If of old it is said, concerning the offering at the altar, "He shall wash the inwards and the legs with water,"[864] so today our conversation must be offered to salvation's science so "that he might sanctify and cleanse it with the washing of water by the word."[865] Because "the blessing of Abraham might come on the Gentiles through Jesus Christ,"[866] and because this blessing is circumcision, it is well to understand that since this promised blessing is the formation of a new *creature* within the conversation, we must take into consideration that "there is a natural body, and there is a spiritual body."[867]

6. Abraham's seed is clearly with a natural body, but his *form* is sealed within a spiritual body. For "that was not first which is spiritual, but that which is natural; and afterward that which is spiritual";[868] therefore there is no debate over the *form* of the Prophet. This man, through the saying of "Jesus Christ," perfected the *body* of the spirit of his mind. By "Jesus Christ," we are to then be "perfect, as pertaining to the conscience,"[869] which is why he says, "I know him, and keep his saying."[870] Now, "we know that he abideth in us, by the Spirit which he hath given us,"[871] and if it says, "If ye be Christ's, then are ye Abraham's seed,"[872] it is that this man first became Abraham's through a commandment of the Spirit, and his example is left for our learning and doing.

7. To be "Christ's" it is to be conceived of the Spirit, and "that which is born of the Spirit is spirit."[873] There is no other form to assume when classed with Abraham than spirit, or mind. There is no other birth to the living God than that through the spirit of the mind, for "God is a Spirit."[874] Therefore, in order for the Spirit to have any offspring, it is that the Spirit must find itself within the *body* of the mind in order to develop a new creature, which is why "if any man be in Christ, he is a new creature."[875] "Christ" entered in to the inward parts is the only way this manner of creation can commence, and there is no such thing

---

864   Leviticus 1:13
865   Ephesians 5:26
866   Galatians 3:14
867   1 Corinthians 15:44
868   1 Corinthians 15:46
869   Hebrews 9:9
870   John 8:55
871   1 John 3:24
872   Galatians 3:29
873   John 3:6
874   John 4:24
875   2 Corinthians 5:17

as any literal or imaginary baptism occurring to fulfill this science, which is why it says, "To be strengthened with might by his Spirit in the inner man."[876]

8. The inner *man*, the character of our conversation, is to find itself strengthened with the *Spirit's might*, and concerning this "might," we read, "I am full of power by the spirit of the LORD, and of judgment, and of might."[877] For the Spirit to fill up the inward parts with "might," it is for the power of the Spirit, which is the judgment of the Spirit, to fill up the inward parts. For this cause, when it says, "Christ in you, the hope of glory,"[878] it is but a reference to the Spirit's counsel resting within and regenerating the conversation's conscience, which is why it says, "Let the word of Christ dwell in you richly in all wisdom,"[879] and, "Wisdom and might are his."[880] The Spirit's *might* is the Spirit's wisdom, and this wisdom is called, in right context, "The Lord Jesus Christ our Saviour,"[881] which Lord is, in all actuality, "the commandment of God our Saviour."[882]

9. "That which is born of the Spirit is spirit,"[883] and in order to embrace this *circumcision*, a commandment is necessary, seeing as how Abraham remained faithful to the words promised to him.[884] For this cause, like as how this man received circumcision of the flesh for his faith in *God's voice*, so too we, by exercising faith on the law of the new covenant promise, will experience a *circumcision* within "the body of the sins of the flesh."[885] The living God explained to us this promise through his chief apostle's *resurrection*, which is why "if the Spirit of him that raised up Jesus from the dead dwell in you, he that raised up Christ from the dead shall also quicken your mortal bodies by his Spirit that dwelleth in you."[886]

10. We have a promise to inherit, and it is to fill of our *flesh's* constitution, which "flesh" is the *body* of our conversation, with "Jesus Christ," for by "Jesus Christ" we are to possess a "spirit that confesseth that Jesus Christ is come in the

---

876   Ephesians 3:16
877   Micah 3:8
878   Colossians 1:27
879   Colossians 3:16
880   Daniel 2:20
881   Titus 1:4
882   Titus 1:3
883   John 3:6
884   Romans 4:20,21
885   Colossians 2:11
886   Romans 8:11

flesh."[887] Neither "Jesus Christ" nor "the flesh" is a literal identification of any *thing*. The Spirit's will is for the circumcision of the body of the conversation's mind, which is no physical body, wherefore to accomplish this, it is necessary for the Spirit to regenerate and reform the spirit of the mind for it to work out salvation between it, its self, and its members. Again, this science is not physical or natural: "the Lord Jesus Christ our Saviour,"[888] which is "the doctrine of God our Saviour,"[889] must find itself washing the conversation's inward parts if it should receive *heaven's* promise.

11. This promise is the living God's new covenant will, which covenant states: "From all your filthiness, and from all your idols, will I cleanse you. A new heart also will I give you, and a new spirit will I put within you: and I will take away the stony heart out of your flesh, and I will give you an heart of flesh. And I will put my spirit within you, and cause you to walk in my statutes, and ye shall keep my judgments, and do them."[890]

12. The offering of the Prophet opened up to every conversation the opportunity to hold communion with the living God's wisdom for newness of thought and feeling, which is why the doer of this will says, "The law of the Spirit of life in Christ Jesus hath made me free from the law of sin and death."[891] When observing conversations after Eden's experiment, "that every imagination of the thoughts of his heart was only evil continually,"[892] a controversy was presented to the living God, that conversations are become their own worst enemy. In order to help minds better their self, the living God created a law for their inward parts, saying, "A law shall proceed from me, and I will make my judgment to rest for a light of the people."[893] In order to better self, the conversation must accept this law within its conscience, and in so accepting, it must bring it into its heart for the accomplishment of its intention.

13. "Circumcision is that of the heart, in the spirit,"[894] leaving it that "every one that doeth righteousness is born of him."[895] When it comes to the seed of Abraham, it is written, "Thou wilt perform the truth to Jacob, and the mercy

---

887   1 John 4:2
888   Titus 1:4
889   Titus 2:10
890   Ezekiel 36:25-27
891   Romans 8:2
892   Genesis 6:5
893   Isaiah 51:4
894   Romans 2:29
895   1 John 2:29

to Abraham, which thou hast sworn,"[896] for that seed is born of "truth" and "mercy," which is conception by "righteousness." "Truth" is "righteousness," even as it says, "The fruit of the Spirit is in all goodness and righteousness and truth,"[897] and, "He that speaketh truth sheweth forth righteousness,"[898] and, "The LORD liveth, in truth, in judgment, and in righteousness."[899] When it says, "To be strengthened with might by his Spirit in the inner man,"[900] and, "I am full of power by the spirit of the LORD, and of judgment, and of might,"[901] it is that "truth" and "righteousness" are to capture the conversation's character, and this capturing through creation's present law and judgment.

14. For this cause, it is our responsibility to be "circumcised with the circumcision made without hands, in putting off the body of the sins of the flesh by the circumcision of Christ."[902] The living God's chief witness opened up the door for this righteousness to occur in the heart of our person, but he did not perform this righteousness within any mind by that offering. The offering only links the conversation to the new covenant will for the intention behind that will; it does not fulfill that will in any way.

15. He or she not experimenting with faith on this promise for devotional newness, examining and doing the law of that promise, will not receive the end of the promise, for did Abraham negligently or lethargically receive his circumcision? Isn't it written, "Abraham believed God, and it was imputed unto him for righteousness: and he was called the Friend of God"?[903] This man believed his *God*, and his belief is witnessed by him mentally and physically exercising faith on the words spoken to him, which is why it says, "Ye are clean through the word which I have spoken unto you."[904]

16. Our responsibility is to the counsel and judgment of that Prophet's *name*, which is the law and commandment of the living God's *name*. His sacrifice did not and could not fulfill this cleansing within any conversation, for an intelligent effort on the part of the human being is necessary. If Abraham received circumcision by his faith, and this equating to the righteousness of *God*, then we, in this

---

896 Micah 7:20
897 Ephesians 5:9
898 Proverbs 13:17
899 Jeremiah 4:2
900 Ephesians 3:15
901 Micah 3:8
902 Colossians 2:11
903 James 2:23
904 John 15:3

"time of reformation,"[905] must rely on no flesh-based manner of circumcision to suffice for *righteousness*, which is why it says, "Except your righteousness shall exceed the righteousness of the scribes and Pharisees, ye shall in no case enter into the kingdom of heaven."[906] The *nature* of *angels* is contrary to that of Abraham, and an "angel" is a human priest or minister, as it says, "Who maketh his angels spirits; his ministers a flaming fire."[907]

17. The *nature* of *angels* is after a scripted and faithless religious practice, which is why it says, "Full well ye reject the commandment of God, that ye may keep your own tradition."[908] The seed of angels is in their reliance on the law or code of a religious tradition, wherefore "that no man is justified by the law in the sight of God, it is evident: for, The just shall live by faith. And the law is not of faith.[909] The nature of the angel cannot comprehend faith's mental and physical exercise, for by strictly adhering to "commandments and doctrines of men,"[910] and "to fables and endless genealogies, which minister questions, rather than godly edifying which is in faith,"[911] they are become "that which is called the Circumcision in the flesh made by hands,"[912] instead of claiming that "circumcision made without hands, in putting off the body of the sins of the flesh by the circumcision of Christ."[913]

18. To one seed, learning of and doing the living God's knowledge leads in to the experience of righteousness; to the other seed, *righteousness* is through the execution of a handwritten religious tradition. Now, "if righteousness come by the law, then Christ is dead in vain,"[914] for he has figuratively liberated the conversation from a flesh-based service to "be filled with the knowledge of his will in all wisdom and spiritual understanding."[915] If we are still *blessed* by a carnal routine and a physical circumcision then he has done no thing at all, but since "that which is born of the flesh is flesh; and that which is born of the Spirit is spirit";[916] we keep and do his *name* for the appointed baptism.

---

905   Hebrews 9:10
906   Matthew 5:20
907   Psalm 104:4
908   Mark 7:9
909   Galatians 3:11,12
910   Colossians 2:22
911   1 Timothy 1:4
912   Ephesians 2:11
913   Colossians 2:11
914   Galatians 2:21
915   Colossians 1:9
916   John 3:6

19. Religious tradition is flesh-based and is for the base conversation, wherefore we may say, concerning that former ethic, what "then serveth the law? It was added because of transgressions, till the seed should come to whom the promise was made."[917] In order to properly preach the experience to come, and the creation that should commence, *God's* host stood by that "which was a figure for the time then present, in which were offered both gifts and sacrifices, that could not make him that did the service perfect, as pertaining to the conscience; which stood only in meats and drinks, and divers washings, and carnal ordinances, imposed on them until the time of reformation."[918]

20. Now, if what they did could do no good thing for the conscience; for it is the living God's will to "purge your conscience from dead works to serve the living God";[919] must we believe that any physical or tangible religious tradition can suffice for what salvation's will is blessed to accomplish? We are today alive during the year of devotional reformation, for if no ancient charge procured blessing, how much less should we obtain blessing under a spiritual dispensation by a physical religious routine? The nature of angels is after this lame manner of worship and service, which manner, when rightly understood, blatantly rejects the endeavor of the living God's wisdom within the conversation.

21. Adherence to the nature of angels involves putting to death the body of the living God's understanding, for "they profess that they know God; but in works they deny him, being abominable, and disobedient, and unto every good work reprobate."[920] If we actually do respect the living God's chief apostle, we would treat his *voice* as a living Savior, meaning that we would actually hear and obey the charge, "If a man love me, he will keep my words."[921] We treat his words as "a merciful and faithful high priest in things pertaining to God"[922] by allowing his *name* to work in our faith's mind, which is why he prays, "Father, glorify thou me with thine own self with the glory which I had with thee before the world was."[923]

22. Now, "in the beginning was the Word...all things were made by him; and without him was not any thing made that was made."[924] This man's *name*

---

917 Galatians 3:19
918 Hebrews 9:10
919 Hebrews 9:14
920 Titus 1:16
921 John 14:23
922 Hebrews 2:16
923 John 17:5
924 John 1:1-3

is an intercessor for the Word or Wisdom appearing within the conversation's conscience, and this appearing is for no thing else but creation. Before the religious world existed, the Word possessed *earth*, and with this man's *name* as "an high priest, who is set on the right hand of the throne of the Majesty in the heavens,"[925] it is become the Captain and Governor of the Word's intention. The "Word," being "the Word of life,"[926] and the Spirit being "the Spirit of life";[927] "because the Spirit is truth";[928] it is that this *name* is become Head over salvation's will by the administration of the living God, and since it says, "Thy law is the truth,"[929] its ministry is the means whereby creation's law is accomplished.

23. The nature of the angel is lazy, which is why Peter warns of them by saying, "Through covetousness shall they with feigned words make merchandise of you."[930] The aim of a right conversation is salvation's *kingdom*, and "flesh and blood cannot inherit the kingdom of God."[931] To adhere to any religious tradition, it is to count flesh and blood worthy of what it is not, which is to take the Author this will as vile and of no value, making this Prophet's *name* nonexistent and our hope in vain.[932] An entirely new religion is sprung up that honors *God's man* by the handwritten religious code, for, if of old it was understood that "the law having a shadow of good things to come, and not the very image of the things, can never with those sacrifices which they offered year by year continually make the comers thereunto perfect,"[933] must we today believe that perfection continues by the same error?

24. "Having begun in the Spirit, are ye now made perfect by the flesh?"[934] I should believe the living God to be a liar if, having established a mental course, and having formerly relayed that course by a natural tradition, one should then consent to the finishing of a philosophical will by a fleshly routine. If it is that our reliance is upon such a sensual manner of worship and service, it is that we have never begun our service in the Bible's wisdom, meaning that we have not obeyed the counsel, "Worship God in the spirit,"[935] and, "True worshippers shall

---

925   Hebrews 8:1
926   1 John 1:1
927   Revelation 11:11
928   1 John 5:6
929   Psalm 119:142
930   2 Peter 2:3
931   1 Corinthians 15:50
932   1 Corinthians 15:13-15
933   Hebrews 10:1
934   Galatians 3:3
935   Philippians 3:3

worship the Father in spirit and in truth."[936] Herein we can understand why a covetous and inordinately affectionate religion should idolize *Jesus*.

25. Creation is by the living God's wisdom within the spirit of the conversation's mind, and is blessed through the "truth," which "truth" is "the word of righteousness,"[937] "the law of truth."[938] Right worship is to the living God by the mind exercising its organs on "the law of the Spirit of life,"[939] for then the heart, passing through this circumcision without hands, will know and love the Father of their consolation, "and this is love, that we walk after his commandments."[940] If we have passed through creation's course of learning, we would have no issue with His commandments, yet to angels, and to their assemblies, it is written, "Full well ye reject the commandment of God, that ye may keep your own tradition."[941]

26. Therefore if we are not willing to shed the perverse nature of *angels*, along with its empty *righteousness*, we cannot enter into creation's classroom to know the living God's benevolence. It is our responsibility, so that we may faithfully and soberly chase after it, to quit our flesh-based conversation to own knowledge of the present promise. This is why we are counseled, "Put off concerning the former conversation the old man...and be renewed in the spirit of your mind; and that ye put on the new man, which after God is created in righteousness and true holiness."[942]

27. This course of learning, as described by Paul, is without self and the religious world's *chain*. The religious age has no knowledge of the *name* of the living God's chief apostle because it remains perpetually crucifying it, and we join in to that crucifixion by having not "escaped the pollutions of the world through the knowledge of the Lord and Saviour Jesus Christ."[943] It is our assignment, to have better relayed to our mind creation's will and wisdom, to stay on the hope of salvation's promise, day by day exercising faith on that *name* for knowledge.

28. There is no greater *nature* than that of Abraham, which is why that Prophet's conversation was fashioned after it. Now Abraham, he received his

---

936　John 4:23
937　Hebrews 5:13
938　Malachi 2:6
939　Romans 8:2
940　2 John 1:6
941　Mark 7:9
942　Ephesians 4:22-24
943　2 Peter 2:20

circumcision in human flesh. Must that Prophet receive his circumcision in the same flesh? What good is the *Spirit's* circumcision to human flesh? If the *LORD* chose *Abraham*, a human with no extra thing in him, to fulfill his will, and if by his *name* one is sealed, must this same *LORD* work by a human being with any extra *thing* in them?[944]

29. There is no in between within the Bible. For if it says, "Let your communication be, Yea, yea; Nay, nay: for whatsoever is more than these cometh of evil,"[945] must the Bible utter both Yes and No at the same time? The *nature* of the living God's chief apostle, in order to fulfill his commission, must be entirely human so that he, by his conversation's character, may seal the example of creation's pattern to every unsound conversation. Thus, his mind lived by the *seed* of Abraham, and by our subscription to Abraham's *name*, we too live by the *name* still giving power to conversations.

---

944   John 3:6; Matthew 12:33
945   Matthew 5:37

10

Our Right God

1. If "in the beginning was the Word, and the Word was with God, and the Word was God,"[946] is not, today, "God" the Word? If "in the beginning was the Word, and the Word was with God, and the Word was God,"[947] is not the Word that "God" if we desire to honor the living God? It does not say that God was with the Word, but that the Word was with God, letting us know that there exists a lawful division between God and the Word, that this *God* of the Word is "the King eternal, immortal, invisible, the only wise God,"[948] and that this Word is as a priest before that *throne*, becoming the *God* of every conversation created by that *throne*.

2. This is crucial to understand. The "Word" is "the Word of life,"[949] and this *Word* is "the Spirit of life."[950] In right context of language, the *Spirit* is *God*, because when it was with its God in the beginning, it created all *things* for its

---

946   John 1:1
947   John 1:1
948   1 Timothy 1:17
949   1 John 1:1
950   Revelation 11:11

God, seeing as how "all things were made by him; and without him was not any thing made that was made."[951] Thus, when hearing that Prophet say, "Have faith in God,"[952] he is making a very plain confession that not only is he not "God," but that there exists a Creator for us and him to have faith on, and if in the beginning the Word was God, and if "God is a Spirit,"[953] then the God that we are counseled to have absolute faith on is that living *Spirit*. This means that the God of the conversation is living God's *Spirit* or *Wisdom*, and since "a spirit hath not flesh and bones,"[954] it is that our devotional conversation is to be governed by this *Wisdom*.

3. Our traditional lapse in judgment, concerning the general *form* of the living God's chief apostle, is based upon a misinterpretation and misunderstanding of the saying, "The Word was made flesh."[955] If the Word is God, and if "God is a Spirit,"[956] then the Word conformed to flesh is of a more sensible outcome than a sensual communion between humanity and *divinity*. Paul once wrote, "Having begun in the Spirit, are ye now made perfect by the flesh?"[957] When he wrote this, was he writing to ministers *naturally* conceived by the *Spirit*? Did his audience physically begin in and by the Spirit? If they were not innately of some negligent amalgamation of the Word and flesh, must that Prophet embrace this tragedy? To have begun in the Spirit is to have commenced one's conversation by the *voice* of the living God's wisdom, and this course is as it was in the beginning, "for he spake, and it was done; he commanded, and it stood fast."[958]

4. The LORD "hath in these last days spoken unto us by his Son,"[959] and by our obedience to that *voice*, we will experience the same end that heaven and earth knew at creation. The Word made flesh is a commandment made flesh, and because "that which is born of the Spirit is spirit,"[960] the Word can only occupy flesh by the spirit of the mind. Again, a commandment is needed for the mind to examine and do if it should know the operation of that working wisdom; personal faith is to find itself corrected for employment by the wisdom

---

951   John 1:3
952   Mark 11:22
953   John 4:24
954   Luke 24:39
955   John 1:14
956   John 4:24
957   Galatians 3:3
958   Psalm 33:9
959   Hebrews 1:2
960   John 3:6

retained within the conversation's mind, which is why it says, "It is the spirit that quickeneth."[961]

5. It makes no sense why the living God's Prophet should preach a doctrine of the regeneration and reformation of the spirit of the mind if he himself did not experience this. Without a fashion that was entirely human, he could not know what end the Spirit should serve, but he kept and dressed his conversation by creation's new covenant will to know its promise, which is why he says, "I know him, and keep his saying."[962] He is counseling his audience to experiment with faith in the living God's commandment. The Word made flesh does not and cannot make that flesh *God*; this is an incorrect interpretation. The Word made flesh makes the *flesh* an instrument of the *Spirit* to the praise of the *Mind* at the center of the scriptures.[963]

6. We understand that he passed through this course of learning because it says, "God was with him."[964] If this man was that *God* then there would be no need for God to be with him, but because the Word of revival and reform dwelt within the spirit of his faith's intellect, the members of his *flesh* embraced a transformation to be of use. The Word, or the Wisdom of the scriptures, became the God of his conversation's character so that he may rightly represent the living God's *name* to a *world* in opposition to the *form* of that *name*, which is why it says of him, "He will magnify the law, and make it honourable."[965]

7. If we had a better understanding of what the Word in flesh meant, the God of our devotion would also be that *Word*, informing us of our responsibility to the Mind that *Word* proceeds out from, seeing as how this is that same "Spirit of truth, which proceedeth from the Father."[966] The word, "God," then, must be better understood, for if the God of our creation is this same Word and Spirit, and if the living God, by this Word, has "created all things by Jesus Christ,"[967] then the God of salvation's assembly is "Jesus Christ," but since this manner of creation is not physical, it is well to understand that "Jesus Christ" is a term

---

961   John 6:63
962   John 8:55
963   Romans 6:19
964   Acts 10:38
965   Isaiah 42:21
966   John 15:26
967   Ephesians 3:9

denoting the law of that Word and Spirit of life making, in right context, "the Lord Jesus Christ our Saviour"[968] "the commandment of God our Saviour."[969]

8. The Word is a commandment or instruction, as it says, "My spirit that is upon thee, and my words which I have put in thy mouth,"[970] and, "The Spirit of the LORD spake by me, and his word was in my tongue."[971] Creation, because it today is accomplished within the spirit of the mind, must occur by a mental commandment, which is why the doer of the Creator's commandment says, "The law of the Spirit of life in Christ Jesus hath made me free from the law of sin and death."[972] Liberty from the law of "sin" is the aim of the living God's wisdom, and this counsel is perfected only within the inward parts. If our conversation is to be "his workmanship, created in Christ Jesus,"[973] and if this creation is not physical, then the *God* of our newness is "Jesus Christ," which "Jesus" is "the doctrine of God our Saviour."[974]

9. Our Savior, then, is just as Paul says, "God." Seeing as how the Word is God, and that "God is a Spirit,"[975] our Savior is the Word, making our salvation through the *Spirit's* saying. This is why it says, "Ye are clean through the word which I have spoken unto you,"[976] and, "If a man love me, he will keep my words."[977]

10. Nowhere is it written, and there is no hint in the scriptures, that the man *Jesus* is become *God*. Such irrelevant conjecture is due to a misunderstanding and a misrepresentation of the scriptures. It is not the man that is become *God*, but rather the knowledge of his *name* is become "God," and his *name* is defined as "Jesus Christ." This should not be thought of as the literal name of a man, but "name" means doctrine, as it says, "And hast kept my word, and hast not denied my name,"[978] and, "Thou holdest fast my name, and hast not denied my faith."[979] There is a clear difference between the *name* of the man and the *flesh* of the man, for there is no instruction in the scriptures, nor is there any hint, to

---

968   Titus 1:4
969   Titus 1:3
970   Isaiah 59:21
971   2 Samuel 23:2
972   Romans 8:2
973   Ephesians 2:10
974   Titus 2:10
975   John 4:24
976   John 15:3
977   John 14:23
978   Revelation 3:8
979   Revelation 2:13

carnally worship the man as *God*, but to rather reverence his *name*, as it says, "We might be justified by the faith of Christ,"[980] and, "There is none other name under heaven given among men, whereby we must be saved."[981]

11. There is a difference in being justified by the *name* of the man and being justified by a supposition on the man's flesh. "Name" is not flesh, but it is wholly spirit or mind, which is why, by the knowledge of his *name*, creation's science is forwarded within the spirit of the conversation's conscience; "that which is born of the Spirit is spirit."[982] This is why it says, "By his knowledge shall my righteous servant justify many."[983]

12. We might therefore find ourselves misled in judgment when hearing, "He worshipped him,"[984] and, "There came a leper and worshipped him,"[985] and, "Then they that were in the ship came and worshipped him."[986] The actions of such individuals are contrary to the speech of the man, who says, "Have faith in God."[987] There is one man who perfectly spoke a conversation that was blessed by this man's *name*, for after healing ten lepers, only "one of them, when he saw that he was healed, turned back, and with a loud voice glorified God."[988]

13. It is well for us to understand, when examining the scriptures, the Bible's process of thinking. All that worshipped this man were *Jews*, but this one leper, "he was a Samar'itan."[989] Not all revered his *words*, but many Jews, after they heard his doctrine, "were all amazed, and glorified God, saying, We never saw it on this fashion."[990] There is then an illustration made of two classes of hearers: the first, being without his doctrine, will worship the man; the second, existing within his doctrine, will glorify the living God by that doctrine.[991] So then scriptures have established the route for them "which say they are Jews, and are not, but do lie,"[992] and it is a conversation founded upon deception; by their hard-

---

980   Galatians 2:16
981   Acts 4:12
982   John 3:6
983   Isaiah 53:11
984   John 9:38
985   Matthew 8:2
986   Matthew 14:33
987   Mark 11:22
988   Luke 17:15
989   Luke 17:16
990   Mark 2:12
991   John 4:23
992   Revelation 3:9

ness of heart to apply self to the law of his *voice*, "God shall send them strong delusion, that they should believe a lie."[993]

14. There is no greater lie than literally worshipping this man as *God*, especially when his *name* today is "a merciful and faithful high priest in things pertaining to God."[994] There is no room for another "God" due to how it says, "Is there a God beside me? yea, there is no God; I know not any,"[995] and, "I, even I, am the LORD; and beside me there is no saviour,"[996] and, "I am the first, and I am the last; and beside me there is no God."[997] There is only one *Mind* behind it all, and there is only one *name* mediating our experience.[998]

15. It would be blasphemy for the living God's chief apostle to claim himself as *God*. Such a profession is contrary to the office of his *name*, seeing as how "he shall stand and feed in the strength of the LORD, in the majesty of the name of the LORD his God."[999] This *name's* responsibility is to magnify the name and doctrine of its *LORD*; it is this *name* that is the personal Savior. Bible salvation is for the inward parts of *Adam*, wherefore to literally take the flesh of *God's man* as being any thing to the inward parts, and to stay on that literal persuasion, is error. Salvation's science is forwarded by his *name*, to the end "the name of our Lord Jesus Christ may be glorified in you, and ye in him."[1000] As the living God's high priest, it is this *name's* responsibility to recover our *eyes* by its *voice* to find harmony with its Author.

16. Service to the living God outside of this man's name is religious error because it removes him from the Creator of that *name*, and in so doing, retards the current mediation of his *name*. With this man as *God*, he is become a force against the character at the heart of the scriptures.[1001] This man's *name* is as Aaron, for when they saw him they said, "Blessed be the King that cometh in the name of the Lord."[1002] There is only one type of man that is fit to appear in the LORD's name, and it is Aaron and his sons, which is why it says, "Aaron

---

993 2 Thessalonians 2:11
994 Hebrews 2:17
995 Isaiah 44:8
996 Isaiah 43:11
997 Isaiah 44:6
998 1 Timothy 2:5
999 Micah 5:4
1000 2 Thessalonians 1:11
1001 2 Thessalonians 2:4
1002 Luke 19:38

was separated...to burn incense before the LORD, to minister unto him, and to bless in his name for ever."[1003]

17. The "King" of the LORD is a reference to nothing but a high priest of the living Creator, which is why it says, "Yet have I set my king upon my holy hill of Zion."[1004] The "hill" of the LORD is the temple of the Spirit, for it says, "Who shall abide in thy tabernacle? who shall dwell in thy holy hill?"[1005] and, "Exalt the LORD our God, and worship at his holy hill."[1006] Removing this man's *name* from its priestly office removes the opportunity for conversations to enter into its *heavenly* Sanctuary to learn of the Ming of that Temple, to the end we may reverence that Mind by its knowledge.

18. We cannot know the Author of creative devotional redemption if we are not found where this *name* is. We only have intercession for the new covenant will through this *name's* mediation, and that mediation, in and of itself, seeing as how "it pleased the Father that in him should all fulness dwell,"[1007] does not exist by its own power. For its ministry to "be filled with all the fulness of God,"[1008] its appointment must "be filled with the Spirit,"[1009] or with the *Word*. This man's prayer, "Father, glorify thou me with thine own self with the glory which I had with thee before the world was,"[1010] is a prayer for the same creation within his conversation's spirit to continue within every conversation joined to his ministry's confidence.

19. Before the *world* was, the *Word* was in the living God's bosom as the saving Creator of the living God's thoughts. With "Christ being come an high priest of good things to come, by a greater and more perfect tabernacle, not made with hands,"[1011] we have the opportunity to receive that "circumcision made without hands, in putting off the body of the sins of the flesh by the circumcision of Christ."[1012] This circumcision is without hands because it occurs within. By experiencing the promised newness through learning of and doing salvation's will, reverence for the *name* of that promise will move the mind to

---

1003   1 Chronicles 23:13
1004   Psalm 2:6
1005   Psalm 15:1
1006   Psalm 99:9
1007   Colossians 1:19
1008   Ephesians 3:19
1009   Ephesians 5:18
1010   John 17:5
1011   Hebrews 9:11
1012   Colossians 2:11

soberly and rightly care for the living God, "and this is love, that we walk after his commandments."[1013]

20. With *God's* man as that *God* to be worshipped, blotting out the *LORD* from view by removing the full weight of his *name's* high priestly appointment, there is absolutely no reason to keep any one of God's commandments. Such a disposition resonates with a delusional conversation. This is understood because "we do know that we know him, if we keep his commandments. He that saith, I know him, and keepeth not his commandments, is a liar, and the truth is not in him."[1014]

21. We cannot know the living God without the *name* of his chief witness, for by this name, the Word is pronounced to our heart and mind, moving our person to love the living God, "and this is love, that we walk after his commandments."[1015] We understand our deviation from salvation's science when we cannot bear to hear or think on any one of the living God's commandments. We cannot stand one of those commandments because our conversation, being flesh-based, owns the rebuke, "Full well ye reject the commandment of God, that ye may keep your own tradition."[1016] Herein is the plight of falsely applying and misinterpreting the Bible, even a stout devotion to a tradition for a pretended *righteousness* that is, in reality, no righteousness at all.

22. This man's *name* without the living God becomes a comic of "Jewish fables, and commandments of men, that turn from the truth."[1017] Thus, if he says, "I can of mine own self do nothing,"[1018] and, "If I bear witness of myself, my witness is not true,"[1019] when found doing all things to witness of *himself*, must we not wonder where the source of *his* pretended power is found?

23. Concerning that false light of *his*, we do not have to think hard about its source, seeing as how "Satan himself is transformed into an angel of light"[1020] to them that do not know creation by the living God's wisdom.[1021] "Satan" is an appellation or term used to highlight a particular religion that deceives self and the religious world. We may understand that, in the beginning, Eden's chosen

---

1013   2 John 1:6
1014   1 John 2:3,4
1015   2 John 1:6
1016   Mark 7:9
1017   Titus 1:14
1018   John 5:30
1019   John 5:31
1020   2 Corinthians 11:14
1021   Philippians 3:9

garden was the only undefiled location of the LORD's *name* by how the serpent said, "Your eyes shall be opened, and ye shall be as gods, knowing good and evil."[1022] In order to say such a thing, this knowledge must already be a living reality.

24. The "gods" mentioned are ministers of the *LORD's* doctrine, for "he called them gods, unto whom the word of God came."[1023] At this time, the religion of the *serpent* ruled among the ministers of *Eden's religion*, for the serpent speaks of the end to be received by negligence in present tense, letting us know that his persuasion has already misled a great host. "The great dragon...that old serpent, called the Devil, and Satan, which deceiveth the whole world,"[1024] is the lot of the individual not willing to bring their faith to the scriptures.[1025] "Satan" is that *Serpent* and *Dragon*, and concerning him, we read, "Pharaoh king of Egypt, the great dragon."[1026] The deception of *Satan* is the religion of *Egypt*, and this religion became that tragedy in the garden wearing *good* and *evil*. That *tree* became the deceiving *angel*, counseling *Adam* to disobey the commandment for the religious vision of *his* own heart.

25. The living God's chief apostle without the Creator is become servant to *Satan*, whose mind is Egyptian, and whose emblem, to distinguish it from the living God's seventh day, is founded on "the third day, which was Pharaoh's birthday."[1027] There should be no contrary or conflicting Remembrance of creation if the conversation is immersed within creation's science. It is by this science that the living God is known and respected, "and this is love, that we walk after his commandments."[1028]

26. When the conversation of the living God's chief apostle was figuratively brought up in to into the living God's heavenly Building, it brought up with it the *name* or the wisdom of its confidence. But the tragedy of the dragon remains on the *earth*. This man's conversation took away and separated religious error from the *world* of the living God's will, purifying the *name* of that will for every willing conversation. But on *earth* the *wisdom* of *good* and *evil* continues, and so much so that we are warned, "Beware lest any man spoil you through philosophy and vain deceit, after the tradition of men, after the rudiments of the world, and not

---

1022   Genesis 3:5
1023   John 10:35
1024   Revelation 12:9
1025   Colossians 3:1
1026   Ezekiel 29:3
1027   Genesis 40:20
1028   2 John 1:6

after Christ."[1029] With his *name* and conversation *above*, the only possible way to know the living God is through the scriptures. If we fail to do so, we will in fact behold a *serpent* elevated between heaven and earth, and having no knowledge of that right *name*, a counterfeit *lord* and *savior* will suffice.

27. The number one commandment confessing the living God's supreme authority over natural and inward creation is the seventh day. If, in the beginning, the Word was with God and was also God, and if of this same Word, who is God and is one with God, it says, "God blessed the seventh day, and sanctified it,"[1030] then we are absolutely wrong when adhering to a *Sabbath* contrary to this. We are wrong because our *God* is not the Word, or is not the law of the living God's Spirit or Wisdom, but is some *lore* because we have not brought salvation's *name* in to our belief's inward parts. If the Word were that God of our conversation, we would confess, "The law of the Spirit of life in Christ Jesus hath made me free from the law of sin and death,"[1031] which is a statement of creation. Being the same creation of the same Word from the beginning of creation, the seventh day appointment of this same Spirit of the same Creator would also be ours.

28. The sign of the present circumcision is entrance in to the Word's seventh-day "rest," which is why it says, "Thou hast given a banner to them that fear thee, that it may be displayed because of the truth."[1032] By doing "the law of truth,"[1033] the "rest" of truth's commandment will dawn upon our conscience. The doer of salvation's law will know that "the seventh day is the Sabbath of the LORD,"[1034] but the conversation without sanctification's commandment, being without reconciliation to creation's throne, will know contrary.

29. It is our conversation's responsibility to honor salvation's science through the *name* of the living God's chief apostle.[1035] Right worship is only by the spirit of the mind, which is why it says, "Live according to God in the spirit,"[1036] and, "Worship God in the spirit."[1037] Our mind is to have its organs exercised on the scripture's truth, and "because the Spirit is truth,"[1038] it is that our mind must

---

1029 Colossians 2:8
1030 Genesis 2:3
1031 Romans 8:2
1032 Psalm 60:4
1033 Malachi 2:6
1034 Exodus 20:10
1035 John 4:23
1036 1 Peter 4:6
1037 Philippians 3:3
1038 1 John 5:6

learn and thoroughly understand the living God's Word if it should soberly and justly honor that Wisdom's *name*. Because "God is a Spirit,"[1039] there is no other satisfactory manner of worship and service, which is why it says, "God is a Spirit: and they that worship him must worship him in spirit and in truth."[1040]

30. Such a strict manner of learning is for the good of our conversation's conscience. The goal of the Bible is to "purge your conscience from dead works to serve the living God."[1041] Dead *works* are lame religious manners, but every right and living work is "through sanctification of the Spirit and belief of the truth."[1042] A right *work* is firstly experiencing the living God's righteousness through the spirit of the mind, which is why it says, "Seek ye first the kingdom of God, and his righteousness."[1043] Our personal faith's primary assignment is to know and experience the living God's goodness; hereafter we will love the *Mind* of this benevolence. If we love the living God, that love will find expression through our obedience to *His* every word. This is why creation is today internal.

31. There is no thing in this scriptures pointing to the *Jesus* as any thing to be worshipped, but rather every witness directs the mind to the living God, and to the *Wisdom* or *Word* of the living God, which is why it says, "The true worshippers shall worship the Father,"[1044] and, "God is a Spirit: and they that worship him must worship him in spirit and in truth."[1045] It is then well for us to do what Bible counsels, for the Word, being that God of the conversation, is to be that law and judgment of our devotion.

32. It is true that the name of the living God's wisdom is "Jesus Christ," and that this "Jesus Christ" is the conversation's "God" and "Savior," but context must not be forgotten. Since the living God's will is creation, and since this creation is not physical, but is entirely mental, "the Lord Jesus Christ our Saviour"[1046] is "the commandment of God our Saviour,"[1047] which commandment our faith must know. The God that is our Savior is the Word or Wisdom of the scriptures that is our Savior, for this salvation, seeing as how "that which

---

1039 John 4:24
1040 John 4:24
1041 Hebrews 9:14
1042 2 Thessalonians 2:13
1043 Matthew 6:33
1044 John 4:23
1045 John 4:24
1046 Titus 1:4
1047 Titus 1:3

is born of the Spirit is spirit,"[1048] is wholly constrained to the spirit of the conversation's conscience. Our conception is therefore by our "God," which is the Wisdom or Counsel of Creation and the Word of Truth, which *birth* is by "the law of the Spirit of life,"[1049] for it says, "Of his own will begat he us with the word of truth."[1050]

1048 John 3:6
1049 Romans 8:2
1050 James 1:18

11

Faith's Good Exercise

1. Because "the Word was with God, and the Word was God,"[1051] when hearing, "Have faith in God,"[1052] the Bible is counseling us to have unwavering faith in the Word. The God of our personal faith should be the Word, and because "God is a Spirit,"[1053] it is that the God of our confidence should be the Bible's Wisdom or *Spirit*. We are to know that it is "the living God, who is the Saviour of all men, specially of those that believe,"[1054] by our careful review of this *Spirit's Wisdom*.

2. The living God is, in the scriptures, that Savior, because its *Spirit*, or *Wisdom*, is the means whereby creation is forwarded. Because the *Spirit* proceeds from the living God, its glory is its chief Wisdom, and because it is the living God's glory that blesses the ministry of that Prophet's *name*, by the knowledge of that *name's* mediation, we return to the *Wisdom* of its consecration. It

---

1051 John 1:1
1052 Mark 11:22
1053 John 4:24
1054 1 Timothy 4:10

will be impossible for us to know the living God if our conversation is without knowledge of the God of our confidence, which God is the Word, which Word is the Spirit, which Spirit is "the law of the Spirit of life,"[1055] which law is "the kindness and love of God our Saviour toward man."[1056] Because it is a law that is our Savior, only faith on the promise of this law can procure the will of that law to the spirit of the mind; "that which is born of the Spirit is spirit."[1057] The good kindness, then, of the *Spirit*, is blessed to the mind, which is why it says, "Be ye transformed by the renewing of your mind, that ye may prove what is that good, and acceptable, and perfect, will of God."[1058]

3. It is therefore become our responsibility to take the Word as that God over our faith. We cannot have faith without knowledge, for if I'm ignorant of what to believe on, what can I believe on? The Word is a law for inward creation, wherefore every doer of that law says, "The law of the Spirit of life in Christ Jesus hath made me free from the law of sin and death."[1059] The creation of a better government within the conversation is the end of the living God's wisdom, which end is understood through the example given by the living God's chief apostle.[1060]

4. Salvation's science is performed when the living God's wisdom is allowed to operate within the spirit of the conversation's conscience. This points to the fact that because the Word is, in reality, "the words of eternal life,"[1061] the mind must keep words in order to obtain faith in the promise of those words, and words are not physical. A physical religious practice cannot suffice for the spiritual renovation to commence by executing faith on a commandment, wherefore it is necessary to mentally discern the living God's will, which is why it says, "Give attendance to reading, to exhortation, to doctrine,"[1062] and, "Take heed unto thyself, and unto the doctrine; continue in them: for in doing this thou shalt both save thyself, and them that hear thee."[1063]

5. The mind, for the sake of acquiring knowledge, is to find itself exercising its organs on salvation's will for material to physically prove. Because if it is

---

1055　Romans 8:2
1056　Titus 3:4
1057　John 3:6
1058　Romans 12:2
1059　Romans 8:2
1060　Romans 8:11
1061　John 6:68
1062　1 Timothy 4:13
1063　1 Timothy 4:16

written, "Thy faith hath made thee whole,"[1064] then it is that our faith needs cultivating if it should ever work for us. Our heart moves, our organs function, our brain works, our muscles loosen or contract, due to their nourishment. By what we feed our organs, they take that substance and function without our noticing, to the end we may stay on our external world and have no thought for what is internal. Our faith has the same structure. Our faith cannot feed itself unless we place nutrition into it for growth. Our faith is made strong by every opportunity we have to prove the Bible's words, and we obtain material to prove by taxing our mind on its words.

6. Our faith saves or delivers our understanding from reproach because "the spirit giveth life,"[1065] but if there is no life added to the spirit or character of our faith, must we believe the spirit within should add life to our confidence? The spirit gives life because of the knowledge it receives when examining the Bible's voice, which is why it says, "The excellency of knowledge is, that wisdom giveth life to them that have it."[1066] Without wisdom, the organs of our conversation receive no *life* to keep our faith sober, and without our faith kept and exercised in knowledge, we will become "idle, wandering about from house to house."[1067]

7. A faith without knowledge is bound to suffer pre-mature death.[1068] Again, the Word is a commandment, as it says, "Whoso despiseth the word shall be destroyed: but he that feareth the commandment shall be rewarded,"[1069] and, "He sendeth forth his commandment upon earth: his word runneth very swiftly."[1070] "Death" is the result of failing to do the Bible's Word or Commandment. This *death* is not literal, but is as it says, "God hath given them the spirit of slumber, eyes that they should not see, and ears that they should not hear."[1071] Our conversation needs to find, for its regeneration, itself exercised in creation's present Commandment.[1072] The crucifixion and resurrection of that *body* of *organs* within the conversation's constitution is the hope of the living

---

1064 Luke 17:19
1065 2 Corinthians 3:6
1066 Ecclesiastes 7:12
1067 1 Timothy 5:13
1068 Proverbs 19:15,16
1069 Proverbs 13:13
1070 Psalm 147:15
1071 Romans 11:8
1072 Romans 6:5,6

God's will and wisdom, to the end we may employ those organs for good use to better serve that understanding, our conversation, and other minds.

8. To do "good" is to edify, which is why it says, "Let every one of us please his neighbour for his good to edification."[1073] The greater our mind is edified by the Bible, the greater our faith can be to keep us on the hope of the reward to appear by faith in its *voice*. It is our faith, and the illustration that our faith draws upon the walls of our heart, that encourages the mind to move forward in salvation's science. The living God's will is an amendment to the conversation for what Eden's experiment revealed, wherefore the Creator thought well to create a law and a judgment for our inward and devotional recuperation.[1074]

9. Seeing as how this creation is inward,[1075] this redemption is for the spirit of the mind at this present time. The iniquity, then, that the living Father desires to firstly handle is not temporal, but is religious or devotional, for by "the washing of water by the word,"[1076] the conversation will, in addition to correcting the members of the heart, pick up a more benevolent scheme for the physical body. The greater our mind is edified by the living God's wisdom, the greater our personal faith may edify our character to properly direct our conversation to know creation's present will.

10. The point of salvation's law is only known by exercising faith on it, for Abraham carried faith in the living God's promise and received the baptism of circumcision, but the living God's chief apostle has prepared, through the intercession of his understanding, a better witness for us.[1077] Our belief, if it is that we care to better serve both the living God's wisdom and other minds, is to rest on the hope of this present circumcision. The "good" that we are to perform must find itself according to the Creator's kindness, which is why it says, "And love one another, as he gave us commandment."[1078]

11. There is a way to "love" that reflects the living God's character, for when it says, "Love one another,"[1079] it means, "Comfort yourselves together, and edify one another."[1080] The Word is made flesh only as the mind is edified,

---

1073 Romans 15:2
1074 Titus 2:14
1075 Ephesians 3:16
1076 Ephesians 5:26
1077 Romans 8:11
1078 1 John 3:23
1079 1 Thessalonians 4:9
1080 1 Thessalonians 5:13

for "that which is born of the Spirit is spirit."[1081] The Word, being a counsel; as it says, "The Spirit of the LORD spake by me, and his word was in my tongue";[1082] can only find itself operating in flesh through the mind calling the limbs of the body into action. The law of the *Spirit* acting within is the full hope of the living God's intention, for by the regeneration of the heart and mind, the organs of the inward person may become instruments to perform a right manner of love.

12. This hope cannot be realized without the strengthening of the mind to educate the heart to have material to exercise through the body. This discipline keeps our faith sincere and its intellect fresh.[1083] "God" is still the Word, and by the life, death, resurrection, and high priestly appointment of that Prophet's conversation, the God of our faith is the *Word* or *Wisdom* of that conversation. We cannot have faith in God, that is, in the Word, if we are ignorant of its will and intention. Righteousness is the end of this *Wisdom's* commandment, and this righteousness should not find itself removed from the charge given to Abraham.

13. This man, seeing nothing of what was promised, continued to move forward, and while keeping every commandment, "he considered not his own body now dead, when he was about an hundred years old, neither yet the deadness of Sara's womb,"[1084] remaining strong in faith, "being fully persuaded that, what he had promised, he was able also to perform."[1085] Again, "by faith Abraham, when he was tried, offered up Isaac...accounting that God was able to raise him up, even from the dead; from whence also he received him in a figure."[1086] And also seeing nothing of what was promised, even before these things, "by faith Abraham, when he was called to go out into a place which he should after receive for an inheritance, obeyed; and he went out, not knowing whither he went."[1087]

14. Abraham is an example for conversations trusting in the regeneration of their conversation.[1088] We may not know where to begin, but with our confidence on the *voice* of the living God's Prophet, it is now well for us to open up the Bible to learn its *name*. This man's *name* is become a *priest* after the ancient

---

1081 John 3:6
1082 2 Samuel 23:2
1083 Romans 6:22
1084 Romans 4:19
1085 Romans 4:21
1086 Hebrews 11:17-19
1087 Hebrews 11:8
1088 Romans 8:11

order, and that priesthood was established to purify the conscience by a routine. The former tradition sought the purification of the flesh by way of a fleshly prescription, and it was lame in that literal blood and offerings could do no good thing for the inward person. Justification was sought by means "that could not make him that did the service perfect, as pertaining to the conscience."[1089] But by offering up his conversation as the mediator to the living God's intention, this man has linked every conversation to the living God's devotional character. It is our responsibility to enter into the *Building* of this intention to receive its kindness.

15. The blood of dumb animals cannot fulfill salvation's science within the conversation, and because "man hath no preeminence above a beast,"[1090] we cannot expect the blood of a man to fulfill that same science within our mind. The blood of a man only does what the blood of Abel accomplished, which blood raised an alarm against what was wrong and solidified what was right. The pledge of our salvation is finished, the down payment for creation is accepted; the only thing left for us to do is to personally adopt and exercise that pledge and down payment.

16. That pledge and down payment for salvation's science is a conversation and a *name*. The philosophy behind that interceding *name* and conversation is the means whereby the living God's will is inwardly sealed and established.[1091] Our course in salvation's science is wholly dependent upon our own mental efforts. In order to experience the Bible's kindness, we must have full and unadulterated faith on "God," which is confidence in the Bible's present Wisdom. This philosophy must become that Sovereign Governor of our conversation, for being that God of our learning, it is the means whereby our faith's development equates to our personal and devotional newness. Exercising our mind on this Wisdom saves or recovers our heart from poor understanding, wherefore if we should have a healthy faith, exercising of our mind on salvation's law must remain a consistent practice.

1089 Hebrews 9:9
1090 Ecclesiastes 3:19
1091 Romans 8:16

12

Where Praise Is Due

1. Seeing as how "the Word was with God, and the Word was God,"[1092] and how that Word is still God, when discerning that "the Word of life"[1093] is "the Spirit of life from God,"[1094] when hearing, "She was found with child of the Holy Ghost,"[1095] it is that we are hearing of a child of the Word, and if by the Word, seeing as how "that which is born of the Spirit is spirit,"[1096] then it is plain to understand that this birth is not physical, but mental. The Spirit mentioned, which Spirit is the same Word is, in reality, a commandment or a judgment concerning the living God's *name*, for it says, "Of his own will begat he us with the word of truth,"[1097] and, "My spirit that is upon thee, and my words which I have put in thy mouth."[1098]

1092 John 1:1
1093 1 John 1:1
1094 Revelation 11:11
1095 Matthew 1:18
1096 John 3:6
1097 James 1:18
1098 Isaiah 59:21

2. All conception by the living God is mental. For God; who is the Word; to conceive any one, it must be by the spirit of the mind as that mind meditates on "the words of eternal life,"[1099] seeing as how this birth is by "that eternal life, which was with the Father."[1100] Because the Spirit infiltrates the spirit, the promised eternal life, "that in every thing ye are enriched by him, in all utterance, and in all knowledge,"[1101] "understanding what the will of the Lord is,"[1102] is by inwardly and mentally exercising the *name* of the living God's chief apostle. Thus, the conversation keeping the saying of the living God's wisdom, their understanding on salvation's benevolent will "may abound yet more and more in knowledge and in all judgment,"[1103] which is why it says, "If a man keep my saying, he shall never taste of death."[1104]

3. The saying of the living God's chief messenger is the knowledge and judgment of the mind at the Bible's core. One impregnated by the *Spirit* is one "filled with the knowledge of his will in all wisdom and spiritual understanding"[1105] by diligently examining and doing that wisdom's will, which is why it says, "He that doeth the will of God abideth for ever."[1106] This language is not speech referencing the body, but the mind, for it was said of John, "If I will that he tarry till I come, what is that to thee?"[1107] "Yet Jesus said not unto him, He shall not die; but, If I will that he tarry till I come, what is that to thee?"[1108]

4. Death will come to the flesh. This man's language is no hint of some *eternal life* for the soul after death, or of some other superstition occurring after death, but is a reference to the ever-developing organs of the conversation's mind. Birth of God, which is birth of the Word, procures everlasting life and strength to the mind because "the Spirit is life."[1109] The Word is the knowledge of the living God's judgment concerning salvation's benevolent will for the conversation's character, and must we believe the Creator to be so low as to produce flesh from words? The Word is "the law of the Spirit of life."[1110] He or

1099 John 6:68
1100 1 John 1:2
1101 1 Corinthians 1:5
1102 Ephesians 5:17
1103 Philippians 1:9
1104 John 8:52
1105 Colossians 1:9
1106 1 John 2:17
1107 John 21:22
1108 John 21:23
1109 Romans 8:10
1110 Romans 8:2

she doing this law receives from "the Spirit of grace"[1111] "the grace of life"[1112] to forward creation's science, and must we take a child of the Spirit to represent a carnal creation?

5. We are "to be strengthened with might by his Spirit in the inner man,"[1113] and concerning this "might," we read, "Wisdom and might are his,"[1114] and, "I am full of power by the spirit of the LORD, and of judgment, and of might."[1115] What is to fill our mind is the same "might" that filled *Mary's* womb, which is why there is no record of any bodily form of God's Spirit or of the LORD descending in to a woman's womb, or having intercourse with *Mary*, but it plainly says, "The Holy Ghost shall come upon thee, and the power of the Highest shall overshadow thee."[1116] Again, the *Holy Ghost* can only come upon the spirit of the mind, and the structure of the *Holy Ghost* is in the form of *power*, which "power" is wisdom, counsel, philosophy, and judgment.

6. Now, is it that wisdom descended in to a literal womb and gave birth to flesh? Or, did judgment fall into the womb of a woman to give birth to a special being? The *Holy Ghost*, who is this same Word and Spirit, falls only onto the spirit of the mind for taxing its organs on the living God's philosophy of creation. The conception of the Spirit is better understood to be one of mental and spiritual impression and comprehension, which is why the *woman* said, "My spirit hath rejoiced in God my Saviour."[1117]

7. Mary rejoiced in God, who is the Word. In order for her to take pleasure in the Word, it is that she must bring the Word's saying into her thoughts and feelings to be "filled with joy, and with the Holy Ghost."[1118] This woman with child of the *Holy Ghost*, she is therefore filled with a certain *joy*. What is to be conceived by her is a child of that *joy*.

8. Now, "God giveth to a man that is good in his sight wisdom, and knowledge, and joy,"[1119] therefore when thinking on this woman Mary, we do fall in to an error when taking her to be a literal woman. Seeing as how this conception of the *Holy Ghost* is not physical or natural, our thoughts must move on from the

---

1111 Hebrews 10:29
1112 1 Peter 3:7
1113 Ephesians 3:16
1114 Daniel 2:20
1115 Micah 3:8
1116 Luke 1:35
1117 Luke 1:47
1118 Acts 13:52
1119 Ecclesiastes 2:26

illustration of a woman to grasp a more sober illustration. Seeing as how it says, "What man is he that feareth the LORD? him shall he teach in the way that he shall choose,"[1120] and seeing as how it was told Mary, "Thou shalt conceive in thy womb,"[1121] it is that the saying is fulfilled, "Shall be afraid in himself,"[1122] and, "Did not our heart burn within us."[1123]

9. The "womb," because the birth spoken of is by the *Holy Ghost*, is no literal womb. A "womb" is language connoting bowels, and one's "bowels" are one's "heart," as it says, "The LORD hath called me from the womb; from the bowels of my mother,"[1124] and, "My bowels are troubled; mine heart is turned within me."[1125] The "womb" spoken of is the heart of a "mother," and this "mother" is no literal woman, even as Paul says, "But Jerusalem which is above is free, which is the mother of us all."[1126] The living God's *Jerusalem* is that "mother" of our conversation, or is the head of salvation's assembly, because it houses the *name* of that Temple, even as it says, "In Jerusalem will I put my name."[1127] A "mother" is a primary church, and every church has a head, even as it says, "The head of the woman is the man."[1128]

10. Mary, that woman impregnated by the *Holy Ghost*, is in reality a church, even as it says, "As the church is subject unto Christ, so let the wives be to their own husbands in every thing."[1129] A "woman," in right context within the Bible, is figurative language denoting a church. What Matthew and Luke's pen has recorded no sensual intercourse between *God* and flesh, but rather the penetration of a mind by the law of the living God's will upon a particular *man* over a particular *woman*, or church. Such a "man" is not the general male person, but is a priest, elder, or father, even as it says, "Rebuke not an elder, but intreat him as a father,"[1130] and, "Seventy men of the elders of the people,"[1131] and, "Then

---

1120 Psalm 25:12
1121 Luke 1:31
1122 Isaiah 19:17
1123 Luke 24:32
1124 Isaiah 49:1
1125 Lamentations 1:20
1126 Galatians 4:26
1127 2 Kings 21:4
1128 1 Corinthians 11:3
1129 Ephesians 5:24
1130 1 Timothy 5:1
1131 Numbers 11:24

pleased it the apostles and elders, with the whole church, to send chosen men of their own company."[1132]

11. We err in understanding when failing to discern the scene established for us by the Bible concerning the origin of that Prophet, for if this birth is of the power and law of the *Holy Ghost* within the spirit of the mind, and if this conception is wholly mental and inward, then it is that the womb imagined is not physical, and that the woman thought of is not literal. In reality, a *man* of the Word, a priest of the living God's wisdom, conceived and apprehended "Jesus Christ" within the bowels of his heart, for "the head of every man is Christ; and the head of the woman is the man."[1133]

12. By how Paul uses the word "Christ," it is evident that he speaks of no literal reference to a man, which is why he teaches, "Wherefore henceforth know we no man after the flesh: yea, though we have known Christ after the flesh, yet now henceforth know we him no more. Therefore if any man be in Christ, he is a new creature."[1134] If "of his own will begat he us with the word of truth, that we should be a kind of firstfruits of his creatures,"[1135] and if Paul is saying that every mind in "Christ" is a new creature, then it is that "Christ" is the "word of truth,"[1136] seeing as how both equate to the same end. "Christ" is in fact that "Word," for birth to the living God cannot commence if not through "Jesus Christ," seeing as how, concerning the living God, "we are his workmanship, created in Christ Jesus."[1137]

13. This creation, because it takes place within the spirit of the mind, allows us to understand that "the Lord Jesus Christ our Saviour"[1138] is, in all actuality, "the commandment of God our Saviour,"[1139] which commandment is "the doctrine of God our Saviour."[1140] To hear *Mary* saying, "My spirit hath rejoiced in God my Saviour,"[1141] it is to hear the *head* of her *body* confessing to a right conversation with the law and commandment of the Word. Thus, the inward parts of this man; of this priest of *Mary*; burned within him as he exercised his mind on the *Spirit's* saying, adding to his understanding a blessing only received

---

1132   Acts 15:22
1133   1 Corinthians 11:3
1134   2 Corinthians 5:16,17
1135   James 1:18
1136   James 1:18
1137   Ephesians 2:10
1138   Titus 1:4
1139   Titus 1:3
1140   Titus 2:10
1141   Luke 1:47

when "rightly dividing the word of truth,"[1142] which is why it says, "I will pour my spirit upon thy seed, and my blessing upon thine offspring."[1143]

14. Herein we are made to understand that the pouring out of the *Spirit*, because we are "to be strengthened with might by his Spirit in the inner man,"[1144] and because "that which is born of the Spirit is spirit,"[1145] is in reality a blessing poured out upon the spirit of the mind. This blessing to be poured out upon the mind, it is "Jesus Christ," which is why it says, "The Lord Jesus Christ be with thy spirit."[1146] Again, concerning the manner in which the Bible speaks, "the Lord Jesus Christ our Saviour"[1147] cannot be any *thing* but "the commandment of God our Saviour."[1148]

15. What Adam's inward parts are to be filled with, according to the Bible, is the knowledge and wisdom of a *name*, which is why it says, "Let the word of Christ dwell in you richly in all wisdom."[1149] This *name* is that Word, and the Word being God, the *name* is that God of personal worship and service to the living God, which is why it says, "Let him trust in the name of the LORD, and stay upon his God,"[1150] and, "Which swear by the name of the LORD, and make mention of the God of Israel."[1151] So when hearing of a woman found with child of "God," is it that the living God's *name* should give birth to literal flesh? "Name" means faith, philosophy, or doctrine.[1152] With the Word being in reality the living God's Name, Wisdom, or Philosophy, is it that this Faith should impregnate flesh to give birth to a human form?

16. To be of the *Holy Ghost* is to be of the living God's *name*, which *name* is the God of the Bible's assembly. Because that creation of the Spirit is spirit, it is that every mind should know newness of character by rightly doing this law, which is why it says, "Live according to God in the spirit,"[1153] and, "Worship God in the spirit."[1154]

1142 2 Timothy 2:15
1143 Isaiah 44:3
1144 Ephesians 3:16
1145 John 3:6
1146 2 Timothy 4:22
1147 Titus 1:4
1148 Titus 1:3
1149 Colossians 3:16
1150 Isaiah 50:10
1151 Isaiah 48:1
1152 Revelation 2:13; Revelation 3:8
1153 1 Peter 4:6
1154 Philippians 3:3

17. It is undeniably true that "Jesus Christ" is "God," but when confessing such a thing, it is well to remember that "henceforth know we no man after the flesh: yea, though we have known Christ after the flesh, yet now henceforth know we him no more."[1155] "Jesus Christ" is an appellation of the living God's *name*, meaning that "Jesus Christ" is the Word of creation, and as that Wisdom, it is that God of every faithful conversation.[1156] The mind is to fully depend on and exercise faith on that Wisdom's saying, for that Prophet was raised and trained by this same saying. Our mortal *body,* or our natural conversation, is to be resurrected and reformed by an experimental faith on salvation's wisdom. The *name* of the living God's chief apostle is to be the means whereby our conversation is born of the *Spirit* for a right approach to the living God, which is why it says, "In that he liveth, he liveth unto God."[1157]

18. It is therefore an eternal fact that if our conversation is buried in death with "Christ," we will honor no thing of self or of the religious world; we are "dead with Christ from the rudiments of the world."[1158] "Death" in "Christ"; because "the Lord Jesus Christ our Saviour"[1159] is "the commandment of God our Saviour";[1160] is a passing away of the mind from an earthy religious conversation to a manner that is in service by the spirit of the mind.[1161] The mind is to be revealed to the conversation through the Word.[1162] This regeneration is to deliver the mind from an unprofitable and earthy religious policy to a benevolent conversation, and this deliverance is only by the knowledge of the living God's *name*, which is why it says, "By his knowledge shall my righteous servant justify many,"[1163] and, "Through knowledge shall the just be delivered."[1164]

19. Because the intended manner of creation is within the mind, it is that deliverance or salvation is from "spiritual wickedness in high places."[1165] To combat inherited and cultivated religious error, "we have received a commandment from the Father"[1166] that we "might be filled with the knowledge of his will

---

1155 2 Corinthians 5:16
1156 Ephesians 3:14
1157 Romans 6:10
1158 Colossians 2:20
1159 Titus 1:4
1160 Titus 1:3
1161 Ephesians 4:22,23
1162 Titus 3:5
1163 Isaiah 53:11
1164 Proverbs 11:9
1165 Ephesians 6:12
1166 2 John 1:4

in all wisdom and spiritual understanding"[1167] to confess, "I will praise thy name, O LORD; for it is good,"[1168] which is why *Mary* says, "Holy is his name."[1169]

20. When we hear, "Glory to God in the highest, and on earth peace, good will toward men,"[1170] it is that we are hearing of the living God's good intention within the conversation's inward parts. Glory and praise is to go to the living God because of this Word, who is that God over the recuperation and reformation of the inward parts. There is no such thing as idolatrously and covetously lusting after *God's man.* Glory and honor is to fall to the living God because of his chief apostle's Wisdom, which is why it says, "At the name of Jesus every knee should bow...to the glory of God the Father."[1171]

21. If we are doers of "Jesus Christ," it is that we will come to rightly admire the Creator of this law by our communion with the intercession of that Prophet's *name.* Our celebration is to be towards God; who is that *name's* saying; for experiencing "the kindness and love of God our Saviour toward man."[1172] This kindness is the living God's good will, which will is the resurrection of the conversation's conscience "that he might sanctify and cleanse it with the washing of water by the word."[1173] This intention is to fulfill in our mind what the former priesthood sought to accomplish, but that "could not make him that did the service perfect, as pertaining to the conscience."[1174] The conscience of our understanding on creation's *name* is the subject and object of the living God's will and affection, for by a sanctified mind, the labor of this wisdom's ministry may find itself perfectly executed.

22. Again, to hear, "Glory to God,"[1175] because "the Word was with God, and the Word was God,"[1176] it is to hear, "Glory to Jesus Christ," wherefore seeing as how "the Lord Jesus Christ our Saviour"[1177] is "the commandment of God our Saviour,"[1178] we are in reality observing the saying, "Glory to the Wisdom and Commandment of the Creator in the Highest." The "highest" spoken of is

---

1167　Colossians 1:9
1168　Psalm 54:6
1169　Luke 1:49
1170　Luke 2:14
1171　Philippians 2:10,11
1172　Titus 3:4
1173　Ephesians 5:26
1174　Hebrews 9:9
1175　Luke 2:14
1176　John 1:1
1177　Titus 1:4
1178　Titus 1:3

in reference to the *heavenly* Sanctuary, which is why it says, "Blessed is he that cometh in the name of the Lord; Hosanna in the highest."[1179] "Hosanna" is an exclamation denoting a rescuer, a savior, or a deliverer, for the one that should appear in the living God's *name* is that Deliverer, and this salvation occurring in the Temple above, which is why it says, "Blessed be he that cometh in the name of the LORD: we have blessed you out of the house of the LORD."[1180]

23. The *one* appearing in the living God's name is as Aaron, for "Aaron was separated...to burn incense before the LORD, to minister unto him, and to bless in his name for ever."[1181] The conversation of the living God's Prophet fulfills Aaron's role.[1182] To hear, "Glory to the living God's will and saying in the highest," is a call for every honest conversation to extend their faith and spirit "above, where Christ sitteth on the right hand of God."[1183]

24. The good intention of the living God's mind cannot find our mind if we are not in communion with that *Jerusalem* and its *name*. Knowledge of "Jesus Christ" can only be obtained by fellowshipping with *heaven*, and "heaven" is a moniker for the living God's heavenly Building.[1184] We are therefore wrong when failing to elevate our thoughts *heavenward*, for our example has fulfilled the saying, "Thy word is settled in heaven."[1185] Our praise is known to be to the living God because our communion is with this Prophet's *name*. If our conversation is not figuratively within this Sanctuary, our practice will follow "the course of this world, according to the prince of the power of the air, the spirit that now worketh in the children of disobedience."[1186]

25. The spirit of the religious world is a mind magnifying religious error against creation's throne, law, and will. The true worshipper will reverence the living God by the wisdom of that chief apostle's *name*, "for Christ is the end of the law for righteousness to every one that believeth."[1187] The living God's good will is righteousness, which righteousness cannot be experienced without examining and doing "the Lord Jesus Christ our Saviour,"[1188] which "Lord" our

---

1179 Matthew 21:9
1180 Psalm 118:26
1181 1 Chronicles 23:13
1182 Hebrews 5:4,5
1183 Colossians 3:1
1184 Psalm 102:19
1185 Psalm 119:89
1186 Ephesians 2:2
1187 Romans 10:4
1188 Titus 1:4

"Savior" is "the doctrine of God our Saviour."[1189] Such a doctrine states, "If we have been planted together in the likeness of his death, we shall be also in the likeness of his resurrection."[1190]

26. The spirit of the mind is to experience a resurrection for newness, which regeneration occurs only by doing the knowledge of this man's *name*, even as it says, "Be ye transformed by the renewing of your mind, that ye may prove what is that good, and acceptable, and perfect, will of God."[1191] That priest set over the *woman Mary* fully proved the living God's will, receiving a more thorough knowledge of the living God's *name* into his *bowels*, and by the knowledge retained, the saying was fulfilled, "A man shall nourish a young cow."[1192]

27. A "cow" is an ox, and oxen are used for plowing, as it says, "Plowing with twelve yoke of oxen,"[1193] and, "The oxen were plowing."[1194] The "cow" and the "oxen," because they plow the ground, they are but figurative illustrations of ministers or servants that toil after the scripture's doctrine, as it says, "Which of you, having a servant plowing or feeding cattle."[1195] The record of Matthew concerning this child of the *Holy Ghost* is one of a young minister of the living God's law conceived by the devotional character of his *mother*. This child took in all that he could from her, but the time came when he should separate from her understanding to learn the full weight of the Creator's *name*, which is why he said, at the appointed time, "By thee have I been holden up from the womb: thou art he that took me out of my mother's bowels: my praise shall be continually of thee."[1196]

28. Our praise is to be according to scripture's instruction, for it says, "Glory to God in the highest,"[1197] and, "Sing unto the LORD, bless his name,"[1198] and, "Give unto the LORD the glory due unto his name; worship the LORD in the beauty of holiness,"[1199] and, "Unto him be glory in the church by Christ Jesus throughout all ages, world without end."[1200] Scripture's testimony is plain.

1189 Titus 2:10
1190 Romans 6:5
1191 Romans 12:2
1192 Isaiah 7:21
1193 1 Kings 19:19
1194 Job 1:14
1195 Luke 17:7
1196 Psalm 71:6
1197 Luke 2:14
1198 Psalm 96:2
1199 Psalm 29:2
1200 Ephesians 3:21

"God is the LORD"[1201] because of the *Word* or the *Commandment* that dwelt within, died within, and revived within, the character of a conversation. The Word made flesh is the ultimate testimony to humbly honoring the living God, for seeing as how "that which is born of the Spirit is spirit,"[1202] and that the Spirit can only fellowship with the devotional *body*, the Word made flesh is but the living God's wisdom operating within the spirit or character of the conversation's conscience.

29. The Word operating through the conversation is the hope of the human being, through a reformed devotional mind, conquering its naturally erroneous constitution. The same experience that the living God's chief apostle knew is to be our same course of learning, which is why his *name* is that chief priest over this science. For this cause, all praise directed to this man reverts to the Architect of redemption's commandment, for by the law of this Mind's devotional character, "we might receive the promise of the Spirit through faith."[1203]

1201 Psalm 118:27
1202 John 3:6
1203 Galatians 3:14

13

A Secured Hope

1. If the Word had not been found with a conversation within the religious world and then consecrated to the living God's wisdom, our conversation would have no present hope or example. Because the Word is the living God's *Wisdom* or *Spirit*, and because "a spirit hath not flesh and bones,"[1204] and because "that which is born of the Spirit is spirit,"[1205] it is well to not think so sensually when hopeful to discern scripture's definition of conception. With the Word being God, because "God is a Spirit,"[1206] to hear that the Word was made flesh is to hear that "God was manifest in the flesh."[1207] To inquire about how the Spirit should appear in the flesh, since "that which is born of the Spirit is spirit,"[1208] is to inquire after how the spirit of the mind was made to demonstrate the Spirit that conceived it.

2. There is no such thing as the Spirit giving birth to human flesh; such a theory is put to rest by the saying, "That which is born of the flesh is flesh; and

---

1204 Luke 24:39
1205 John 3:6
1206 John 4:24
1207 1 Timothy 3:16
1208 John 3:6

that which is born of the Spirit is spirit."[1209] This means that if the Spirit should capture any flesh, then that flesh must be of a form or nature similar to it, and concerning this manner of conception, "God giveth it a body as it hath pleased him."[1210] Therefore "there is a natural body, and there is a spiritual body,"[1211] and because "the natural man receiveth not the things of the Spirit of God,"[1212] "that which is born of the Spirit is spirit."[1213] Herein we are made to view a more intelligent transaction than what is traditionally accepted. Because "the LORD is a God of knowledge,"[1214] it says, "By his knowledge shall my righteous servant justify many,"[1215] which is why "we might be justified by the faith of Christ."[1216]

3. Justification is sanctification; the two are one and the same. Justification, which is sanctification, is a process of cleansing after the manner of the saying, "Take away the dross from the silver, and there shall come forth a vessel for the finer."[1217] Sanctification is an educational course of learning where the mind, by proving creation's will and saying, is regenerated after the likeness of that saying to own its labor and person, which is why it says, "Be ye transformed by the renewing of your mind, that ye may prove what is that good, and acceptable, and perfect, will of God."[1218] For this cause, sanctification cannot commence without material to purify, which is why it says, "Not the hearers of the law are just before God, but the doers of the law shall be justified,"[1219] and, "Be ye doers of the word."[1220]

4. Sanctification occurs only through the knowledge of that Prophet's *name*, which *name* is the law and word of the living God's *Spirit*. Therefore if it says, "By his knowledge shall my righteous servant justify many,"[1221] and, "We might be justified by the faith of Christ,"[1222] it is evident that "Jesus Christ" is that "knowledge" to commence justification's course of learning. For this cause, "Jesus Christ," in the manner that the Bible uses this phrase, should move us

---

1209 John 3:6
1210 1 Corinthians 15:38
1211 1 Corinthians 15:44
1212 1 Corinthians 2:14
1213 John 3:6
1214 1 Samuel 2:3
1215 Isaiah 53:11
1216 Galatians 2:16
1217 Proverbs 25:4
1218 Romans 12:2
1219 Romans 2:13
1220 James 1:22
1221 Isaiah 53:11
1222 Galatians 2:16

to remember that "henceforth know we no man after the flesh: yea, though we have known Christ after the flesh, yet now henceforth know we him no more. Therefore if any man be in Christ, he is a new creature."[1223]

5. Sanctification is for the creation of a new person within the conversation, and since this creation is not physical but mental, and is by the law of the Spirit through the spirit of the mind, it is that wisdom is to possess our mind "that he might sanctify and cleanse it with the washing of water by the word."[1224] No literal washing of the physical body is herein referenced; doesn't it say, "He shall baptize you with the Holy Ghost"?[1225] How is this baptism possible? If not for the natural body, then to what body will please the Spirit for baptism? "There is a natural body, and there is a spiritual body,"[1226] and because "that which is born of the Spirit is spirit,"[1227] it is that the organs and instruments of the heart and mind are the object of the *Spirit's* enterprise.

6. Justification is through the *name* of the living God's chief apostle, which *name* is "the knowledge of the Lord and Saviour Jesus Christ."[1228] Therefore when hearing the name, "Jesus Christ," it is well to remember that "the Lord Jesus Christ our Saviour"[1229] is, in right context, "the knowledge of the Lord and Saviour Jesus Christ,"[1230] which knowledge is "the commandment of God our Saviour."[1231] Justification is by an experimental faith on this commandment's will, which commandment is "the doctrine of God our Saviour."[1232] By bringing this commandment in to the spirit of the mind for its establishment by the living God's creative wisdom, "The law of the Spirit of life in Christ Jesus hath made me free from the law of sin and death,"[1233] every doer of this saying will confess.

7. Herein is witnessed the Spirit's righteousness, even the hope of having engraved within our conversation's natural constitution a law for a good and sober conversation. Our conversation has no naturally "good" precept within it,

---

1223 2 Corinthians 5:15,16
1224 Ephesians 5:26
1225 Luke 3:16
1226 1 Corinthians 15:44
1227 John 3:6
1228 2 Peter 2:20
1229 Titus 1:4
1230 2 Peter 2:20
1231 Titus 1:3
1232 Titus 2:10
1233 Romans 8:2

for there is no rule in it saying, "Let every one of us please...to edification."[1234] The first part of the human that should be edified is self, but there is no mind within the human being to benevolently exhort and counsel self, but rather a mind fulfilling the saying, "That which I do I allow not: for what I would, that do I not; but what I hate, that do I."[1235] Ministers, in the beginning, had a choice to make between which parts of their being they would rather have: either the natural law of religious error or the law of *life* from the *tree* of *life*. Whichever they chose would be their predominant conversation in the flesh.

8. They chose the nature of a lower conversation above a conversation founded upon the cultivation of their higher faculties, wherefore "by one man sin entered into the world, and death by sin; and so death passed upon all men."[1236] This "death" is not literal, but is entirely philosophical. From this point forward, a slumbering spiritual understanding kept the science of the living God's *name* hidden, the impulse of the human being becoming guide to the mental and the spiritual perception. Yet, at the time appointed, the living God's chief apostle, so every doer of that commandment may share in its promise, was raised up to advance salvation's saying.

9. With the Word made flesh and offered for flesh, or with a "spirit that confesseth that Jesus Christ is come in the flesh"[1237] and offered for *flesh*, or for conversations, every thinking and feeling human being may experience the living God's promise for newness, and that promise beginning when once investigating and executing the knowledge of that promise. The Word made flesh is the knowledge of salvation's commandment working within the conversation. A mind confessing that "Jesus Christ" is come in to the *flesh*; because "the Lord Jesus Christ our Saviour"[1238] is, in proper context, "the knowledge of the Lord and Saviour Jesus Christ";[1239] is a mind perfectly executing the nature of that commandment.[1240] The Word made flesh is the living God's wisdom demonstrated through the limbs of the body. That Prophet fully demonstrated this science by learning of and doing that will, which is why he says, "I know him, and keep his saying."[1241]

1234 Romans 15:2
1235 Romans 7:15
1236 Romans 5:12
1237 1 John 4:2
1238 Titus 1:4
1239 2 Peter 2:20
1240 1 Timothy 1:5
1241 John 8:55

10. Herein the living God's chief apostle witnesses for the character of the living God. In his ministry, he never once says, "I am a God, I sit in the seat of God,"[1242] but rather says, "Have faith in God,"[1243] and, "I know him, and keep his saying."[1244] His faith is in God, and he allows us to understand what keeps and dresses his faith by pointing us to the saying of that God. Therefore seeing as how it is written, "In the beginning was the Word, and the Word was with God, and the Word was God,"[1245] to counsel us to have faith on God is to advise us to exercise faith on the Word, that is, on the saying of the Word, which saying is "the Lord Jesus Christ our Saviour,"[1246] or rather, "the commandment of God our Saviour."[1247]

11. We are to "live according to God in the spirit,"[1248] meaning that the Word is to be that God of the conversation for the reception of that Word's promise. There is nothing in the scriptures pointing to a man called *Jesus* as being *God*, but rather the "Christ" of the Creator has definitely led the careful observer to its God, which God and Christ is that wisdom over its *spirit*, which wisdom is the saying of the living God's *Spirit* or *Wisdom*. This man knew the living God through the living God's wisdom, pointing the active thinker to this wisdom's *name* for serving the true and living Wisdom of the Creator. By keeping this wisdom, "I have kept my Father's commandments, and abide in his love,"[1249] he says, this blessing being an example for the conversation keeping that same saying.

12. Worship is to be directed to the living God of creation's science, which is why every doer of this *Wisdom's* law knows that "the true worshippers shall worship the Father in spirit and in truth: for the Father seeketh such to worship him."[1250] Again, there is no thing in the Bible pointing to any idolatrous or inordinate service to *God's man*, for even the man himself directs our attention to his God.

13. It is because of the Creator's observation, after religious error entered into that *garden's* philosophy, that he was moved to place into that *earth* a law

1242 Ezekiel 28:2
1243 Mark 11:22
1244 John 8:55
1245 John 1:1
1246 Titus 1:4
1247 Titus 1:3
1248 1 Peter 4:6
1249 John 15:10
1250 John 4:23

of regeneration, saying, "A law shall proceed from me, and I will make my judgment to rest for a light of the people."[1251] When the time came, that prophesied minister appeared and fully demonstrated that law through his natural religious conversation, which is why it says, "My righteousness is near; my salvation is gone forth."[1252] The Word made flesh is the revealed righteousness and salvation of the living God's Spirit or Mind. The righteousness or the pleasure of this Mind is the resurrection and reformation of the conversation's understanding on the living God's character by "the knowledge of his will in all wisdom and spiritual understanding."[1253] This righteousness, seeing as how it is "the grace of God that bringeth salvation,"[1254] is a benevolent gesture over the conversation's inward parts by grace's creative power.

14. Creation's force is only for the spirit of the mind and is obtained through "Jesus Christ," as it says, "The grace of our Lord Jesus Christ be with your spirit,"[1255] and, "They which receive abundance of grace and of the gift of righteousness shall reign in life by one, Jesus Christ."[1256] Again, the manner in which "Jesus Christ" is referenced must keep the mind in remembrance that no literal person is mentioned,[1257] but rather a commandment. Grace forwards the promise of creation within the conversation, but grace is not given without the mind discerning "the Lord Jesus Christ our Saviour,"[1258] which is "the commandment of God our Saviour."[1259]

15. The Spirit's righteousness is advanced by grace, and this justification cannot commence unless this counsel is patiently and temperately fulfilled: "In his law doth he meditate day and night."[1260] In order for the Word to be made flesh, the mind must digest and execute its saying, for then the righteousness of its intention will shine forth through the conversation, uttering a song of its kindness to every conscience and witnessing to the justness of its thoughts. It is therefore well that, when thinking on that Word made flesh, to understand that, in reality, the righteousness of the Word found itself perfectly revealed by a human being through the reformed members of its devotional conversation,

---

1251 Isaiah 51:4
1252 Isaiah 51:5
1253 Colossians 1:9
1254 Titus 2:11
1255 Galatians 6:18
1256 Romans 5:17
1257 2 Corinthians 5:16
1258 Titus 1:4
1259 Titus 1:3
1260 Psalm 1:2

for "God anointed Jesus of Nazareth with the Holy Ghost and with power: who went about doing good."[1261]

16. The Word manifested in flesh is the salvation of the living God's *Spirit* witnessed by a conversation, for if, concerning ministers within the religious world, it was known "that every imagination of the thoughts of his heart was only evil continually,"[1262] yet the living God anointed that Prophet's ministry,[1263] then a great mystery has happened. What we observe in this man is the exchanging of "sin's" law for a new *law*, which is why it says, "The life was manifested...that eternal life...."[1264] That "eternal life" was observed within a conversation. Must we think so low of the Bible to imagine some carnal intercourse between *eternal life* and human flesh? That eternal life of the Father is that "eternal Spirit,"[1265] and seeing as how "that which is born of the Spirit is spirit,"[1266] the life of the Father found itself manifested by a spirit or mind working out "the words of eternal life."[1267] Herein we may understand that this was the first "spirit that confesseth that Jesus Christ is come in the flesh,"[1268] for by doing the Spirit's *law*, "the grace of life"[1269] was added to his mind for creating his conversation after "the image of the invisible God, the firstborn of every creature."[1270] Because "every one that loveth is born of God, and knoweth God,"[1271] he could not help but demonstrate to others that Word's good will.

17. Because the Spirit's righteousness is in procuring to the conversation's conscience a more benevolent government than what it is naturally born with, every spirit created by the Spirit will care that others know the same *name* and saying refreshing their faith and mind. This is why he counsels every convert of that righteousness to love others as they have been loved by it, for where it says, "Love one another,"[1272] in reality the counsel is, "Comfort yourselves together, and edify one another."[1273] The intercession of *heaven's* current manner of

---

1261 Acts 10:38
1262 Genesis 6:5
1263 Acts 10:38
1264 1 John 1:2
1265 Hebrews 9:14
1266 John 3:6
1267 John 6:68
1268 1 John 4:2
1269 1 Peter 3:7
1270 Colossians 1:15
1271 1 John 4:7
1272 1 Thessalonians 4:9
1273 1 Thessalonians 5:11

salvation is for edifying *Adam's* devotional understanding to secure in them a more sober conversation to live by, even as it says, "Then had the churches rest...and were edified; and walking in the fear of the Lord, and in the comfort of the Holy Ghost, were multiplied."[1274]

18. The comfort of the Holy Ghost is the learning of the Holy Ghost, as it says, "All may learn, and all may be comforted."[1275] The Spirit's learning is the living God's "fear," and "the fear of the LORD is the beginning of knowledge."[1276] Edification appears through the Spirit's knowledge, for when it says, "I will not leave you comfortless: I will come to you,"[1277] the counsel is not physical but spiritual, for the living God will appear only by mental revelation, which is why it says, "If a man love me, he will keep my words,"[1278] and, "Ye are clean through the word which I have spoken."[1279] Right "love" is therefore mentally refreshing the understanding on the Bible's will so that the conversation may no longer misunderstand or misinterpret it.

19. The conversation blessed to pass through salvation's course has a responsibility to a religious world practicing *death*, which is why it says, "As my Father hath sent me, even so send I you,"[1280] and, "As thou hast sent me into the world, even so have I also sent them into the world."[1281] This man was sent to fully demonstrate creation's righteousness, which is why it says, "He will magnify the law, and make it honourable."[1282] The Word made flesh is the righteousness of the Spirit's *law* proceeding from the heart and mind by the conversation, and for every mind formed by this righteousness, there is a special vocation and employment awaiting them.

20. The highest knowledge is charity, and every conversation blessed to "love one another, as he gave us commandment,"[1283] is a conversation safely guiding another conversation on its journey of recovery.[1284] Right charity is edifying a mind through "the doctrine which is according to godliness,"[1285] which

---

1274 Acts 9:31
1275 1 Corinthians 14:31
1276 Proverbs 1:7
1277 John 14:18
1278 John 14:23
1279 John 15:3
1280 John 20:21
1281 John 17:18
1282 Isaiah 42:21
1283 1 John 3:23
1284 3 John 1:5-7
1285 1 Timothy 6:3

doctrine is "the commandment of God our Saviour."[1286] The living God's chief apostle preached the Word or the Wisdom because he had that Commandment within his conversation's conscience. By his own faith's higher learning, he experienced this will to love after the commandment of that will. This classroom is for our discipline that many should say of us, "They have refreshed my spirit and yours."[1287]

21. For this cause, we rightly display our joy and awe of the living God's chief minister by keeping the same saying that he kept. Because of him, our conversation has the opportunity to know the science of the living God's righteousness through the development of our mind by that science's will and commandment. This man is the savior or deliverer of the living God's Wisdom because by the offering of his conversation, other conversation may experience "the kindness and love of God our Saviour toward man"[1288] to hear, "The very God of peace sanctify you wholly; and I pray God your whole spirit and soul and body be preserved."[1289]

22. By one sacrificed mind and conversation fully dawning the righteousness of the living God's *Wisdom*, every conversation may now know the same pleasure to possess a similar ministry and conversation. The full sanctification of our conversation's character and conscience will, through this *Wisdom* or *Word*, undergo a transformation, but in order to begin this training, the conversation must adopt this man's *blood*, struggle, or experience.[1290] The conversation must be sanctified. To sanctify, in this context, is to separate or consecrate for a good or just purpose. This man's *blood*, or his conversation's experience, separates the one exercising faith on it for the purpose of commencing creation's science within their inward person; the only issue is who will mentally discern that consecration for the reception of its promise.

23. To every doer of creation's science, Paul counsels, "Faithful is he that calleth you, who also will do it."[1291] What is it that the living God is faithful to do? It says, "The very God of peace sanctify you wholly."[1292]

1286 Titus 1:3
1287 1 Corinthians 16:18
1288 Titus 3:4
1289 1 Thessalonians 5:23
1290 Hebrews 13:12
1291 1 Thessalonians 5:24
1292 1 Thessalonians 5:23

24. The sanctification to appear occurs at none other time than when humanity is functioning, for when did our example experience creation?[1293] So also it is our responsibility to condemn personal and religious error while alive, and this condemnation is through the Word being made flesh, or by a "spirit that confesseth that Jesus Christ is come in the flesh."[1294]

25. The kindness or the righteousness of salvation's science functioning through the conversation is the greatest condemnation to the natural religious persuasion, which is why it says, "Put ye on the Lord Jesus Christ, and make not provision for the flesh."[1295] The only way we can put on "Jesus Christ" is by our mind, for it says, "The Lord Jesus Christ be with thy spirit."[1296]

26. Again, the Bible references no man or figure living within our mind. Because we cannot forget that "the Lord Jesus Christ our Saviour"[1297] is "the commandment of God our Saviour,"[1298] and that by this commandment the living God's salvation is discerned and the conversation's Deliverer pronounced, the conversation's conscience is to be bettered by the creative power within the Bible's present wisdom, and we should never lose sight of this.

1293 Romans 8:3
1294 1 John 4:2
1295 Romans 13:14
1296 2 Timothy 4:22
1297 Titus 1:4
1298 Titus 1:3

14

By The Act Of One

1. By the sacrifice of one, every conversation may freely experience the living God's new covenant will. Because the living God's chief apostle has given his conversation as that offering,[1299] it is our responsibility to know just what was sacrificed so that we may be able to benefit from that oblation.

2. Anciently, it was that "the blood of bulls and of goats, and the ashes of an heifer sprinkling the unclean, sanctifieth to the purifying of the flesh,"[1300] the liberty and the sober stabilization of the conversation being the *Creator's* intention. From the moment religious error against the living God's *name* occurred, "unto Adam also and to his wife did the LORD God make coats of skins, and clothed them,"[1301] for they became concerned with their conversation. Covering their conversation's error by the *apparel* of a certain sacrifice was always the intention.

1299 Ephesians 5:2
1300 Hebrews 9:13
1301 Genesis 3:21

3. It is not as though they had no knowledge of their *nakedness*, for "they were both naked, the man and his wife, and were not ashamed."[1302] But the *death* that blessed their negligence exposed some *thing* that made them hide self from the living God.[1303] The "death" that they suffered was to their *eyes*; that is, the eyes of their understanding;[1304] for if at first they saw their plight and felt no thing, but then after disobedience they not only saw it, but also felt it, then the *eyes* of their spiritual perception had suffered a great wound, which wound *God* sought to make better by covering what had come under assault.

4. *Adam's* new mind made them hide their conversation from the living God's *presence*, and concerning what that presence is, we read, "To present you faultless before the presence of his glory,"[1305] and, "Who shall be punished with everlasting destruction from the presence of the Lord, and from the glory of his power,"[1306] and, "Glory and honour are in his presence; strength and gladness are in his place,"[1307] and, "My presence shall go with thee...I will make all my goodness pass before thee, and I will proclaim the name of the LORD before thee."[1308]

5. The living God's presence is the living God's *name*, which *name* is a glory and power. To hide self from the living God's presence is to hide the mind from discerning that presence's *Mind*, and every conversation joined to that *Wisdom* says, "Truly I am full of power by the spirit of the LORD, and of judgment, and of might."[1309] *Adam's* violation put them against the *law* or the judgment of the Creator's wisdom which, because of their conversation's new supremacy over their thoughts and feelings, caused them to not only hide their conversation from the living God, but to artificially clothe it to hide self from their own conscience.

6. What they hid themselves from was the living God's *voice* acting upon their faith's mind, and that *voice* is not physical or tangible, seeing as how "a spirit hath not flesh and bones."[1310] The heightened stimulus of the conversation's constitution moved *Adam* to remove their mind from exercising faith

---

1302   Genesis 2:25
1303   Genesis 3:8
1304   Ephesians 1:18
1305   Jude 1:24
1306   2 Thessalonians 1:9
1307   1 Chronicles 16:27
1308   Exodus 33:14-19
1309   Micah 3:8
1310   Luke 24:39

on a *voice* for righteousness to unlawfully labor after faith for *righteousness*. This moves the careful observer to question why, if the living God seeing and knowing their emptiness and did nothing about it, should *Adam* have cared to hide their *self*? An unstable devotional mind now reigned over *Adam*, but the living God, through one offering, would do well by them.

7. *Adam* is created with a naturally devotional government within their conversation. Their conversation is their assignment from the day that they are born and until they pass away, for we are all "as one dead, of whom the flesh is half consumed when he cometh out of his mother's womb."[1311] Being creatures from the *earth*, must we expect any other foundational religious nature to exist within our conversation? We innately suffer the *earth's* original mind within our conversation, for when the *earth* was founded, was it in a good or in a degenerate condition?

8. The Creator may have regenerated the *earth* by *sound*, and the *earth* may have accepted regeneration by that *voice*, but this transformation is not transferable. *Adam* has the *earth's* natural spiritual persuasion within their conversation, which disposition is void of any "good" *thing* in and of itself, and is without any "good" understanding of how to better itself from that mind, which is why it says, "That the soul be without knowledge, it is not good,"[1312] and, "Hath spoken without knowledge, and his words were without wisdom."[1313]

9. The conversation has within it a law that is without wisdom and knowledge of how to care for the self and its character, but it is the living God's righteousness to raise up conversations from this natural standard to a more benevolent commandment that they may learn how to keep their self, and that by learning right government, they may better care for that commandment's *name*, self's person, and the character of other persons. *Adam's* task is in overcoming self's thoughts and feelings by this *voice*, but since their error naturally removes the mind from creation's *voice*, this course of learning is not only become difficult, but useless and impossible without the living God's *Spirit*.

10. *Adam's* error stripped the living God's *Spirit* or *Wisdom* from them because, by one mistake, faithlessness towards this *voice* came in to existence. Their lot was to study creation so that they may better understand the creative redemption to occur within their conversation for the good of its conscience. As they discerned how the living God's *voice* not only brought all things into

1311 Numbers 12:12
1312 Proverbs 19:2
1313 Job 34:35

existence, but also continued to keep all things in existence, they were to learn creation's science for the transformation of their mind and person. But their failure to examine and do creation's law proves that even before they knew of their lacking, their inward nature took hold of them. It is because they did not retain knowledge of creation's wisdom for their inward parts that they chose a doctrine contrary to it, gaining the revelation, "Woe is me! for I am undone; because I am a man of unclean lips, and I dwell in the midst of a people of unclean lips."[1314]

11. *Adam's* disobedience opened up their understanding not only to how far they were from their Creator's character, but of how far, for this entire time, they were from that personal and devotional character. Knowledge of their lethargic conversation had surfaced, letting them now understand the reason why creation's course of learning was so mentally taxing and strict against the natural law within the conversation. This new mind troubled *Adam*, and being troubled, they hid their self from the living God's *voice*, saying, "There is no hope."[1315]

12. Our task for personal and devotional liberty is not easy or simple, for if *man*, being unconscious of their devotional condition, failed to find correction in that condition, how much more trying should this course be with a conversation that is already conscious of its sinful or erroneous character? What made *Adam* special was that his mind knew no deviation from the Commandment or Spirit of creation. They had no thoughts to disobey or disregard any commandment of the Creator, for they were *born*, although with a naturally troubled conversation, in a state of mind confessing, "I will worship toward thy holy temple, and praise thy name for thy lovingkindness and for thy truth."[1316] But their violation perverted their perception of self and of the living God. The woman was the first to deviate, and there was, after her disobedience, no sign of *death* in her, causing them to think of the living God as a liar and his words as without power, which only worked to forward negligence.

13. But the living God's covenant was with the *man* and not with the *woman*, wherefore his *voice's* promise should be expected to find fulfillment within the one under covenant. Therefore, as soon as he consumed what was given to him by his wife, "the eyes of them both were opened, and they knew that they were

---

1314   Isaiah 6:5
1315   Jeremiah 18:12
1316   Psalm 138:2

naked."[1317] This opening is in reality a tragedy, for their *eyes* were not opened to a regenerative personal devotion, but to a degenerative conversation. The pure *eye* of their spiritual understanding was put to sleep, and so this *death* is made to pass upon all conversations from the moment they are born to the *earth*. By their decision to magnify their base spiritual nature above the higher faculties of their conversation, every conversation should find itself born to a lesser estate, leaving the person to take the conversation's natural mind to be that rule of personal and devotional government.

14. So *Adam*, in the beginning, sacrificed his mind for the perversion of their faith's inward parts, and by that sacrifice passing that illness to every other conversation mindful of *Eden's* philosophy thereafter. But at the time appointed, the last *Adam* sacrificed his mind for the regeneration of the conversation's inward parts, and by that sacrifice passing that refreshing to every mind desiring Eden's philosophy thereafter. By one act, *Adam* relinquished his understanding on self and on high *things* not only to a certain *sleep*, but to a slumber under the speech and tradition of the *serpent*, but by the act of another conversation created by the living God, sanctification of the conversation's inward parts is established by that justified conversation sacrificed for conversations.

15. *Adam's* first sacrifice was for the deadening of the mind to the conversation's detriment, but the last *Adam's* sacrifice, because it was offered in a *body*, or in a conversation, filled with the living God's righteousness, was accomplished for the renewing of the mind for the conversation's reformation to again find harmony with the living God's *voice*. The *LORD God* may have covered physical flesh with the skin of an animal, but because Adam's error is wholly mental and inward, what physically occurred was only done to "serve unto the example and shadow of heavenly things."[1318] The body of Adam represents the invisible law within the conversation; the skin of the animal represents the living God's *voice* covering the members of the body; the blood of the slain animal represents the means whereby Adam may obtain the privilege to have his flesh hidden and his mind recovered. For this cause, "Put ye on the Lord Jesus Christ, and make not provision for the flesh."[1319]

16. The spirit of our mind is to put on "the Lord Jesus Christ our Saviour,"[1320] which is, in reality, the *voice* of the Creator through "the commandment of God

---

1317   Genesis 3:7
1318   Hebrews 8:5
1319   Romans 13:14
1320   Titus 1:4

our Saviour."[1321] This commandment is the law of God, and seeing as how the Word is plainly acknowledged as God, and because "God is a Spirit,"[1322] to put on the Lord Jesus Christ is to put on "the law of the Spirit of life"[1323] to say, "I delight in the law of God after the inward man."[1324] This law of God is the law of the Word, and this law is to be that God of the conversation moving its doer to say, "With the mind I myself serve the law of God."[1325]

17. The Word made flesh is the Spirit made flesh, which is the law of the Word's righteousness finding expression by the members of the conversation through the limbs of the body. By the performance of one, the conscience of all conversations was sacrificed to slumber. But now every living soul should know an opening of the *eyes* that is contrary to the original plan. But by the actions of another, and after the same *build* of the first, by the righteousness of the living God's *Spirit* within the conscience of his conversation, upon every mind the same righteousness of the same Word may find itself reproduced in their conversation, which is why it says, "Thy righteousness is an everlasting righteousness, and thy law is the truth,"[1326] and, "My salvation shall be for ever, and my righteousness shall not be abolished."[1327]

18. Because "the Spirit is truth,"[1328] and because "the Spirit is life,"[1329] the law of the Spirit's *life* and *righteousness* is decreed for the willing conversation. We have this higher learning freely opened up to us by the *blood*, or by the devotional fellowship of the living God's chief apostle. Like as how blood sealed the first covenant to that former congregation,[1330] so also to ratify this new covenant promise to every conversation, the *blood*, or the inward struggle of the living God's chief apostle was a necessary representative to share the Spirit's promise with every conversation. The Word made flesh is the new covenant promise of the living God's *Spirit*, which is why it says, "I the LORD have called thee in righteousness, and will hold thine hand, and will keep thee, and give thee for a covenant of the people, for a light of the Gentiles."[1331] This new covenant is a

1321 Titus 1:3
1322 John 4:24
1323 Romans 8:2
1324 Romans 7:22
1325 Romans 7:25
1326 Psalm 119:142
1327 Isaiah 51:6
1328 1 John 5:6
1329 Romans 8:10
1330 Hebrews 9:19
1331 Isaiah 42:5

light, and seeing as how "the law is light,"[1332] and "that God is light,"[1333] it is that the Spirit's new covenant is a law of Wisdom, and this covenant states: "A new heart also will I give you, and a new spirit will I put within you."[1334]

19. The living God's intention is after a revival and reform of the inward person in manners of personal worship and service. This promise of sanctification cannot commence until the aim of the new covenant is personally embraced. Thus, without our sincere "acknowledging of the truth which is after godliness";[1335] which "truth" is "the faith of God's elect";[1336] the covenant of the *Spirit* is not activated.

20. Creation's new covenant will is for godliness according to the living God's standard of holiness, to the end we may pray, "Holy is his name,"[1337] and, "I will praise thy name, O LORD; for it is good."[1338] Isn't it that Prophet who says, "Why callest thou me good? there is none good but one, that is, God"?[1339] He would not take the living God's *name* for himself because he understood that no good thing of himself rested within himself. He can do nothing for the conversation, for he even confesses, "I do nothing of myself,"[1340] and, "I can of mine own self do nothing,"[1341] and, "The Son can do nothing of himself."[1342] There is no indication that he would have any mind inordinately affectionate towards him, for he can, in all actuality, do nothing for anyone because he is not the Creator. There is only one that is good, and that one is *God* who is, in reality, a Wisdom, which is why he doesn't say, "Have faith in me," but rather, "Have faith in God."[1343]

21. Thus, as that chief apostle, he can say no *thing* for anyone, but instead says, "Why callest thou me good? none is good, save one, that is, God."[1344] The Word is that good and benevolent God, and the reason why salvation's Word is "good" is because it replenishes the inward parts for the good of the conver-

---

1332 Proverbs 6:23
1333 1 John 1:5
1334 Ezekiel 36:26
1335 Titus 1:1
1336 Titus 1:1
1337 Luke 1:49
1338 Psalm 54:6
1339 Mark 10:18
1340 John 8:28
1341 John 5:30
1342 John 5:19
1343 Mark 11:22
1344 Luke 18:19

sation. "Good" is another term for "holy" and "godly," and the good and holy will of the Spirit is in resurrecting and reforming man's heart and mind to better care for self; this is the living God's righteousness, even "the kindness and love of God our Saviour toward man."[1345] If our affection towards this man is right, if our respect for him is sober, our love for him would move us to honor what he has labeled as good for the person, which is why he says, "I know him, and keep his saying."[1346]

22. The devotion of the true worshipper is to learn of and do the saying of the Word's righteousness; doesn't it say, "Seek ye first the kingdom of God, and his righteousness"?[1347] Herein we may understand that since the Word is God, that the kingdom spoken of is not literal or tangible. The kingdom of the Word is the righteousness of the Spirit, and for the Word to be made flesh, it is that the Spirit's kingdom is made flesh, and "flesh and blood cannot inherit the kingdom of God."[1348] A better *body* is therefore pronounced for the new covenant, for "there is a natural body, and there is a spiritual body,"[1349] wherefore "that which is born of the Spirit is spirit."[1350]

23. We therefore greatly err when taking the speech of the Bible to be so sensual. To hear that the Word was manifested in flesh is not to hear of some fanatical superstitious folklore, but is to observe the kingdom and righteousness of the Word existing "through the faith of the operation of God"[1351] in and by the conversation's members. This is why we are counseled, "Mortify therefore your members which are upon the earth,"[1352] for by the Spirit's *law* of regeneration, the conversation's constitution is become silent to own the character of that *law*.[1353]

24. By one conversation's failure to mortify its *earthly* members, those members are become the primary organs of its spiritual being, and are therefore become the dominant agents of conversations similar to its own. But by one minister's obedience to mortify the mind of his conversation; as it says, "If ye through the Spirit do mortify the deeds of the body, ye shall live";[1354] every

1345 Titus 3:4
1346 John 8:55
1347 Matthew 6:33
1348 1 Corinthians 15:50
1349 1 Corinthians 15:44
1350 John 3:6
1351 Colossians 2:12
1352 Colossians 3:5
1353 Galatians 5:22,23
1354 Romans 8:13

conversation honoring the *build* or the *nature* of *Adam* may now share in the *life* of that presently sacrificed conversation, making it well to know that "the Spirit is life."[1355] "To be carnally minded is death,"[1356] and by one conversation, this carnal mind passed to every living *soul*, "but to be spiritually minded is life and peace,"[1357] and by one minister consenting to tame the *death* within his natural devotional character, all conversations may harmoniously embrace his devotional mind, for by this minister the law of the Spirit's mind is sealed to the willing conversation.

25. Because his conversation was sacrificed with the Word's righteousness within its conscience, his *blood,* or the reforming vocation of his conversation, is the means whereby conversations are bound to this course for experiencing the new covenant promise. The literal blood shed by this man did and does nothing. But his *blood,* figuratively illustrating the struggle and the conflict his conversation embraced when living by the wisdom within the scriptures, is set for an example of how to maintain the devotional experience.

26. The blood of *man* is of no greater value than that of an animal, for "a man hath no preeminence above a beast."[1358] This minister[1359] is herein observed to be, in stature, no better than a beast. Therefore the blood of this man, being of similar value to that of the dumb animal can, in and of itself, do nothing to persuade human minds to claim the living God's kindness.[1360] As that blood of old served a symbolic purpose, so today this man's *blood* is to be thought of in a higher way, even as in a context revealing the conflict the conversation must know in order to have the fulfillment of the new covenant will within its conscience.

27. A greater work is therefore demanded if the person should be convinced to know the living God's righteousness, which is why it says, "Except ye eat the flesh of the Son of man, and drink his blood, ye have no life in you."[1361] The Bible speaks in no solid terms, but in philosophical.

28. It is our assignment to eat and drink the *flesh* and *blood* of the living God's chief apostle, and concerning his *flesh,* he says, "The bread that I will give

1355 Romans 8:10
1356 Romans 8:6
1357 Romans 8:6
1358 Ecclesiastes 3:19
1359 Philippians 2:7,8
1360 Philippians 3:14
1361 John 6:53

is my flesh."[1362] His flesh is that "bread" of his offering ratified for us, which "bread" is even "the law of the Spirit of life,"[1363] the "commandment from the Father."[1364] It is our responsibility to do the Spirit's commandment in order to obtain entrance into the promised creative redemption. This is where his *blood* becomes valuable, for the "blood" spoken of is in reference to the mentally and spiritually trying ordeal born by lawfully doing salvation's will, which is why we are counseled, "Be thou partaker of the afflictions of the gospel according to the power of God."[1365]

29. This Prophet instructs us to have faith in God, and to acknowledge God as good, meaning that mental and physical exercise on the living God's charge is the means whereby we may have "the grace of life"[1366] to seal up the righteousness of that charge's *name* in us. "Blood" is imagery connoting pain, hardship, and perseverance in creation's present higher education, which is why, for our learning, it says of Abraham, "After he had patiently endured, he obtained the promise."[1367]

30. We today have a good promise sealed to us; the only issue is in patiently and temperately opening up that sealed promise to receive the gift within it. The gift of that promise is not freely given, but rather by the course of one conversation, that gift, so long as we faithfully pass through the course the Bible's intended wisdom, is ours to freely claim.

31. This wisdom's chief minister, having the mystery of its righteousness finished within the character of his conversation, opened up the manner of this learning and sanctification to every conversation by one sacrifice, giving to every conversation the hope of their regeneration from the first religious error.[1368] Herein is our faith's promise for complete and perpetual newness.

32. It is our lot to, while holding firm to this hope, examine the Bible for knowledge to apply so that grace, which is a *substance* for active creation, may be added to our conversation for experiencing the living God's righteousness, which is why it says, "Grow in grace, and in the knowledge of our Lord and Saviour Jesus Christ."[1369] The offering of the living God's chief apostle provides

---

1362 John 6:51
1363 Romans 8:2
1364 2 John 1:4
1365 2 Timothy 1:8
1366 1 Peter 3:5
1367 Hebrews 6:15
1368 Romans 8:11
1369 2 Peter 3:18

us the opportunity to *eat* and *drink* his *name*, to the end we may boldly confess, "The law of the Spirit of life in Christ Jesus hath made me free from the law of sin and death."[1370] The exchanging of one devotional nature and conversation for a more benevolent nature and conversation is the living God's righteousness. By having our inward parts refreshed, "we should be holy and without blame before him in love,"[1371] even as it should have been in the beginning.

1370 Romans 8:2
1371 Ephesians 1:4

15

Eden's Continuing Mystery

1. Because a conversation that perfected the righteousness of the living God's *Wisdom* was sacrificed, it is that both the conversation and the mind of the individual is returned to the living God. The living God's endeavor for conversation's through his chief apostle's conversation, because of the position his conversation now holds before the living God, that they may love and find harmony with the Creator's character, returns the heart of every conversation back to the throne of that ascended conversation's *name*, "and this is love, that we walk after his commandments."[1372]

2. To "be holy and without blame before him in love,"[1373] it is to exist in harmony with every word of the Mind at the core of the Bible. Because it is this *Spirit* or *Wisdom* that formed *Adam*, and because this same Adam violated this same Commandment, and because the chief apostle of this same Creator was raised up by the same *Wisdom* of this same Creator, whosoever should know the same resurrection by this same Commandment will also know the same Creator, which is why it says, "I know him, and keep his saying."[1374]

1372   2 John 1:6
1373   Ephesians 1:4
1374   John 8:55

3. The entire aim of the living God's desire is to personally bring the ancient *garden's* right philosophy to the person. *Man* may have been forbidden access to it, but now, by the offering of the living God's chief apostle, that garden's wisdom may now enter in to *man*, fulfilling the saying, "God was manifest in the flesh,"[1375] and, "The Word was made flesh,"[1376] and, "The life was manifested."[1377] The spirit of the mind is to become the Creator's new *garden* by the saying of his *Wisdom*, for like as it was said of that garden, "Joy and gladness shall be found therein, thanksgiving, and the voice of melody,"[1378] so the conversation's conscience should experience "righteousness, and peace, and joy in the Holy Ghost"[1379] to sing, "Thou wast slain, and hast redeemed us to God by thy blood out of every kindred, and tongue, and people, and nation."[1380]

4. The will of the living God's Spirit is for the conversation's full conversion to Eden's devotional philosophy, meaning that, in order to advance such a desire, the person must find their understanding, and without self and the religious world, "above, where Christ sitteth on the right hand of God."[1381] The sacrificed conversation of the living God's chief apostle was offered for a very real and serious purpose, even for regenerating our conversation's conscience to that free estate originally intended. For this cause, a very great science must find itself employed within the person, for the conversation's constitution is now naturally against that ancient *garden's* practice.

5. In a *sinless* state, the conversation's members conquered the human being to reveal that they are innately built to challenge the living God's *name* and *voice*, therefore *man*, in a consciously sinful devotional condition, must have a better spiritual service with better promises to more perfectly uphold what *Adam* failed to keep and dress. It is therefore well to understand the definition of "sin," and it says, "If a soul shall sin through ignorance against any of the commandments of the LORD."[1382]

6. Because the Bible is a philosophical book correcting religion, it is unlawful to firstly define "sin" secularly. "Sin" is against the *voice* of the living

1375   1 Timothy 3:16
1376   John 1:14
1377   1 John 1:2
1378   Isaiah 51:3
1379   Romans 14:7
1380   Revelation 5:9
1381   Colossians 3:1
1382   Leviticus 4:2

God's commandment; "sin is the transgression of the law";[1383] when in a sinless condition, *Adam* knew no thing contrary to the law or commandments of his Creator. Yet when under a sinful religious constitution, it is that they knew all things contrary to the living God's *voice* and did govern their spiritual conversation by that diet and appetite.

7. As student-laborers of salvation's will, it is that our conversations are to be blameless towards the living God's wisdom; this is the point behind the offered conversation of the living God's chief witness. If our desire is not to know and keep every word of the garden's Mind, then not only is the Bible's philosophy not for us, but "if any man have not the Spirit of Christ, he is none of his,"[1384] disqualifying their conversation from obtaining a right character. The living God is that Mind behind the new covenant will, and the conversation inclined to learn of and do that will has a mind wanting to say, "I have kept my Father's commandments, and abide in his love.":[1385]

8. A living and personal religion is the Creator's intention for us, wherefore if *man* originally failed to hear and keep the commandment, seeing as how "of his own will begat he us with the word of truth, that we should be a kind of firstfruits of his creatures,"[1386] then it is that this same Creator will bring that commandment in to *man* for it to hear and keep them. Herein we are made to observe a controversy, because if the conversation did not keep *his* charge when it had no mind to unlawfully agitate itself, how much more difficult should it be to bring the conversation, in a now perpetual state of conscious agitation, to hear that *voice*? "The carnal mind is enmity against God,"[1387] and because the Word is that God, "the natural man receiveth not the things of the Spirit of God."[1388] Wherefore to confess, "I delight in the law of God after the inward man,"[1389] is to relay the greatest miracle in existence.

9. The natural devotional conversation dislikes right service to the Bible's *Mind* because that devotion is wholly mental and inwardly strenuous. The human being does not like to think, nor is there any good thing within it to naturally move its self to rationalize any *thing*, especially to rationalize by an

---

1383 1 John 3:4
1384 Romans 8:9
1385 John 15:10
1386 James 1:18
1387 Romans 8:7
1388 1 Corinthians 2:14
1389 Romans 7:22

experimental faith. The counsel, "Come now, and let us reason together,"[1390] is absolute foolishness to *man's* innate constitution, for "the natural man receiveth not the things of the Spirit of God: for they are foolishness unto him: neither can he know them, because they are spiritually discerned."[1391]

10. All things of the Bible, because they proceed from the *Word*, which is its *Spirit*, are comprehended by spending brainpower, by "comparing spiritual things with spiritual."[1392] If hopeful to understand any *thing* in the Bible, the mind must find itself taxed and diligently reviewing its sayings. "The things of God knoweth no man, but the Spirit of God,"[1393] wherefore if we are desiring to mysteriously know some thing by failing to exercise our mental faculties, or are taking in spiritual prescriptions from *men*, it is well to know that because right learning is "not in the words which man's wisdom teacheth, but which the Holy Ghost teacheth; comparing spiritual things with spiritual;"[1394] we exist in the *death* of the first *Adam*. This conveys to the careful observer that learning is personal and only obtained by holding communion with the *Mind* of the scriptures.

11. What the living God asks of us is not unreasonable. If we want anything, we'll spend the energy to research it, and if we know that our budget is tight, we may, while continuing our research, save up until we have enough funds to buy what we want. The issue, then, is who really wants what the living God is offering, or who does not, and who is satisfied with a counterfeit. It is more than natural, after innocent and childlike belief is had on the living God's chief apostle that, truly wanting want him, the person will spend energy to diligent run through the Bible to draw nearer to him, and drawing nearer, they learn to "draw nigh unto God."[1395] It is God that the true worshipper comes to delight in, or rather the Word or the *Wisdom* of the scriptures, because they are, simply put, sick, and are tired of their *illness*.

12. We can't buy, or cannot desire to buy, what does not convince us of its need in our life. Seeing as how "Christ Jesus came into the world to save sinners,"[1396] if we would value the Word, it is that we actually value our conversation enough to understand that we don't know how to value it, and by that

---

1390 Isaiah 1:18
1391 1 Corinthians 2:14
1392 1 Corinthians 2:13
1393 1 Corinthians 2:11
1394 1 Corinthians 2:13
1395 Hebrews 7:19
1396 1 Timothy 1:5

ignorance have mistreated it, and are therefore ready to learn how to better care for it, praying, "That which I see not teach thou me: if I have done iniquity, I will do no more."[1397] The conversation rejoicing in the Word only does so because they acknowledge their deviation from the Bible's *voice* has enflamed their *disease*, and by exercising faith on its present will, they will know only a recovered heart and mind.

13. The only point of the *Spirit's* sacrifice was to rescue conversations violating the living God's will and wisdom. The conversation failing to correctly hear and do that commandment, and those devotional principles enjoined to it, are the "sinners" and the "wicked" against the living God. The correction of the natural devotional disposition is only by *creation's* present Word upon the spirit of the mind, which is why it says, "Live according to God in the spirit,"[1398] and, "Worship God in the spirit,"[1399] and, "Be renewed in the spirit of your mind."[1400] If the person can quiet their heart and mind to sincerely mediate on the Spirit's *law*,[1401] a right understanding of salvation's knowledge will capture the mind for bettering the personal and the devotional conversation.

14. The issue at hand is on convincing the conversation's thoughts and feelings that it not only needs rescuing from its own character, but also deliverance according to the intended manner, and for this revelation, only the heart of the person can humble the conversation's disposition, which is why it says, "Give me thine heart, and let thine eyes observe my ways."[1402] There is a twofold work mentioned in order to begin *creation's* training, namely, giving up the heart and observing the manners of the living God's chief apostle. Too often the conversation moves the heart to care for his manners without first offering the heart to comprehend them, and this is wrong, which is why "many are weak and sickly... and many sleep."[1403]

15. It is because of a false love and ambition that many "will not endure sound doctrine; but after their own lusts shall they heap to themselves teachers, having itching ears; and they shall turn away their ears from the truth, and shall be turned unto fables."[1404] Conception is to occur through the saying of the

---

1397 Job 34:32
1398 1 Peter 4:6
1399 Philippians 3:3
1400 Ephesians 4:23
1401 Psalm 1:2
1402 Proverbs 23:26
1403 1 Corinthians 11:30
1404 2 Timothy 4:3,4

Bible's words within the mind, meaning that our mental faculties must wrestle with and endure its doctrine until a clear vision of its *name* is understood. It is because of an unwillingness to review the Bible's words that the conversation lowers in character to subscribe to "Jewish fables, and commandments of men, that turn from the truth."[1405]

16. The true worshipper doesn't know this contrary course of learning, but will only confess, "I applied mine heart to know, and to search, and to seek out wisdom, and the reason of things."[1406] Right learning is proving the Word or Wisdom of the Bible. Right learning is proving the living God's *Wisdom* to be that Creator of the inward parts. Right learning is proving that the living God's chief apostle didn't lie when saying, "Have faith in God."[1407] It is our assignment to worship the *Word* by the spirit of the mind so that our faith may experience its righteousness to praise its *name* as "Intercessor." We absolutely make the priestly ministry of this *Wisdom* of no value by failing to receive from its intercession that promise to appear by an experimental faith on its *name*. It is because of a heart that is too lazy and a faith that is too depressed that the person allows its human being to rule their conversation, which only serves to encourage the conversation to abuse the mind for the violation of the body.

17. It is wrong, after there is any confidence on the living God's chief apostle; whether great or small; to turn the conversation over to the human being that is either within or without us.[1408] Our inclination towards this man is by no natural occurrence. Because our heart, in the moment it heard whatever it heard concerning him, freely opened up, the silencing of the natural inclination by the living God's influence is the reason our heart was able to retain whatever it should to persuade it to trust on whatever it heard. We may have heard, from another, some thing about him, but it was not them that convinced us of any thing. The little information our spirit received when our heart was permitted to open up to the living God's *voice*, that is what blessed our heart.

18. We heard some *thing* that was us. We heard some *thing* that knew us. We heard some *thing* that comforted our heart. We heard some *thing* that made our person tremble. For a moment, our thoughts were silent. For a time, our feelings did not speak. But our inward person experienced stillness, and that quietness is what we have never known, but do desire to consistently have. And

---

1405 Titus 1:4
1406 Ecclesiastes 7:25
1407 Mark 11:22
1408 Galatians 3:3

herein is the honest conversation separated from the dishonest conversation, for no *thing* will stop the honest mind from perpetually experiencing stillness, but all *things* will thwart the dishonest from quietness. The honest soul, attributing their experience not to another person, will return to the words it heard to know its *name* and *force*, and by "comparing spiritual things with spiritual,"[1409] will not run after a flesh-based stimulus.

19. Must the body finish what the mind experienced? Must the superstition of a religious tradition finish what is first known by no religious tradition? Well, "if righteousness come by the law, then Christ is dead in vain,"[1410] "but that no man is justified by the law in the sight of God, it is evident: for, The just shall live by faith. And the law is not of faith."[1411] No law of any religious tradition can suffice for the reception of salvation's benevolent will, for that promise is above the religious world, and so much so that the doer of that science says, "Thou wast slain, and hast redeemed us to God by thy blood out of every kindred, and tongue, and people, and nation."[1412]

20. To be redeemed or purged from out of every denomination is to embrace a *birth* and *baptism* by the *Word* "to the general assembly and church of the firstborn, which are written in heaven."[1413] Seeing as how "God sent forth his Son, made of a woman, made under the law, to redeem them that were under the law,"[1414] it is the Bible's every intention that we pass away from "the pollutions of the world through the knowledge of the Lord and Saviour Jesus Christ,"[1415] which is why we are to "be dead with Christ from the rudiments of the world."[1416] Herein are two persuasions: the first is the *death* of *Christ* and the second, the *life* of the religious world. In the way "Christ" and "the world" are mentioned, it is well to know that both represent a specific brand of philosophy. For, "the Lord Jesus Christ our Saviour"[1417] is "the commandment of God our Saviour,"[1418] and concerning "the world," it says, "The tradition of men, after the rudiments of the world."[1419]

1409 1 Corinthians 2:13
1410 Galatians 2:21
1411 Galatians 3:11,12
1412 Revelation 5:9
1413 Hebrews 12:23
1414 Galatians 4:5
1415 2 Peter 2:20
1416 Colossians 2:20
1417 Titus 1:4
1418 Titus 1:3
1419 Colossians 2:8

21. "The world" is linked to the religious tradition of elders and priests, and there is no clean *thing* in the religious world, which is why "the whole world lieth in wickedness."[1420] The sacrificed conversation of the living God's chief apostle is ordained to purify the inward parts for the very purpose of possessing self away from the mind and lore of the religious world. This is why, to the end his offering may fulfill in every willing conversation the philosophy of righteousness to quit the conversation within the religious world, he was born under the tradition of the philosophy of the religious law.

22. Having a mind sacrificed under the operation of the living God's will within his conversation, and having also that same mind removed from the common religious tradition to the living God's *heavenly* Sanctuary, the living God's Prophet has secured for every conversation the opportunity to become a partaker of the confidence within the *Temple* above. When we hear him say, "I proceeded forth and came from God; neither came I of myself, but he sent me,"[1421] he is confessing his conversation's origin from the *Word*, and that conversation occurring by the mind, for "that which is born of the Spirit is spirit."[1422] To proceed from the Word is to cultivate a conversation to the living God by the law and judgment of a Wisdom within the spirit of the mind, allowing us to know that "the word of God is not bound,"[1423] and is even "gone into heaven, and is on the right hand of God."[1424] This is the reason why his conversation said, "I leave the world, and go to the Father."[1425] Thus, with the Creator and this man's conversation not in the religious world, what good is in and of the *world*? With both in the Building above, what tradition can suffice?

23. The living God's goal is the right philosophy of the original *garden* engraved upon the heart and established within the mind, which is why this mystery is known as, "Christ in you, the hope of glory."[1426] The hope of glory is "Christ" in the heart of the conversation's thoughts and feelings, wherefore it is well to remember that "Christ" is but a term denoting a specific counsel.[1427] "Christ," as is here mentioned, seeing as how "Christ is the end of the law for

---

1420 1 John 5:19
1421 John 8:42
1422 John 3:6
1423 2 Timothy 2:9
1424 1 Peter 3:22
1425 John 16:28
1426 Colossians 1:27
1427 2 Corinthians 5:16

righteousness to every one that believeth,"[1428] is the full will of the living God for conversations. This man willingly suffered crucifixion to show that every mind examining and doing "Christ," just as be also both did and examined, will inwardly transcend the religious world's institution.

24. He, being born under the weight of a religious tradition, and cultivating within the mind of his conversation the understanding of the scripture's *Word*, and conquering his conversation's mind by that wisdom, being slain with that right devotional condition resting within his naturally erroneous religious conversation, has set forth an example to follow.[1429] The tradition of the honest conversation is in that *Building* this man's regenerated conversation was brought up to, for it is today "a merciful and faithful high priest in things pertaining to God"[1430] that we might love the Creator behind this mediation,[1431] and the creation attached to that ministry.

25. Every law of the living God's mind, in the beginning, pointed to the fact that this mind's *voice* not only promoted creation, but also that creation continued due to that *voice*. We today have no knowledge of our faith's Creator, and it is because we fail to do what was done in the beginning, namely, to listen, perceive, do, and live out the present philosophy of the living God's *voice*, which is why it says, "Keep my commandments, and live; and my law as the apple of thine eye,"[1432] and, "Let thine heart retain my words: keep my commandments, and live."[1433]

26. Our heart must retain the living God's words in order to have any knowledge on how to faithfully carry out our conversation. This retaining; because words are not physical; must come by mental exercise, which is why it says, "I will meditate in thy precepts, and have respect unto thy ways."[1434] Herein is witnessed that no love or respect for the Bible can appear without scrutinizing its sayings, which is why it says, "If a man love me, he will keep my words."[1435]

1428　Romans 10:4
1429　2 Peter 2:20
1430　Hebrews 2:17
1431　2 John 1:6
1432　Proverbs 7:2
1433　Proverbs 4:4
1434　Psalm 119:15
1435　John 14:23

16

Seek First His Word

1. We should know that it is well to quit self's religious policies with the standards of the religious world to learn the Bible's philosophy. To hear, "Live unto God,"[1436] and, "Live according to God,"[1437] is to hear, "Live unto righteousness,"[1438] for it is written, "Uphold me according unto thy word, that I may live."[1439] Our conversation's primary responsibility is to *God*, which is the Word, and to the righteousness or charity of that Word. Our assignment is to first make sure that the living God's intention enters in to the *flesh*, or the body of our devotional understanding. That good will, because "that which is born of the Spirit is spirit,"[1440] is only by one means, as it says, "Live according to God in the spirit,"[1441] and, "Worship God in the spirit."[1442]

1436 Galatians 2:19
1437 1 Peter 4:6
1438 1 Peter 2:24
1439 Psalm 119:116
1440 John 3:6
1441 1 Peter 4:6
1442 Philippians 3:3

2. It is well to personally discern the wisdom of the living God's science; there is no *thing* more important to our conversation than the benevolence of the Bible's words. Our devotion, because we are counseled to carry our mind by the Bible's present experience, should therefore accept *creation's* Word over and within it. If ever without this Wisdom; who is that God of the conversation; we are bound to serve an empty practice equal to the void within the conversation.[1443] The hope of *God's* philosophy is the implanting of a *good thing* wherein no good thing exists, wherefore the doer of the Spirit's *law* says, "With the mind I myself serve the law of God."[1444]

3. To hear, "With the mind I myself serve the law of God,"[1445] is to hear, "God is my witness, whom I serve with my spirit in the gospel of his Son."[1446] The *law* of *God*; the Bible's philosophy being God; is the doctrine of its chief apostle, which counsel is "the righteousness of God which is by faith of Jesus Christ."[1447] Herein we must discern the language presented to us in order to grasp just what to consider. With the Word being God, and as "God is a Spirit,"[1448] the righteousness to appear by faith of "Jesus Christ" is the kindness and righteousness of the *Spirit*. Because this righteousness is only for the spirit of the mind, it is that faith must find itself exercised by a specific charge. This charge is called "Jesus Christ," and it is well to consider that, due to how the scriptures are using the term "Jesus Christ," that no man is referenced.[1449]

4. We are to understand, due to the context of "Jesus Christ" in the scriptures, that "the Lord Jesus Christ our Saviour"[1450] is, in reality, a "commandment of God our Saviour"[1451] equating to "the kindness and love of God our Saviour toward man."[1452] Therefore, the righteousness of the Word occurs by experimenting with faith on the living God's commandment for creation, which is the reason why "we have received a commandment from the Father."[1453] Our consistent investigation and execution of this saying is the only means whereby we may experience the intended righteousness, which is why it is necessary to

1443 Romans 7:18
1444 Romans 7:25
1445 Romans 7:25
1446 Romans 1:19
1447 Romans 3:22
1448 John 4:24
1449 2 Corinthians 5:16
1450 Titus 1:4
1451 Titus 1:3
1452 Titus 3:4
1453 2 John 1:4

quit self's spiritual mind and the theories of the religious world to learn of and do the Bible's present will.

5. If it is that we are touched by any thing concerning the living God's chief apostle, this counsel should not pass us by: "For in that he died, he died unto sin once: but in that he liveth, he liveth unto God."[1454]

6. His physical body suffering death is a figurative illustration of our conversation's members experiencing a certain silence to live unto the living God's *Word* or *Wisdom* and to no other *God*. Thus, like as how "there is no work, nor device, nor knowledge, nor wisdom, in the grave,"[1455] so also the naturally irrational religious inclination that keeps the conversation tied to the religious world, and to its own stubborn religious interpretations, must quit every self-cultivated labor, device, knowledge, and understanding in order to claim a conversation entirely consecrated to the Bible's science. If it is that we are actually *dead* with *Christ*; that is, having the mind of our faith silenced by "the Lord Jesus Christ our Saviour";[1456] which "Lord" is "the knowledge of the Lord and Saviour Jesus Christ";[1457] then it is that the spirit of our mind is free to worship the living God by the Word.

7. Death to the conversation's constitution, then, by the living God's knowledge, must occur within the mind and not within the conversation, meaning that, above a traditional religious routine, the mind, in order for it to have wisdom to exercise for strengthening its faith, must thoroughly and consistently review the Bible's *voice*. The knowledge of the living God's chief apostle is herein witnessed to be that instrument used to deliver the person from "profane and vain babblings, and oppositions of science falsely so called,"[1458] which is why it says, "Through knowledge shall the just be delivered."[1459]

8. The "just" are the justified, which is why it says, and by no accident, "By his knowledge shall my righteous servant justify many."[1460] "Death" by "Christ" is the means whereby justification commences. Sanctification is the living God's educational learning whereby the conscience of the conversation is translated from *earth* in to *classroom* above.[1461] The deliverance wrought by studying "Jesus

---

1454 Romans 6:10
1455 Ecclesiastes 9:10
1456 Titus 1:4
1457 2 Peter 2:20
1458 1 Timothy 6:20
1459 Proverbs 11:9
1460 Isaiah 53:11
1461 Colossians 1:13

Christ" is mental deliverance from self's misunderstanding and the religious world's misconception "to the general assembly and church of the firstborn, which are written in heaven, and to God the Judge of all."[1462]

9. *God* only exists within the *heavenly* Sanctuary, which is why it says, "For ever, O LORD, thy word is settled in heaven."[1463] God is that Counsel, and in order for us to properly reverence the philosophy of this Temple, it is that we must apply our mind to the philosophy of the *Word* or *Spirit* of this Temple, which is why we have "a merciful and faithful high priest in things pertaining to God."[1464] The high priest of this temple is the *name* and *conversation* of the living God's chief apostle. This mediation is ordained to forward creation within our conversation's inward parts, wherefore it is necessary to extend our faith into this *Building*, "for without are dogs, and sorcerers, and whoremongers, and murderers, and idolaters, and whosoever loveth and maketh a lie."[1465]

10. This is why Paul counsels, "Beware of dogs, beware of evil workers, beware of the concision. For we are the circumcision, which worship God in the spirit, and rejoice in Christ Jesus, and have no confidence in the flesh."[1466] To hear, "God was manifest in the flesh,"[1467] is to hear, "Jesus Christ is come in the flesh,"[1468] for with "God" being "Jesus Christ," it is necessary to remember that no man is referenced.[1469] We cannot forget that since "the Word was with God, and the Word was God,"[1470] that the Word will always be God, and that the appellation or moniker of the Word is "Jesus Christ."

11. "Jesus Christ," like "the Word," is immaterial or intangible, representing no fleshly man, for "God is a Spirit,"[1471] and "a spirit hath not flesh and bones."[1472] For this cause, "Jesus Christ," who is the Word and God, must dawn a better form than that of flesh in order to bless the mind, for "that which is born of the Spirit is spirit."[1473] This is why it is written, "My spirit that is upon

---

1462 Hebrews 12:23
1463 Psalm 119:89
1464 Hebrews 2:17
1465 Revelation 22:15
1466 Philippians 3:2,3
1467 1 Timothy 3:16
1468 2 John 1:7
1469 2 Corinthians 5:16
1470 John 1:1
1471 John 4:24
1472 Luke 24:39
1473 John 3:6

thee, and my words which I have put in thy mouth,"[1474] and, "I will pour out my spirit unto you, I will make known my words unto you."[1475] The Spirit appears in the form of words, for "that which is born of the Spirit is spirit."[1476] Thus, to take joy in "Jesus Christ" is to worship God or the Word in the spirit of the mind, and this delight occurring as the mind chews and digests the Bible's words, even as it says, "I will meditate in thy precepts, and have respect unto thy ways."[1477]

12. Our principal vocation is in bringing the Word in to our mind for acquiring a "spirit that confesseth that Jesus Christ is come in the flesh,"[1478] which is why we are counseled, "Wisdom is the principal thing; therefore get wisdom: and with all thy getting get understanding."[1479] The Word made flesh is "Christ the power of God, and the wisdom of God,"[1480] conquering the conversation's conscience. "Christ" is the power and wisdom of the Word, which Word is the Spirit, who is God, or who is primary philosophy, wherefore every conversation entered in to creation's higher education is told, "The Holy Ghost shall come upon thee, and the power of the Highest shall overshadow thee."[1481]

13. Seeing as how we are "to be strengthened with might by his Spirit in the inner man,"[1482] the power of the Holy Ghost can only appear within the inward person, and that appearance by the living God's wisdom refreshing the mind.[1483] We can therefore understand how it may be difficult to embrace the Bible's course of learning while devoted to the religious world, for "no servant can serve two masters: for either he will hate the one, and love the other."[1484] The stimulus of the religious age, because it is the same natural force working within the human being, is contrary to the intended devotional pleasure or experience.

14. It is well to understand that the author, when recording their narrative of the living God's chief apostle, fairly wrote, "I leave the world, and go to the Father."[1485] This is mentioned to let us know that there should be no spiritual *thing* in the religious world for our conversation, seeing as how we are to "be

---

1474 Isaiah 59:21
1475 Proverbs 1:23
1476 John 3:6
1477 Psalm 119:15
1478 1 John 4:2
1479 Proverbs 4:7
1480 1 Corinthians 1:24
1481 Luke 1:35
1482 Ephesians 3:16
1483 Psalm 51:6
1484 Luke 16:13
1485 John 16:28

dead with Christ from the rudiments of the world."[1486] His conversation was removed from this realm and brought into salvation's sphere.[1487] Hereafter the philosophy of the Bible should no longer find itself within any religious age, for that right understanding once consecrated to the *earth* now rests by the right hand of the living God and under the supervision of a vetted conversation.

15. This same "LORD God made the earth and the heavens,"[1488] and fashioning them, decreed the same Faith of the *heavens* for the *earth*. An error then occurred among *heavens* host, and this LORD sanctified his *name* by his *heavens*, sending forth that religious error to the *earth*.[1489] With the *heavens* free of religious error, the *dragon* sought an entrance in to the LORD's *earth*, and it prevailed. For ages and for generations the dragon's religion frustrated the living God's philosophy on *earth*, but then, at the appointed time, that Messenger finished a work for the *earth*, securing the living God's philosophy above, away from the *earth*.

16. In order for us to properly honor the living God, it is necessary for our conversation to learn of and do the philosophy that is above the religious world.[1490] The high priestly appointment of that Messenger's conversation secures to every conversation the original philosophy placed within ancient *garden*, leaving every *thing* under the heaven and on *earth* in service to the *spirit* of error. This is why we are counseled, "Love not the world, neither the things that are in the world...For all that is in the world, the lust of the flesh, and the lust of the eyes, and the pride of life, is not of the Father, but is of the world."[1491]

17. If the living God's chief messenger is on our mind, it is well to cultivate what we have so that we may have a knowledgeable confidence in the promise to appear by an experimental faith. There is a reason why he had to die, for we now have a witness revealing the intended conversation for our faith.[1492] Our confidence on him should not leave us sitting in limbo. His death figuratively opened up the door of the Sanctuary above so that our conversation might have the Bible's present righteousness fulfilled within its inward parts. Our conversation has no *hope* outside of this Building, but when within it, regeneration's will is ours to know.

1486 Colossians 2:20
1487 Galatians 1:1
1488 Genesis 2:4
1489 Revelation 12:9
1490 Colossians 3:1,2
1491 1 John 2:15,16
1492 Hebrews 10:19,20

18. For this cause, it is well to learn of *God's* philosophy, to do it, for we may then pick up the prayer, "Whom have I in heaven but thee? and there is none upon earth that I desire beside thee."[1493] Herein is the fulfilling of the saying, "The Word was made flesh";[1494] the alteration within the conversation's constitution to wholeheartedly serve the Word is a great miracle, even a work "contrary to nature."[1495] There is then a greater Institution to be apart of, even like as it says, "Thou wert cut out of the olive tree which is wild by nature, and wert graffed contrary to nature into a good olive tree."[1496]

19. Our conversation, naturally "having the understanding darkened, being alienated from the life of God,"[1497] is to be with "the spirits of just men made perfect."[1498] Where on *earth* may it be said that there are minds justified? Where under the *heavens* can I find this assembly? Where in the religious world is that *Wisdom* and God of right judgment? There is only one *Building* in existence for finishing the mystery of the living God's will, and within it, we have "a minister of the sanctuary, and of the true tabernacle, which the Lord pitched, and not man."[1499]

20. We must; as student-laborers of that *administration* above; come up higher in our faith and in thoughts. If the living God would have been pleased to leave salvation's commandment on *earth*, it would have been done, but this isn't the case. He didn't leave it on *earth* because it is the living God's intention to supply the honest conversation with a sure hope, and with a sure *Forerunner* of that hope, to the end they may say, "I therefore so run, not as uncertainly; so fight I, not as one that beateth the air."[1500]

21. The removal of that Prophet's conversation from the *earth* witnesses to the fact of a spiritual dominion for a spiritual science by great and precious spiritual gifts and promises for the spirit of the mind, which is why it says, "Blessed be the God and Father of our Lord Jesus Christ, who hath blessed us with all spiritual blessings in heavenly places in Christ."[1501] The "places" of *heaven* connote the two rooms of the sanctuary.[1502] These "places" or "rooms" make up

---

1493 Psalm 73:25
1494 John 1:14
1495 Romans 11:24
1496 Romans 11:24
1497 Ephesians 4:18
1498 Hebrews 12:23,24
1499 Hebrews 8:2
1500 1 Corinthians 9:26
1501 Ephesians 1:3
1502 Hebrews 9:2,3

the *heavenly* Sanctuary, for like as how "the first covenant had also ordinances of divine service, and a worldly sanctuary,"[1503] so also the new covenant is regulated by a *service* within *Temple*. The living God raised up this conversation to be that chief priest over this Temple's assembly.[1504]

22. If we are without this intercession, we are without the living God of this ministry and are therefore "without Christ, being aliens from the commonwealth of Israel, and strangers from the covenants of promise, having no hope, and without God in the world."[1505] There is absolutely no reason why any conversation should exist in this condition, especially since "we have such an high priest, who is set on the right hand of the throne of the Majesty in the heavens."[1506] The issue, then, is not with the living God, but with us.

23. The longer we refuse to personally learn of and do creation's present will, the longer the influence of *heaven's Spirit* is removed from our conversation, keeping our person in a state of slow burning for a pre-mature *death*. There is no good *thing* on the *earth* or within the religious world, for both *creation's* Word and the conversation of its Messenger exist above. It is for this reason that our learning within that *Building* above is important, for we are to not grow comfortable in this *House* of *Prayer*, but are to be found, after a period of learning, descending from *heaven* to *earth*, even as it says, "A ladder set up on the earth...and behold the angels of God ascending and descending on it."[1507] Minds are justified for training as *angels* or as messengers of wisdom, being.[1508] They ascend by the knowledge of salvation's science only to travel back to *earth* "to give the light of the knowledge of the glory of God in the face of Jesus Christ."[1509]

24. It may appear that heaven's course of learning is too strict or too narrow, or too grievous upon the person; even as some anciently said, "The place where we dwell with thee is too strait for us";[1510] but the weight of this learning is greater than our individual experience. Creation is the point, and every creation of the Word is employed for a good labor to bless its environment, which is why,

---

1503 Hebrews 9:1
1504 Hebrews 7:25
1505 Ephesians 2:12
1506 Hebrews 8:1
1507 Genesis 28:12
1508 1 Corinthians 4:1
1509 2 Corinthians 4:6
1510 2 Kings 6:1

in the beginning, "God saw every thing that he had made, and, behold, it was very good."[1511]

25. The vocation of the Spirit's creation is to do "good" according to the saying, "Let no corrupt communication proceed out of your mouth, but that which is good to the use of edifying,"[1512] and, "Let every one of us please his neighbour for his good to edification."[1513] Our course in faith's higher learning is only preparing our conversation to execute a ministry of healing within the religious world. This is the manner and mission in which that Prophet was brought up by the living God, and concerning it, he says, "As thou hast sent me into the world, even so have I also sent them into the world."[1514]

26. Today, it is well to begin to refrain from self's spiritual notions and the religious world's fables to cultivate a living faith in the Bible's present science. The God of a right discipline to the Creator; as pronounced by the scripture; is the philosophy of creation's Wisdom, for by our diligent communion in its *law*, sober affection for its conversation and godly reverence towards its Creator will serve to correct the conversation on how to love and possess its self. It is our faith's experience of possessing its self under the supervision of this wisdom that will fashion it after the likeness of its *Mind*, becoming a champion, to the praise of what is above, of its will among *earth's* inhabitant.

1511 Genesis 1:31
1512 Ephesians 4:29
1513 Romans 15:2
1514 John 17:18

17

By His Hair

1. When thinking on the living God's chief apostle, and when hopeful to discern the saying, "With child of the Holy Ghost,"[1515] it is well to review the history of another, and who, in similar fashion, was pronounced and conceived. Concerning Samson, his mother was told, "Thou shalt conceive, and bear a son; and no razor shall come on his head: for the child shall be a Nazarite unto God from the womb."[1516]

2. Samson's hair made him special. Samson's strength came from his hair, for this child, although prophesied to be Israel's deliverer, and although prophesied to be one particularly and peculiarly blessed above all, was no sensual or carnal creation of the LORD. Because like as the living God's chief messenger especially found himself blessed above all, so too concerning Samson we know that "the child grew, and the LORD blessed him. And the Spirit of the LORD began to move him at times in the camp of Dan."[1517]

1515   Matthew 1:18
1516   Judges 13:5
1517   Judges 13:24,25

3. The blessing of the LORD came through his Spirit moving upon Samson, and this movement is not to find itself perversely understood, for "that which is born of the flesh is flesh; and that which is born of the Spirit is spirit."[1518] Samson, being wholly flesh, must find himself moved by his LORD's Spirit only by the spirit of his mind, for he was not ignorant of how the LORD once said of a man, "I have filled him with the spirit of God, in wisdom, and in understanding, and in knowledge."[1519]

4. The living God's Spirit moves today as it moved of old, which is why it says, "I am the LORD, I change not."[1520] To be filled with the Spirit is to have the wisdom, knowledge, and understanding of the living God's *name* within the spirit of the mind, which is the experience the living God's Prophet knew.[1521] A child of the *Holy Ghost* is a mind conceived to the living God's philosophy by the wisdom, knowledge, understanding, fear, and counsel at the heart of the scriptures.[1522] This is important to comprehend because there is a pattern that the LORD establishes by Samson to explain the excellent brilliance of that Prophet.

5. Although born of flesh, the LORD pronounced, before his birth, a special blessing upon a natural part of Samson. If this natural part should find itself damaged, then his Spirit could not tend to this deliverer, but if that *part* of Samson should find itself without any injury, then the promise of blessing, and the fellowship of his Spirit, should find itself perfectly fulfilled in Samson. Samson's mother was counseled to keep a clean diet[1523] because if her constitution suffered, then her connection to Samson would harm his strength, for his body was to be in a condition having no unnecessary burden, and especially his *hair*, which was that *part* especially blessed.

6. Should Samson's hair know injury, the channel that he should have to the LORD's throne by his Spirit would fail, but if his hair found itself without any burden added to it, then his strength would be made sure, allowing him to fulfill the mission devised for him concerning Israel's liberation. It is well to think on this link between flesh and the LORD's Spirit because, like as his Spirit only found itself prominent in Samson's growth and development by a body within Samson already attached to his fleshly form, so too for every child of the *Holy*

1518   John 3:6
1519   Exodus 31:3
1520   Malachi 3:6
1521   Isaiah 11:2,3
1522   Exodus 3:18
1523   Judges 13:4

Ghost, the living God's *Wisdom* or Spirit must find itself working in and through a *body* already joined to an *earthy form*.

7. Samson was no product of the Spirit by the spirit, but was rather a product of the Spirit by the flesh, in that the LORD pronounced a specific blessing and a strict regimen upon a natural part of Samson. The birth of the living God's chief apostle is no different than this, except instead of pronouncing a blessing upon a physical body, the blessing was constrained to a spiritual body. Since "there is a natural body, and there is a spiritual body,"[1524] it is well to never forget that "that which is born of the flesh is flesh; and that which is born of the Spirit is spirit."[1525] As that prophesied deliverer of the living God, he was to find, as was Samson in relation to his hair, his conversation born with a character ordained for blessing. And the Bible foreshadowed the excellent spirit of this man through Samson, for like as hair sprouts from the head, so it should be that "the head of Christ is God."[1526]

8. Blessing found itself attached to Samson by a physical body, yet by the vision preached through Samson, it is that we should understand why it was necessary that the living God's chief apostle should have his mind regenerated.[1527] The "head" is figurative language denoting the "eyes"; that is, "the eyes of your understanding";[1528] for, "the wise man's eyes are in his head."[1529] Samson may have had his physical head blessed, but this was only accomplished to illustrate the promised blessing for the eyes through the offering of that Prophet.

9. As the first *child* of the *Holy Ghost* through the new covenant will, hair was not to be the means whereby a deliverer should be trained, but rather the *eyes* of his comprehension. His eyes, in order to receive the promised conception, should be filled with the living God's Spirit, for his head should be God, which is why he says, "I know him, and keep his saying."[1530] Herein it is well to never lose sight of the fact that "the Word was with God, and the Word was God,"[1531] and that the Word is that God.

1524 1 Corinthians 15:44
1525 John 3:6
1526 1 Corinthians 11:3
1527 1 Corinthians 15:45
1528 Ephesians 1:18
1529 Ecclesiastes 2:14
1530 John 8:55
1531 John 1:1

10. Because "God is a Spirit,"[1532] the head of the living God's chief minister is the Spirit, which Spirit is the same "Word of life."[1533] Again, "that which is born of the Spirit is spirit,"[1534] and in order for him to obtain birth of the Spirit, it is that his spirit, or his *eyes*, must receive words to forward that conception within his mind. This is why, concerning *birth* by the living God's Spirit, it says, "I will pour out my spirit unto you, I will make known my words unto you,"[1535] and, "My doctrine shall drop as the rain."[1536]

11. The outpouring of the living God's Spirit is the outpouring of the living God's doctrine, and this shower is only poured out upon the spirit of the mind, seeing as how "that which is born of the Spirit is spirit."[1537] A *child* of the *Holy Ghost* is a mind learning how to consistently "put on the new man, which is renewed in knowledge,"[1538] which is why we are counseled, "Put ye on the Lord Jesus Christ."[1539] "Jesus Christ" is that "new man" our mind is to put on, therefore it is well to understand, by the language of the Bible, that "Jesus Christ" is a reference to the same saying that the living God's chief apostle kept and dressed his conversation with. This saying is even "the Word of life,"[1540] which "Word" is "the law of the Spirit of life."[1541]

12. Again, "the Lord Jesus Christ our Saviour"[1542] is understood to be "the commandment of God our Saviour,"[1543] which law and commandment is "the doctrine of God our Saviour."[1544] Therefore when it says, "I will pour my spirit upon thy seed, and my blessing upon thine offspring,"[1545] it is that it is saying, "My doctrine shall drop as the rain, my speech shall distil as the dew."[1546] The blessing to be received by the living God's wisdom is the filling of the conversation's heart and conscience with the doctrine of the knowledge of that Prophet's *name*, even as it says, "Thou desirest truth in the inward parts: and in the hidden

---

1532 John 4:24
1533 1 John 1:1
1534 John 3:6
1535 Proverbs 1:23
1536 Deuteronomy 32:2
1537 John 3:6
1538 Colossians 3:10
1539 Romans 13:14
1540 1 John 1:1
1541 Romans 8:2
1542 Titus 1:4
1543 Titus 1:3
1544 Titus 2:10
1545 Isaiah 44:3
1546 Deuteronomy 32:2

part thou shalt make me to know wisdom."[1547] Conception is then understood to be by truth within the mind, and seeing as how it says, "Thy word is truth,"[1548] and, "Thy law is the truth,"[1549] the word and instruction of the Spirit's law of creative redemption rests in the spirit of the mind, which is why it says, "With the mind I myself serve the law of God."[1550]

13. Because the *body* of his faith; housing within its members the new covenant will; was sacrificed in that regenerated and reformed estate, the promise of "the blood of the everlasting covenant"[1551] is for ever bound to conversations for acceptance and experimentation. Samson's blessing died with him, for the flesh-based routine of a Nazarite only found itself blessed within that one man, the peculiar blessing of his hair beginning and ending with him. But by the *blood* of the living God's chief apostle, by one sacrifice, every conversation may share in the benefit of communion with the *Holy Ghost* to obtain devotional newness by chewing and digesting "God," which "God" is "Jesus Christ," "the Lord Jesus Christ our Saviour"[1552] being "the commandment of God our Saviour."[1553]

14. Because "that which is born of the Spirit is spirit,"[1554] the Spirit's commandment is that Deliverer for the conversation to more perfectly serve living God, self, and other minds. Our conversation is, by learning of and doing this present will and saying, to be created "perfect, as pertaining to the conscience,"[1555] that we may properly uphold a benevolent or empathic conversation.[1556] By the offering of God's chief apostle, we all have the opportunity to share in and obtain this hope. Because his conversation lived and died in this saying, and was then revived to become that high priest over creation's present promise and experience, every conversation has sealed to it the commandment, the Spirit or the *Wisdom*, and the priesthood, of heaven-appointed and heaven-accepted devotional *perfection*.

15. Like as it was necessary that Samson's hair find itself blessed above all, so too it was necessary that the mind of God's Prophet should find itself especially blessed to fully comprehend and do the hidden will; this is why "we have

---

1547 Psalm 51:6
1548 John 17:17
1549 Psalm 119:142
1550 Romans 7:25
1551 Hebrews 13:20
1552 Titus 1:4
1553 Titus 1:3
1554 John 3:6
1555 Hebrews 9:13
1556 1 Timothy 1:5

not an high priest which cannot be touched with the feeling of our infirmities; but was in all points tempted like as we are, yet without sin."[1557] Having his hair blessed did not make Samson any more "holy" or "divine" than any other person then alive, for we find this man consistently tempted and fallen away from the LORD, and "God cannot be tempted with evil, neither tempteth he any man."[1558] Likewise we also find God's chief minister bitterly tempted.[1559] Herein we are made to observe the victory secured for us by that Prophet.

16. As blessed as Samson was by *God's* Spirit, the members of his flesh still failed, but in God's chief witness we see victory over the conversation's mind, which is a mind naturally inclined to reject the living God's will for self's desire, and this is why it says, "They that are Christ's have crucified the flesh with the affections and lusts."[1560] God's Prophet clearly had no advantage over his flesh or mind above Samson, but we know that "God was with him,"[1561] and that "the head of Christ is God,"[1562] because he resisted the temptation to disregard the Creator's will. Herein the aim of the new covenant promise is revealed, even a mind that hates being "not subject to the law of God."[1563]

17. There is no thing in God's chief apostle that is naturally greater than any thing within any of us.[1564] But what distinguishes him above all others is the care and transformation his mind knew, for he was "declared to be the Son of God with power, according to the spirit of holiness"[1565] "because of the words of his holiness,"[1566] even "the words of eternal life,"[1567] which is why it says, "Be ye transformed by the renewing of your mind."[1568] This man exercised control over his self when tempted to disobey the living God because he possessed his self by the character of his conversation, "for God was with him."[1569]

18. "God" is "the Word," therefore within the conscience of his inward parts rested "the law of truth,"[1570] which law is "the Lord Jesus Christ our

---

1557 Hebrews 4:15
1558 James 1:13
1559 Matthew 26:13
1560 Galatians 5:24
1561 Acts 10:38
1562 1 Corinthians 11:3
1563 Romans 8:7
1564 Hebrews 2:14
1565 Romans 1:4
1566 Jeremiah 23:9
1567 John 6:68
1568 Romans 12:2
1569 Acts 10:38
1570 Malachi 2:6

Saviour,"[1571] which "Savior" is "the doctrine of God our Saviour."[1572] The living God's new covenant is the promise of a functioning mind for the good order of self and of the members of the heart. This man demonstrates self-restraint to the praise of the living God, which act both Adam and Samson failed at because the *flesh* is innately lame and without any good *thing* in it. But when once the good commandment of the Father is rightly divided by the mind for government over the conversation's appetite, and is carried out by the body, "The law of the Spirit of life in Christ Jesus hath made me free from the law of sin and death,"[1573] we will confess.

19. Imagine if the living God's chief apostle had failed to learn of and do creation's present will! Imagine if he had no living and personal knowledge of the living God's science! Surely we should be "as water spilt on the ground, which cannot be gathered up again"![1574] He was prophesied to appear for one reason, and that reason was to finish heaven's will within his own conversation that by the offering of that finished *body* of faith, we might have knowledge to "seek those things which are above, where Christ sitteth on the right hand of God,"[1575] and that we "might be filled with the knowledge of his will in all wisdom and spiritual understanding"[1576] to say, "The law of the Spirit of life in Christ Jesus hath made me free from the law of sin and death."[1577]

20. The entire point of this man's sacrifice is for every conversation to share in the same victory over self and the religious world, and that victory cannot find itself benefiting the human being until the person should confess, "I delight in the law of God after the inward man."[1578] Like as how Samson only flourished as the hair on his head was permitted to suffer no harm, so too our involvement with salvation's science cannot commence until the *eyes* of our understanding are permitted to only behold *creation's* Word, which is why, for our observation, it is written, "I will meditate in thy precepts, and have respect unto thy ways,"[1579] and, "In his law doth he meditate day and night."[1580] *Birth* from the *Holy Ghost*

1571 Titus 1:4
1572 Titus 2:10
1573 Romans 8:2
1574 2 Samuel 14:14
1575 Colossians 3:1
1576 Colossians 1:9
1577 Romans 8:2
1578 Romans 7:22
1579 Psalm 119:15
1580 Psalm 1:2

is only by examining and doing salvation's law or saying, for not even *God's* Prophet rejected this learning, saying, "I know him, and keep his saying."[1581]

21. If our conversation refuses any commandment of the living God, or if we fail to give the Creator's *voice* attention, it is due to a tempted heart, and "God cannot be tempted with evil, neither tempteth he any man: but every man is tempted, when he is drawn away of his own lust, and enticed."[1582] How odd would it be to observe a man tempted to stand against *God* while professing to know that *Wisdom*? If this Wisdom's chief apostle beat back the conversation's oppressive waves to commit no violence against the living God's will, if he disciplined his own mind to honor the commandment at the cost of his life, encouraging himself by saying, "I know that his commandment is life everlasting,"[1583] who are we claiming to profess when tempted to disregard any commandment of the living God?

22. Truly "we do know that we know him, if we keep his commandments. He that saith, I know him, and keepeth not his commandments, is a liar, and the truth is not in him."[1584] The end or the point of "Jesus Christ" engraved upon the heart is witnessed by the living God's chief apostle, which end is for unswerving allegiance to every word and commandment that passes out of the Creator's mouth. This is why we are counseled, "Man shall not live by bread alone, but by every word that proceedeth out of the mouth of God."[1585] Man's issue within their conversation is against faithfully obeying the will and wisdom within the scriptures, but the living God's chief witness fully demonstrates salvation's intention by his course of learning.

23. The Word; who is God; is to find itself penetrating the organs of the conversation to enlighten its mind on the good behind doing that its *voice*. If we fail to exercise faith on the living God's will and saying, we will not love the Creator of that saying, "and this is love, that we walk after his commandments."[1586] If we fail to know of the living God's precepts, we do not have the saying fulfilled in our heart, "God was with him";[1587] for we are not doers of salvation's *law* and counsel. With the living God's doctrine within and covering the organs of his mind, that Prophet was able to possess self for the good of his

1581 John 8:55
1582 James 1:13,14
1583 John 12:50
1584 1 John 2:3,4
1585 Matthew 4:4
1586 2 John 1:6
1587 Acts 10:38

conversation, which is why he could experience temptation yet never draw back from the living God's charge; this lesson is for us.

24. The actions of our example when pressed by his conversation confesses the manner of the living God's love toward us, that it is his good intention to revive and reform our mind for the purpose of benevolently correcting and caring for self, and to the end we may receive knowledge of his name to love his *voice*.[1588] What is on our Father's mind; from observing the actions of his chief witness; is the memory of Adam in Eden, to correct the mistake. In our example, that *garden's* philosophy was made *flesh* to devour the conversation's natural mind, and this example is left for our learning and doing.

25. The Word made flesh is God, or the living God's *Wisdom*, devouring the natural devotional mind to remain justly loyal to the living God, self, and others. Thus, by his example, a right definition of the Word made flesh is understood, for since "that which is born of the Spirit is spirit,"[1589] the Word made flesh is the Spirit's law within the mind for conquering and re-educating the members of the personal and the devotional conversation to care for creation's *voice*. Herein we may understand just how our Father loves us, and that the living God has not left us to perpetually experience self-abuse by the irrational members of our human being, but that by the offering and the intercession of this man's conversation, we have secured for us a course of learning to correct our natural human and religious mind.[1590]

26. Not only is the Bible's wisdom authored by the living God's Mind, but the Ten Commandments are also the product of that Mind; to learn this fact we read, "Two tables of testimony, tables of stone, written with the finger of God,"[1591] and, "If I with the finger of God cast out devils,"[1592] and, "If I cast out devils by the Spirit of God."[1593] God's Prophet explains that the *finger* of God is the *Spirit* of God, wherefore we may know that this same *finger* is the Author of the living God's ten precepts. This is why "we do know that we know him, if we keep his commandments."[1594]

1588   2 John 1:6
1589   John 3:6
1590   1 Corinthians 2:14
1591   Exodus 31:18
1592   Luke 11:20
1593   Matthew 12:28
1594   1 John 2:3

27. The living God's chief apostle tells us that he knows the living God because he kept salvation's saying; "I know him, and keep his saying,"[1595] he said; and because he kept that saying, he also kept the living God's commandments to remain in the intended manner of love.[1596] The living God's science is for our loyalty to every word of the Bible's philosophy, and if we keep that science, we will never fail of love to value its commandments, "for this is the love of God, that we keep his commandments."[1597]

28. The love of God equals the keeping of the commandments of God because of the Word living within the spirit of the mind, which is why it says, "Live according to God in the spirit,"[1598] and, "Worship God in the spirit."[1599] Creation's course of learning; which is "the kindness and love of God our Saviour toward man";[1600] is for the purpose of bringing devotional conversations in harmony with every one of the living God's laws and judgments, which is why it says, "A new heart also will I give you, and a new spirit will I put within you: and I will take away the stony heart out of your flesh, and I will give you an heart of flesh. And I will put my spirit within you, and cause you to walk in my statutes, and ye shall keep my judgments, and do them."[1601] Herein is the parameter of the new covenant.

1595 John 8:55
1596 John 15:10
1597 1 John 5:3
1598 1 Peter 4:6
1599 Philippians 3:3
1600 Titus 3:4
1601 Ezekiel 36:26,27

18

That Right Nature

1. We should stand in awe of the prayer, "O my Father, if this cup may not pass away from me, except I drink it, thy will be done."[1602] Herein is witnessed an absolutely amazing feat, namely, the overturning of the saying, "The carnal mind is enmity against God: for it is not subject to the law of God, neither indeed can be."[1603] In this man, we are made to observe an irrational conversation as the subject to *creation's* will. Through him, we find the conversation serving the Father's Mind above its own. In him, the saying is vanquished, "I see another law in my members, warring against the law of my mind, and bringing me into captivity to the law of sin which is in my members,"[1604] for his natural mind is become a constitution confessing, "I delight in the law of God after the inward man."[1605]

2. This is an accomplishment highlighting a great miracle. In this man, the irrational human being is silenced, the mind breathes and speaks, the heart

---

1602 Matthew 26:42
1603 Romans 8:7
1604 Romans 7:23
1605 Romans 7:22

is reformed, self is in possession of a benevolent conscience, and the inward person is subject to the Creator's *voice*. The conversation of this man did not want the experience that it should know, and its members so abused his heart that, "being in an agony he prayed more earnestly: and his sweat was as it were great drops of blood falling down to the ground."[1606] Instead of violating the living God's charge, the conversation of *Adam* did what it has no natural mind to do, and that is to pray for *strength* to keep God's *voice*. Herein is witnessed the fulfillment of the new covenant promise.

3. *Adam* originally failed to stay faithful to the Spirit's *voice* when tempted, allowing us to know that Adam, being created in the LORD's image, did not actually attain to the image that they were created in. It is written, "God cannot be tempted with evil, neither tempteth he any man,"[1607] and when hearing of Eve, how that "she took of the fruit thereof, and did eat, and gave also unto her husband with her; and he did eat,"[1608] we are hearing of two conversations failing to evince the image of their Creator. God's Prophet, when under duress, reveals the *image* of creation's wisdom by the exercising of his faith. And it is well to remember that the Word is God, for this man displays for us the character of that Wisdom by its engraving upon his heart and mind.

4. The image of the living God is the image of *creation's* Word or *Wisdom*, which is an image of edification for right government. Adam fell victim to their flesh-based mind because they never passed through the Spirit's good learning. Because, since it says, "Let no corrupt communication proceed out of your mouth, but that which is good to the use of edifying,"[1609] and, "Let every one of us please his neighbour for his good to edification,"[1610] it is expected that whosoever is edified by the living God will edify as the living God has edified them.

5. To do "good" is to edify the inward parts. The Spirit's will is in bringing up a mind perpetually edified to consistently care for self and the members of the heart. We would have known that the first Adam dwelt with his LORD when refusing Eve's temptation, "for God cannot be tempted with evil, neither tempteth he any man."[1611] Observing Eve blatantly challenging not only his conscience, but also the *voice* of the *garden*, should have been enough proof for

---

1606   Luke 22:44
1607   James 1:13
1608   Genesis 3:6
1609   Ephesians 4:29
1610   Romans 15:2
1611   James 1:13

Adam to say, "The LORD rebuke thee, O Satan."[1612] She did not display the image of the garden's *Mind*, for if she did sit with it, she would have been able to possess self when her *body* challenged its understanding.

6. It was Adam's responsibility to rightly examine the *voice* of their *God*, to the end they "may be able by sound doctrine both to exhort and to convince the gainsayers."[1613] Why is there no record of Adam correcting Eve? Where is *his* exhortation? And Eve, why was she not able to convince a contrary *voice*? Where was *her* exhortation? Why are we made to see an irrational *figure* subjecting *man* to its *voice*, when it is in *man* to rule the *creature*? Adam failed by their appetite, and *creation's* Prophet, sharing the constitution of their conversation, also owned the passion of their *stomach*, yet he obtained victory over that conversation and the religious world to keep the living God's saying. He had sense to admonish his self because of the spirit he cultivated by the living God's promise. In him the saying is fulfilled, "I keep under my body, and bring it into subjection."[1614] Herein is the will of the new covenant, even to "purge your conscience from dead works to serve the living God."[1615]

7. The living God's aim is our conversation's alleviation from "dead works." We understand what these *works* are by the actions of the pair in the *garden*, for their "death" is witnessed to be no literal demise, but one that is mental, inward, and philosophical. This is why, concerning these labors of *death*, it says, "Alienated and enemies in your mind by wicked works."[1616]

8. "Dead works" are "wicked works," and to be "wicked" is to be rebellious, inflexible, self-willed, or stubborn against the living God's devotional character, as it says, "Look not unto the stubbornness of this people, nor to their wickedness, nor to their sin,"[1617] and, "Them that walk after the flesh in the lust of uncleanness, and despise government. Presumptuous are they, selfwilled."[1618] Herein we are made to view the spirit and the nature that God's chief apostle displayed when tempted.

9. The issue at hand, concerning the inherited *works* and mind of *Adam*, is over government. Adam's error was not physical, but mental. They fell to temptation because that law within their conversation found itself enticed

---

1612 Zechariah 3:2
1613 Titus 1:9
1614 1 Corinthians 9:27
1615 Hebrews 9:14
1616 Colossians 1:21
1617 Deuteronomy 9:27
1618 2 Peter 2:10

by agitation through a sensual imagination. If they had knowledge of the living God's creative operation for their mind, they would have another law to direct their faith by. But they both failed to bring the Creator's commandment in to their inward person so that they "might be filled with the knowledge of his will in all wisdom and spiritual understanding."[1619] Having no right perception of that *voice* made it easy to question its authority over them, which disposition ultimately weakened their conversation and made their mind obstinate.

10. *Adam's* disease is obstinacy, for this plague is that persuasion of their conversation's religious constitution. *Adam's* original error unleashed wrath against the devotional conversation, making its stubbornness to the living God's *voice* the natural intent of the human devotional conversation, which purpose serves to affect the heart and spirit of the mind, even as it says, "Thou art obstinate, and thy neck is an iron sinew, and thy brow brass,"[1620] and, "The LORD thy God hardened his spirit, and made his heart obstinate."[1621] What the Bible describes as becoming obstinate or stubborn is the mind, the heart, or the brow, and the "brow" is pointing to the eyebrow, denoting the mind, for it is seated behind the brow. Wrath from the living God fell in to the heart of the religious mind by *Adam's* mistake, and this wrath is best understood from how it says, "He hath shut their eyes, that they cannot see; and their hearts, that they cannot understand."[1622]

11. What is now naturally shut are the *eyes* of our faith,[1623] for by the hardheartedness of one, all conversations are become hardhearted. *Adam's* choice to disregard both *God* and their conscience is mental, therefore it is only right that when the living God promised, "I will put enmity,"[1624] that a good and more benevolent law than that innately existing and enflamed within the conversation should come in to the heart for establishing a new rule. *Man* lost their conscious ability to retain their faith's conscience; a wrath conquering natural rebellion being that chain over their conversation; but today we may know that "God hath not appointed us to wrath."[1625]

1619 Colossians 1:9
1620 Isaiah 48:4
1621 Deuteronomy 2:30
1622 Isaiah 44:18
1623 Ephesians 1:18
1624 Genesis 3:15
1625 1 Thessalonians 5:9

12. This wrath is not physical, but is mental and philosophical; wrath, fulfilled by *one*, perpetually rests on the conversation for the degeneration of the inward person. Yet by one minister, it is today possible "to be strengthened with might by his Spirit in the inner man."[1626] We do not have wonder about what our faith is delivered from, for the living God's chief apostle "delivered us from the wrath to come,"[1627] which wrath appears through devotional negligence, as it says, "Let no man deceive you with vain words: for because of these things cometh the wrath of God upon the children of disobedience."[1628] And what is that "disobedience" our conversation is redeemed from? It says, "Christ hath redeemed us from the curse of the law,"[1629] that is, has rescued our conversation from the philosophy of the handwritten religious law.

13. *Adam's* course is still a reality if we are not willing to reclaim what they sacrificed without our personal consent, even the sacrifice of the spirit of the mind and the conscience of the conversation. The living God thought well of us to devise a decree for our perpetually regaining the stabilization of our faith's intellect, for we today have a law at enmity with the natural law of our conversation, and it is one moving the doer of it to say, "The law of the Spirit of life in Christ Jesus hath made me free from the law of sin and death."[1630] Herein is witnessed our reasonable escape from *wrath*.[1631] Seeing as how the Word was and still is God, it is that the Word silences *wrath's* operation within the conversation, and this is what it means to observe the Word made flesh, for it is that "the life was manifested,"[1632] and "the Spirit is life."[1633]

14. The *Word* made flesh is the *life* manifested. The *life* manifested is the living God's intention demonstrated through the conversation's members, and because "that which is born of the Spirit is spirit,"[1634] the *life* magnified is the Spirit's *law* devouring that law within the conversation's constitution. Herein is the image of God, or of the Word, even a character possessing self to rightly govern the heart and body to accomplish a good and edifying labor, and to the injury of the conversation's *chain* or burden instead of the mind's wellbeing.

1626 Ephesians 3:16
1627 1 Thessalonians 1:10
1628 Ephesians 5:6
1629 Galatians 3:13
1630 Romans 8:2
1631 1 Thessalonians 5:9
1632 1 John 1:2
1633 Romans 8:10
1634 John 3:6

15. Our highest aim and aspiration should be owning the experience of the Word swallowing up the conversation, wherefore our labor should pick up where *Adam* left off at, even the revival and reform of our inward parts, for which cause we are counseled, "Let the word of Christ dwell in you richly in all wisdom,"[1635] and, "Be renewed in the spirit of your mind."[1636] The Spirit can fulfill its new covenant promise only as we exercise faith on its saying, and because *Adam* lost their self by neglecting their understanding, it is our responsibility to regenerate our mind for a new and living conscience towards the living God.[1637] This manner of newness cannot commence until the word of "Christ," which is the wisdom of the living God's *Spirit*, rests within our mind.

16. *Adam* failed to retain knowledge, being overcome by a law that they had no full knowledge of, yet the conversation of *God's* Prophet, owning a mind free of wrath by salvation's higher learning, was offered so that every conversation, sharing his same naturally sick conversation, may have the opportunity to wholly possess self to better honor the living God's *voice*, self, and one another. We, because he perfectly upheld creation's law without any error or schism, not only have the hope of his conversation's victory secured to our conversation, but his flawless conversation means our betterment by trial and error, "for the judgment was by one to condemnation, but the free gift is of many offences unto justification."[1638]

17. We do not have to think about forcing a perfect conversation because, by the willingly perfect conversation of *God's* Prophet offered for us, we have room to fall down, to get back up, to check and to correct self, to learn sorrow, to do well, to move forward, and to exercise faith on creation's regenerating wisdom.[1639] As we mentally discern the living God's will and doctrine, our application of what is retained is the means for adding knowledge to our conversation for the development of its character.[1640] His conversation is that judge and savior because by it being sacrificed for the recovery of our conversation, we have the hope of adding *strength* to our higher faculties to sensibly govern the lower, wherefore it is well to know that "wisdom strengtheneth."[1641]

1635 Colossians 3:16
1636 Ephesians 4:23
1637 Hebrews 9:14
1638 Romans 5:16
1639 Romans 4:24
1640 Proverbs 11:9
1641 Ecclesiastes 7:9

18. We may now understand why it says, "I can do all things through Christ which strengtheneth me,"[1642] for, "wisdom strengtheneth."[1643] Herein it is evident that, according to scripture's language, "Christ" is "wisdom," confirming to us that "Jesus Christ," in right context, ought to be thought of as no man.[1644] Wisdom is not fleshly or tangible, but is as spirit, and "a spirit hath not flesh and bones."[1645] Having no physical form, "Christ" must strengthen another *body*, for "there is a natural body, and there is a spiritual body."[1646] Seeing as how "that which is born of the Spirit is spirit,"[1647] it is clear that we are to "to be strengthened with might by his Spirit in the inner man"[1648] by "the Lord Jesus Christ our Saviour,"[1649] which means, in reality, being strengthened by "the commandment of God our Saviour."[1650]

19. It is our assignment to know the decreed deliverance by investigating and doing the living God's commandment. The stance of the Bible's chief apostle when tempted reveals that he kept and dressed the spirit of his conversation with "Jesus Christ," for which cause it is written, "Put ye on the Lord Jesus Christ, and make not provision for the flesh, to fulfil the lusts thereof."[1651] Herein it is explained how he subjected his human being to reason, and it was due to possessing a "spirit that confesseth that Jesus Christ is come in the flesh."[1652] This man, wearing the Spirit's enmity, overcame human and devotional delusion to stay on creation's present will, and this is demonstrated through him that we may know the certainty of the living God's intention.

20. If he did not humble his mind under the Word's direction, we today would have no good example for our conversation's conscience. But it is his experience in the Bible's wisdom that moved him to counsel, "The true worshippers shall worship the Father in spirit and in truth: for the Father seeketh such to worship him. God is a Spirit: and they that worship him must worship him in spirit and in truth."[1653] By his speech, he allows us to understand that God,

---

1642 Philippians 4:13
1643 Ecclesiastes 7:9
1644 2 Corinthians 5:16
1645 Luke 24:39
1646 1 Corinthians 15:44
1647 John 3:6
1648 Ephesians 3:16
1649 Titus 1:4
1650 Titus 1:3
1651 Romans 13:14
1652 1 John 4:2
1653 John 4:23,24

being that Word, is a Spirit, wherefore the only acceptable worship of the living God is by honoring the Word, which occurs only as the mind is diligently and consistently challenged by its *truth*.

21. Now, it is written, "Thy law is the truth,"[1654] and, "Thy word is truth,"[1655] and it is that the spirit of the mind is to find itself refreshed by the law of the Word's revelation on inward creative redemption, which is why it says, "Sanctify them through thy truth."[1656] He says, "Sanctify them through thy truth,"[1657] but in another place he says, "Ye are clean through the word which I have spoken,"[1658] sanctification being ordained for the mind, and this cleansing through "the washing of water by the word."[1659] The mind must then find itself "justified" by thorough meditation, reflection, and application of the Word's *law* for deliverance from the *curse* of the disobedient conversation. Because *man* lost feeling within his mind, the mind must find itself sanctified in order to regain that feeling, wherefore the living God did well to invent a law of promise, and that law's chief example did well to suffer through its fulfillment that we may have it for our faith's wellbeing.

22. We today have a good hope to aspire to, even the likeness of the revelation of one praying, "O my Father, if this cup may not pass away from me, except I drink it, thy will be done."[1660] Our attention is made to view *Adam* governed by a rule contrary to their natural persuasion. The Spirit's will is here of a greater importance than the conversation's desire; which desire aims to draw the person from the Creator's *voice* to the religious world's philosophy; this is truly the fulfilling of the saying, "Is not this a brand plucked out of the fire?"[1661] Surely he was *born* from *fire*,[1662] and doesn't it say of him, "Upon whom thou shalt see the Spirit descending, and remaining on him"?[1663] The Spirit fell and stayed upon his conversation, for since "that which is born of the Spirit is spirit,"[1664] his mind perpetually embraced the intended baptism by his diligent meditation on creation's commandment.

1654 Psalm 119:142
1655 John 17:17
1656 John 17:17
1657 John 17:17
1658 John 15:3
1659 Ephesians 5:26
1660 Matthew 26:42
1661 Zechariah 3:2
1662 Matthew 3:11
1663 John 1:33
1664 John 3:6

23. The *fire* of the *Spirit* is the means whereby wrath passed away from his understanding, which opened up his mind to embrace the commandments of the living God. With a mind no longer stubborn towards the Creator's *voice*, it will become easy to understand how and why the heart fails when ignorant of that *voice's* counsels. By doing salvation's commandment with refreshed and hopeful thoughts, the mind comes to realize the health behind its instruction, which wholeness is the reason why the conversation confesses, "I know him, and keep his saying."[1665]

24. The doctrine that this man speaks by his prayer is *heaven's* good miracle towards us, even a heart and mind caring to violate self instead of the living God's *voice*. The experiment in Eden reveals that the plague within our mind needs more help than what the human will can give or afford, which is why we have a philosophy that says, "For judgment I am come into this world."[1666] Although that minister of that judgment, it is well to know that since he says, "Sanctify them through thy truth,"[1667] and, "Ye are clean through the word which I have spoken,"[1668] and, "If a man love me, he will keep my words,"[1669] that he has not personally delivered the end of that word to any conversation, but has only opened up the experience to every mind, establishing a *ladder* for us to climb up in to that Sanitarium.

25. The fact that sanctification must commence by words allows us to understand that, since he is not here to physically train or educate any one, the person must engage their own mind on the saying of his *voice* if they should find their conversation ultimately delivered from Adam's curse. The *blood* of this man has secured to every conversation a course of learning whereby it may find itself under the power of its conscience, and in this sense he is that savior or deliverer who has provided our faith an example to obtain the intended devotional recovery and rescue, having secured for us the gift of his *name* by the offering of his conversation. Yet it is evident that we, by our cooperating with the living God's law of creation, determine our own resurrection, for "through knowledge shall the just be delivered."[1670]

1665 John 8:55
1666 John 9:39
1667 John 17:17
1668 John 15:3
1669 John 14:23
1670 Proverbs 11:9

19

But To The Jews

1. When they "set up over his head his accusation written, THIS IS JESUS THE KING OF THE JEWS,"[1671] what was written was no mistake, but was a foreshadowing of the age soon to appear. In right context, a "king" is a term that should be understood as representing a "kingdom," as it says, "The king of the south shall come into his kingdom,"[1672] and, "His king shall be higher than A'gag, and his kingdom shall be exalted."[1673] Again, the scriptures speak of one, in the line of prophecy, fulfilling the saying, "And in the latter time of their kingdom, when the transgressors are come to the full, a king of fierce countenance, and understanding dark sentences, shall stand up."[1674] This "king" appears after three kingdoms have passed away, and concerning this "king," Moses warned the congregation by saying, "The LORD shall bring a nation against thee from far, from the end of the earth, as swift as the eagle flieth; a nation whose tongue thou shalt not understand; a nation of fierce countenance."[1675]

1671   Matthew 27:37
1672   Daniel 11:9
1673   Numbers 24:7
1674   Daniel 8:23
1675   Deuteronomy 28:49,50

2. This "king" was not an individual man, but was rather a kingdom or a nation, even the fourth beast of Bible prophecy. When Pilate asked the living God's chief apostle, "Art thou the King of the Jews?"[1676] the question wasn't gendered towards the man, as if the man claimed to be a personal king of the Jews, but was towards his speech, as if to inquire about a religious kingdom or denomination over the Jews, for Rome ruled the Jews, and an insurrection warranted death.

3. The Jews, when they would hear him speak, failing to rightly understand Moses' speech, took this man's words literally. He preached what he called, "The kingdom of heaven," or, "The kingdom of God," or, "The kingdom of the Son of God." This is what he called his doctrine, and because the Jews could not understand that he spoke of no literal reign, growing frustrated at his language, "when he was demanded of the Pharisees, when the kingdom of God should come, he answered them and said, The kingdom of God cometh not with observation: neither shall they say, Lo here! or, lo there! for, behold, the kingdom of God is within you."[1677] The Jews wanted an uprising to take place against Rome. They imagined a *Christ* that should liberate them from their Roman yoke to establish a temporal reign above all kingdoms of the *earth*. But, because "God is a Spirit,"[1678] this Prophet frustrated that plan.

4. The "kingdom of God" is in reality the kingdom of the Spirit, and because "a spirit hath not flesh and bones,"[1679] "flesh and blood cannot inherit the kingdom of God."[1680] The *kingdom* that this man preached was no literal royal religious government, but was, because "that which is born of the Spirit is spirit,"[1681] a reign of the Creator's Mind within the spirit of the mind. This is why he could only say, "The kingdom of God is within you,"[1682] because it is written, "God is with us,"[1683] that is, "God hath said, I will dwell in them, and walk in them."[1684]

5. Now, we cannot forget how it is written that "in the beginning was the Word, and the Word was with God, and the Word was God."[1685] "God" was and

---

1676 Luke 23:3
1677 Luke 17:20,21
1678 John 4:24
1679 Luke 24:39
1680 1 Corinthians 15:50
1681 John 3:6
1682 Luke 17:21
1683 Isaiah 8:10
1684 2 Corinthians 6:16
1685 John 1:1

still is today "the Word." The kingdom of God is the reign of the Word within the conversation's inward parts, which is why we are "to be strengthened with might by his Spirit in the inner man."[1686] The question, then, becomes, "How is the Word to be or to dwell within us?" Seeing as how "that which is born of the Spirit is spirit,"[1687] and that this same Spirit is "the Word of life,"[1688] the only way the *Spirit* can be within our spirit is through words of a commandment, which is why it says, "I am full of power by the spirit of the LORD, and of judgment, and of might,"[1689] and, "He hath filled him with the spirit of God, in wisdom, in understanding, and in knowledge."[1690]

6. The reign of God, or the dominion of the Word, is the rule of "the law of the Spirit of life,"[1691] "the word of righteousness,"[1692] "the doctrine of Christ,"[1693] over and within the inward parts of the conversation's conscience, which is why it says, "Thou desirest truth in the inward parts: and in the hidden part thou shalt make me to know wisdom."[1694] The Spirit's law is that wisdom or judgment to rest within the heart of the character of our belief, for, "because the Spirit is truth,"[1695] and because it says, "Thy law is the truth,"[1696] the kingdom of God is in reality the government of "the law of truth"[1697] over the spirit of the mind. This is why, because this *law* is for the good revival and reformation of the conversation's members, it says, "The Word was made flesh."[1698]

7. The swallowing up of the conversation's constitution for the re-education of its heart and mind is the living God's will, for "if Christ be in you, the body is dead because of sin; but the Spirit is life because of righteousness."[1699] Herein we are made to understand that "God with us," or "the Word within us," or "the law of the Spirit within the spirit of the mind," "is Christ in you, the hope of

---

1686 Ephesians 3:16
1687 John 3:6
1688 1 John 1:1
1689 Micah 3:8
1690 Exodus 35:31
1691 Romans 8:24
1692 Hebrews 5:13
1693 2 John 1:9
1694 Psalm 51:6
1695 1 John 5:6
1696 Psalm 119:142
1697 Malachi 2:6
1698 John 1:14
1699 Romans 8:10

glory."[1700] Thus, if the *body* of an invisible body is to pass away for a resurrection by "Christ," it is evident that "Christ" is no reference to any man.[1701]

8. The kingdom of God is the "kingdom of Christ," and it is well to understand that, in right context, "the Lord Jesus Christ our Saviour"[1702] is "the commandment of God our Saviour,"[1703] which commandment is "the doctrine of God our Saviour."[1704] The *name* of the Word is "Jesus Christ," and because the Word is called both "God" "Jesus Christ," "Jesus Christ," because the Word was and still is God, is "God." When thinking of "Jesus Christ," it is a carnal practice to take "Jesus Christ" as the figure of a man; this is incorrect. "Jesus Christ" is a form of speech that the living God's slain chief apostle taught, which speech is the dominion and perpetual reign of the Creator's spiritual priesthood within conversation for the creation of a "spirit that confesseth that Jesus Christ is come in the flesh."[1705]

9. "Jesus Christ" is to come in to the *flesh's* or the conversation's empty constitution, and this is what it means to say, "The Word was made flesh,"[1706] and, "God was manifest in the flesh,"[1707] and, "The life was manifested."[1708] "The Word," "God," "the Life," and "Jesus Christ," they all represent the same *Spirit* or *Wisdom* of the same Creator, which *Wisdom* is a law, a saying, a judgment, a commandment, or a "doctrine which is according to godliness."[1709] The reign of the Word is the transformation of the mind to keep and dress the conversation with creation's right *discipline*, which is why the kingdom of the Spirit is also known as the kingdom of *heaven*.

10. The living God's chief witness didn't just preach the established deliverance of the conversation from the wrath of *Adam's* error, but he also taught the people the *Place* where this great mystery is to occur. "Heaven" is language denoting the *heavenly* Sanctuary, as it says, "He hath looked down from the height of his sanctuary; from heaven did the LORD behold the earth,"[1710] and,

---

1700 Colossians 1:27
1701 2 Corinthians 5:16
1702 Titus 1:4
1703 Titus 1:3
1704 Titus 2:10
1705 1 John 4:2
1706 John 1:14
1707 1 Timothy 3:16
1708 1 John 1:1
1709 1 Timothy 6:3
1710 Psalm 102:19

"The LORD is in his holy temple, the LORD'S throne is in heaven."[1711] "The kingdom of heaven" is the reign of the living God's throne within the spirit of the mind, and seeing as how this throne is within a *heavenly* Temple, it is that the mind, because "our conversation is in heaven,"[1712] should "seek those things which are above, where Christ sitteth on the right hand of God."[1713]

11. Creation's science cannot commence until the spirit and personal faith of the person is found in the *Spirit's Sanctuary*. This Prophet's conversation was consecrated by the *LORD* of this Temple to be its high priest for the intercession of newness within other conversations, which is why "we have such an high priest, who is set on the right hand of the throne of the Majesty in the heavens."[1714] Herein we are made to understand that the man's literal blood is not enough for redemption's creative endeavor.

12. This man's conversation, as the first creature of the Spirit by his spirit, and being sacrificed in that condition within an erring *body* of faith, has bound conversations to the work and to the effect of righteousness. The new covenant's intention is a promise of righteousness, and the righteousness of the Spirit is the resurrection of the naturally erring religious conversation.[1715] This man sacrificed to the living God is a conversation sacrificed to the living God for other conversations to claim the same victory of regeneration within their own heart, even as Adam's error secured for *us* a free obstinacy against the Creator's *voice*.

13. No conversation is automatically written to receive the end of *heaven's* will. If it says, "He that is unjust, let him be unjust still: and he which is filthy, let him be filthy still: and he that is righteous, let him be righteous still: and he that is holy, let him be holy still,"[17:6] it is evident that the living God does not, and will never control one's choice to begin *heaven's* course of learning, even as the Creator did not rule over *Adam's* mind in the beginning. This man's spilt blood figuratively binds the experience of every conversation to his own; there is no thing more or less than this.

14. When, in the beginning, conversations existed, did the *LORD* persuade them either to the right or to the left? The *LORD* communed with the pair about his *name* and the creative operation he decreed for their inward parts,

1711   Psalm 11:4
1712   Philippians 3:20
1713   Colossians 3:1
1714   Hebrews 8:1
1715   Romans 8:11
1716   Revelation 22:11

"for unto us was the gospel preached, as well as unto them."[1717] The *LORD* did not interfere with their conscience, for he took absolute faith on the fact that they would not violate the *garden's name*, and whether they did or not, the consequence would be what the consequence should be. Nothing has today changed. The living God's chief apostle has set the example for conversations. Because he upheld *heaven's* new will and philosophy within his mind for the good recovery of his conversation, our fellowship with the *Spirit* is, and for this same end, because of him. But while this will for the conversation is established, it is not complete if the conversation is without the *Building* and *name* to finish the Creator's intention.

15. His *blood*, or the experience of his labor with salvation's law, is the only means whereby *heaven's* Sanitarium is opened up to our conversation. We express our satisfaction with his sacrifice, and do write our *name* on the new covenant's contract, when allowing our faith and mind to pass through *heaven's* doors to see "one like unto the Son of man, clothed with a garment down to the foot, and girt about the paps with a golden girdle."[1718] The doctrine of this man's conversation is the reign and the communion of *heaven's* Temple within the soul temple of the conversation's conscience, for there is a work and assignment for us to do, even as it says, "I know him, and keep his saying."[1719]

16. We cannot know this saying if without its *Building*, for it is written, "For ever, O LORD, thy word is settled in heaven."[1720] The Word only found itself within him because his mind remained in communion with the *Spirit* and *Temple* of the living God, and he was not shy to tell us this fact, saying, "I came down from heaven."[1721] He speech is not literal, for the time of *his* fellowship within the Sanctuary of the Creator blessed his faith, and after that refreshing appeared, a ministry was given to him, causing him to demonstrate the living God's benevolence; this is what it means when saying, "Ye shall see heaven open, and the angels of God ascending and descending upon the Son of man."[1722] The "Son of man" is that ladder delineating the knowledge of the living God's saying; which saying is the law of the Word; and this wisdom is found only in *heaven*, where messengers of its *name* are raised up to shower the *earth* with blessing.

1717 Hebrews 4:2
1718 Revelation 1:13
1719 John 8:55
1720 Psalm 119:89
1721 John 6:38
1722 John 1:51

17. The aim of salvation's higher learning is not to put the conversation through such a strict course of learning for no reason, but we are to be "his workmanship, created in Christ Jesus unto good works, which God hath before ordained that we should walk in them."[1723] The student-patient of *heaven's Building* is receiving a baptism to train them in the labor that they should pick up under the ministry of *heaven's* high priest, even a self-sacrificing service "to give the light of the knowledge of the glory of God in the face of Jesus Christ."[1724] Such a vocation is a high calling, for by this man's offering, conversations now have the opportunity to share in *heaven's* ministry.

18. This man offered his faith and conversation in a finished regenerative condition that satisfied the living God. By consecrating this conversation over creation's science, the living God, seeing as how that, by exercising faith on the Spirit's *law* we are "to be conformed to the image of his Son,"[1725] has set his *name* over the project preparing conversations for *work*. When therefore hearing, "A merciful and faithful high priest in things pertaining to God,"[1726] it is that we are hearing a philosophy beginning at "Jesus Christ, and him cruci-fied,"[1727] and ending at the saying, "We have a great high priest, that is passed into the heavens."[1728]

19. But to the Jews it is written, "Behold your King!"[1729] "And Pilate wrote a title, and put it on the cross. And the writing was, JESUS OF NAZARETH THE KING OF THE JEWS."[1730]

20. Pilate was right in what he wrote, and it is our responsibility to compre-hend the language used to frame the illustration that the scriptures rightly portray. This speech tells of them "which say they are Jews, and are not, but do lie,"[1731] for their "king," or "kingdom," should find itself idolatrously formed around one on a tree. These same Jews that "cried, saying, Crucify him, crucify him,"[1732] would later become a "certain of the sect of the Pharisees which

---

1723 Ephesians 2:10
1724 2 Corinthians 4:6
1725 Romans 8:29
1726 Hebrews 2:17
1727 1 Corinthians 2:2
1728 Hebrews 4:14
1729 John 19:14
1730 John 19:19
1731 Revelation 3:9
1732 Luke 31:21

believed,"[1733] who beforehand desired of him a form of speech confirming a temporal reign.

21. We must remember how it is written, "The men that held Jesus mocked him, and smote him,"[1734] for they "led him, and brought him into the high priest's house."[1735] The "men" that held "Jesus," these were Jewish priests and elders that handled the *body* of the living God's knowledge. When they had within their hands the *body* of *heaven's* understanding, they smote its *voice* and mocked its doctrine, and this act Luke does record to speak to what should afterward occur against his *name*. The "king" of the *Jews* should become a mocked version of the Creator's wisdom, for the tradition of these people, and of their offspring, should be an imitation, a farce, a deception, a delusional ridiculing of the living science of the living God. Thus Pilate spoke the fact of the matter, that a sect should arise proclaiming one on a tree, or on a cross, to be the image of *their* Jewish kingdom or denomination.

22. We may understand that the man's accusation centered around the establishment of a religious throne from how "Pilate saith unto them, Shall I crucify your King? The chief priests answered, We have no king but Caesar."[1736] The Jews put forth a lie to their State, asserting that the man preached a doctrine of heresy not only against their *God*, but also against the State of Rome, of whom Caesar is a symbol.

23. The Jewish leadership understood what he was trying to do, which was to get people thinking on *heavenly things*. The foundation of his doctrine is, "Have faith in God,"[1737] and since "God is a Spirit,"[1738] and since the Word is God, and since "a spirit hath not flesh and bones,"[1739] to have faith in the Word means to mentally discern the *voice* of the scriptures to "be filled with the knowledge of his will in all wisdom and spiritual understanding."[1740] This is something the Jewish leadership cannot entertain because when the people realize that their *LORD's* intention is inward renovation by mental and spiritual discernment, then their temporal reign, with all of their flesh-based traditional customs, will pass away,

---

1733 Acts 15:5
1734 Luke 22:63
1735 Luke 22:54
1736 John 19:15
1737 Mark 11:22
1738 John 4:24
1739 Luke 24:39
1740 Colossians 1:9

and this they so realized that upon one occasion they said, "Perceive ye how ye prevail nothing? behold, the world is gone after him."[1741]

24. Now, concerning "the world," it is defined in the saying, "I spake openly to the world; I ever taught in the synagogue, and in the temple, whither the Jews always resort."[1742] "The world," to the Bible's mind, is the religious world, and at this time, the LORD's earth was drawing away from the lame traditional structure of Jewish elders to a resurrection by understanding for the kingdom of the Word.

25. No man had authority over what the living God's chief apostle preached, namely, the regeneration and the reformation of the conversation's conscience. Religious tradition is a slumber enslaving the devotional mind and conscience, but this man's doctrine liberates the devotional self's bondage to the conversation's irrational religious form, and from its servitude to the religious world. This is why it was necessary that "when the fulness of the time was come, God sent forth his Son, made of a woman, made under the law, to redeem them that were under the law, that we might receive the adoption of sons."[1743]

26. To be made under the law is to be baptized under the rule of a traditional religious standard. Concerning this man, it was prophesied, "The LORD thy God will raise up unto thee a Prophet from the midst of thee, of thy brethren,"[1744] for his philosophy was to own the then religious heritage of the Hebrews in devotion to the LORD of the Hebrews. Being born as a minister of the LORD in the midst of the Hebrews means being born as one under the dominion of a religious tradition of elders. This man, finding himself bound under a traditional religion, and yet receiving his training from heaven, sets the standard for us all, that salvation's law transcends every and all spiritual persuasions, leaving the doer of its will singing, "Thou wast slain, and hast redeemed us to God by thy blood out of every kindred, and tongue, and people, and nation."[1745]

27. Pilate was right in what he wrote, and in thus writing, he pronounces "the blasphemy of them which say they are Jews, and are not."[1746] For, it should be that "he is a Jew, which is one inwardly; and circumcision is that of the heart, in the spirit";[1747] but we find ourselves observing a people who confess themselves to

---

1741 John 12:19
1742 John 18:20
1743 Galatians 4:4,5
1744 Deuteronomy 18:15
1745 Revelation 5:9
1746 Revelation 2:9
1747 Romans 2:29

be Jews outwardly, and through the foundation of a mockery. *Creation's* Prophet was slain; as the host of *heaven* sing in the quoted verse from the Revelation; for our conversation's deliverance from every religious denomination for membership "to the general assembly and church of the firstborn, which are written in heaven."[1748] The Jews understood that this was the intention of his philosophy, and so a false accusation was raised against him.

28. To save their earthy denomination, the Jewish leadership put forth a lie, saying that he not only preached a State above Rome, but a religious State above Rome. The government of Rome was both secular and religious, and being the then world-ruling kingdom, to utter such speech of rebellion against Rome was to challenge Rome's divine estate; both secularly and spiritually; and this warranted death. The Jews saw that this was that Prophet who appeared "to bind up the brokenhearted, to proclaim liberty to the captives, and the opening of the prison to them that are bound,"[1749] and to preserve their tradition, they turned his *name* in to a lie, which act reveals that these same priests would be "who changed the truth of God into a lie."[1750]

29. We must also pay attention to the fact that his title "was written in Hebrew, and Greek, and Latin."[1751] This signifies the people or the religious families that should take the *one* on the tree and confined to the earth to be their *kingdom*, and they are of the *Hebrews*, the Jews of the seventh day, the Greeks, pagan philosophers, and the Latin, who are the sun worshipping Romans. These *Jews*, and their elders, should all have "Jesus" in their hands to handle, and by their employment, the saying will be fulfilled, "They crucify to themselves the Son of God afresh, and put him to an open shame."[1752] Herein we should take knowledge of how it says, "The truth is in Jesus,"[1753] for when hearing, "The men that held Jesus mocked him, and smote him,"[1754] it is that we, in reality, are observing religious priests mishandling the truth constrained to this man's *name*.

30. It says, "Thy word is truth,"[1755] and, "Thy law is the truth,"[1756] for when hearing the name, "Jesus," it is that, in right context, we are hearing an epithet

---

1748 Hebrews 12:23
1749 Isaiah 61:1
1750 Romans 1:25
1751 John 19:20
1752 Hebrews 6:6
1753 Ephesians 4:21
1754 Luke 22:63
1755 John 17:17
1756 Psalm 119:142

of *creation's* law and commandment. The *title* of this Prophet should be, "The living God's will and wisdom within our faith's intellect," but a contrary title was erected to the satisfaction of Pilate to relay the spirit of the Jews, which spirit only foreshadowed the perpetual slaying of *heaven's* will by priests who despised both the man and his philosophy, along with the Mind behind the *law* that his *voice* magnified. It is our assignment to transcend the religious world's mockery, for we are to "have escaped the pollutions of the world through the knowledge of the Lord and Saviour Jesus Christ."[1757]

1757 2 Peter 2:20

20

Our Necessary Reform

1. Because we are to "have escaped the pollutions of the world through the knowledge of the Lord and Saviour Jesus Christ,"[1758] it is a fact that we can trust no spiritual *thing* on *earth* and under the *heavens*, which is why it says, "Set your affection on things above, not on things on the earth."[1759] So long as our *eyes*; "the eyes of your understanding";[1760] are found in the *heavenly* Sanctuary, our "love may abound yet more and more in knowledge and in all judgment."[1761] All things without knowledge and right judgment exist outside of this Sanctuary, for if it says, "Thy way, O God, is in the Sanctuary,"[1762] must we believe that we should discover any good *thing* outside of it?

2. This *Building* is so dear to our conversation that the living God brought up that delivering conversation in to this *Place* to forward a ministry of healing. If the conversation of the living God's chief apostle is in this *Place*, is there any

---

1758   2 Peter 2:20
1759   Colossians 3:2
1760   Ephesians 1:18
1761   Philippians 1:9
1762   Psalm 77:13

other *place* more desirable than this? If the living God brought up this *name* from the religious world to hold an office beside creation's throne, must our faith remain where that *name* is not? The "way" of the Word is in this *Building* where that conversation is "a minister of the sanctuary, and of the true tabernacle, which the Lord pitched, and not man."[1763] This *name* and conversation is not in the religious world, and if *he* is nowhere to be found, we may know that the living God is also absent from every *thing* under the heavens.

3. The "way" of the Word is the operation of the Spirit, and when it says, "I am the way, the truth, and the life,"[1764] it is that the *heavenly* Sanctuary holds that *Wisdom's* "way," which "way" is a route pronouncing the Spirit's truth, which truth is the "life" of the conversation. Now, it says; since "he whom God hath sent speaketh the words of God";[1765] "I am the resurrection, and the life."[1766] "The life" is "the resurrection," and "the resurrection" is the "way" of the Spirit's "truth," for "if Christ be in you, the body is dead because of sin; but the Spirit is life because of righteousness."[1767] Herein we may understand that the operation of *heaven's* mediating *name* is for resurrection by righteousness, and that righteousness, seeing as how "that which is born of the Spirit is spirit,"[1768] is a course of learning whereby the mind is regenerated and reformed to pass newness to the members of the heart for government over the body.

4. This manner of creation within the inward parts of the conversation is located only within the *heavenly* Sanctuary, which is why, seeing as how his *name* "is able also to save them to the uttermost that come unto God by him, seeing he ever liveth to make intercession for them,"[1769] the living God anointed this Prophet's *name* to be that guide over salvation's will and science. This intercession is for salvation, and salvation is righteousness, and this righteousness occurring within the spirit of the mind, and this occurrence is by a *law* resting within the mind, as it says, "Be ye transformed by the renewing of your mind, that ye may prove what is that good, and acceptable, and perfect, will of God."[1770]

5. Without that anointed *name*, our conversation is nonexistent. This man's sacrifice did not procure to any mind the end of the living God's saying, but

---

1763 Hebrews 8:2
1764 John 14:16
1765 John 3:34
1766 John 11:25
1767 Romans 8:10
1768 John 3:6
1769 Hebrews 7:25
1770 Romans 12:2

only opened up divine fellowship to the conversation's experience. The blood of the man, although physically spilt, represents no physical thing to ignorantly and idolatrously covet, for "the life of the flesh is in the blood."[1771] Intercession for receiving the precious gifts and spiritual promises of the living God is for cleansing the *life* existing within the conversation.

6. The *life* naturally existing within the conversation is injurious to the human being, but having one whose *life* was mixed with *water*, and having the *blood* of that one spilt, bears witness to the fact that it is now the living God's will that the illness within the conversation's constitution find resolution by a better ministry under a better covenant and though better promises than that of old. The ancient priesthood of Aaron depended on the blood of animals to satisfy the LORD as a right substitute for the illness within human flesh. The blood of animals could not satisfy that illness because, although both are of the ground, being equal in stature, the blood of man is singular only to his kind, and the slaying of animals could not truly bless the spiritual renovation that the ritual imagined. Yet by the saying of that anointed conversation, the *blood* of a perfect conversation is now linked to *heaven* for the alleviation and the reform of other conversations.

7. It was necessary that this man perform salvation's will within his conversation so that other conversations may not only have a representative, but that there may also be an advocating *name* before the living God; this is why "we have not an high priest which cannot be touched with the feeling of our infirmities; but was in all points tempted like as we are, yet without sin."[1772] We need to know that this Prophet's conversation is presently our faith's high priest. If without knowledge of its current operation, the *blood*, or the labor of reconciliation is wasted. This *name* conducts service on behalf of the Creator, and to take the earthly mission of this man to be the end of the work in *heaven* is gross religious error.

8. Earth's mission is absolutely complete. A conversation bearing within its members the *Word* and *Wisdom* of the living God's Mind is sacrificed for every mind to experience; yet the full will of the living God's throne is nowhere near finished if there are no conversations to benefit by that offering. The labor of the living God's chief apostle was for spiritually coarse and intoxicated conversations. This man's mission was to give an example of the *life* within the conversation's devotional experience. Thus, it was necessary that a natural devotional

---

1771 Leviticus 17:11
1772 Hebrews 4:15

manner swallow up that Prophet's inward person, to the end his sacrifice, so that other minds may claim a useful conversation to the living God, should link conversations to the philosophy that delivered his conversation from the plague of the religious world.

9. Today, the *life* within the conversation has a remedy. The mission of the living God's chief witness was for that empty and enflamed *life* within the mind of our being and, like as how Adam's act forwarded that agitation within the conversation for the slumbering of its mind, so the offering of this man's conversation serves to quiet the agitation of the conversation for regenerating its mind to rightly care for wellbeing's *voice*, self, and the condition of other minds. His sacrifice, therefore, only ratified the conversation's higher learning for devotional betterment, meaning that it is the responsibility of that individual mind to examine and do *creation's* will and commandment if it should hope to receive the promise of that discipline, which promise is, "God was manifest in the flesh,"[1773] or, "The Word was made flesh."[1774]

10. "The Word was made flesh,"[1775] which is a "spirit that confesseth that Jesus Christ is come in the flesh,"[1776] is the Bible's righteousness, which is the righteousness of the Word, which is the righteousness of the living God's *Spirit*. This Prophet finished that mission for conversations on *earth*, which mission was to only join the *life* of the unsanctified conversation to the ministry of the living God's wisdom, but the end of that ministry, and the promise of that ministry, seeing as how "we might receive the promise of the Spirit through faith,"[1777] is by no means automatically fulfilled within any mind. There is yet a work for the individual to accomplish in order to receive the Creator's intention.[1778]

11. Justification is sanctification; the two mean the same thing. The spirit of the mind; because this conception is by the Spirit, and because "that which is born of the Spirit is spirit";[1779] is privileged to experience sanctification only as the mind diligently exercises faith on the wisdom of "Christ." There is then a blatant difference between exercising faith on the man *Christ*; which amounts to nothing due to the ignorant worshiping of an imagination; and exercising faith and confidence on the faith of the living God's chief apostle. Paul is not saying,

---

1773 1 Timothy 3:16
1774 John 1:14
1775 John 1:14
1776 1 John 4:2
1777 Galatians 3:14
1778 Galatians 2:16
1779 John 3:6

"We are justified by Christ," which is why he goes out of his way to say, "We might be justified by the faith of Christ."[1780] It is our responsibility to comprehend just what the "faith" of our example conversation is, and we do not have to think too hard because it counsels us, "Have faith in God."[1781]

12. The philosophy of the living God's chief apostle is the Word; if we are to be sanctified by the faith of "Christ," it is that we are to be justified by the Word of "Christ." Now, "Christ," in proper context, is that "Word."[1782] Seeing as how "the Lord Jesus Christ our Saviour"[1783] is "the commandment of God our Saviour,"[1784] justification by the faith of "Christ" is sanctification by the commandment of the Word. This allows us to understand that since it says, "Ye are clean through the word,"[1785] that our mind must find its understating given to a certain wisdom for cleansing "with the washing of water by the word."[1786]

13. This clarifies for us the responsibility and the duty of the reforming conversation. Words cannot clarify any thing but the mental and the moral faculties, therefore if sanctification appears by patiently and temperately examining and doing words, it is that the salvation promised is wholly ordained for the mind, and that the mind must act out its part in creation's science. The part that the mind must consent to in redemption's plan is "rightly dividing the word of truth,"[1787] and "not in the words which man's wisdom teacheth, but which the Holy Ghost teacheth; comparing spiritual things with spiritual."[1788] This pronounces to us a mental labor that the heart and mind must consent to, for although God's Prophet did what he did, he has by no means labored within our mental and moral faculties by that offering.

14. He is the deliverer or savior of the natural or traditional devotional conversation, in that by one sacrificed conversation, the mind may find its self delivered in to the *heavenly* Sanctuary for newness to govern the devotional conversation's conscience.[1789] Herein is the reason why the Word must find itself within the conversation's mind, and it is so that the individual may work out the wisdom that the living God impresses upon the character of their conversation,

---

1780 Galatians 2:26
1781 Mark 11:22
1782 2 Corinthians 5:16
1783 Titus 1:4
1784 Titus 1:3
1785 John 15:3
1786 Ephesians 5:26
1787 2 Timothy 2:15
1788 1 Corinthians 2:13
1789 John 6:63

for "the spirit giveth life."[1790] By cooperating with creation's present will and saying, the conversation is to receive power and wisdom to correct and reform its own individual character, and the living God's chief minister, by such an offering, has not accomplished this internal work within any one, but has only opened up the door for that science to the conversation caring to cooperate with the intercession of his *name* for the living God's manner of *love*.

15. We should think that the living God is fraudulent if, by the experience and actions of that Prophet, irrational humanity, without any acting and taxing consent on the part of the person, is automatically cleansed or sanctified by his individually sacrificed body. Experience is as transferable as character, and there is no transaction in the flesh concerning either, but "he that tilleth his land shall be satisfied with bread."[1791] Hereafter this man's conversation says, "The bread that I will give is my flesh, which I will give for the life of the world."[1792]

16. We, as individual souls, are not the religious world; nevertheless it is that we are all born to *women* or to churches of the religious world that are without right devotional health. Our conversations are not the law of our inherited or self-cultivated religious tradition; "Christ hath redeemed us from the curse of the law, being made a curse for us: for it is written, Cursed is every one that hangeth on a tree."[1793]

17. Our celebration of this man, if it is sober, should find itself centered upon the fact that Paul establishes, namely, that his death figuratively educates on alleviation from bondage to every traditional religious chain. Hereafter the conversation is become one that is passed away from a dark curse; which curse is traditional religious misconception; to pick up fellowship with the living God by a liberated devotional mind. His crucifixion only represents a conversation that is passed away from the philosophy of the religious law so that the mind may awaken to the experience within *heaven's* Sanctuary, which is why the Creator's host sings, "Thou wast slain, and hast redeemed us to God by thy blood out of every kindred, and tongue, and people, and nation."[1794]

18. We are therefore wrong; according to the wisdom of the living God's chief apostle; to idolize one slain on a tree. Paul's illustration of the man crucified is one pronouncing creation and regeneration from the religious world.[1795]

1790 2 Corinthians 3:6
1791 Proverbs 12:11
1792 John 6:51
1793 Galatians 3:13
1794 Revelation 5:9
1795 Galatians 6:14

The reforming conversation, by subscribing to a course of learning whereby the mind is sanctified by an experimental faith on the commandment of *creation*, is made to experience liberty of heart and mind to justly care for the Bible's *voice*, self, and other minds. Liberty expresses freedom from religious chains and deliverance from philosophical oppression, and seeing as how "where the Spirit of the Lord is, there is liberty,"[1796] and that this is that "Spirit of life from God,"[1797] because it says, "Is not God in the height of heaven?"[1798] because "the LORD is in his holy temple, the LORD'S throne is in heaven,"[1799] it is that we must find the person of our conversation in this *heavenly* Temple if it should know the liberty promised to it.

19. The chains that we are to be liberated and enlightened from are not physical, but are mental and spiritual. This is why the saying, "To bind up the brokenhearted, to proclaim liberty to the captives, and the opening of the prison to them that are bound,"[1800] means "the eyes of your understanding being enlightened; that ye may know what is the hope of his calling, and what the riches of the glory of his inheritance in the saints, and what is the exceeding greatness of his power to us-ward who believe...which he wrought in Christ, when he raised him from the dead, and set him at his own right hand in the heavenly places."[1801]

20. The illustration, although an allegory, is plain. The living God explained the will and righteousness of his *Spirit* for conversations by the resurrection of his Prophet's conversation.[1802] The regeneration and reform of the conversation's constitution is the end of "Jesus Christ," but that sanctification cannot commence until the mind rightly observes and accepts just what that body hanging on the tree represents. It was necessary that this man suffer this instrument of torture to forward the notion that death to the law and order of earthy religious tradition, and to spiritual prescriptions "after the commandments and doctrines of men,"[1803] is come to an end by that *name* "who is gone into heaven, and is on the right hand of God."[1804]

1796 2 Corinthians 3:17
1797 Revelation 11:11
1798 Job 22:12
1799 Psalm 11:4
1800 Isaiah 61:1
1801 Ephesians 1:18-20
1802 Romans 8:11
1803 Colossians 2:22
1804 1 Peter 3:22

21. The person, when rightly accepting the transaction occurring on that tree, will understand that the conversation shed for them is the means whereby the *life* of their own conversation may find itself recovered to a more wholesome experience under the direction of that *name's* intercession. Discerning that by this man's conversation and *name* our conversation is redeemed, purged, and delivered from the religious world to know the operation within *heaven's* Temple for the self and the mind, personal faith should find itself encouraged to climb the ladder of the knowledge of this man's *name* to for ever hear and reverence the counsel, "Stand fast therefore in the liberty wherewith Christ hath made us free, and be not entangled again with the yoke of bondage."[1805]

22. The bondage that Paul speaks of is a slavery that anointed conversation on the tree liberates from, namely, that *mind* which is according to the saying, "Bondage under the elements of the world,"[1806] and, "Our old man is crucified with him, that the body of sin might be destroyed, that henceforth we should not serve sin."[1807] That tree, and the one on it, because his mind is a creation of the salvation's present will, is a figurative delineation of every creation after him, in that the spirit of the former flesh-based religious conversation is passed away into the heavenly *Sanctuary* to become a creature of that Building's *name*.[1808]

23. Herein we are made to observe that creation's science is the work of creative redemption within the inward parts of the conversation by its *Word* or Philosophy resting within and engraved upon the heart and mind to own the confession, "The law of the Spirit of life in Christ Jesus hath made me free from the law of sin and death."[1809] The sacrifice of this man's conversation, and the illustration of one suspended between heaven and earth, when rightly observed and accepted, is the beginning of a new *life* and conversation without the religious world, and by a reformed and refreshed self and spiritual confidence. All pure and honest acceptance of this man should therefore prompt the sincere reformer to say, "I leave the world, and go to the Father."[1810] His crucifixion means none other thing than the ultimate passing away of the former conversation to the intended devotional experience for the refreshing of its character

---

1805   Galatians 5:1
1806   Galatians 4:3
1807   Romans 6:6
1808   Romans 6:9,10
1809   Romans 8:2
1810   John 16:28

so that it might exist "unto all pleasing, being fruitful in every good work, and increasing in the knowledge of God; strengthened with all might, according to his glorious power."[1811]

24. If we truly honor the living God's chief apostle, if our respect for him on the tree is right, our faith will no longer be found on the earth and under the heavens, but "above, where Christ sitteth on the right hand of God."[1812] The new covenant's promise cannot be obtained in any other fashion than a passing away from inherited and self-cultivated religious tradition, for with the Bible's philosophy bringing up its *high priest* to its own throne within its own *Building*, it is that the choice is ours: we will either choose *heaven*; where the model conversation is and where our faith's hope is accomplished; or we will choose *earth*, where there is no hope, no *Wisdom*, no *Creator*, no *Sanctuary* for creation, and where the *name* of the living God's chief apostle is no high priest, but rather an empty *land* with *one* on a cross, even "JESUS OF NAZARETH THE KING OF THE JEWS."[1813]

25. We must understand that if we are to "have escaped the pollutions of the world through the knowledge of the Lord and Saviour Jesus Christ,"[1814] that all things within the religious world and under the heavens are erroneous. This title was not written in that place where the living God's *name* is, but "the place where Jesus was crucified was nigh to the city,"[1815] and this is that city wherein it says, "Jerusalem, the city which I have chosen me to put my name there."[1816]

26. By this *man's* sacrifice, the person is to not quit self's mind and the foolishness of the religious world to find themselves homeless, for the Spirit's Building that this man's *name* today ministers in is within that "city of the living God, the heavenly Jerusalem."[1817] This is the *City* that his conversation was brought up to, where the living God anointed his *name* to be that high priest over "the general assembly and church of the firstborn, which are written in heaven."[1818] But on *earth* today, there is *one* upon a cross that is near to the Spirit's *City* and *Building*, but who is not that conversation of that *City* and

---

1811 Colossians 1:10,11
1812 Colossians 3:1
1813 John 19:19
1814 2 Peter 2:20
1815 John 19:20
1816 1 Kings 11:36
1817 Hebrews 12:22
1818 Hebrews 12:23

Building. Pilate; a symbol of a Roman minister for the Jewish State; wrote this title, and he wrote it; and would not make any amendment to it; for every *Jew* under Rome's dominion to see and observe, "and it was written in Hebrew, and Greek, and Latin."[1819] Rome rules the then world, and because this crucifixion is a religious event, Pilate's act witnesses to the fact that every Roman by Hebrew, Latin, and Greek descent will observe this title on *earth*, forsaking the conversation above the religious world.

27. The living God's chief apostle plainly says, "I leave the world, and go to the Father,"[1820] allowing us to know that, not only is his conversation and philosophy no longer within the religious world, but that he doesn't lie when saying, "I am not of the world."[1821] Herein we are made to observe two ministers who, as Jacob and Esau, on the surface appear to be twins, for while one is born right, the other is known to wear a *red* garment.

28. When the conversation of the living God's chief apostle left this *earth*, it brought up the living God's philosophy with it, leaving the *earth* and the *sea* to the will of the *dragon*, which "dragon" is a deceptive religious conversation, as it says, "Pharaoh king of Egypt, the great dragon."[1822] This same *Egyptian* religion then gained an entry into Christian folds, for "his tail drew the third part of the stars of heaven, and did cast them to the earth."[1823] On this *earth*, the *kingdom* or the denomination of the *Jews* remains suspended on a cross, and every *Hebrew* under Rome; every seventh day *people* under *Roman* authority; and every *Greek* people, or every superstitious philosophical *people* under *Roman* authority; and every *Latin* people; every first day or sun-day keeping *people*; will honor the title that Pilate wrote.

29. The *Jews* that observe this title are them that say, "We have no king but Caesar,"[1824] for their religious heritage will find itself submerged in handwritten *Roman* paganism while taking on the religious kingdom of *one* on a cross, even as the head of their practice says, "Behold the man!"[1825] It is therefore well to examine scripture's tongue, for by Pilate's actions, we observe one perpetually under the heavens and covered in a *red* garment, who is nigh unto Jerusalem, but who is not that one "that died, yea rather, that is risen again,

---

1819 John 19:20
1820 John 16:28
1821 John 17:16
1822 Ezekiel 29:3
1823 Revelation 12:4
1824 John 19:15
1825 John 19:5

who is even at the right hand of God, who also maketh intercession for us."[1826] If we are sincere, if we respect *heaven's* interceding *name* and conversation, we will consider how that "Christ hath redeemed us from the curse of the law, being made a curse for us,"[1827] "that we might receive the promise of the Spirit through faith."[1828]

1826 Romans 8:34
1827 Galatians 3:13
1828 Galatians 3:14

21

A Meaningful Relation

1. It is written, "The LORD God formed man of the dust of the ground, and breathed into his nostrils the breath of life; and man became a living soul,"[1829] and, "Whatsoever God doeth, it shall be for ever: nothing can be put to it, nor any thing taken from it."[1830] As *Adam* said, "Bone of my bones, and flesh of my flesh,"[1831] so no thing that the Creator has decreed or created can and will change shape unless he overturns it.

2. The devotional *frame* of Adam remains, and will continue to remain. We understand this fact from how that, even though the living God's man has informed conversations on how to justly honor the living God, it is still needful to remain cautious of the religious world. This is why we are counseled, "Beware lest any man spoil you through philosophy and vain deceit, after the tradition of men, after the rudiments of the world, and not after Christ."[1832]

1829 Genesis 2:7
1830 Ecclesiastes 3:14
1831 Genesis 2:23
1832 Colossians 2:8

3. This quote reveals what the mission of the living God's Prophet was. If we are hearing Paul advise against religious philosophical commandments and traditions, it is that this Prophet's offering did not render to the flesh any immediate blessing, nor did it vanquish religious error from the *earth* or the *sea*. What this offering did was, in addition to opening up *creation's* door for the mind of our conversation, it purged the living God's philosophy of religious error, separating the *name* of that philosophy from the *wisdom* within the religious world.

4. Religious error against the Creator's doctrine remains alive, and we should not think that it should not be alive; doesn't it say, "Of the tree of the knowledge of good and evil, thou shalt not eat of it: for in the day that thou eatest thereof thou shalt surely die"?[1833] The LORD pronounced a curse of *death* to Adam for their consumption of the cursed tree. The LORD's *spoke* this promise, therefore no thing can be done about this promise's effect, for in this tree the saying is fulfilled, "So shall my word be that goeth forth out of my mouth: it shall not return unto me void, but it shall accomplish that which I please, and it shall prosper in the thing whereto I sent it."[1834]

5. *Adam's* curse for spiritual disobedience is a permanent fixture in their devotional conversation. That wrath attached to the *law* within their spiritual understanding perpetually keeps their inward parts asleep by that curse. The LORD spoke this promise of lethargy and slumber, and if this is "the word of God, which liveth and abideth for ever";[1835] and it is; must we expect this illness to naturally find itself reversed? Every mind owning a flesh-based conversation will for ever own a *body* housing wrath-filled *members* against the *voice* of the living God. There is no other alternative to any one born within the *dragon's earth*, or within the religious world. Therefore "God sending his own Son in the likeness of sinful flesh,"[1836] or as possessing *Adam's* degenerate conversation, is enough to inform us that this man had no thing more or less than *us*.

6. There is one whose profession is founded on lies.[1837] A *Christ* born to a sensual form becomes a *Savior* of no value. Such lore is in no right service to the Mind of Eden's *garden* because it fails to take in to account the aim of that *garden's* thoughts and the perpetual weight of its counsel, which is what the *serpent* specializes in. The *serpent's* speech will stimulate the conversation for the slumbering of the mind, making it appear as though the scriptures lie, "and

---

1833 Genesis 2:17
1834 Isaiah 55:11
1835 1 Peter 1:23
1836 Romans 8:3
1837 John 8:44

for this cause God shall send them strong delusion, that they should believe a lie."[1838]

7. The religion of the *dragon* is one where confidence is placed on a cursed tree, for that tree is founded upon the saying, "Ye shall not surely die."[1839] The *serpent* despises the living God's commandment and will persuade its congregation to disregard *creation's* words, thus, if it says, "Thou shalt surely die,"[1840] it is the goal of this contrary *philosophy* to deceive its assembly to believe that what is said is not so. This counterfeit religion will then remove the *eyes* from right words to an *image* of its own devising, causing the mind to dwell upon a mind-numbing vision for stillness. At this point the conversation may impulsively direct its self to accomplish its own religious desires and imaginations.[1841]

8. No thing spoken or formed by the living God can change unless by its will, and it, by its chief apostle's sacrifice, has spoken no thing concerning the removal of the natural impulse of the human and the devotional conversation from *Adam*, or the removal of the *dragon's* philosophy from the *earth*. If *God's Christ* did appear in the popularly accepted Greco-Roman form, what value is there in the saying, "I will put enmity between thee and the woman, and between thy seed and her seed"?[1842] A blatant division between the Bible's thinking and feeling conversation and the servants of the *dragon's* religion is here pronounced.

9. Now, with *Christ* owning a form carnally superior to the human's form, what value is he to their fractured condition? What right salvation can come to mankind from flesh perversely housing *divinity* when mankind is but flesh and blood? The outcome is a lazy hope established by the *serpent's* inspiration. The Bible's philosophy involves mental and spiritual discernment for inward renewal, but the *serpent* is found encouraging Eve to quit learning for a cheap route to an ascent to truth. And the end of Eve's course is well deserved, for she proves that there is actually no natural intention to better self or the spirits of others within the human being. It was only after this failed experiment that a thought for *Adam's* plight surfaced. It was then said, "I will put enmity."[1843]

10. Hereafter a division between them that would know the *garden's* philosophy, and them that would know Eden's contrary *wisdom*, would take place.

1838 2 Thessalonians 2:11
1839 Genesis 3:4
1840 Genesis 2:17
1841 Ephesians 2:3
1842 Genesis 3:15
1843 Genesis 3:15

The LORD didn't blot out the serpent; he couldn't and wouldn't, for it says, "The serpent...which the LORD God had made";[1844] neither did his promised curse fail, for "as by one man sin entered into the world, and death by sin; and so death passed upon all men."[1845] But this wasn't right. This pair deserved the promise of their negligence, but what about them that should come after them? The living God thought well to devise a decree for our return to that *garden's* wisdom, for while it could not and would not erase any thing that its *voice* had brought into existence, an amendment for the error committed against that garden's *name* was made.[1846]

11. The new covenant's offering demanded *flesh* in likeness to the flesh that *Adam* sacrificed to the serpent. This should be necessary to establish a course of learning to ensure *Adam's* separation not only from the wrath pronounced against their conversation, but also from the *dragon's* religious world. This sacrifice cannot, and should not end religious error from the *world* under the heavens, or from that naturally enflamed agitation within the human being, but it should, and it does, offer the opportunity to know an amendment within the human and the devotional constitution to quit the *serpent's wisdom* for a right conversation.

12. If the Bible should prophesy of a *Christ* contrary to Adam in any way, the entire plan of creative redemption is retarded. The serpent's persuasion is to depend upon a *tree* for knowledge without exerting any right mental and physical labor for understanding, depending upon that tree to be the means wherein *salvation* and *righteousness* is achieved. The experiment in Eden was given to examine the *garden's* host, to understand if *Adam* would cry after knowledge or if they would quit efforts to learn and depend upon a *tree* given for a law of *righteousness*.

13. There is no such thing as obtaining any thing from the living God without mental and spiritual discernment.[1847] The Bible does not own a lazy character. This living God owns no negligent mind, seeing as how "the Spirit searcheth all things, yea, the deep things of God."[1848] The conversation possessing a character similar to the Bible's mental character will diligently examine its voice.[1849] Knowledge must be found, and finding knowledge involves searching for

---

1844   Genesis 3:1
1845   Romans 5:12
1846   Isaiah 51:4
1847   1 Samuel 2:3
1848   1 Corinthians 2:10
1849   Proverbs 2:3-5

knowledge, and searching for knowledge involves prayer, taxation of mind, the exercising of the inward person, and fasting from self.

14. *Adam* was created fraudulent so that their experience could better seal salvation's science within them. Should Adam engage their faith's intellect, should Adam examine creation, should they respectfully and thoughtfully question creation and their Creator they, by the brainpower spent discerning his *voice*, and by the anguish their soul should know when quitting temptation by the engrafted wisdom upon their heart, would have known the Creator's wisdom, the praise of its *name*, and the perpetuity of its *voice*. But they never willingly and wholeheartedly sat with *it*. Their challenge would have been easy if they had learned of and executed a right *light*.

15. "The law is light,"[1850] and if they had, by caring for the living God's commandment, studied the labor of his hands, they would have understood life's law, which "law" is creation's science, that like as how by a *voice* the *earth* resurrected and reformed, so by digesting the Creator's words, the devotional conversation should know a similar newness. Had they studied creation's law, and the redemption of the *earth*, they would have understood not only the definitive weight of the living God's *voice*, but also the aim dressing its tone.

16. No thing given by the living God is for our injury. If by his *voice* the *earth* was made better, then what wrong can be found in any thing coming from his mouth? To take any *thing* from the living God to be perverse or without credibility is to expose our allegiance to the *serpent's* mind and *tree*. We do not know the good intention behind any of the Creator's commandments because we have failed to do his *light*.[1851] Thus, as it says of that *father* of lies, so the living God's chief apostle says of its offspring, for neither the *dragon* nor his assembly care for the Bible's fact. Seeing as how it says, "Thy word is truth,"[1852] and, "Thy law is the truth,"[1853] the *dragon* must lead the mind away from salvation's law if he should capture the imagination. It is this spiritual delusion that encourages illness within the conversation to increase.[1854]

17. Having our higher faculties removed from the living God's devotional character and our inward parts numb to its influence, "fables and endless genealogies, which minister questions, rather than godly edifying which is in

---

1850 Proverbs 6:23
1851 1 John 2:4
1852 John 17:17
1853 Psalm 119:142
1854 Hebrews 3:12

faith,"[1855] will govern the conversation. This is what occurred to both Adam and Eve. Because they failed to retain personal knowledge of the Creator, they fulfilled the saying, "The time will come when they will not endure sound doctrine; but after their own lusts shall they heap to themselves teachers, having itching ears; and they shall turn away their ears from the truth, and shall be turned unto fables."[1856]

18. That *tree* of promised *death* was a fable endorsed by the *serpent*. Sensing that they were not willing to mentally persevere through the living God's instruction, and by their bodily language evinced their distaste for actively engaging self in right labor, he moved them to trust on what, by all outward appearances, concealed a free and harmless *salvation*. This *tree*, like them, had both good and evil within it. The fruit of this tree was a perfect sacrifice to supposedly attain just what the LORD preached. The tree spoke no different doctrine than any other tree, for it was a tree of Eden, but they perceived it to be above every other tree, containing within it a seemingly *divine* remedy to satisfy their natural and spiritual ignorance. Therefore, when hopeful to gain their allegiance, the serpent took advantage of their thoughts and feelings, convincing them of a false sense of security.

19. Now, to believe such foolishness is to forget that "all flesh is not the same flesh: but there is one kind of flesh of men, another flesh of beasts, another of fishes, and another of birds. There are also celestial bodies, and bodies terrestrial: but the glory of the celestial is one, and the glory of the terrestrial is another."[1857] There is allotted to *man* only one *flesh*. This flesh does not and cannot change for any one. This *flesh*, or devotional body, was not only established in the beginning, but it is sealed to the human being by wrath for their negligence.

20. There is a different body for the celestial, or for the *divine*. This body is not that body of flesh, nor can it find itself translated to flesh, which is why "that which is born of the flesh is flesh; and that which is born of the Spirit is spirit."[1858] The living God's chief apostle, allowing us to know that the flesh of *man* is unalterable, but that what can find itself under right construction is the spirit of the mind, has drawn a very plain line between "bodies."

21. The Word, or the living God's wisdom, made in to the flesh is the flesh cooperating with that wisdom, and in order for the flesh to find itself continuing

---

1855 1 Timothy 1:4
1856 2 Timothy 4:3,4
1857 1 Corinthians 15:39,40
1858 John 3:6

in and by that wisdom, it is that the spirit of the mind must exercise itself on that philosophy; this birth is not physical, but is mental. Man owns one physical form, and within that body are two bodies, for "there is a natural body, and there is a spiritual body."[1859] The Word, or the living God's Wisdom, being *God*, cannot fellowship with what is fleshly and natural because *God* is *Spirit*. That other body, the spiritual or the devotional, must therefore become the subject of communion.[1860]

22. For flesh and blood; which is *corrupt*; to inherit what is not corrupt, does not make right sense. If we are taking a professed *tree* of the *LORD* to house within it both corruption and incorruption, then what good is that sensual tree to us who are wholly corrupt, both naturally and spiritually? Should I put confidence in a tree of good and evil, or of *divinity* and humanity, to deliver me from my low estate?

23. This tree is humble, yet prideful. It, being both good and evil, is erroneously spiritually wealthy, and must I believe it understands what I am and what I need? What confidence should I then have in *it*? Maybe if I were created as it is my confidence would then be found in it, and for a very good reason. It, being like me, and being equal to me, can make up for my failure before *God*, but if it, being above me, is not found as low as me, but mocks my illness by thinking it can help me by being only half of me, then what good is this *tree* to me?

24. What is its *salvation*? What is its mission if it already wonderfully possesses humanity's *remedy* within its natural core? I should take the *LORD* that sent it to be a liar, and as one that absolutely hates humanity, loathes *Adam*, and despises its own self. This is why the living God edified his chief apostle. It was necessary that this man should be as we are both naturally and devotionally, for if he weren't, then we would have no right reason to better the culture of inward person.

25. Because this Prophet partook of Adam's conversation, perfecting within his conversation the living God's commandment to know the hope of the new covenant will, and was slain with this movement upon his heart, his experience is ours to mimic for knowing the promise, "I will put enmity between thee and the woman, and between thy seed and her seed."[1861] The conversation rightly honoring that offering will find its self owning a conscience in direct opposition to the *dragon's* lie.

1859 1 Corinthians 15:44
1860 1 Corinthians 15:50
1861 Genesis 3:15

26. We should bear in mind that while this man's conversation has permanently relocated, and by that translation bringing salvation's science with it,
that the *dragon* remains on the *earth*, and that the illustration in the *garden*
only served to foreshadow the appearing of "the idol shepherd that leaveth the
flock."[1862] This is that *tree* whose host cries, "They have taken away my Lord,
and I know not where they have laid him,"[1863] who has "set up over his head his
accusation written, THIS IS JESUS THE KING OF THE JEWS."[1864] Herein is
the true fulfillment of the serpent's tree, which *tree* fulfills the saying, "The man
that made the earth to tremble, that did shake kingdoms; that made the world
as a wilderness, and destroyed the cities thereof; that opened not the house of
his prisoners."[1865]

27. The living God's chief apostle took away the religious error of the Jews
and of the *dragon* from the Bible's *name* and philosophy, destroying that "which
was contrary to us, and took it out of the way, nailing it to his cross."[1866] But this
does not mean that religious error against the living God is put away from that
realm infected by the *dragon*. This man silenced the deceptive religion of the
serpent by his offered conversation, binding to conversation's *heaven's* course
of learning to lawfully honor salvation's science, self, and other minds, but that
does not mean self and mankind are forcefully bound to *heaven's* will. If we
were bound to that will, there would be no need to say, "Beware lest any man
spoil you through philosophy and vain deceit, after the tradition of men, after
the rudiments of the world, and not after Christ."[1867]

28. Today, the religious world may hear and apply to the counsel, "Either
make the tree good, and his fruit good; or else make the tree corrupt, and his
fruit corrupt."[1868] A promise of human and devotional newness awaits the doer
of salvation's science, but it is our decision to either apply for it or not. Nevertheless, whether we should choose heaven's will or not, and however long it takes
us to choose, the training of the new covenant's intention is sure, wherefore it
is well to "account that the longsuffering of our Lord is salvation."[1869] This does

---

1862   Zechariah 11:17
1863   John 20:13
1864   Matthew 27:37
1865   Isaiah 14:16,17
1866   Colossians 2:14
1867   Colossians 2:8
1868   Matthew 12:33
1869   2 Peter 3:15

not mean that we put off salvation's science, "for what is your life?"[1870] Eden's experiment proves that the longer we put off mentally and spiritually discerning the Bible's words, the greater the chance to have that right influence pass away from us, keeping us ignorant in understanding, our conversation becoming fit for the *dragon's* train of thought.

29. We should understand that the living God's Prophet upon a tree is no idol to revere, or is no *thing* to irrationally covet. That illustration is of a conversation passing away from its naturally erroneous spiritual understanding. This is why it says, "Christ hath redeemed us from the curse of the law, being made a curse for us: for it is written, Cursed is every one that hangeth on a tree."[1871]

30. The illustration of this man's sacrifice condemns every law of a religious tradition professing service to the *Mind* within the Bible. Every conversation rightly discerning that crucifixion refrains from unlawfully handling its self, its mind resting "above, where Christ sitteth on the right hand of God."[1872] Thus, no *thing* on *earth*, because it is all to devour our faith's character, can and should be trusted.[1873] This devouring isn't literal, but is mental. For this cause our *eyes*, to avoid the snare of that sensual *tree*, whose "superscription also was written over him in letters of Greek, and Latin, and Hebrew, THIS IS THE KING OF THE JEWS,"[1874] should behold the conversation of the living God's chief apostle as its high priest.[1875]

1870 James 4:14
1871 Galatians 3:13
1872 Colossians 3:1
1873 1 Peter 5:8
1874 Luke 23:38
1875 Revelation 1:1

22

From Legal Craft

1. A clearer and more sober understanding of the illustration behind the sacrifice of the living God's chief apostle is necessary. Religious tradition has perverted the liberty forwarded by this event, which perversion is strictly advised against by the Bible.

2. That Prophet suspended between heaven and earth is a message that "Christ hath redeemed us from the curse of the law, being made a curse for us."[1876] What does this mean? This means that by this one act, the authority of any law of any religious tradition concerning the Bible, this man having "abolished in his flesh the enmity, even the law of commandments contained in ordinances,"[1877] is perpetually passed away.

3. All commandments and ordinances that "have indeed a shew of wisdom in will worship, and humility, and neglecting of the body,[1878] are abolished by this Prophet's crucifixion. This means that no religious code of elders constricts

---

1876 Galatians 3:13
1877 Ephesians 2:15
1878 Colossians 2:23

the reformer's conversation. This means that religious tradition, to the eyes of the living God, is grotesque. This means that the handwritten religious tradition is a curse to the mind of the believer, which is why "Christ hath redeemed us from the curse of the law, being made a curse for us."[1879] If it is that we rightly value this man willingly offering his self to make a philosophical statement, we will understand that our former superstitious tradition is come to an end for properly acknowledging our belief's betterment. By this man's blood, it is well to know that there is no salvation by our religious tradition.[1880]

4. There are two *forces* at play. If there is now redemption from the handwritten religious law, then if we honor any religious tradition, we admit *redemption* by that commandment. Peter counsels us that we are not cleansed by what is handwritten, but Paul informs us of what we are redeemed by, even by "Christ."

5. Now, this man's sacrifice did not extinguish religious error against the living God; if it did, there would be no need for us to hear, "Many false prophets are gone out into the world,"[1881] and, "Let no man deceive you with vain words."[1882] Clearly, then, this man's conversation, by dying and reviving, did not perform any automatic redemption within the inward parts of mankind, wherefore when we hear Paul say that "Christ" redeemed from the curse of manmade religious ethics, it is well to remember that "henceforth know we no man after the flesh: yea, though we have known Christ after the flesh, yet now henceforth know we him no more. Therefore if any man be in Christ, he is a new creature."[1883]

6. The former creature is one "in bondage under the elements of the world,"[1884] being crafted "after the commandments and doctrines of men."[1885] But the new creature of "Christ" is one honoring the advice, "Live according to God in the spirit."[1886] The image of the cross is therefore a revelation of necessary reformation in manners of worship and in service, moving the heart of the person to purchase liberty for the spirit of their personal devotional conversation.

1879 Galatians 3:3
1880 1 Peter 1:18
1881 1 John 4:1
1882 Ephesians 5:6
1883 2 Corinthians 5:16,17
1884 Galatians 4:3
1885 Colossians 2:22
1886 1 Peter 4:6

7. This redemption, seeing as how "of his own will begat he us with the word of truth, that we should be a kind of firstfruits of his creatures,"[1887] appears only as the mind examines the law of the Creator's *name*. All in "Christ" are regenerated and reformed creatures to the *name* and praise of the living God, and if this creation is by "the law of truth,"[1888] then it is evident that, in right context of language, "the Lord Jesus Christ our Saviour,"[1889] being no reference to a literal figure, is "the commandment of God our Saviour."[1890]

8. The living God's manner of redemption, because it occurs by the Word or Wisdom of creation, can only take place by the commandment of that philosophy. Because this Word is "God," and because God is Spirit, because "that which is born of the Spirit is spirit,"[1891] the result of *creation's* science is that "the Word was made flesh,"[1892] or is the Creator's present wisdom living within and through the devotional conversation. This cannot occur if the conversation is subject to and regulated by a handwritten religious standard.

9. The Creator's redemption must take place within the spirit of the mind. The conversation learning of and doing that redemption's commandment will receive the privilege of becoming a new and ever-living creation of its wisdom to confess, "The Spirit of God hath made me."[1893] The law and commandment of salvation's philosophy for "the washing of regeneration"[1894] must have the opportunity to commence within the mind; this is, in all actuality, "the washing of water by the word."[1895]

10. Words are not physical. No word is bound. Words, in order to benefit the person, must find themselves mentally examined. In order to know the deliverance that the Bible highlights, it is that the mind must discern the *voice* behind its wisdom's intercession.

11. If it is that we are "doers of the word, and not hearers only,"[1896] then "Christ hath redeemed us from the curse of the law,"[1897] yet who can claim deliverance from a curse while under it? If it is that our mind has rightly exam-

---

1887 James 1:18
1888 Malachi 2:6
1889 Titus 1:4
1890 Titus 1:3
1891 John 3:6
1892 John 1:14
1893 Job 33:4
1894 Titus 3:5
1895 Ephesians 5:26
1896 James 1:11
1897 Galatians 3:13

ined the Bible's *voice* through the mediation of that wisdom's intercession, our findings will match Paul's, who counsels, "Put off concerning the former conversation the old man, which is corrupt according to the deceitful lusts; and be renewed in the spirit of your mind; and that ye put on the new man, which after God is created."[1898]

12. Our initial conversation, it is traditional and superstitious, being drowned in inordinate and illogical religious affection.[1899] If the conversation was created by "the Lord Jesus Christ our Saviour";[1900] that is, was purified by "the doctrine of God our Saviour";[1901] a new conversation would have emerged, and one that was created by *God*, that is, by the Bible's Wisdom. His Prophet abolished, by the sacrifice of his conversation, necessary obedience to flesh-based prescriptions. Possessing *heaven's* will within the members of his conversation, having his conversation sacrificed with those members conquered by the law of the Word, every conversation after him should, and by the same law, share in the same victory. This man's sacrificed and regenerated conversation means the regeneration and reformation of every conversation owning a routine spirituality. Achieving this liberty and purpose within the religious world, his sacrifice means our fellowship with this same commandment without the religious world.

13. "We have received a commandment from the Father,"[1902] and concerning this decree, it says, "I know that his commandment is life everlasting,"[1903] and, "I know him, and keep his saying."[1904] The fact that this man was slain, and with salvation's saying within the members of his conversation, allows every one taking confidence on his act to know that they have a resurrection to experience.

14. He does not say, "I am of 'the perfect manner of the law of the fathers,'"[1905] or, "I came from 'the Jews' religion,'"[1906] but he plainly says, "I proceeded forth and came from God,"[1907] and, "I came out from God."[1908] His language does not provoke any sensual or perverted sentiment. If "the Word of

---

1898 Ephesians 4:22-24
1899 Colossians 2:8
1900 Titus 1:4
1901 Titus 2:10
1902 2 John 1:4
1903 John 12:50
1904 John 8:55
1905 Acts 22:3
1906 Galatians 1:13
1907 John 8:42
1908 John 16:27

life"[1909] is "the Spirit of life,"[1910] and if "God is a Spirit,"[1911] and if "that which is born of the Spirit is spirit,"[1912] then to come out from "God" is to obtain birth within the spirit of the mind by the living God's Wisdom.

15. The birth that he experienced was through the new covenant's commandment washing his conversation's inward parts, which is why it says, "Thou desirest truth in the inward parts: and in the hidden part thou shalt make me to know wisdom."[1913] This man received circumcision and baptism by a word, counsel, or wisdom,[1914] and having a conversation sacrificed through the baptism and circumcision of the living God's wisdom, he fully destroyed all fear and respect of religious tradition, giving us an example of how to carry our conversation.[1915]

16. The living God's chief apostle took the philosophy of *righteousness* by the handwritten religious law from out of the new covenant's science. Error, by this man's sacrifice, may not be removed from the religious world or from the human condition, nor did he, by that offering, place within any one a spirit to lawfully adhere to the Creator's commandment, but he did absolutely remove and smear every possible handwritten religious tradition from the living God's *name*. The way, then, that leads to the manner of redemption at the heart of the Bible, which is "salvation through sanctification of the Spirit and belief of the truth,"[1916] is not "through philosophy and vain deceit, after the tradition of men, after the rudiments of the world,"[1917] but rather by learning of and doing the will of the intended devotional experience, seeing as how "if any man will do his will, he shall know of the doctrine."[1918]

17. The Bible's concern is over our personally knowing its *name*, and that impression cannot take place until we mentally comprehend its words, that "they are spiritually discerned."[1919] Paul's speech to the Colossians openly shuts down whatever traditional religious thought we believe to be superior or flawless, for by this one act, that Prophet has abolished every legal religious ethic of

---

1909   1 John 1:1
1910   Revelation 11:11
1911   John 4:24
1912   John 3:6
1913   Psalm 51:6
1914   Isaiah 11:2
1915   Colossians 2:14
1916   2 Thessalonians 2:13
1917   Colossians 2:8
1918   John 7:17
1919   1 Corinthians 2:14

priests for every conversation to have its thoughts "above, where Christ sitteth on the right hand of God."[1920] Herein the illustration of him suspended between heaven and earth is perfectly relayed, for the vision is one of spiritual regeneration to embrace "the time of reformation."[1921]

18. This man took out of salvation's law every religious ordinance concocted by *men* for devotional salvation, wherefore we may know that we entertain religious error when our heart is ruled by "philosophy and vain deceit, after the tradition of men, after the rudiments of the world."[1922] Paul, by rightly educating us on what this man on the tree represents, is warning us to let no thing of the religious world halt our faith's growth and development; in us the saying should be fulfilled, "The life was manifested."[1923]

19. The manifestation of "the life," "the truth," and "the way" within our heart, is damaged by the curse or illness that religious tradition consumes the heart of the conversation with, which is why "Christ hath redeemed us from the curse of the law, being made a curse for us: for it is written, Cursed is every one that hangeth on a tree."[1924] If we truly respect the illustration connected to this man's act, it is that we will express reverence towards his *name* by quitting inherited and cultivated religious tradition; this is why he was slain and willingly sacrificed himself.

20. If he was not sacrificed, and if, within the members of his conversation "the law of the Spirit of life"[1925] did not flourish, then we would have free license to continue to adhere to handwritten religious traditions and *spiritual* charges. There is then no thing "abolished in his flesh"[1926] and "blotting out the handwriting of ordinances that was against us, which was contrary to us."[1927] We may freely idolize this *Christ*, for seeing as how his force is flesh-based, "every man should eat and drink, and enjoy the good of all his labour."[1928]

21. But the living God thinks higher of us. When observing such covetous and negligent error against salvation's *name*, it is the living God that says, "How turn ye again to the weak and beggarly elements, whereunto ye desire again to

1920 Colossians 3:1
1921 Hebrews 9:10
1922 Colossians 2:8
1923 1 John 1:2
1924 Galatians 3:13
1925 Romans 8:2
1926 Ephesians 2:15
1927 Colossians 2:14
1928 Ecclesiastes 3:13

be in bondage?"[1929] and, "Received ye the Spirit by the works of the law, or by the hearing of faith? Are ye so foolish? having begun in the Spirit, are ye now made perfect by the flesh?"[1930]

22. Our current conduct towards the living God and towards the *name* of his chief apostle is nothing short of disrespectful, for if he, by one act, removed the stumblingblock of hard religious prescriptions from the salvation's benevolence, how then, by picking up that stumblingblock, do we honor that *name*? This man on the tree symbolizes the liberty of the conversation's conscience from the religious world, which is why it says, "Let no man therefore judge you in meat, or in drink, or in respect of an holyday, or of the new moon, or of the sabbath days."[1931]

23. That word "judge," as Paul uses it, means, "have dominion over," or, "have command or control over." Paul is counseling us, because that Prophet has openly vanquished from out of the living God's *name* every handwritten commandment and ordinance, to let no elder or teacher have dominion over our mind in matters of meat, drink, and especially of the Sabbath, which Sabbath is not a handwritten law, even as the Bible says, "My holy day."[1932] Today, no religion professing the Bible may, according to the speech of that Prophet, dictate to any conversation any religious charge, and especially any charge regarding any other Sabbath than that of the seventh day.

24. Because this man perished on the tree, there is no rule of *men* over *meat*, and "meat" is figurative language denoting "bread," as it says, "When all the people came to cause David to eat meat while it was yet day, David sware, saying, So do God to me, and more also, if I taste bread,"[1933] and, "The bread that I will give is my flesh."[1934] "Bread," being a symbol of flesh, is a symbol of meat, and "meat" is a symbol of doctrine, as it says, "Be not carried about with divers and strange doctrines. For it is a good thing that the heart be established with grace; not with meats."[1935]

25. When Paul counsels us to let no teacher have dominion over the mind by "meat," it is that he is giving instruction to let no priest rule the spiritual

---

1929 Galatians 4:9
1930 Galatians 3:2,3
1931 Colossians 2:16
1932 Isaiah 58:13
1933 2 Samuel 2:35
1934 John 6:51
1935 Hebrews 13:9

understanding, for "of his own will begat he us with the word of truth."[1936] All conception to the living God is through the impression of the new covenant's commandment upon the spirit of the mind. No one rules where the living God is sovereign, and no minister is more potent than the *voice* of the living God's Wisdom; no conversation except his Prophet's conversation is an expert.[1937] This is why it says of the wisdom belonging to this man's conversation, "He is the head of the body, the church...that in all things he might have the preeminence."[1938]

26. Because this man's conversation is that high priest over the economy concerning salvation's science, every law of the living God is become the commandment of its priesthood. No priest is ordained for the congregation to worship, but this man, seeing as how his conversation fulfills Aaron's role, follows after Aaron's manner, in that it says, "Aaron was separated...to burn incense before the LORD, to minister unto him, and to bless in his name for ever."[1939] "No man taketh this honour unto himself, but he that is called of God, as was Aaron. So also Christ glorified not himself to be made an high priest; but he that said unto him, Thou art my Son, to day have I begotten thee."[1940]

27. This is why every *angel* is subject to the *voice* of this man's spiritual understanding, "for unto which of the angels said he at any time, Thou art my Son, this day have I begotten thee?"[1941] The Bible commits creation's assignment to none other but to its Prophet's conversation, wherefore, concerning the living God's doctrine, and concerning its experience, no minister rules the mind of any one, but only that commandment of salvation's chief priest governs creation's present experience. It is therefore our personal responsibility to eat and drink the *meat* and *blood* of that Prophet. This counsel, because this man is not physically or tangibly available for consumption, embraces terms of a mental reform, which is why we are counseled, "Worship God in the spirit."[1942]

28. Salvation's science, by that Prophet's offering, is become a spiritual or philosophical dispensation. It is truly no lie, in reference to the new covenant, how it says, "They shall all know me."[1943] It was necessary that this man find

---

1936 James 1:18
1937 1 Peter 3:22
1938 Colossians 1:18
1939 1 Chronicles 23:13
1940 Hebrews 5:4,5
1941 Hebrews 1:5
1942 Philippians 3:3
1943 Jeremiah 31:34

himself on the tree for the liberty of every conversation to know the *name* this oblation is devoted to.

29. The new covenant will is a promise to bring the believer in to full "knowledge of his will in all wisdom and spiritual understanding,"[1944] and our Father is serious about this promise. The creature of the new covenant is conceived within their mind; the mind is to become "an habitation of God through the Spirit,"[1945] which is why "circumcision is that of the heart, in the spirit, and not in the letter."[1946] The "letter" is the handwritten rule of a religious tradition.

30. Anciently, many took their blessing and claimed *righteousness* by that *baptism* "in the flesh made by hands,"[1947] yet the living God's chief apostle, by one sacrifice, abolished this manner od devotion, opening up to every conversation "the circumcision made without hands."[1948] The *baptism* of the religious world is with hands, yet that baptism of the living God is without hands; if "of his own will begat he us with the word of truth,"[1949] what physical routine can suffice? A "word" is discerned only by the mental faculties, which is why "that which is born of the Spirit is spirit."[1950] Thus, if any teacher should replace the labor of the mind with a routine flesh-based prescription, we may know that this is not from the Word, and that they are not of that Wisdom's mind.

31. If we did rightly know the Bible's *meat* and *blood*, we would not, for example, allow any religious tradition to remove our minds from the Bible's seventh day. Paul exposes the heresy of maintaining a first day *sabbath*, for if no man should have dominion over the mind of any one concerning *meat*, *drink*, and any *holy* day, or new moon, then we must admit to religious error when lending our affection to a *sabbath* tradition found nowhere in the Bible.

32. "Sabbaths" are linked to new moons, as it says, "When will the new moon be gone, that we may sell corn? and the sabbath, that we may set forth wheat,"[1951] and, "From one new moon to another, and from one sabbath to another,"[1952] and, "It is neither new moon, nor sabbath."[1953] When Paul says, "Let no man therefore judge you...in respect of an holyday, or of the new

---

1944 Colossians 1:9
1945 Ephesians 2:22
1946 Romans 2:29
1947 Ephesians 2:11
1948 Colossians 2:11
1949 James 1:18
1950 John 3:6
1951 Amos 8:5
1952 Isaiah 66:23
1953 2 Kings 4:23

moon, or of the sabbath days,"[1954] he is advising every one professing "love in the Spirit"[1955] to let no priest have dominion over their mind concerning any Sabbath, or solemn assembly, and there is only one solemn assembly, above all others that may be invented, in existence that matters.

33. Now, the living God's Prophet smeared every handwritten commandment of *men*, whether that commandment exists in his day or ours. Every commandment of *men* is written in the name of a compromised religious conversation, which is why "the letter killeth, but the spirit giveth life."[1956] Anciently, the *LORD* worked "by the hand of Moses,"[1957] and there is a difference between the hand of a man and that of the living God. Therefore we may know what *man* is of the Word by their understanding that "God blessed the seventh day,"[1958] for, in the beginning, only the *voice* of a philosophy existed.

34. No man has the right to have any rule over our conversation in respect of *rest's* appointment because "God blessed the seventh day, and sanctified it."[1959] The entire point of the new covenant promise is creative redemption from the conversation's irrational condition and from the religious world's spiritual negligence, wherefore the doer of this promise says, "The law of the Spirit of life in Christ Jesus hath made me free from the law of sin and death."[1960] Any other *sabbath* devoted to this *new covenant will* is thus exposed as a fraudulent *feast*, which is why we understand that "the seventh day is the Sabbath of the LORD"[1961] and why none other *sabbath* exists.

35. If the *LORD* raised up that Prophet on the first or the second day, and not on the third, we may have license to subject our conversation to religious tradition, but since the *LORD*, "in the end of the Sabbath, as it began to dawn toward the first day of the week,"[1962] was moved to act, the Bible has linked its seventh-day to the philosophy within that Prophet's conversation. Because this man suffered the fate of the tree, no *angel* has the right to declare any other *sabbath*, or to preach any other *sabbath*, than that which is in celebration of

---

1954   Colossians 2:16
1955   Colossians 1:8
1956   2 Corinthians 3:6
1957   Nehemiah 9:14
1958   Genesis 3:2
1959   Genesis 3:2
1960   Romans 8:2
1961   Exodus 20:10
1962   Matthew 28:1

salvation's new covenant, which is why, by this man's offering, it is an indisputable fact that "God blessed the seventh day, and sanctified it."[1963]

36. We have been given, by one sacrifice, the opportunity to fully know the living God, and we cannot know our Creator if not passing through creation's course of learning, even as our example did. Why does our natural realm continue to follow the natural course given to it? Why did the living God have enough confidence in nature to say, "While the earth remaineth, seedtime and harvest, and cold and heat, and summer and winter, and day and night shall not cease"?[1964] It is because creation took the time to know its Maker by becoming a subject of creation through *his* voice.

37. When *he* spoke, and when the commandment fell in to the atmosphere, the *world* opened up and that commandment fell in to heaven and earth's core. What he said manifested itself within heaven and earth. We are told, "He spake, and it was done; he commanded, and it stood fast."[1965]

38. All of this was done without a hand, and must we not discern from this act a lesson for our own conversation by the same *voice*? Creation is but a revelation of the Bible's new covenant, and if, at the end of the new covenant's exhibition, the living God sealed creation's new assignment with his seventh day, should not the conversation created after the same power and wisdom within the same covenant, and by the same Mind, know that "God blessed the seventh day, and sanctified it"?[1966] It is written of every creature of salvation's will, "Thou hast given a banner to them that fear thee, that it may be displayed because of the truth";[1967] by patiently learning of and doing creation's wisdom, the sign of creation's righteousness will be given to that faithful mind: the person will know that "the seventh day is the Sabbath."[1968]

39. The illustration of that Prophet on the tree is a reminder to "beware lest any man spoil you through philosophy and vain deceit, after the tradition of men, after the rudiments of the world, and not after Christ."[1969] Salvation's higher education is personal and intimate, existing "not in the words which man's wisdom teacheth, but which the Holy Ghost teacheth; comparing spiritual things with spiritual. But the natural man receiveth not the things of the

---

1963 Genesis 2:3
1964 Genesis 8:22
1965 Psalm 33:9
1966 Genesis 2:3
1967 Psalm 60:4
1968 Exodus 20:10
1969 Colossians 2:8

Spirit of God: for they are foolishness unto him: neither can he know them, because they are spiritually discerned."[1970]

40. We may know the erroneous guide from that conversation grounded and settled in *heaven's* benevolent knowledge, for "we do know that we know him, if we keep his commandments."[1971] The traditions of priesthoods will for ever stand against and challenge the Bible's character, but that Prophet on the tree reveals a different mind. The *body* of his faith is no longer on that tree. The *name* of his conversation is not within the religious world. Our mediating wisdom for the intended devotional experience is next to the living God.[1972] The figurative illustration of the Creator bringing up this wisdom to himself, and anointing it as high priest over his assembly, allows us to know that this mediation is for the living God's will, that we may come to know and love the living God, "and this is love, that we walk after his commandments."[1973]

1970 1 Corinthians 2:13,14
1971 1 John 2:3
1972 Hebrews 8:1,2
1973 2 John 1:6

23

A Right Passing

1. It is written, "He that is hanged is accursed of God."[1974] Now, there is a reason why "when the fulness of the time was come, God sent forth his Son, made of a woman, made under the law,"[1975] and it was to "redeem them that were under the law."[1976] "What things soever the law saith, it saith to them who are under the law,"[1977] but when that binding religious law is become separated from them that are under it, then there is no more service to the religious law, but to the purpose of liberty from that law.[1978]

2. "Wherefore, my brethren, ye also are become dead to the law by the body of Christ,"[1979] for before this man's death, the law of a religious tradition ruled the conversation, but after this man's sacrifice, the conversation is freed from every philosophical religious tradition to personally know the living God.

1974 Deuteronomy 21:23
1975 Galatians 4:4
1976 Galatians 4:5
1977 Romans 3:19
1978 Romans 7:2
1979 Romans 7:4

This man, being born under the rule of a religious tradition, and then found on a tree in that spiritual condition, represents the slaying of religious tradition for whosoever should care to "live according to God in the spirit."[1980] As one born under the rule of religious law, and being found on that tree, he represent the fact that prescribed religious ordinances and ethics in devotion to *the Mind* of the *Bible* are accursed and categorized as "sin." By one sacrifice, the living God has cursed the spirit of the religious world, teaching, "The strength of sin is the law."[1981]

3. Herein we observe the fact that the living God has kept and fulfilled its promise, which promise was, "I will put enmity between thee and the woman."[1982] When speaking of creation's new covenant act, the prophet records, "Thou wentest forth for the salvation of thy people, even for salvation with thine anointed; thou woundedst the head out of the house of the wicked, by discovering the foundation unto the neck."[1983]

4. A complete separation between the seed of the Spirit and the power of the serpent is established through this sacrifice, for the serpent flourishes by religious tradition. It is of the serpent to put his own will ahead of the *LORD's*, and to even challenge the *LORD's* commandment by his own tradition. The serpent may have moved Adam to curse the *LORD's* conversation, but the living God's Prophet delivered a mighty wound to the serpent's wisdom; this man was persuaded by salvation's science to curse the serpent's philosophy.

5. It was by a religious tradition that Eve was seduced. She obeyed the *serpent*, whose speech convinced her to see "that the tree was good for food, and that it was pleasant to the eyes, and a tree to be desired to make one wise,"[1984] even though they were told, "In the day that thou eatest thereof thou shalt surely die."[1985] The serpent propounded an ordinance stating *righteousness* by the works of the hands, which commandment was contrary to that of the *LORD's*, who preached the reception of knowledge's blessing without force. Their error set the stage for the course of priesthoods in the *earth*, but the living God had a plan to redeem *them* from the *serpent's* contrary wisdom.

6. It was that, after their failure to exercise and experiment with faith for regenerative knowledge, "by one man sin entered into the world, and death

---

1980 1 Peter 4:6
1981 1 Corinthians 15:56
1982 Genesis 3:15
1983 Habakkuk 3:13
1984 Genesis 3:6
1985 Genesis 2:17

by sin; and so death passed upon all men."[1986] Hereafter the religious world within the living God's *earth* should find itself governed by laws and charges that prevented the Creator's right intention from advancing. The serpent's philosophy had crept into the living God's wisdom and every conversation honoring that wisdom was made to err by the same error of Eden's first *priest*, causing every generation thereafter to fulfill the saying, "This people draw near me with their mouth, and with their lips do honour me, but have removed their heart far from me, and their fear toward me is taught by the precept of men."[1987]

7. But the *LORD* was not content with what his thinking and feeling creation must experience. He made a promise, saying, "I will put enmity,"[1988] and by that promise, it should be fulfilled, "I will proceed to do a marvellous work among this people, even a marvellous work and a wonder: for the wisdom of their wise men shall perish, and the understanding of their prudent men shall be hid."[1989] A plan to abolish the wisdom and understanding of priests fraudulently professing his *name* was created. The *LORD* would wound the *serpent* by ending its reign over conversations. He would permanently seal minds to his Mind, and this conversion by their obedience to a specific law or commandment, which is why it says, "A law shall proceed from me."[1990]

8. No longer would any man claim devotion or piety to the *LORD* by flesh-based works. Enmity against the spirit of the serpent would arise by the law and judgment of the living God working within the mind of its student, which is why that Prophet said, "For judgment I am come into this world."[1991]

9. The living God swore, "A law shall proceed from me, and I will make my judgment to rest for a light of the people,"[1992] and at the appointed time, a prophet gave mention to the Creator's new will and promise for the personal devotional conversation. This man was trained by this Wisdom to place into the religious world a judgment that would separate its *name* from the living God's *name*. This judgment is "the law of the Spirit of life,"[1993] and because he

---

1986 Romans 5:12
1987 Isaiah 29:13
1988 Genesis 3:15
1989 Isaiah 29:14
1990 Isaiah 51:4
1991 John 9:39
1992 Isaiah 51:4
1993 Romans 8:2

kept and dressed his conversation with it; as he says, "I know him, and keep his saying";[1994] "the Word was made flesh."[1995]

10. The Word made flesh is the living God's "face in the flesh,"[1996] and concerning this "face," it says, "They shall walk, O LORD, in the light of thy countenance,"[1997] and, "Thy right hand, and thine arm, and the light of thy countenance."[1998] The living God's *face* is the light of the living God's countenance, "and the law is light";[1999] this is why it says, concerning this same law, "His arm shall rule for him,"[2000] and, "On mine arm shall they trust."[2001] The Word made flesh is the commandment of the living God *arm* and right *hand* come in to the members of the conversation; this is the kingdom and righteousness of the Word.

11. By the Word, or by this Wisdom working within the spirit of the mind, right manners of worship and service is to proceed from the conversation, even as it says, "As ye have yielded your members servants to uncleanness and to iniquity unto iniquity; even so now yield your members servants to righteousness unto holiness."[2002] With the Word come into the flesh, or into the conversation, the organs of the conversation may learn of and continue in that righteousness, and this executed through "the words of his holiness,"[2003] which is why it says, "Worship the LORD in the beauty of holiness."[2004]

12. Before the Word's sacrifice, the Bible said, "Their fear toward me is taught by the precept of men,"[2005] but soon a great mystery was to commence. By the Word's oblation, it was to be fulfilled, "Give unto the LORD the glory due unto his name; worship the LORD in the beauty of holiness."[2006] Worship to the living God is to hereafter commence in the beautiful design of "holiness," which refinement is according to the saying, "Be not conformed to this world: but be ye transformed by the renewing of your mind, that ye may prove what

---

1994 John 8:55
1995 John 1:14
1996 Colossians 2:1
1997 Psalm 89:15
1998 Psalm 44:3
1999 Proverbs 6:23
2000 Isaiah 40:10
2001 Isaiah 51:5
2002 Romans 6:19
2003 Jeremiah 23:9
2004 Psalm 96:9
2005 Isaiah 29:13
2006 Psalm 29:2

is that good, and acceptable, and perfect, will of God."[2007] The religious world, due to the *serpent's* influence, moves conversations to depend on tradition for validation, but a right devotion is according to the mind's continual personal devotional revival and reform.

13. "Holiness" is "godliness," and "godliness" is "goodness," and "goodness" is "righteousness," and "righteousness" is benevolent kindness, which is why the wisdom of the living God's chief apostle is after "the kindness and love of God our Saviour toward man."[2008] To worship the living God in the beauty of holiness is to honor the living God in a manner where experiencing the benevolence of the Bible's words yields resurrection in heart and in mind.[2009] The living God's righteousness is in blessing the conversation's inward parts, and concerning this blessing, it says, "I will pour my spirit upon thy seed, and my blessing upon thine offspring."[2010]

14. The outpouring of the living God's Spirit or Mind upon the conversation is the blessing decreed for the reformer, and this outpouring is explained in the saying, "I will pour out my spirit unto you, I will make known my words unto you."[2011] Without the outpouring of his words upon our mind, the correct form of righteousness cannot take place within our person, for "that which is born of the Spirit is spirit."[2012] The living God would halt religious foolishness by bringing the mind into complete fellowship with *his* wisdom, and this it would do by sealing to the conversation a certain law and a judgment.

15. Above flesh-based traditional laws and policies, it is our privilege to honor our Father in the beauty of holiness by learning of and doing his *name*. With his Prophet *born* under the rule of tradition, and with him killing that tradition by the Word entered in to his conversation and influencing the mind of its heart, by him suffering that tree, the *mind* enslaved by its religious conversation is become liberated, opening up the way for it to bring its conversation to its Creator. The revelation of this man upon the tree witnesses to the fact that the Word is become that God of the conversation, for with every handwritten religious ethic silenced through the tree, the only means left to know the Father

---

2007 Romans 12:2
2008 Titus 3:4
2009 Romans 8:11
2010 Isaiah 44:3
2011 Proverbs 1:23
2012 John 3:6

by is through the mind, which is why it says, "Live according to God in the spirit,"[2013] and, "I serve with my spirit in the gospel of his Son."[2014]

16. Our conversation is therefore erroneous when placing confidence in idols, in ceremonies, in guides, in "days, and months, and times, and years"[2015] "after the commandments and doctrines of men."[2016] Right worship is today in service to "holiness," which "holiness" is the living God's benevolence, which kindness, seeing as how "that which is born of the Spirit is spirit,"[2017] occurs only within the spirit of the mind. This is why it says, "God is a Spirit: and they that worship him must worship him in spirit and in truth."[2018]

17. The living God's chief apostle appeared under the law of a *woman* professing service to the *LORD*, and it is well to know that a "woman," to the Bible's mind, figuratively illustrates a church, as it says, "As the church is subject unto Christ, so let the wives be to their own husbands."[2019] In right language, this man's conversation was brought up in a church and bound to the religious tradition of that assembly, and this was done so that his course above the religious world should transfer to every conversation caring to rightly honor the Creator. Having a conversation under the law of a church and being found upon the tree, he represents the passing away of the conversation's mind from "bondage under the elements of the world."[2020] Every religious law of every professed church claiming service to the *Bible* is herein put in check by this man, who has truly "abolished in his flesh the enmity, even the law of commandments contained in ordinances; for to make in himself of twain one new man."[2021]

18. The entire point of this offering is to forward the creation of a new conversation by the *name* that was sacrificed. Because the Word existed within the members of his conversation, and because this man's mind, passing away in that conversation was revived by the living God in that very same *body* of faith, it is that every conversation after him, when rightly taking confidence on the new covenant's experience to subscribe to his *name*, will know a similar resurrection. Hereafter "if Christ be in you, the body is dead because of sin."[2022]

2013 1 Peter 4:6
2014 Romans 1:9
2015 Galatians 4:10
2016 Colossians 2:22
2017 John 3:6
2018 John 4:24
2019 Ephesians 5:24
2020 Galatians 4:3
2021 Ephesians 2:15
2022 Romans 8:10

19. By this man's sacrifice, the living God opened up a course of learning for our conversation to better honor salvation's science without committing any religious error. This man's example educates on the refreshing of the devotional mind from the religious world, for this man, in order to fulfill his ministry, had "Christ" within him. This man's faith, passing away with "Christ" within its conversation's conscience, was resurrected with a mind consecrated to a new office, for our Father blessed his conversation to "be a merciful and faithful high priest in things pertaining to God."[2023] Thus, having passed away from the religious world and finding itself before the living God, this conversation is ever alive.

20. As this man's conversation figuratively died through "Christ" to the religious world and revived to know the living God's *face*, so too our conversation is to be dead to the religious world by the same "Christ" existing within it, and since this existence is not natural or physical, it is written, "Though I be absent in the flesh, yet am I with you in the spirit."[2024] There is no other way, seeing as how "of his own will begat he us with the word of truth,"[2025] for "Christ" to dwell in *us* but by the spirit of our mind, placing us in good remembrance that "the Lord Jesus Christ our Saviour"[2026] is, because this creation is wholly mental and inward, "the commandment of God our Saviour."[2027] By bringing the Spirit's commandment into the spirit of our conversation, by examining and doing that will, "Christ," being a term representing salvation's commandment, so that our understanding may be refreshed to birth a new and right conversation, will exist within our thoughts to crucify the former *body* of our confidence. This is why the faithful pray, "Create in me a clean heart, O God; and renew a right spirit within me."[2028]

21. Like as this man's conversation was slain under a *woman* and under the law of a religious tradition, yet was raised up from that slumber to know only the living Father,[2029] so too our conversation is also ordained to pass through a course of learning to own a conversation wholly consecrated to the wisdom at the core of the Bible. This man, by his conversation, represents the perverse renderings of the *LORD's voice* by priesthoods, wherefore being slain, he

---

2023 Hebrews 2:17
2024 Colossians 2:5
2025 James 1:18
2026 Titus 1:4
2027 Titus 1:3
2028 Psalm 51:10
2029 Micah 5:4

represents the fact that such confidence is permanently removed out of the way of the living God's manner of kindness, even as it says, "The LORD hath rejected thy confidences, and thou shalt not prosper in them."[2030]

22. There was no wrath decreed by the *LORD* for lame traditional and ceremonial prescriptions anciently, but with this man's conversation become accursed, everything has changed. This man's conversation being connected to every other conversation professing devotion to the living God, with his conversation crucified, under the rule of religious law, and being accursed, every conversation maintaining any religious law is just as accursed as that one on the tree. We have to remember that within this man's *body* of belief dwelt both the right and the wrong form of devotion. Him on the tree represents a delusional religion forwarded by a contrary religious impulse and appetite, and by his placement, a plain rebuke from the living God against such a flesh-based conversation is uttered.

23. But there is hope. Although this man carried a wrong conversation, and that this *body* of faith became accursed when found on the tree, within the members of that same conversation dwelt "Christ." What is here represented by the illustration of the crucifixion is the passing away of a wrong body of devotion and the resurrection of a right body of devotion. This is why it says, "If the Spirit of him that raised up Jesus from the dead dwell in you, he that raised up Christ from the dead shall also quicken your mortal bodies by his Spirit that dwelleth in you."[2031]

24. This is truly a great philosophical mystery, how that one may pass away by a mind injurious against self and the Wisdom of creation to own a more benevolent conversation towards self and the Wisdom of creation, and this creation being without any hands. This man's conversation, although a symbol of religious error, being resurrected from *death*, and in that same conversation becoming *alive* for the second time, has set forth the example of our resurrection in heart and in mind from a lame religious conversation to the living God's intended manner of worship and service.[2032] This Prophet, although possessing an accursed conversation, had his conversation raised up to revere the living God's *name*, having none of his former conversation's errors remembered or held against it. And this is an example for us. There is, by this man's philosophy,

2030 Jeremiah 2:37
2031 Romans 8:11
2032 Romans 6:10

patience and forgiveness with the living God towards our conversation, to the end we may, like him, freely capture creation's present will.

25. The fact that his conversation passed away in error, but was brought up to only know and regulate righteousness, reveals the express desire of our Father. Through this act is preached the perpetual pardon of offenses against the *name* and throne of the living God by the renewal of our devotional mind, which is another promise of the new covenant, which states, "I will forgive their iniquity, and I will remember their sin no more."[2033] We should not expect this man, bearing devotional illness and passing away while under the law of religious tradition, to receive the office of *Aaron's sons* while on earth, but this man's faith died to religious error and was raised up with a new mind of devotion. This was accomplished so that we may know when once we sincerely and soberly embrace what the sacrifice represents, we may freely enter into the Bible's course of learning to obtain the promised newness for our promised employment.

26. Our willingly passing away from the religious world by salvation's higher education means that our devotional past no longer exists, and that what remains is our own forgetting of what was before. We are pardoned to advance in the living God's Wisdom when once we honestly accept that the experience of the new covenant is for bringing that instruction into our person; such a mind evinces that we, like our example, are dead to former spiritual appetites and passions to "live according to God in the spirit."[2034] Truly, then, "you, being dead in your sins and the uncircumcision of your flesh, hath he quickened together with him, having forgiven you all trespasses."[2035]

27. This act of quickening our conversation together with his revived conversation finds itself rightly honored when we actually take advantage of what this quickening is for. Because, if this quickening does not benefit me, in what do I celebrate? The living God has performed a great mystery where I, by the act of this man, may have my former ignorance against his *name* ignored and amended. Why has this happened? Is it to idolatrously celebrate *one* on a tree? If it is, and if all things on a tree are accursed, then by my empty celebration of that *man* on the tree, I too am become accursed. Must I not, then, care to investigate just what I am quickened in to, and where I am quickened to, and how I am freely connected to his victory?

2033 Jeremiah 31:34
2034 1 Peter 4:6
2035 Colossians 2:13

28. This man has opened up to us creation's course of learning so that we may know the same victory over self and over the religious world. The personal victory of this man is the personal victory of no one, but is simply a pledge encouraging the individual to pick up that discipline and its victory through his conversation's *name*. If his victory were personally our achievement, it would not say, "Be renewed in the spirit of your mind,"[2036] and, "Put on the new man."[2037] There is a work and training for every individual mind to pass through, all that is missing is our involvement with "the power of his resurrection, and the fellowship of his sufferings, being made conformable unto his death."[2038]

29. It is our responsibility, being blessed with such an opportunity to intimately know the Bible's character, to hear and keep the counsel, "Acquaint now thyself with him, and be at peace: thereby good shall come unto thee. Receive, I pray thee, the law from his mouth, and lay up his words in thine heart."[2039]

30. The Bible's counsel is, so that we "might be filled with the knowledge of his will in all wisdom and spiritual understanding,"[2040] to acquaint self with, and to receive in to the spirit of the mind, the law of regeneration at the heart of the Bible. Herein "the prince of this world is judged,"[2041] for the serpent's routine, seeing as how we are "to be strengthened with might by his Spirit in the inner man,"[2042] is put to sleep by a mind supported by salvation's wisdom. This judgment entered into the conversation means the hope of *Adam's* curse being reversed. We then do well to familiarize self with the benefit of that Prophet's ministry, to the end "we should be holy and without blame before him in love."[2043]

2036 Ephesians 4:23
2037 Ephesians 4:24
2038 Philippians 3:10
2039 Job 22:21,22
2040 Colossians 1:9
2041 John 16:11
2042 Ephesians 3:16
2043 Ephesians 1:4

24

That Lifted Up

1. It says, "Moses lifted up the serpent in the wilderness."[2044] The serpent upon a pole become a great idol to the people of Israel, wherefore when Hezeki'ah came into office, "he removed the high places, and brake the images, and cut down the groves, and brake in pieces the brasen serpent that Moses had made: for unto those days the children of Israel did burn incense to it."[2045]

2. What took place of old was only a figurative illustration of our present day. The idolatry of the brass serpent upon a pole continues. This serpent being brass should send the mind to think on Nebuchadnez'zar's image; "this image's head was of fine gold, his breast and his arms of silver, his belly and his thighs of brass."[2046] The head of the image, it is taken to represent Babylon; its chest and arms, the kingdom of the Medes and the Persians; his belly and thighs, the Grecian kingdom founded by Alexander the Great. The serpent is brass for a

---

2044   John 3:14
2045   2 Kings 18:4
2046   Daniel 2:32

very specific reason, for it represents that Greek *savior*, even "the image which fell down from Jupiter."[2047]

3. Jupiter, while a Roman god, is derived from the Greek god Zeus. This Greek image illustrated by that brass serpent is a perverted version of Samson, of whom it says, "The Philis'tines took him, and put out his eyes, and brought him down to Ga'za, and bound him with fetters of brass."[2048] As that deliverer blessed of the *LORD's Spirit*, when we find Samson bound with brass chains, we are but witnessing, in the context of what is *brass*, the chains of Greek philosophical mythology restraining the brilliance of this *governor*. For this cause, it is well to understand that to observe a brass serpent upon a pole is to view a crucified Greco-Roman *Samson*.

4. Individuals claiming service to *the LORD* of the *Bible* have a habit of worshipping the image of this false deliverer. Hezeki'ah performed the work that the living God's Prophet should accomplish, for when he says, "As Moses lifted up the serpent in the wilderness, even so must the Son of man be lifted up,"[2049] it is that he is calling for a reform that will abolish the lame work of that serpent for the right work of the living God.

5. "The Son" must be lifted up, and this lifting is not literal, for then he must forever remain on the tree, and "he that is hanged is accursed of God."[2050] If all that we are doing is idolizing one accursed of *God* on a tree, then we are become as accursed as that one on the tree. This is why that Prophet points to the lifting up of "the Son," for this lifting up is entirely by "the eyes of your understanding being enlightened,"[2051] allowing us to understand that "the Son" is but a commandment or a saying to take knowledge of. This we may rightly conclude because before referencing Moses, he says, "No man hath ascended up to heaven, but he that came down from heaven, even the Son of man which is in heaven."[2052]

6. To lift up "the Son" is to magnify the *heaven* that it not only came down from but, according to what is written, presently resides in. "The Son" is a body of knowledge that does not ultimately exist on earth, but rather *above*. To lift up "the Son" is to celebrate a doctrine of heaven, and "heaven" is that Building

2047 Acts 19:35
2048 Judges 16:21
2049 John 3:14
2050 Deuteronomy 21:23
2051 Ephesians 1:18
2052 John 3:13

of salvation's ministry, as it says, "He hath looked down from the height of his sanctuary; from heaven did the LORD behold the earth."[2053]

7. It was Moses that first created and lifted up the serpent, but the time would come when the *LORD* should resurrect and bring up to his throne that *Son* of his *heavenly* Sanctuary. Flesh can only rise so far, for flesh is limited to what is under the heaven, yet the *Son* and *Spirit* of the scriptures transcends what is under heaven to own a residence above the *earth*, for "the heaven, even the heavens, are the LORD'S: but the earth hath he given to the children of men."[2054] "Heaven" is become "heavens" because the heavenly Sanctuary has two rooms.[2055] When the conversation of the living God's Prophet ascended,[2056] this same conversation was consecrated to be a priest over creative redemption.[2057] When we then hear that "the Son" must be lifted up, we are hearing about a law of redemption experienced only within the heavenly Sanctuary.[2058]

8. Herein we may discern the error in holding our understanding to what exists on *earth*, for if our conversation's mediator says, "I leave the world, and go to the Father,"[2059] allowing us to know that *he* is no longer within the religious world, what good can be found within the religious world? "The Son"; that is, "the knowledge of the Son of God";[2060] must find itself lifted up not before our literal eyes, but before the *eyes* of our spiritual comprehension. The living God's chief apostle, in his speech, is pleading for no vain idolatry of an accursed image; he afterwards explains right manners of worship by saying, "True worshippers shall worship the Father in spirit and in truth."[2061]

9. Worship is by the spirit of the mind. For this man to call us to honor the living God by that brass serpent upon the pole is to contradict his own speech, exposing it to be contrary to the scriptures.[2062] The call to lift up "the Son" is a call for every conversation to say, "I will meditate in thy precepts, and have respect unto thy ways."[2063] Because the living God "hath in these last days

---

2053   Psalm 102:19
2054   Psalm 115:16
2055   Hebrews 9:2-4
2056   Psalm 11:4
2057   Hebrews 7:25
2058   Hebrews 4:14
2059   John 16:28
2060   Ephesians 4:13
2061   John 4:23,24
2062   James 1:8
2063   Psalm 119:15

spoken unto us by his Son,"[2064] our assignment is to "hear the voice of the Son of God,"[2065] even "the voice of the words of the LORD,"[2066] which words are "the words of eternal life,"[2067] "the words of his holiness."[2068]

10. Thus, to lift up "the Son" takes on more than carnally relying on an accursed tree, for if the accursed *thing* should today benefit any one, "then is Christ not risen: and if Christ be not risen, then is our preaching vain, and your faith is also vain."[2069] Our faith is become vain because by unlawfully coveting what is accursed, we are become accursed by it, expressing our fondness for what in reality does not exist, fulfilling within ourselves the rebuke, "And for this cause God shall send them strong delusion, that they should believe a lie: that they all might be damned who believed not the truth, but had pleasure in unrighteousness."[2070]

11. The present brass Greek *Samson* upon a tree is but an image of unrighteousness expressing unbelief in the Bible's fact. Seeing as how it says, "Thy word is truth,"[2071] and, "Thy law is the truth,"[2072] to believe on Bible fact is to exercise and experiment with faith in "the law of truth,"[2073] and "because the Spirit is truth,"[2074] "the law of the Spirit of life"[2075] is become the diet of the living reformer. Because "that which is born of the Spirit is spirit,"[2076] belief can only commence within the spirit of the mind, allowing us to understand why it was promised, "By his knowledge shall my righteous servant justify many,"[2077] and why it says, "Ye are clean through the word which I have spoken."[2078] Knowledge, because it is not firstly physical, firstly cleanses the mind, wherefore the baptism of "the Son's" *voice* is "with the washing of water by the word."[2079]

2064 Hebrews 1:2
2065 John 5:25
2066 1 Samuel 15:1
2067 John 6:68
2068 Jeremiah 23:9
2069 1 Corinthians 15:13,14
2070 2 Thessalonians 2:11,12
2071 John 17:17
2072 Psalm 119:142
2073 Malachi 2:6
2074 1 John 5:6
2075 Romans 8:2
2076 John 3:6
2077 Isaiah 53:11
2078 John 15:3
2079 Ephesians 5:26

12. Right service to *heaven's* ministry is herein a more perfect manner than that of ancient and even modern *Israel*. There is no hint of the living God's Prophet advocating the worship of any *thing* connected to any image of one on a tree. Being one who prayed, "Create in me a clean heart, O God; and renew a right spirit within me,"[2080] he fully understands that every mind doing *creation's* present commandment will pray, "Whom have I in heaven but thee? and there is none upon earth that I desire beside thee."[2081]

13. Right devotion to the *voice* of *heaven's* "Son" will move the mind to confess, "When I saw him, I fell at his feet as dead,"[2082] for "if Christ be in you, the body is dead,"[2083] that is, "the body of the sins of the flesh."[2084] The entire point of the doctrine of the Father's "Son" come in to our conversation is for the crucifixion of a lame and deceiving religion. Such a religion must pass away because we are to observe the vision of our high priest before the living God. As he confessed a passing away of his conversation from the religious world into the Creator's *heavenly* Temple, so too the mind, "rightly dividing the word of truth,"[2085] receives the opportunity to bring its faith "above, where Christ sitteth on the right hand of God."[2086] A right reception of this man upon the tree is one where the conscience understands that its present manner of worship and service is false, and that it is time for it to enter into that *heavenly* Building to receive the promised consolation.

14. No other illustration is drawn by this man upon a tree than that of a necessary passing away from one religious conversation in to a more mindful manner of devotion to receive the Creator's will. To stay upon the image of one upon a tree is herein understood to be a practice of spiritual death, "for he that is hanged is accursed of God."[2087] There is only *wrath* by what is accursed of *God*, for of old, when it said, "There is an accursed thing in the midst of thee,"[2088] after they found that *thing*, and the family that hid it, "all Israel stoned him with stones, and burned them with fire, after they had stoned them with stones."[2089] "He that is taken with the accursed thing shall be burnt with fire, he

---

2080 Psalm 51:10
2081 Psalm 73:25
2082 Revelation 1:17
2083 Romans 8:10
2084 Colossians 2:11
2085 2 Timothy 2:15
2086 Colossians 3:1
2087 Deuteronomy 21:23
2088 Joshua 7:13
2089 Joshua 7:25

and all that he hath,"[2090] and, today, concerning the willingly negligent conversation, it is well to know that the same fate, yet upon our mind, will occur.[2091]

15. Our mind must take in personal knowledge of the living God's will through the intercession of that Prophet's conversation, or by learning of and proving the higher education that he experienced with the scriptures. If there is no labor to spiritually discern the *name* of "the Son," and we are found lazily prostrated before an accursed tree and its image, it is well to know that, because our actions evince a mind contrary to what is within the scriptures, our heart and mind must find their members filled with a degenerative wrath. This is why, because it is contrary to our human and devotional growth and development, that such confusion is forwarded by *heaven's* counterfeit ministry.

16. This manner of worship is not of the living God's devotional character. Seeing as how "the Spirit searcheth all things, yea, the deep things of God,"[2092] the living God is openly against a lame image-driven religion. The living God's righteousness is creative redemption within the conversation's inward parts, which is why his man, when hoping to refresh the mind of elders, said, "Did not he that made that which is without make that which is within also?"[2093]

17. What is within the person is, to the Bible, of the greatest concern, which is why we are "to be strengthened with might by his Spirit in the inner man";[2094] this is why the faithful pray, "Thou desirest truth in the inward parts: and in the hidden part thou shalt make me to know wisdom."[2095] In order to know the righteousness of the Bible, the wisdom of the Bible must find itself within the mind, which is why our example said, "I know him, and keep his saying."[2096]

18. The mind, because "that which is born of the Spirit is spirit,"[2097] must keep salvation's saying if its praise should be experienced. This allows us to understand that the redemption promised is for our understanding on *heavenly* things, and that the deliverance promised is for our exodus from the religious world to the living God's *heavenly* Sanctuary. This is why the mind is the main subject of salvation, and why "through knowledge shall the just be delivered."[2098]

2090   Joshua 7:15
2091   Romans 1:28,29
2092   1 Corinthians 2:10
2093   Luke 11:40
2094   Ephesians 3:16
2095   Psalm 51:6
2096   John 8:55
2097   John 3:6
2098   Proverbs 11:9

19. The conversation negligent towards *heaven's* righteousness is refusing to bring the knowledge of the living God's chief apostle into its mind. The negligent conversation will not personally examine the Bible for knowledge of how to cooperate with creation's science. Without agitating the heart and soul by the wisdom retained, and without disturbing its conscience by the wisdom obtained, our conversation fails of fulfilling prerequisite obligations to know "the kindness and love of God our Saviour toward man."[2099] This kindness is the Creator's right benevolence to our faith's growth and development."[2100]

20. The key to unlocking this praise is in allowing the living God's words to rest within our mind, and because "that which is born of the Spirit is spirit,"[2101] only the spirit of the mind is desired for creation's science. The character of the living God's mind appears within our conversation's mind by no odd mystery, for it says, "I am full of power by the spirit of the LORD, and of judgment, and of might,"[2102] and, "I have filled him with the spirit of God, in wisdom, and in understanding, and in knowledge."[2103] The living God's *Spirit* dwells within our mind by knowledge and understanding, and if this same *Spirit* refreshed the living God's Prophet, then our conversation, by the knowledge of this same *Spirit's* operation resting within our inward parts, "shall be also in the likeness of his resurrection."[2104]

21. There is a call to inwardly exist by the example of how this man's conversation resurrected and not to vainly idolize an illustration hiding the Creator's wisdom. Because like as this resurrection has a spiritual definition, so also the death of the man owns a vision to be understood, "for if we have been planted together in the likeness of his death, we shall be also in the likeness of his resurrection."[2105]

22. The likeness of his resurrection is one born of the living God's mind to wholeheartedly serve the living God through the mind, wherefore the likeness of his death is a conversation passed away from the mind and lore of the religious world, and from its illogical and unsanctified understanding. This man upon the tree, his body representing the flesh-based tradition of righteousness by the religious law, is a symbol of an accursed religious tradition. Passing away

---

2099 Titus 3:4
2100 Romans 8:11
2101 John 3:6
2102 Micah 3:8
2103 Exodus 31:3
2104 Romans 6:5
2105 Romans 6:5

in such a body on the tree, he represents the passing away of the conversation's religious constitution from the religious world: now the handwritten religious tradition is become an accursed thing.

23. To literally stay on this image of one upon the tree is to, in reality, keep the conversation on what is accursed. Him on the tree represents what is accursed of *God*; conversations in service to this image of sin and religious error are against the living God and are also become as accursed as the image. This is why it says, "To whom ye yield yourselves servants to obey, his servants ye are to whom ye obey; whether of sin unto death, or of obedience unto righteousness."[2106]

24. Right obedience is in embracing the revelation of the death and resurrection of the man's devotional conversation. "Death" is in quitting creation's course to covet a supposed image of *salvation*, refusing to spend brainpower for the development of faith, which only adds wrath to the understanding. By him on that tree, we are made to understand how negligent a carnal religious routine is now become, and how such a routine is abolished from the living God's devotional character, which is why we are counseled, "Live according to God in the spirit."[2107]

25. Our conversation is to be, according to the Bible, in devotion to the living God's Word or Wisdom by the mind. This wisdom blatantly speaks against any practice that does not firstly involve, for examining self and the conversation's conscience, thoroughly bringing in to the mind the sayings of the scriptures. If to the Bible we are to uphold our conversation, how then can we do so when wisdom is not physical? *Peter* speaks of a higher learning for *heaven's* student-patient, for if we are planted after the likeness of the death this man's conversation suffered, we will operate our conversation after the likeness of his resurrected mind. This resurrected mind of his has no trace of the religious world within it.[2108] This man on the tree symbolizes the religious *death* supported by the Bible. Passing away from the death of religious tradition and being raised to salvation's science is an illustration of our present work, that we too are to quit the slumber of the religious world to only know the Bible's Wisdom.

26. If our conversation has been established after the manner of his death, it is true that we will dawn the likeness of his newness. This man is then set forth

---

2106 Romans 6:16
2107 1 Peter 4:6
2108 Romans 6:10

as an example of our Father's will. When found on the tree, his body represents what is accursed, even like as it says, "Christ hath redeemed us from the curse of the law."[2109] But within that body dwelt another more important *body*. Hanging upon the tree, and owning within the members of his conversation "the law of the Spirit of life,"[2110] this man symbolizes, in one body, the passing away of one manner of religious devotion and the regeneration of a new mind of devotion created after the living God's character.

27. The death of his body figuratively illustrates the conversation joining into *heaven's* promised newness to quit former religious habits to perfectly reverence the living God, which is why every doer of *heaven's* will says, "The law of the Spirit of life in Christ Jesus hath made me free from the law of sin and death."[2111] "Knowing that Christ being raised from the dead dieth no more; death hath no more dominion over him";[2112] with "death" being religious manners "after the commandments and doctrines of men,"[2113] it is that we too, by rightly taking hold of this illustration, are become numb to every *thing* but the Bible's philosophy, having our mind no longer in "bondage under the elements of the world."[2114] Thus, by this man, we have the opportunity to lift up "the Son" before the *eyes* of our understanding to know the Creator's great kindness towards our inward person.

28. It is therefore crucial to the development of our faith and to the training of our conversation that we find our mind in *heaven's* Sanctuary, "for our conversation is in heaven; from whence also we look for the Saviour."[2115] We cannot trust any image that is on *earth*, for the conversation of that Prophet forwarding this kind ministry is not on earth. This man's saved conversation is become that primary minister of the Creator's *heavenly* Building, which is why that Building's assembly sings, "Blessed be the God and Father of our Lord Jesus Christ, who hath blessed us with all spiritual blessings in heavenly places in Christ."[2116]

29. What is accursed of *God* does not forward creation's science. Creation's science is not accomplished or executed by that accursed figure on the tree.

2109 Galatians 3:13
2110 Romans 8:2
2111 Romans 8:2
2112 Romans 6:9
2113 Colossians 2:22
2114 Galatians 4:3
2115 Philippians 3:20
2116 Ephesians 1:3

The Father, concerning that risen conversation, began salvation's will "when he raised him from the dead, and set him at his own right hand in the heavenly places."[2117] We cannot believe any thing appears by that figure on the tree because it is without that anointing credential to pick up creation's new office. Creation's age began in name when he said, "It is finished,"[2118] yet in reality it began when his wisdom ascended "into heaven itself, now to appear in the presence of God for us."[2119]

30. If all we have is the image of *one* accursed of *God* before our *eyes*, we are become a most sorry and miserable people. But our Creator thought well of us, for by figuratively bringing up that Prophet's conversation and anointing it as that Son, our conversation has an assembly to become a member of and a right course of learning to fulfill. Our personal devotional conversation should consistently find itself in creation's *Building*, and we receive perpetual entrance into this Sanctuary by mentally discerning the *voice* of that anointed conversation. This is why we are counseled, "Be renewed in the spirit of your mind."[2120]

31. If it is that we have not "escaped the pollutions of the world through the knowledge of the Lord and Saviour Jesus Christ,"[2121] it is that we are members of that *church* honoring a brass *Savior* upon a pole, whose "superscription also was written over him in letters of Greek, and Latin, and Hebrew, THIS IS THE KING OF THE JEWS."[2122] Herein we are made to understand the present religious error against the living God's will and wisdom, for with that will and wisdom no longer within the religious world, but ascended to its Creator, all *things* on *earth* are left to a contrary wisdom.

32. The Present *Israel*, like ancient Israel, has an addiction to that brass serpent upon a pole. With that Prophet dead and no longer found on a tree, his conversation figuratively brought into the direct presence of the living God, rampant heresy exists within the religious world. He is passed away from the tree, but when we observe voices weeping for that figure put to death on a tree, and by that crucified figure creating commandments and traditions to adhere to, which ordinances plainly stand in conflict with salvation's science, we may understand that, because what is on *earth* is under the *serpent's* persuasion,

---

2117　Ephesians 1:20
2118　John 19:30
2119　Hebrews 9:24
2120　Ephesians 4:23
2121　2 Peter 2:20
2122　Luke 23:38

within this religious world "Satan himself is transformed into an angel of light."[2123] Just as *he* formerly coerced *Adam*, and just as ancient Israel burned incense to that brass serpent upon a pole, so today the *serpent's* deception is in service to *one* upon a tree and believed to offer *salvation*, when in reality this "image which fell down from Jupiter"[2124] preaches a lie of *good* and *evil*.

2123 2 Corinthians 11:14
2124 Acts 19:35

25

A Right Revelation

1. The living God's chief apostle did not sacrifice himself with the intention that we would mindlessly venerate him for that sacrifice, but rather to highlight a promise whereby we may transcend devotional vanity. This man did not endure the ordeal of the tree, or the cross, for us to persist in a devotional experience lacking spiritual renewal and inward integrity. Instead, he willingly embraced such suffering to enable us to engage in an experience transformed by the influence of his mind. The Bible's narration of his sacrifice is no intimation of any coarse or carnal form of worship.[2125]

2. And truly, if "Christ hath redeemed us from the curse of the law, being made a curse for us,"[2126] then any charge forwarding any traditional law is not of the living God. The Bible blatantly advises us that the illustration of this man on that tree is made to represent the redeeming of our mind from the handwritten religious ethics, and concerning the definition of "redemption," it says, "Concerning redeeming and concerning changing."[2127] To be "redeemed"

2125 Jeremiah 32:35
2126 Galatians 3:13
2127 Ruth 4:7

from flesh-based religious rule is to be "changed" from the law of flesh-based religious rule, and we "are changed into the same image from glory to glory, even as by the Spirit of the Lord."[2128] Now, if "that which is born of the Spirit is spirit,"[2129] then it is evident that our "changing" is to occur within the spirit of our mind. For this cause, it is impossible to render such a "change" to be by physical or temporal *things*, "for a spirit hath not flesh and bones."[2130]

3. The living God's Prophet upon that tree represents our faith's liberty from the dominion of elders, which is why "flesh and blood cannot inherit the kingdom of God."[2131] Taking into account that the living God's Wisdom is God,[2132] the kingdom of God is, in reality, the reign of the living God's Wisdom within the spirit of the mind.[2133] This man's death teaches that every conversation under the rule of a religious tradition professing service to the Bible has the opportunity to obtain victory over that rule. His conversation, being bound to the code of a religious tradition, and also having within the members of that same conversation the dispensation of salvation's science, delineates the fact that the conversation has a remedy for its sickness, and that this remedy is for elevating our faith's spirit into *heaven's* Sanctuary.[2134]

4. It is the living God's righteousness, so that all praise may flow to the living God's Wisdom through the conversation of his chief apostle, to circumcise the conversation's heart. This liberty we obtain through the *name* of his Prophet by learning of and doing "the law of the Spirit of life."[2135] Should we patiently and temperately examine this judgment for creation, we will obtain the promised deliverance of our mind to not only experience "the kindness and love of God our Saviour,"[2136] but to also "love one another, as he gave us commandment."[2137]

5. It is known that "the letter killeth, but the spirit giveth life,"[2138] wherefore the living God so despised the bondage placed upon the mind by religious law that "when the fulness of the time was come, God sent forth his Son, made of a

---

2128 2 Corinthians 3:18
2129 John 3:6
2130 Luke 24:39
2131 1 Corinthians 15:50
2132 John 1:1
2133 John 4:24
2134 Romans 2:29
2135 Romans 8:2
2136 Titus 3:4
2137 1 John 3:23
2138 2 Corinthians 3:6

woman, made under the law, to redeem them that were under the law."[2139] As we observe this man upon the tree, it is that our mind should discern the opportunity to embrace a change of conversation, for through him is pronounced "the time of reformation."[2140] Thus, when we take into account the established tradition of ministers professedly in service to the *Bible*, and the openly contrary commandments and doctrines of these elders, as we soberly digest the revelation of this man's devotional character, we will enter into a higher sphere of communion with the Bible's words.[2141] The changing or the redeeming of our mind, by the impression of this man upon the tree, should allow us to discern his *name* as "a merciful and faithful high priest in things pertaining to God,"[2142] and that this *name* magnifies the Bible's core philosophy. Truly, then, by such a vision, we are purged from that demeanor within the religious world.

6. The excellent knowledge behind this man upon that tree is the work and effect of righteousness within the conversation's inward parts, to resurrect it into *heaven's* Building. In this Place, every conversation sings, "Thou wast slain, and hast redeemed us to God by thy blood out of every kindred, and tongue, and people, and nation."[2143]

7. When redeeming any thing, that redeemed thing finds itself translated in to another form. The only thing the Bible primarily decrees redemption over is the devotional character, for it says, "He shall redeem their soul from deceit and violence,"[2144] and, "That which is born of the Spirit is spirit."[2145] This violence and deceit, it is not physical or natural, therefore redemption from it cannot be physical or natural, which is why this manner of deliverance occurs within the mind, and why we are counseled, "Be renewed in the spirit of your mind."[2146] The violence and deceit to be delivered or ransomed from is religious error, and the only way for this to commence is by the mind personally exercising its organs on salvation's commandment. By doing so, the heart may know just what its will is, for by mentally handling the Bible's *voice*, the impression of that *voice* has the opportunity to react upon the mind.[2147]

2139 Galatians 4:4,5
2140 Hebrews 9:10
2141 Hebrews 12:22,23
2142 Hebrews 2:17
2143 Revelation 5:9
2144 Psalm 72:14
2145 John 3:6
2146 Ephesians 4:23
2147 1 John 2:17

8. The "letter," or the handwritten religious bill, kills the mind; the law of a religious tradition poisons faith; this is why "Christ hath redeemed us from the curse of the law, being made a curse for us."[2148] If we truly take this man to be any thing to us, we would understand "clean" from "unclean." This man's sacrifice has rendered it an eternal fact that no religious tradition supposedly in favor or in devotion to the living God is legitimate, but is rather an invention of them that "serve not our Lord Jesus Christ, but their own belly; and by good words and fair speeches deceive the hearts of the simple."[2149] Herein it is well to remember that we are told "Christ" redeems from such a perverse endeavor, making it also well to remember that "the Lord Jesus Christ our Saviour,"[2150] because this redemption is not physical, but rather mental and inward, is "the commandment of God our Saviour."[2151]

9. The sacrifice of this man did not purge any conversation or mind of any violence against its self or the living God; it simply teaches redemption's course to every mind and conversation. Redemption, then, or the expected changing, must appear by "Christ," and from how the Bible uses the term "Christ," it is evident that it is in no way referencing a man or an individual.[2152] "Christ" is, in all actuality, an appellation or term used to denote the living God's commandment for creation, wherefore our changing or redeeming from the religious world and to the living God's mind occurs by a specific commandment, philosophy, or saying. If theologians upheld *heaven's* will, a contrary wisdom to that doctrine witnessed by that man upon a tree would halt.

10. The mind that executes "Christ" and does "Jesus Christ" will understand why the Word is that God and Savior of the conversation, for even the living God's Prophet said, "I know him, and keep his saying."[2153] With the saying of the Word become the Governor and Physician of the heart and mind, redemption is inevitable, for then the conscience sings, "Thou shalt guide me with thy counsel, and afterward receive me to glory. Whom have I in heaven but thee? and there is none upon earth that I desire beside thee."[2154] The right manner of worship and service to the Creator is thus witnessed to be by the Word, that is,

---

2148 Galatians 3:13
2149 Romans 16:18
2150 Titus 1:4
2151 Titus 1:3
2152 2 Corinthians 5:16
2153 John 8:55
2154 Psalm 73:24,25

by the wisdom of the new covenant's instruction concerning devotional newness and reform.

11. No counsel or judgment is physical or tangible, but is rather discerned by the faculties associated with the mind, which is why our right baptism is "with the washing of water by the word."[2155] Having our understanding refreshed, being soberly "filled with the knowledge of his will in all wisdom and spiritual understanding,"[2156] and learning how to carry self and the conversation without flesh-based "philosophy and vain deceit, after the tradition of men, after the rudiments of the world,"[2157] it is that the scriptures are become new to our perception. This is why it says, "If any man be in Christ, he is a new creature: old things are passed away; behold, all things are become new."[2158] Blessed revelation!

12. Herein is the fact of the matter, that the mind should experience a certain creation moving the heart in to a new and more benevolent experience with the Bible. The conversation executing "the Lord Jesus Christ our Saviour";[2159] that is, who is proving "the doctrine of God our Saviour";[2160] will experience the exchanging of one manner of thought and feeling for another that is seven times more beneficial. Creation is the end of "Jesus Christ," and that creation beginning within the conversation when once the mind examines salvation's saying, and when once the person accepts the liberty behind the illustration of that man upon the tree.

13. The doctrine of the Word entered in to the spirit of the mind is the living God's will and righteousness, and this, in order to handle the illness within our own heart and character, is ordained for our faith's resurrection from the sickness within self-cultivated and inherited religious tradition. Right and reverent worship towards the Creator of this benevolent privilege is not witnessed by idolatrously observing an accursed image, but by embracing the fact behind the vision of that man's suffering to prove the living God's will. That philosophy nailed to the tree is regarded as poisonous to the Bible, meaning that the Bible and this image have absolutely no thing in common. For the conversation delighting in what is separated for and devoted to the destruction of its character, the Bible says, "Ye have turned judgment into gall, and the fruit of

---

2155 Ephesians 5:26
2156 Colossians 1:9
2157 Colossians 2:8
2158 2 Corinthians 5:17
2159 Titus 1:4
2160 Titus 2:10

righteousness into hemlock."[2161] Truly, then, by the turning upside down of its voice, "the mystery of iniquity doth already work."[2162]

14. It is a mystery how that a philosophy to purify the conversation is become a poison to deaden the human being. The vision of the that Prophet on a tree is a revelation explaining a judgment to experiment with by faith, and yet this judgment of the Creator's praise is become trash by "the enemies of the cross of Christ: whose end is destruction, whose God is their belly, and whose glory is in their shame, who mind earthly things."[2163] We may know how these ministers are understood to be enemies, for our it says, "Those mine enemies, which would not that I should reign over them."[2164]

15. The reign of this man is not physical, which is why it says, "Be ye transformed by the renewing of your mind."[2165] *His* reign is by the impression of his *name's* knowledge upon the spirit of the mind; this is why it says, "By his knowledge shall my righteous servant justify many."[2166] It is a great mystery how that the vision of this man on a tree rightly represents deliverance from spiritual vanity, yet this vision is somehow made to represent a furthering of spiritual negligence. It is a mystery how that this man upon the tree illustrates the transformation of the mind to the philosophy within the heavenly Sanctuary, yet somehow this vision keeps the mind earthy and spiritually vain. Isn't it that "as we have borne the image of the earthy, we shall also bear the image of the heavenly"?[2167] If inwardly receiving what is *heavenly* is the point of this man suffering the tree, how then is it become the norm to remain *worldly* while professing *this man* on the tree?

16. A terrible tragedy has occurred against this man and against the Bible's philosophy. This injustice is hidden by that *mind* deceiving the religious world. We are wrong; because "Christ hath redeemed us from the curse of the law, being made a curse for us";[2168] for maintaining the philosophy that tree has accursed. Right and sober reverence towards the illustration put forth by the Bible concerning this man's crucifixion is found in the saying, "The law of the

---

2161 Amos 6:12
2162 2 Thessalonians 2:7
2163 Philippians 3:18,19
2164 Luke 19:27
2165 Romans 12:2
2166 Isaiah 53:11
2167 1 Corinthians 15:49
2168 Galatians 3:13

Spirit of life in Christ Jesus hath made me free from the law of sin and death,"[2169] therefore "having begun in the Spirit, are ye now made perfect by the flesh?"[2170]

17. What begins in the Spirit only ends in and is finished by the Spirit, which is why it says, "That which is born of the Spirit is spirit."[2171] If it is that we believe it is right to adhere to the conscience of theologians to finish what is wholly internal and mental, and if we do hold this belief by the notion that *God's Christ* has authorized this form of devotion, we evince our understanding to be sensual and erroneous. The Bible plainly says, "Christ hath redeemed us from the curse of the law, being made a curse for us: for it is written, Cursed is every one that hangeth on a tree."[2172]

18. The fact that this man found himself upon a tree reveals that every one professing thanksgiving by his act is a mind "forgetting those things which are behind, and reaching forth unto those things which are before."[2173] What is left behind are useless practices by former and present handwritten religious tradition in service to a flesh-based stimulus. "But after that the kindness and love of God our Saviour toward man appeared, not by works of righteousness which we have done, but according to his mercy he saved us, by the washing of regeneration..."[2174]

19. Herein *Paul* explains just what this man's sacrifice renders poisonous, and it is deeds and works of *righteousness* accomplished by the devotional conversation's deceptive impulse, which is why we are counseled, "Put off concerning the former conversation the old man, which is corrupt according to the deceitful lusts; and be renewed in the spirit of your mind."[2175] If it is that our desire is for experiencing the Bible's righteousness, it is that the mind must embrace that washing by the Bible, even "the washing of water by the word."[2176] The mind must examine and do the principles it learns when proving the Bible's words, for then the understanding may find its body edified by experience.

20. The regeneration of the devotional mind is the Bible's concern, where-fore to say, by any idolatrous commandment, or by any law of any religious tradition, that regeneration of the mind is evidently accomplished by it, what

---

2169 Romans 8:2
2170 Galatians 3:3
2171 John 3:6
2172 Galatians 3:13
2173 Philippians 3:13
2174 Titus 3:4,5
2175 Ephesians 4:22,23
2176 Ephesians 5:26

then did this man suffer for? Why even waste time as "a man of sorrows, and acquainted with grief"?[2177] Truly "if righteousness come by the law, then Christ is dead in vain."[2178] To observe this man on that tree is to understand what "sin" is, and what "death" removes the mind from embracing *heaven's* right will, even like as it says, "The strength of sin is the law."[2179] A right observation of this man is to lead to a change in mind, that our conversation may "be dead with Christ from the rudiments of the world."[2180]

21. It is therefore well to soberly perceive this man upon that tree, to the end we may have the opportunity to discern "one like unto the Son of man, clothed with a garment down to the foot, and girt about the paps with a golden girdle."[2181] John caught vision of this revelation, and concerning his experience, he writes, "When I saw him, I fell at his feet as dead."[2182] This understanding is synonymous with what that man, and those that were around him did when observing the living God's chief apostle between heaven and earth.[2183]

22. The number one reaction that this vision of that Prophet upon the tree will provoke is the puncturing of the *breast*, or the wounding of the heart. Every conversation arriving at a right sight or vision of this man suffered damage within their self, and that scene is written to illustrate just what a right perception of this man's offering is to perform. This sight injures the heart because the conversation now understands its spiritual error against the Bible's devotional character.[2184] Herein the heart is dropped by a right observation, for "if Christ be in you, the body is dead."[2185]

23. The vision of that Prophet on the tree preaches the death and resurrection of a clearly irreverent conversation before the living God. If our celebration of this man is honest, it is that our vision of him on that tree will move us to embrace a death in similar fashion, that is, a complete separation from the philosophy within the religious world to experience a regeneration similar to his. Such regeneration is the renewing of the spirit of the mind to rightly honor the living God.

2177   Isaiah 53:3
2178   Galatians 2:21
2179   1 Corinthians 15:56
2180   Colossians 2:20
2181   Revelation 1:13
2182   Revelation 1:17
2183   Luke 23:47,48
2184   Psalm 38:17,18
2185   Romans 8:10

24. He willingly obliged to a death by the tree to witness for what should thereafter be understood as accursed.[2186] For this cause, if this offering was put forward with the intention of bringing conversations into personal knowledge of the living God, if by subscribing to what this offering categorizes as being accursed, are we made to advance in any understanding? The mind soberly experiencing this man's conversation is welcomed into *heaven's* Sanctuary to begin the intended redemption, wherefore we may understand that our handling of this man's conversation is improper when we are taking confidence on what this sacrifice has forever put away, namely, a devotion through what is handwritten. Herein we are made to understand the error behind the handwritten charge[2187]

25. Our conversation needs a better understanding of the redemption preached through the illustration of this man suffering the tree. The blatant idolatry presently framed around that brass serpent on the pole is an evident token that the living God is not in our mind. If the Bible were in our thoughts, a full and knowledgeable separation between clean and unclean manners of devotion would take place, but a great tragedy exists. Presently, all attention is given to an empty religious philosophy preaching *good* and *evil* by a *figure* upon the tree. It is as if we have no sense to think, "What fellowship hath righteousness with unrighteousness? and what communion hath light with darkness?"[2188]

26. If the living God, by this man's sacrifice, has not only decreed handwritten religious laws to be accursed, but has also decreed our purging from them to know his *name*, then who, clamming this man to be their salvation's captain, is right to celebrate the deadness of an abolished state of mind? By our celebration of what is abolished, we in fact expose our conversation to be nonexistent.[2189] We then prove, by how we handle our conversation, because the philosophy of the religious world is opposed to "rightly dividing the word of truth,"[2190] that we own the *world's* devotional character.

2186 1 John 5:20
2187 Jeremiah 14:14
2188 2 Corinthians 6:24
2189 Ephesians 2:12
2190 2 Timothy 2:15

26

Creation's Perpetual Remembrance

1. Due to the obvious evidence of creation from the saying, "Christ hath redeemed us from the curse of the law, being made a curse for us: for it is written, Cursed is every one that hangeth on a tree,"[2191] the philosophy of the living God's chief apostle is brilliantly highlighted by the seventh day's perpetual celebration of redemption's science. If this man, through the act of willingly offering himself to death for the living God's will for the conversation, encourages a manner of devotion apart from the routine of maintaining handwritten religious laws, then today, seeing as how this man's conversation became "the mediator of the new testament...for the redemption of the transgressions that were under the first testament,"[2192] there exists the same ten precepts of old for our conversation to presently know.

2. The redemption secured to us by this man is only from errors committed against the ten laws of the first covenant, wherefore we may understand that we subscribe to religious error when any one of our religious principles are in

---

2191 Galatians 3:13
2192 Hebrews 9:15

direct conflict with those ten counsels. We are purged from erroneous handwritten spiritual policies that we may have the opportunity to personally learn
of those commandments they fail to take knowledge of, which is why a plain
separation from the religious world is necessary if we should embrace *heaven's*
higher learning. The clearest error in violation of the redemption encouraged
by that Prophet is against the Bible's seventh-day, which *rest* commenced before
a Jew, a Hebrew, or a Christian took a breath. In the beginning, before any
other popular religious sect existed, "God blessed the seventh day, and sanctified it."[2193]

3. Have we not wondered why redemption is so important to the Bible?
Have we not wondered what kind of redemption is important to the scriptures?
Have we not thought about how the living God expects to carry out that manner
of redemption? If we begin the story with that Prophet on the tree, we have no
rational understanding as to why redemption is necessary; if we begin at him
on the tree, we fail to discern the type of savior we ought for to know. Our
journey must begin in Eden, where tragedy struck, and where the *serpent* originally wounded the *body* of the living God's knowledge.

4. *Eden's* host found themselves compromised because they failed to rightly
discern their Creator's doctrine. It was their responsibility, seeing as how "in
the beginning was the Word, and the Word was with God, and the Word was
God,"[2194] to examine their living God's operation by his Word, or by the instruction of his primary devotional philosophy. The living God set in motion a plan
to recover the *earth* from its error, to the end it may become a useful *realm*.
The living God pronounced *heaven* and *earth's* commandment, leaving their
creation to his doctrine. The inward parts of *heaven* and *earth* received the living
God's *voice*, and in so doing, all that was pronounced became as imagined.
Creation was not by hand, but by the vibration of a *voice* entering in to the
realm's elements. By investigating creation, thee *garden's* assembly was to learn
of their own inward deficiency, along with the training they must embrace in
order to know the consolation perpetually edifying *heaven* and *earth*.

5. Such a manner of learning was to also pronounce to their understanding
why "God blessed the seventh day, and sanctified it."[2195] With the Word, or
the living God's chief philosophy, being "God," and with the Word being that

2193 Genesis 2:3
2194 John 1:1
2195 Genesis 2:3

Creator, since "God is a Spirit,"[2196] it is the Word, or Spirit, or Wisdom of the living God that blessed the seventh day. Herein is witnessed a plain decree for the seventh day's appointment, for if this same Word of creation was found within the conversation of the living God's chief apostle, and if this same man found himself upon a tree and slain for every handwritten commandment put forth by religious tradition; and he was; then what is passed away is human religious tradition, but what remains is every commandment put forth by the mouth of the living God, and there is no dispute that "God blessed the seventh day, and sanctified it."[2197] Thus, we are made to comprehend the religious error advertised by priests utterly foreign to the fact that "Christ hath redeemed us from the curse of the law, being made a curse for us: for it is written, Cursed is every one that hangeth on a tree."[2198]

6. Seeing as how no religious law of the first day, or of any other period of time has ever proceeded out of the living God's mouth, any other primary appointment is religious error. What witnesses against this error, especially from them that would link this falsehood to that *one* on the tree, is the fact that this illustration of him on the tree condemns handwritten religious laws and ordinances. With this man on that tree as a symbol of the official passing away of handwritten religious standards from the Bible's philosophy, we are made to observe only the *garden's* precepts, along with a law of devotional resurrection, from the same *Word*.

7. There is no difference between the Word and the living God, for this Word is that same "Spirit of truth, which proceedeth from the Father."[2199] To hear, "God was in Christ,"[2200] is to hear, "The Word was in Christ." With the living God's Mind resting within this man's mind; for, "that which is born of the Spirit is spirit";[2201] this man sacrificed upon the tree means our newness of heart to the living God by the philosophy hiding within his devotional character. By this man's sacrificed conversation; because his crucified body symbolizes the fact that handwritten religious tradition is become "sin"; all things regarding creations Word or Counsel are for the conversation.

2196 John 4:24
2197 Genesis 2:3
2198 Galatians 3:13
2199 John 15:26
2200 2 Corinthians 5:19
2201 John 3:6

8. The same finger that figuratively engraved those stones is the same editor of our conversation's conscience.[2202] This *finger* is that same Word, for by the Word entered in to our conversation's conscience, we are to be "written not with ink, but with the Spirit of the living God; not in tables of stone, but in fleshy tables of the heart."[2203] Thus, if the scriptures confess that our conversation is to be written by the living God's wisdom, it is because this wisdom's chief apostle first experienced that newness, which is why his conversation "is the image of the invisible God, the firstborn of every creature."[2204] Now, every *creature* of the living God understands that "if any man be in Christ, he is a new creature,"[2205] for this Prophet also had to keep and do "Christ" in order to obtain the promised regeneration. This is why he says, "I know him, and keep his saying."[2206]

9. Like as how Adam's error passed upon all conversations, so too the sacrificed conversation of the living God's chief apostle ratifies the Word's right devotional manners for every conversation to know. On that tree, this man represents the end of a religious world bound by flesh-based prescriptions, for when we next see *him*, *he* is become "a great high priest, that is passed into the heavens,"[2207] and is become an illustration of the fact that every conversation has a course of learning prepared for it through his offered conversation. This man's wisdom, being sacrificed in an erroneous *body* of understanding, and with the Word yet resting within that *body*, preaches a division between the living God's wisdom and the *wisdom* within the religious world. This illustration preaches the blotting out the religious world's *wisdom* by one offering, to the end the *eyes* of our understanding would comprehend his conversation as creation's mediator.[2208]

10. There is no other point behind his sacrifice than to bring the mind in harmony with the Creator's devotional character, which character is understood through the Ten Commandments. The living God's new covenant is a promise to bind every conversation to his *name* by the law of his chief apostle's intercession, which law is "the law of the Spirit of life."[2209] By this law, the doer of it will find their conversation in opposition to the serpent's manners of worship and

---

2202   Exodus 31:18
2203   2 Corinthians 3:3
2204   Colossians 1:15
2205   2 Corinthians 5:17
2206   John 8:55
2207   Hebrews 4:14
2208   Hebrews 9:15
2209   Romans 8:2

service, for it is promised, "I will put enmity between thee and the woman."[2210] The living God's chief witness on the tree represents the fulfillment of that enmity, for by abolishing; through his crucified flesh; the *serpent's* legal religious routine, a new way commenced to rightly approach the living God.

11. Being able to presently enter into creation's present experience by learning of and experiencing this man's conversation,[2211] it is our assignment to draw nearer to the living God, to love our Father, "and this is love, that we walk after his commandments."[2212] *Man* originally sacrificed his mind to the *serpent's* devotional conversation, and by that *mind*, the *garden's* philosophy found its self destroyed by "Jewish fables, and commandments of men, that turn from the truth."[2213] But by the service of one minister, and by the brilliance of that experience impressed upon his mind, the offering of this mind is the means whereby the organs of conversations may be transformed to better honor the living God, self, and others.

12. The offering of his conversation was a necessary sacrifice, for with the Word within his conversation, and with that conversation sacrificed, a new and living way is established to obtain the promised redemptive creation, even like as it says, "Of his own will begat he us with the word of truth, that we should be a kind of firstfruits of his creatures."[2214] With his flesh-based conversation put to rest and that conversation edified by the living God's wisdom regenerated, through this man is preached what the living God would redeem, and why. This man, whose flesh symbolizes "the enmity, even the law of commandments contained in ordinances"[2215] for every age, by tasting death in that flesh, preaches the death of such handwritten procedures. But his conversation raised from that death and brought in to creation's *heavenly* Building informs us of the binding perpetuity of the Word's ten counsels by the philosophy of his conversation's *heavenly* ministry.

13. The commandment, then, most illuminated before our *eyes*, when correctly comprehending the illustration of him suffering the tree, is that of the fourth precept, which teaches us that "the seventh day is the Sabbath of the LORD."[2216] The conversation doing salvation's law understands its obligation to

---

2210 Genesis 3:15
2211 Hebrews 10:19-21
2212 2 John 1:6
2213 Titus 1:14
2214 James 1:18
2215 Ephesians 2:15
2216 Exodus 20:10

this commandment because they have experienced redemption by the *voice* of its Word or Wisdom. The same Word that, in the beginning, blessed the seventh day and regenerated *heaven* and *earth*, is the same Word that has blessed their inward parts, allowing them to pick up the statement, "The law of the Spirit of life in Christ Jesus hath made me free from the law of sin and death."[2217]

14. By experiencing the redemption of "the Lord Jesus Christ our Saviour";[2218] which is deliverance from the religious world by no *figure*, but by "the commandment of God our Saviour";[2219] the conversation is blessed to understand what Adam failed to discern about the Creator, even that "he is the living God, and stedfast for ever, and his kingdom that which shall not be destroyed, and his dominion shall be even unto the end."[2220] Every creation of the living God says, "We trust in the living God, who is the Saviour of all men,"[2221] for by their training with the Word, they understand that this Word is that Savior, and that because of their service to the Word, they are become servants to "the King eternal, immortal, invisible, the only wise God."[2222] The revelation of this man's conversation as salvation's high priest forwards this understanding, for by the philosophy of that conversation's mediation, they understand that it is its lot to "stand and feed in the strength of the LORD, in the majesty of the name of the LORD his God."[2223]

15. Thus, by one sacrifice, the living God's chief apostle has bound every conversation owning religious error with the opportunity to possess self for rightly demonstrating love to the Word and to the Creator, "and this is love, that we walk after his commandments."[2224] Thus, our evident love to Eden's Creator cannot be witnessed if not through willing obedience to his *voice*, for if Adam deviated by refusing to bring the living God's commandment in to his heart, then we too should understand a deviation from this same Creator by refusing to bring his wisdom's commandment of redemption in to our heart.

16. The philosophy of *heaven's* ministry is ordained to work within the inward person for their harmony with the living God's commandments; "this

---

2217 Romans 8:2
2218 Titus 1:4
2219 Titus 1:3
2220 Daniel 6:26
2221 1 Timothy 4:10
2222 1 Timothy 1:17
2223 Micah 5:4
2224 2 John 1:6

is the love of God, that we keep his commandments."[2225] The definition of the Father's manner of love is the keeping of *creation's* commandments, for his Prophet found himself upon a tree to make a statement for the need to philosophically abolish the philosophy of the religious law from those commandments. Creation's science; which is "the kindness and love of God our Saviour toward man";[2226] is established to purge the mind from the religious world to observe that resurrected conversation rendering service to the *garden's Mind*. Thus, if we are claiming this man's sacrifice as any thing to us, but are yet found subscribing to handwritten tenets, we may understand that we condone religious error; "we do know that we know him, if we keep his commandments."[2227]

17. Our witness to the fact that we know the living God is by our passage in to the "rest" of the seventh day. The reason why the knowledge of *his* Prophet should purge conversations from traditional religious laws is for their acquaintance with salvation's *name*. Without flesh-based standards and policies, without any religious *thing* falsely comforting the human being, without any *thing* directing the conversation, the person is left to operate only by the words within the Bible. By taking self in hand and quietly sitting with the Bible without an aid,[2228] a map of understanding is created within the mind, and by that map the person learns the living God. This map will, because "his understanding is infinite,"[2229] never stay underdeveloped.

18. Religious tradition limits devotional understanding, leaving faith to the human being, and what can the human being do for what is wholly mental and spiritual? A handwritten or scripted religion kills the person by limiting experience, wherefore it was necessary that that man, to expose this fact, willingly sacrifice himself to death.[2230] Hereafter no commandment should exist but that philosophy of the *garden's* Creator, and our comprehension of this fact through that garden's Word. Because this Prophet perfectly experienced the Word's righteousness, and because his conversation passed away and was resurrected with this correct wisdom within its character, the discipline of the Word is passed on to our conversation, along with the saying, "If thou wilt enter into life, keep the commandments."[2231]

2225 1 John 5:3
2226 Titus 3:4
2227 1 John 2:3
2228 Psalm 1:2
2229 Psalm 146:5
2230 Galatians 3:13
2231 Matthew 19:17

19. Now, entrance in to "life" is entrance in to "that eternal life, which was with the Father,"[2232] and "the Spirit is life."[2233] The "life" that we are to enter in to is the conversation of "the Word of life,"[2234] which entrance we cannot receive if failing to do "the law of the Spirit of life,"[2235] which is "the law of truth."[2236] The entire purpose of the Spirit's law; which "law" is the Father's manner of love; is for us to keep and love the living God's commandments.[2237] Thus, when hearing that the Word was made flesh, it is that we are hearing that the love of the Word continued in and was demonstrated by the members of a conversation, allowing us to discern every other contrary government working within the conversation.

20. The living God's Spirit or Wisdom come in to the spirit or mind is the righteousness of the Word working through the members of the conversation, which labor is according to the saying, "Let every one of us please his neighbour for his good to edification."[2238] The religious world is not of this mindful labor. Instead of edifying the mind, the priests of the religious world "speak great swelling words of vanity, they allure through the lusts of the flesh, through much wantonness."[2239] Thus, because the natural estate of *man*; as evinced by the *garden's* pair; is in abusing self and others through spiritual lies, the Word conforming the conversation's mind to that of its chief apostle is herein understood to be a very great and wonderful mystery.

21. The mind of the religious world is not that of the living God's Spirit, but it is the righteousness of his Spirit to transform the mind bound to the spirit of the religious world to know a more benevolent form of devotion. By the sacrifice of one conversation, all conversations are made to own a mind preferring self's persuasion and the *serpent's* religious craft above the living God's *voice*, but by the offering of another conversation, all conversations are given the opportunity to claim redemption from the *serpent's* routine to possess self. The creation of a new mind within a dead conversation is the illustration taught by this man who was put to sleep with an accursed conversation, yet whose inward conversation was brought up by the living God's Wisdom.

2232 1 John 1:2
2233 Romans 8:10
2234 1 John 1:1
2235 Romans 8:2
2236 Malachi 2:6
2237 1 John 2:4,5; 1 John 5:3
2238 Romans 15:2
2239 2 Peter 2:18

22. Such a great will and intention deserves a celebration, and this man, having proven the abolishment of every spurious charge and ordinance written by hand, has left the faithful hearer and doer of *heaven's* will in vision of creation's seventh-day remembrance, praying, "The desire of our soul is to thy name, and to the remembrance of thee."[2240] Herein it is well to know how it is written, "In death there is no remembrance of thee,"[2241] wherefore we may know that we are in fact members of *death's institution* when lacking, or when finding our self in conflict with that blessed appointment of the Word's seventh day. This man has established our course of learning to find self purged from what is handwritten. By this sacrifice, there exists no other commandments supposedly in devotion to the Creator, "and hereby we do know that we know him, if we keep his commandments."[2242]

23. Seeing, then, how that the former religious world is come to an end by one offering, and that "the prince of this world is judged,"[2243] we can understand why the *living God* waited until "the end of the Sabbath, as it began to dawn toward the first day of the week,"[2244] to move. Herein is witnessed a blatant division between the first day of the week and the seventh day. If the living God was moved to act on the second day, we may have liberty to do away with *his* Sabbath. And if his Prophet revived on the first day, we may then have a license to quit the seventh day. But since he brought up his conversation on the third day,[2245] keeping himself and this man silent during the seventh day, the Bible has forever linked its seventh-day "rest" to the living God's *heavenly* ministry.

24. The living God's chief apostle, because he was dead, could not resurrect his conversation from the grave, and especially during the hours of the seventh day. If, by dying for the separation of the commandments of the living God from the *serpent's* religious tradition, he were seen rising up during that precept pronouncing the living God's *name*, then this man would be a liar. But, having cancelled and overthrown every lame handwritten charge by the passing of his flesh, all that remains is what is without and above flesh, for by his conversation's stillness on the seventh day, the saying is fulfilled, "All thy commandments are righteousness."[2246]

2240 Isaiah 26:8
2241 Psalm 6:5
2242 1 John 2:3
2243 John 16:11
2244 Matthew 28:1
2245 Galatians 1:1
2246 Psalm 119:172

25. If this man's conversation is our salvation's Captain, it is well for us to keep not only what his Father had him reverence when in the grave, but also what his Word pronounced in the beginning as a perpetual law; it plainly says, "God blessed the seventh day, and sanctified it."[2247] This man upon that tree represents the perpetual separation of handwritten religious policies from the living God's devotional character, wherefore if we are beguiled to believe that this same Creator sanctions commandments contrary to himself, we are grossly misled. It is the *serpent's* intention to mislead, and there is no clearer misconception than any charge contradicting the *garden's* intended devotional character. The living God's *name* is without end,[2248] allowing us to know that his *voice* of commandments contains the same everlasting life of his *throne*.

26. His Prophet on that tree is a witness to the continual force of his *voice* among his congregation. His conversation becoming a curse, conversations born under the dominion of handwritten ethics; which is every conversation; those ethics, so that we may know the Creator's will,[2249] are hereafter become accursed. Herein is the reason why that man must find himself on the tree, because if he did not, our conversation would remain compromised. It is because of our reconciliation to the living God's devotional character that we endure *creation's* training, thus, by our diligence we are privileged to understand the celebration of this training, delighting in the fact that "God blessed the seventh day, and sanctified."[2250]

2247 Genesis 2:3
2248 Isaiah 40:28
2249 2 John 1:6
2250 Genesis 2:3

27

Until The Seed Should Appear

1. Seeing as how "Christ hath redeemed us from the curse of the law, being made a curse for us,"[2251] it is well to inquire about the function of such hand-written religious ordinances. If, by this man's sacrifice, all flesh-based traditional commandments are nullified, if we are found servants to any handwritten law, it is evident that we are in direct conflict with the Bible's present philosophy. Recognizing the error that the Christian tribe was falling into, inventing rituals and ceremonies for *the new covenant*, Paul sought to expound upon the value of the former age by saying, "Wherefore then serveth the law? It was added because of transgressions, till the seed should come to whom the promise was made."[2252]

2. The laws of Moses were invented to correct the people on right service to the *LORD's* ten laws. The diverse rules and ordinances compiled by Moses were introduced to instruct the people on what constituted lawful and harmful conduct in their *LORD's* sight, and they were intended to be in effect for a

---

2251   Galatians 3:13
2252   Galatians 3:19

specific period of time, even until that *seed* should appear.[2253] This people needed regulatory laws and precepts, for how else would they remember their *LORD* and *God* after such a long season of *captivity*? Because the spirit of the human being is naturally weak, the organs of the natural devotional conversation are also weak and lame, therefore it was necessary that rules and commandments govern the people. But after that knowledge of the living God's *name* should appear, this manner of government should find itself passed away, for then a new covenant experience should arise.

3. These individuals, for whom religious laws were ordained, had recently been liberated from Egypt, where their spirituality had been ensnared by Egyptian customs, necessitating a renewal of their spiritual comprehension. Over four centuries, the Hebrews endured subjugation under Egyptian governance, and what notably suffered within them was the integrity of their ancestral faith. Egypt is known and recognized in the Bible as the *dragon*; it says, "Pharaoh king of Egypt, the great dragon";[2254] wherefore when hearing of the Hebrews under Egyptian rule, it is that we are hearing of the Hebrews in subjection to a *house* of pagan bondage. A "house" is figurative language denoting a church, as it says, "The house of God, which is the church of the living God."[2255]

4. When it says, "I am the LORD thy God, which have brought thee out of the land of Egypt, out of the house of bondage,"[2256] it is an announcement that the living God is redeeming or delivering from bondage out of the *dragon's* devotional character, or from a church whose *wisdom* is contrary to the philosophy at the heart of the scriptures. This Hebrew people found their spiritual understanding in a similar condition as Moses' former estate, of which it says, "Moses was learned in all the wisdom of the Egyptians."[2257] This Egyptian wisdom is "the wisdom of their wise men"[2258] and "the understanding of their prudent men,"[2259] for the Hebrews honored the religion of their *fathers* by Egyptian idols and laws. Thus, to remove them from a pagan approach, and to challenge their mind on *heavenly* things, a legal religious code was instituted for the time being.

2253 Galatians 3:16
2254 Ezekiel 29:3
2255 1 Timothy 3:15
2256 Exodus 20:2
2257 Acts 7:22
2258 Isaiah 29:14
2259 Isaiah 29:14

5. Upon their exit from the *dragon's* lore; which dragon is also "Satan, which deceiveth the whole world";[2260] their *LORD* sought to demonstrate to their senses the living majesty of his throne, counseling them to appear before him that they may hear his *voice*. The essence of the Egyptian religion is aimed at gratifying natural religious desires, leading the mind to concoct a false reality for worship, devoid of a genuine benefit except for what is crafted by human hands. In order to demonstrate to this populace his sovereignty as a living authority and his identity as "LORD," he instructed Moses to assemble the people. Hereafter "it came to pass on the third day in the morning, that there were thunders and lightnings, and a thick cloud upon the mount, and the voice of the trumpet exceeding loud; so that all the people that was in the camp trembled."[2261]

6. At this time, "from his right hand went a fiery law,"[2262] for his own *finger had* engraved, and upon stone, ten laws, "and he added no more."[2263] Now, the *LORD*, knowing the spirit within this people, and understanding that flesh cannot keep these laws, moved Moses to appear before him, saying, "Stand thou here by me, and I will speak unto thee all the commandments, and the statutes, and the judgments, which thou shalt teach them."[2264] Thus, Moses received supplementary commandments for maintaining a right service to those ten precepts.[2265]

7. During this period of time, the *LORD* shared with Moses a vision of the *heavenly* Sanctuary, counseling Moses to form a tabernacle after the fashion of that *Building* in *heaven*. Moses also developed various laws, judgments, and statutes from the *LORD* concerning, for example, daily ministerial life and religious appointments, and this is what the Bible means when saying, "And commandedst them precepts, statutes, and laws, by the hand of Moses thy servant."[2266] What is written by flesh is written by flesh, but what is decreed by the living God is decreed by the living God, and the only laws not written of Moses were those that were engraved upon stone, and especially that law of the seventh day's "rest."

2260 Revelation 12:9
2261 Exodus 19:16
2262 Deuteronomy 33:2
2263 Deuteronomy 5:22
2264 Deuteronomy 5:31
2265 Exodus 24:15-18
2266 Nehemiah 9:14

270 • The Dawn of Devotion

8. After they left Egypt, the *LORD* promised them *bread* from his own *oven*, saying, "This is that which the LORD hath said, To morrow is the rest of the holy Sabbath unto the LORD: bake that which ye will bake to day, and seethe that ye will seethe; and that which remaineth over lay up for you to be kept until the morning."[2267] Now, concerning the Egyptian *sabbath*; which *sabbath* is still today adhered to by the *dragon's* rule; it is known that it is honored on "the third day, which was Pharaoh's birthday."[2268] Herein we may understand why the *LORD* chose the third day to give his people those laws personally engraved by his *finger*, and why at this time he let them know, "The seventh day is the Sabbath of the LORD."[2269]

9. The living God chose to demonstrate his glory before the people on the third day for the same reason he did not resurrect *his chief witness* during the seventh day, for "God blessed the seventh day, and sanctified it."[2270] Herein the Bible should settle any debate between its seventh day and the *dragon's* third day, which day is *Egypt's* first day *sabbath*. This Hebrew people had come to admit in to their religion Egypt's *third day*, so the living God, on the third day, and in two separate ages of the world, witnesses for his own *name* by first descending upon the mount with his ten counsels, pronouncing to the people that ancient *garden's* devotional character, and by secondly bringing up that conversation to himself "in the end of the Sabbath, as it began to dawn toward the first day of the week."[2271]

10. The Bible gives a very clear and blatant statement about its thoughts of the third or the first day, for if the seventh day meant no thing at all to it, why not *resurrect* that conversation during the seventh day? Or, why not cause the magnificence of Si'nai to appear during the seventh day? Because "God blessed the seventh day, and sanctified it,"[2272] not even he would violate that good appointment, allowing us to understand that "what therefore God hath joined together, let not man put asunder."[2273] The Creator, by his own devotional philosophy, joins *his* "rest" to the seventh day, wherefore we may understand religious error by what seeks to divide what the living God has put together.

2267 Exodus 16:23
2268 Genesis 40:20
2269 Exodus 20:10
2270 Genesis 2:3
2271 Matthew 28:1
2272 Genesis 2:3
2273 Mark 10:9

11. Thus, to help the people better understand the *LORD's voice*, Moses was instructed on what laws and ordinances must be given for increasing their knowledge and loyalty to *God's* ten laws. The *LORD* therefore put forth a covenant to this people that was based upon their compliance to the handwritten laws of Moses. *God* had given this people ten laws that he knew they could not keep, wherefore he made them a promise that if they honored the laws of Moses, because the keeping of his laws should direct their attention to maintaining those ten precepts, he would bless them.[2274] The plan was to keep and do the laws of Moses, that by obeying Moses' handwritten tradition, the promise to keep the Ten Commandments would be met. Devotion to the *LORD* ran through the pen of Moses, which is why it says, "Keep therefore and do them; for this is your wisdom and your understanding in the sight of the nations."[2275]

12. The covenant made with Israel was, "Obey my voice, and do them, according to all which I command you: so shall ye be my people, and I will be your God: that I may perform the oath which I have sworn unto your fathers,"[2276] "and all the people answered together, and said, All that the LORD hath spoken we will do."[2277] Herein is that old covenant, even a promise of blessing for obeying the handwritten craft of a man. So long as the people kept what was written by Moses, they would do well, for by examining the nature of those statutes, they would have right knowledge added to their confidence for sincerely regarding *God's* ten laws, and this is exactly what makes the first covenant a weak testament.

13. There was no sure manner of conversion to *heaven's* wisdom by this covenant, for if all I must do to receive blessing is engage my conversation with a handwritten tradition, then my entire focus should be on that handwritten tradition. Suddenly *God* or the Deity becomes the handwriting of flesh, and the one by whom this handwriting came, a *savior* to be worshipped. This people, because of their devotion to what Moses had written, greatly perverted that handwriting, bogging down their *LORD's name* with commandments and ordinances of their own. All of a sudden those ten laws, and the character within those precepts, were not the ambition of the elders, but rather a religion crafted by their own imagination. It then became necessary to tell them, "Full well ye reject the commandment of God, that ye may keep your own tradition."[2278]

2274 Deuteronomy 26:15-19
2275 Deuteronomy 4:6
2276 Jeremiah 11:4,5
2277 Exodus 19:8
2278 Mark 7:9

14. When the time was therefore right, a minister uttering the scripture's philosophy against the handwritten standard then appeared.[2279] The law of Moses "was added because of transgressions, till the seed should come to whom the promise was made,"[2280] therefore when we observe that man upon that tree, it is that we are observing the passing away of the rule of any religious law or tradition from the living God's devotional conversation. These laws of a Mosaic tradition were given for increasing spiritual amendment in heart and in mind towards the ancient *garden's* Mind, but with that Wisdom of the living God manifested, it is that every law after the intention that Moses' handwriting served is abolished by the sacrificed conversation of the Bible's philosophy.

15. The first covenant failed because it sought the conversion of the conversation by what stimulated the human being, and since "we know that the law is spiritual,"[2281] it is absolute foolishness to expect the human being to honor what is entirely mental. But the LORD had faith in his people. If they could just soberly honor what Moses gave them, by the time that chief apostle should appear, they would be a people ready and prepared to cast away a lame handwritten obligation for a better promise through the spirit of their mind. But they, instead of honoring what was given, perverted that routine, causing their *eyes* to fail to comprehend the new will to appear by an experimental faith.

16. This living God's chief apostle taught a philosophy without subjection to religious laws, directing his audience to the inward labor of words.[2282] The former manner was physical and encouraged the human being to care for a temporal religious government, but the that Prophet preached a doctrine where, by the reign of the living God's wisdom within the inward parts, salvation's will would find itself engraved upon the heart of the conscience. This is why he taught, "Receive with meekness the engrafted word."[2283]

17. No longer would the conscience of religious leaders rule the conscience of the conversation, but a new covenant would find itself within the *world* of the living God's wisdom, which covenant was a promise of devotional newness within the conversation's inward parts. The first covenant sought worship to the LORD by forcing upon the human being a rule to live by, but the new covenant seeks reverence to the Creator's *name* by the conversion of the mind through

---

2279 Galatians 4:4,5
2280 Galatians 3:19
2281 Romans 7:14
2282 Luke 17:20,21
2283 James 1:21

that *name's* Philosophy, which Word is "the law of the Spirit of life,"[2284] which is why it says, "Of his own will begat he us with the word of truth."[2285] Anciently, *birth* was by a handwritten tradition, and such conception was a *baptism* "which stood only in meats and drinks, and divers washings, and carnal ordinances."[2286] Today, we live during the *year* of reformation, which reformation we understand should commence when "the seed should come to whom the promise was made."[2287]

18. If, by the appearance and sacrifice of the living God's chief apostle the saying is fulfilled, "Blotting out the handwriting of ordinances that was against us,"[2288] and we are found adhering to that what is handwritten,[2289] we blatantly confess to the fact that the Bible's philosophy has not come and is not offered, making an open mockery of the new covenant's labor and ministry. This is why it says, "Unto which of the angels said he at any time, Thou art my Son, this day have I begotten thee? And again, I will be to him a Father, and he shall be to me a Son?"[2290]

19. An "angel" is a human messenger of the philosophy at the heart of the scriptures. If we find any *angel* ordaining any law for any one to adhere to, we may understand that this is no steward of that philosophy. There is only one wisdom blessed to govern the living God's host, and this wisdom tells us, "I will declare the decree: the LORD hath said unto me, Thou art my Son."[2291] This wisdom and conversation of the Creator is today on no tree, but is "a merciful and faithful high priest in things pertaining to God,"[2292] which is why it says, "He shall stand and feed in the strength of the LORD, in the majesty of the name of the LORD his God."[2293] As that chief priest of the living God's wisdom, it was necessary that it find itself born to a contrary tradition, to the end that, by its passing, all that should remain is what is of the living God. This is why it is written, "For in that he died, he died unto sin once: but in that he liveth, he liveth unto God."[2294]

2284 Romans 8:2
2285 James 1:18
2286 Hebrews 9:10
2287 Galatians 3:19
2288 Colossians 2:14
2289 Galatians 3:19
2290 Hebrews 1:5
2291 Psalm 2:7
2292 Hebrews 2:17
2293 Micah 5:4
2294 Romans 6:10

20. This man's conversation represents "sin" against the living God's will and wisdom, and this "sin" is "the enmity, even the law of commandments contained in ordinances."[2295] "Having abolished in his flesh the enmity, even the law of commandments contained in ordinances,"[2296] it is that no handwritten law rules over the promise of the new covenant, which is why we are counseled, "Live according to God in the spirit,"[2297] and, "Worship God in the spirit."[2298] Right service to the living God and to that decreed conversation is today through the spirit of the mind, which is why, in this "time of reformation,"[2299] we are counseled, "Be renewed in the spirit of your mind."[2300]

21. Herein we have defined for us just what religious error to be aware of, and it is the ordaining of and the adhering to ordinances "after the commandments and doctrines of men."[2301] We may therefore understand that we have a lying conversation when claiming wellbeing by the living God's chief apostle and found subjected to what is handwritten, and Paul, understanding this spirit of error within the Christian camp, wrote to their elders, "Wherefore if ye be dead with Christ from the rudiments of the world, why, as though living in the world, are ye subject to ordinances...after the commandments and doctrines of men?"[2302]

22. If the Word governs the spirit of our conversation's mind, there will be as great of a rebellion against the religious laws of *men* as is the sensual or natural mind against salvation's science.[2303] As "the natural man receiveth not the things of the Spirit of God,"[2304] so the mind created by the living God's will and commandment does not receive any handwritten *thing*, "for his seed remaineth in him: and he cannot sin, because he is born of God."[2305] The living God's Prophet on that tree is a symbol of "sin" against the living God's philosophy, and that "sin" is articulated in the saying, "The strength of sin is the law."[2306]

2295 Ephesians 2:15
2296 Ephesians 2:15
2297 1 Peter 4:6
2298 Philippians 3:3
2299 Hebrews 9:10
2300 Ephesians 4:23
2301 Colossians 2:22
2302 Colossians 2:20-22
2303 Romans 8:7
2304 1 Corinthians 3:14
2305 1 John 3:9
2306 1 Corinthians 15:56

23. If it is that we are today servants to what is handwritten, it is that we confess the conversation of the living God's chief apostle has yet to appear. Our willingness to lend our conversation to the rule of what is abolished only pronounces our service to the *dragon*, which encourages his host to do contrary to what the living God has decreed. The living God has today, by the sacrifice of his Prophet's conversation; "for he that is hanged is accursed of God";[2307] declared every handwritten charge and ordinance to be accursed, making the conversation doing that tradition just as abominable as that policy. For this cause we are counseled, "Neither shalt thou bring an abomination into thine house, lest thou be a cursed thing like it: but thou shalt utterly detest it, and thou shalt utterly abhor it; for it is a cursed thing."[2308]

24. Now, as stated earlier, a "house" figuratively denotes a church, even as it says, "The house of God, which is the church of the living God."[2309] When we find a church bringing in to it whatsoever the Bible has categorized as abominable, we may know that this church is in gross religious error, fulfilling the saying, "Her end is bitter as wormwood, sharp as a twoedged sword. Her feet go down to death; her steps take hold on hell."[2310] That church of *hell* and of *death*, she is in service to that *dragon*, which is the religious tradition of Pharaoh, whose celebration is honored on "the third day, which was Pharaoh's birthday."[2311]

25. If it is that we are today honoring the *house* of *death* and of *hell*, we should know that such a religious institution is forwarded by elders "who changed the truth of God into a lie,"[2312] and so much so that it had to be said of them, "The name of God is blasphemed among the Gentiles through you, as it is written."[2313] And truly such open blasphemy against the name and will of the Bible is evident, for if our example, by one sacrificed conversation, has abolished one manner of worship and service, yet conversations professing service to that *name* and *will* are caught honoring what is abolished, then a great violation has occurred. This *people* professing *the Word* are found to be misled by their consent to the standards of the old covenant, for when "he saith, A new

---

2307 Deuteronomy 21:23
2308 Deuteronomy 7:26
2309 1 Timothy 3:15
2310 Proverbs 5:4,5
2311 Genesis 40:20
2312 Romans 1:25
2313 Romans 2:24

covenant, he hath made the first old."[2314] "That which decayeth and waxeth old is ready to vanish away,"[2315] and should our conversation not also perish when honoring what no longer exists?

26. Truly our conversation should perish, and it will, but it says, "Whosoever believeth in him should not perish, but have eternal life."[2316] If we are counseled, "Live according to God in the spirit,"[2317] since "that which is born of the Spirit is spirit,"[2318] the perishing to appear should not be literal perishing, but rather a decaying and waxing old of "the eyes of your understanding."[2319] The "eternal life," then, to appear by believing on this man's *name*, is but for the spirit of the mind, to the end we should never fail to achieve "knowledge of his will in all wisdom and spiritual understanding."[2320] Mental and spiritual discernment is herein the subject of the Bible; seeing as how the promise of the new covenant is a new heart and mind, creation is the living God's intention, and this creation is by "the grace of life."[2321]

27. The power of grace is only for the spirit of the mind, even as it says, "The grace of our Lord Jesus Christ be with your spirit."[2322] Grace is secreted into the conversation's conscience by "the Lord Jesus Christ," and in the context of the Bible's language, we may understand that since this creation is not physical, but is wholly mental and spiritual, "the Lord Jesus Christ our Saviour"[2323] is rightly understood to be in reference to no man or figure, but to "the commandment of God our Saviour."[2324] The mind must, seeing as how it is "the grace of God that bringeth salvation,"[2325] mentally comprehend the living God's commandment if grace should be given to forward salvation's science.

28. This salvation occurs only within the spirit of the mind, wherefore we may understand that to fail to mentally discern salvation's will means to mentally pass away from a right Bible understanding. Herein, by our clear refusal to bring the law and judgment of the *Word* into our heart and mind for

---

2314 Hebrews 8:13
2315 Hebrews 8:13
2316 John 3:15
2317 1 Peter 4:6
2318 John 3:6
2319 Ephesians 1:18
2320 Colossians 1:9
2321 1 Peter 3:6
2322 Philemon 1:25
2323 Titus 1:4
2324 Titus 1:3
2325 Titus 2:11

the intended manner of creation, the saying must find fulfillment in us, "For this cause God shall send them strong delusion, that they should believe a lie."[2326] This lie is that mockery of *one* on a cross and taken for natural and spiritual *health*, which *one* is not that Prophet, but is that *serpent* upon a pole. If it is that we find ourselves tied to a *house* honoring what is handwritten, we may know that this church serves this lie.

2326 2 Thessalonians 2:11

28

A Right Regard

1. We need to come up higher in our devotional understanding. "Whoso-ever transgresseth, and abideth not in the doctrine of Christ, hath not God,"[2327] and seeing as how the Word is "God," our violation against the knowledge of "God's" chief apostle removes us from the benevolent will at the heart of the Bible. A major transgression against the Word's knowledge is in falling back in to formerly accursed manners of worship and service, which manners state: "If ye walk in my statutes, and keep my commandments, and do them; then I will give you rain in due season,"[2328] and, "It shall be our righteousness, if we observe to do all these commandments before the LORD our God, as he hath commanded us."[2329]

2. *Blessing* and *righteousness*, under the former covenant, appeared by the conversation keeping the commandment through its human being. Of old, it was the responsibility of the conversation to do the handwritten commandment to

---

2327 2 John 1:9
2328 Leviticus 26:3,4
2329 Deuteronomy 6:25

278

persuade the heart and mind of its *holy* appointment. With such a standard for *righteousness*, it is no surprise that they should take the tradition of command-ments to be that rule whereby *blessing* is given. It was formerly our *righteousness* to keep and do what was handwritten, but today, "if righteousness come by the law, then Christ is dead in vain."[2330] That old covenant was predicated upon the saying, "You are justified by the law,"[2331] but concerning the new will, "By his knowledge shall my righteous servant justify many,"[2332] it says. The offering of that Prophet pronounced a reform in manners of personal worship and service; the experience is no longer flesh-based, but is mental.

3. *Justification* formerly appeared by the labor of the conversation, but today, with justification appearing by knowledge, it is that the conversation's baptism must occur within the spirit of the mind through "the washing of water by the word."[2333] Justification, because it is to occur within the inward parts, must therefore occur by an experimental faith on some *thing*, which is why it says, "Thou desirest truth in the inward parts: and in the hidden part thou shalt make me to know wisdom."[2334]

4. The Bible does not lie when saying that justification is through the appli-cation of knowledge. The conversation's sanctification occurs by the wisdom of the living God's *name* working within the conversation's conscience.[2335] Such sanctification, because it did not entirely rely on the application of an exer-cised faith for knowledge, was not apparent under the former testament.[2336] The *righteousness* forwarded by the handwritten tradition is no righteousness at all; by it being a physical routine, no faith is needed, and if no faith is needed, no mental activity is required, and where no mental activity exists, no knowledge can appear. The entire point of the new will is to, by the knowledge of salva-tion's present philosophy, "purge your conscience from dead works to serve the living God."[2337]

5. The former will was to obtain *righteousness* by doing acts, but today, righ-teousness is forwarded by the mind's engagement with the Bible's present *voice*. The former will was without any sure commandment for the mind; if by doing

---

2330 Galatians 2:21
2331 Galatians 5:4
2332 Isaiah 53:11
2333 Ephesians 5:26
2334 Psalm 51:6
2335 Colossians 3:16
2336 Galatians 3:11
2337 Hebrews 9:14

what I am told I can attain *righteousness*, and if by Moses' hand this *righteousness* is given, then I can not only attain *righteousness* by doing what Moses says, I can even create my own *righteousness* to achieve the *righteousness* advocated by Moses. This people was not given a handwritten tradition to spoil their conversation, but because "the LORD is a God of knowledge, and by him actions are weighed,"[2338] by rightly doing the commandment, knowledge of the charge was to find itself relayed to the mind to keep the person subject to what was retained. The former testament put the conversation in charge of a spiritual understanding, trusting the human being to cultivate within itself a mind to patiently and temperately hear *God's voice*.

6. This testament was lame, for every conversation setting their heart to it said, "The good that I would I do not: but the evil which I would not, that I do."[2339] What then should be the solution to this illness for not keeping what is "good"? It should be, through measures against the conversation, the creation of more laws and traditions to subject a naturally unruly heart. The former will found itself perverted by ministers that "did not like to retain God in their knowledge,"[2340] but that did like to invent *knowledge* of *God*, for which cause it says, "My people would not hearken to my voice; and Israel would none of me. So I gave them up unto their own hearts' lust: and they walked in their own counsels."[2341]

7. Thus, the former covenant, established with a seemingly good intention, was grossly perverted, but if they had lent their mind to the understanding contained within the ordinance, they would have known that these laws were given to them "because of transgressions, till the seed should come to whom the promise was made."[2342] When that *seed* should appear, and when that *seed* should find his mind sacrificed, a reformation would occur in the conversation's blessing, for it would no longer be, "You are justified by the law,"[2343] but rather, "Through the Spirit wait for the hope of righteousness by faith."[2344] After this man's offering, inwardly waiting on the living God's *voice* for righteousness should appear, meaning that the righteousness to appear should be a manner of kindness for the spirit of the mind.

2338 1 Samuel 2:3
2339 Romans 7:19
2340 Romans 1:28
2341 Psalm 81:11,12
2342 Galatians 3:19
2343 Galatians 5:4
2344 Galatians 5:5

8. This "waiting," because the activity is inward, must find itself executed by faith on some *thing*. Because "that which is born of the Spirit is spirit,"[2345] and because we are "to be strengthened with might by his Spirit in the inner man,"[2346] and because we are counseled, "Be ye transformed by the renewing of your mind,"[2347] it is that the spirit of the mind must faithfully wait upon some *thing* in order to receive the intended experience, and this is why it says, "The isles shall wait for his law."[2348] The living God, when initially referencing his chief apostle, says of him, "I have put my spirit upon him: he shall bring forth judgment to the Gentiles."[2349] The reforming mind is to wait on the law of this chief apostle's spiritual understanding, which law is "the knowledge of the Son of God."[2350]

9. Again, concerning the reception of this righteousness, it says, "By his knowledge shall my righteous servant justify many,"[2351] for the mind must examine and do the law of this man's conversation in order to qualify for its kindness. This righteousness to obtain from such a discipline is plainly witnesses by the passing and the regeneration of this man's conversation. With his crucified body representing the philosophy of *righteousness* by handwritten religious laws, the passing away of that body means the decaying of such a philosophy from *heaven's* conversation. The resurrection of that conversation means the redemption and the sanctification of the conversation's mind from that former flesh-based practice to soberly reverence the philosophy of this benevolent will.

10. This man's sacrificed conversation; seeing as how "God sent forth his Son, made of a woman, made under the law, to redeem them that were under the law";[2352] means that *righteousness* by any handwritten law, and the former sway that religious practices may have anciently had, is for ever abolished, letting us know that the re-establishment of such flesh-based routines means a blatant transgression against *creation's* doctrine; "if I build again the things which I destroyed, I make myself a transgressor."[2353] Herein we make the living God to be a liar by not only subscribing to flesh-based tenets, but by the creation

2345 John 3:6
2346 Ephesians 3:16
2347 Romans 12:2
2348 Isaiah 42:4
2349 Isaiah 42:1
2350 Ephesians 4:13
2351 Isaiah 53:11
2352 Galatians 4:4,5
2353 Galatians 2:18

of tenets to follow. If the living God figuratively destroyed that former manner through the illustration of this man's sacrificed conversation, only to recover those former manners, then he is absolutely fraudulent, but it is well to know that when "he saith, A new covenant, he hath made the first old."[2354]

11. When was the Creator's new covenant ratified? The new covenant will took that old will away when that Prophet said, "It is finished."[2355] What was finished was the establishment of *creation's* new cause for the inward parts of conversations.[2356] Thus, it is an indisputable and an eternal fact that the passing away of this man's body meant the ratification of a new testament, which covenant blotted out the old, for which cause it says, "Blotting out the handwriting of ordinances that was against us, which was contrary to us, and took it out of the way, nailing it to his cross."[2357]

12. What was taken out of the way of the new covenant's philosophy was all reliance upon "the enmity, even the law of commandments contained in ordinances."[2358] Hereafter every handwritten law and ordinance should find itself accursed, for they are now contrary to the Bible's wisdom, whose intention is to be within our conversation's conscience.

13. What is contrary to "us," because "that which is born of the Spirit is spirit,"[2359] is contrary to the growth and development of our conversation's conscience. Handwritten standards are against to the mind because they depend upon the body for execution, making knowledge of no value to the conversation. Such a conversation laboring for *righteousness* through deeds and acts encourages vanity and spiritual negligence, moving the heart to "be desirous of vain glory, provoking one another, envying one another."[2360]

14. It is easy to believe that the heart is in a "good" condition by the demanding routine of a tradition, and this was never the reality that the *garden's Mind* sought to portray. It was the comfort of a tradition, and of self-crafted traditional laws, that moved Adam to reject the *LORD's* commandment, wherefore it was only right that, at the appointed time, liberation from what Adam

2354 Hebrews 8:13
2355 John 19:30
2356 Hebrews 9:16,17
2357 Colossians 2:14
2358 Ephesians 2:15
2359 John 3:6
2360 Galatians 5:26

willingly enslaved their self to should appear through the illustration of that Prophet suffering the tree.[2361]

15. This man upon that tree allows us to understand that no conversation is in a good condition by the handwritten charge, for "if righteousness come by the law, then Christ is dead in vain."[2362] Open mockery against the living God is therefore committed when any religious law is created and followed, this is why it says, "God is a Spirit: and they that worship him must worship him in spirit and in truth."[2363] Because service is to God, or is to the Bible's Wisdom, and because God is Spirit, right service can only take place through the exercising of the spirit of the mind on the Bible's "truth." Seeing as how it says, "Thy word is truth,"[2364] and, "Thy law is the truth,"[2365] because "that which is born of the Spirit is spirit,"[2366] it is that the mind must examine and do the law of the living God's science if it should experience "the kindness and love of God our Saviour toward man."[2367]

16. The old will was ordained for doing commandments so that temporal blessing may appear. This will was given to foreshadow the benevolence to appear after it. The new will is ordained for spiritual blessings within the spirit of the mind for mentally discerning the judgment or the philosophy behind salvation's conversation, to the end the mind may govern the members of the conversation to rightly direct the body.

17. Of old, Moses gave a promise of blessing through doing what his hand had put together,[2368] but today we are to be "built up a spiritual house, an holy priesthood, to offer up spiritual sacrifices,"[2369] and if we should achieve this by learning of and doing the Bible's present will, "Ye are a chosen generation, a royal priesthood, an holy nation, a peculiar people,"[2370] we are counseled. The old will was based upon the labor of the conversation for a spiritual revelation, but today the labor is for the mind so that the conversation may be edified."[2371] Instead of relying upon what is flesh-based, this present time of reformation

---

2361 Galatians 3:12
2362 Galatians 2:21
2363 John 4:24
2364 John 17:17
2365 Psalm 119:142
2366 John 3:6
2367 Titus 3:4
2368 Deuteronomy 28:1,2
2369 1 Peter 2:5
2370 1 Peter 2:9
2371 1 Peter 1:13

demands absolute service to the character of our faith; the regeneration of our mind is to engrave within our heart "the knowledge of his will in all wisdom and spiritual understanding."[2372]

18. This hope found no place under the first covenant, for what knowledge can the human being obtain through a mindless routine? But under the second and last will, all routines and ceremonies are abolished from creation's science, and this fact is prophesied by the saying, "I will bring the blind by a way that they knew not; I will lead them in paths that they have not known: I will make darkness light before them, and crooked things straight. These things will I do unto them, and not forsake them."[2373]

19. The entire point of Moses' religious philosophy was to help portray to the people their shortcoming to that character engraved upon stone. But instead of rightly examining self by the imposed routine, they reverted to the ways of their *mother* and *father*, of whom it says, "They sewed fig leaves together, and made themselves aprons."[2374] A new way to approach the living God's intended edification would find itself ratified for experiencing creation's righteousness, and it would be a training without hands, to the end the experience would serve to fulfill the saying, "They shall be turned back, they shall be greatly ashamed, that trust in graven images, that say to the molten images, Ye are our gods."[2375] The former covenant could not cleanse the inward parts, for what tradition can cleanse the heart? But under the new covenant, there is a promise to create a new *person* within the conversation in harmony with the devotional character at the core of the scriptures, the aim being to forward a love for the living God's *name*, "and this is love, that we walk after his commandments."[2376]

20. This manner of spiritual learning commenced when the living God's chief apostle took his last breath. This man giving up the ghost, because his body represents the curse of a handwritten religious philosophy, is but an illustration of the source of life passing away from such a philosophy. This man gave up the ghost of a false manner of devotion on that tree, signifying that the former flesh-based routine is not only accursed, but that the living God's manner of learning for the intended manner of righteousness is without it.

21. Therefore as that Prophet's conversation gave up the life of those standards under the old will, was raised up by the *Spirit* of a better *Philosophy*, and

---

2372 Colossians 1:9
2373 Isaiah 42:16
2374 Genesis 3:7
2375 Isaiah 42:17
2376 2 John 1:6

was brought in to the *heavenly* Sanctuary, so too the same experience, within the spirit of our conversation's conscience, is to occur,[2377] the only issue being our willingness to give up the *ghost* of the religious world's devotional approach. Like as this man could not find his conversation regenerated without giving up that ghost within it, so also we should not find ourselves experiencing the living God's righteousness if we are not willing to know that "circumcision made without hands, in putting off the body of the sins of the flesh by the circumcision of Christ."[2378] This man on that tree represents the officially fallen will of the old covenant, and if sincerely drawn to his conversation's intercession, it is that we are "dead with Christ from the rudiments of the world."[2379]

22. The creation and the following of handwritten religious commandments witness to an open violation of salvation's philosophy. If the living God sanctioned such an endeavor under the new will, such a philosophy would not have been offered and accepted as a fit sacrifice. If today the mind is *blessed* by what anciently could procure no blessing, then this *LORD* is a liar, that Prophet's conversation is no mediator for righteousness, and the living God's wisdom is no Savior. If today we may continue an empty religion under the old covenant, especially since that man made himself an example that "hath redeemed us from the curse of the law, being made a curse for us,"[2380] then truly such a *Prophet* has not yet come, making the inflammation of the conversation and the slumber of the mind a most acceptable condition for *blessing*.

23. But, if of old, such a practice "could not make him that did the service perfect, as pertaining to the conscience,"[2381] seeing as how the cleansing and the dressing of the conversation's conscience is the living God's aim, must such a lame sensual conversation suffice for what is offered? We find ourselves honoring another *Lord* and *God* when hearing, "You are justified by the law."[2382] Such an open challenge against the living God's wisdom, who says, "No man is justified by the law in the sight of God,"[2383] is forwarded only by priests captured by the spirit and religion of the *serpent*; "these be they who separate themselves, sensual, having not the Spirit."[2384]

2377 Romans 8:11
2378 Colossians 2:11
2379 Colossians 2:20
2380 Galatians 3:13
2381 Hebrews 9:9
2382 Galatians 5:4
2383 Galatians 3:11
2384 Jude 1:19

24. To have no communion with the *Spirit* is to have no fellowship with the Word, making the mind willingly negligent against the Bible's ultimate devotional character and philosophy.[2385] Conversations inclined to continue the manners of the old covenant are not followers of *creation's* Word, for they are, seeing as how "of his own will begat he us with the word of truth,"[2386] no creation of the Bible's sure wisdom. A different religious faction is then arisen in direct conflict with salvation's will and doctrine when preaching, "Righteousness come by the law,"[2387] for to such a sect, no *Savior* is among them, no *Deliverer* has rescued them, and no *Wisdom* is in the heart of their conversation.

25. The members of such a sect "profess that they know God,"[2388] but at the same time "blaspheme his name, and his tabernacle, and them that dwell in heaven."[2389] Somehow, that accursed philosophy upon the tree is transformed into an idol, and an abolished religious approach, even when that approach and idol does not exist,[2390] is unlawfully given a voice to speak. Something is very wrong within the religious world who, while professing that *Prophet*, is found subject to what is handwritten, along with "days, and months, and times, and years."[2391]

26. There are opened up before us two manners of devotion that self may keep: the first, that philosophy of the religious world, and the second, that philosophy of the living God's wisdom.[2392] The world's religious conversation is a flesh-based ascent to truth, but the Bible embraces a contrary sentiment, which manner of learning involves mentally and physically proving the philosophy of its will. This is why we are counseled, "Except your righteousness shall exceed the righteousness of the scribes and Pharisees, ye shall in no case enter into the kingdom of heaven."[2393]

27. That *righteousness* of the Jews was found in keeping and doing a tradition, wherefore in order to know the righteousness of the living God; which righteousness is "the kindness and love of God our Saviour toward man";[2394] it is necessary to quit flesh-based commandments and doctrines to personally pick

---

2385　2 John 1:9
2386　James 1:18
2387　Galatians 2:21
2388　Titus 1:16
2389　Revelation 13:6
2390　Hebrews 8:13
2391　Galatians 4:10
2392　Romans 12:2
2393　Matthew 5:20
2394　Titus 3:4

up the Bible for understanding that right will. The old will convinced the people that a pure conversation occurred by doing a written charge of the council, wherefore the people sought *favor* through commandments and traditions, but this was never their *LORD's* intention. The conversation moves to such a lazy conclusion of the living God's *voice* due to its hardheartedness. That *voice*, being ultimately spiritual, is only understood when spiritually discerned.

28. David, who passed his time under the first will, perfectly comprehended the new will to appear, which is why he prayed, "Thy way, O God, is in the sanctuary,"[2395] and, "Create in me a clean heart, O God; and renew a right spirit within me."[2396] This man did not rely upon the mind of Moses, but rather relied upon what was unwritten within his laws, which mental learning moved him to write, "Blessed is the man that walketh not in the counsel of the ungodly, nor standeth in the way of sinners, nor sitteth in the seat of the scornful. But his delight is in the law of the LORD; and in his law doth he meditate day and night."[2397]

29. Here was one who actually taxed his brain on the philosophy behind sayings to render right worship and service to the philosophy within those sayings. This man, existing under the old covenant, had the privilege of observing the new. Concerning his conversation, it was said of him, "The soul of my lord shall be bound in the bundle of life with the LORD thy God,"[2398] for he learned that "the Spirit is life because of righteousness."[2399] It is because of his experience in the kind will within the scriptures that he, looking ahead to its official ratification, wrote, "Mercy and truth are met together; righteousness and peace have kissed each other."[2400] By the offering of that foreshadowed conversation, our conversation is to know the same pleasure that David knew, for this man lived in a time when *heaven's* pleasure was not fully known, but we today have that great promise available for our understanding.

30. The living God's devotional manners are today of greater importance than the religious world's approach. We do make a full confession of gratitude towards that Prophet's offering when allowing his conversation's *name* to work in our heart. When we give our confidence to the religious world, it is that we are upholding a former manner that is now categorized as "sin." The old manners

---

2395   Psalm 77:13
2396   Psalm 51:10
2397   Psalm 1:1,2
2398   1 Samuel 25:29
2399   Romans 8:10
2400   Psalm 85:10

of devotion do not care for the condition of the inward person, and they, being firstly flesh-based and sensual, cannot. The new covenant will is to create within the mind and conscience of the conversation a person liberated from the religious world and in possession of self to the praise of the living God's *name*, which is why it says, "Ye are not under the law, but under grace."[2401]

31. Because grace is ordained only for the spirit of the mind, a turning to grace is a turning of the mind to a mental devotional conversation, which is why it says, "In that he died, he died unto sin once: but in that he liveth, he liveth unto God."[2402] With the body of that man symbolizing a conversation governed by that former religious error, him being dead means his conversation being unconscious to the former religious manner. But being figuratively regenerated to life, it is that the conversation once governed by religious prescriptions is now free from spiritual slavery to know the *Mind* within the scriptures. This is why it is well to remember how it says, "The sting of death is sin; and the strength of sin is the law."[2403]

2401 Romans 6:14
2402 Romans 6:10
2403 1 Corinthians 15:56

29

Judged Ethics

1. Our supporting handwritten doctrines and commandments, and especially philosophical traditions in blatant opposition to the Bible, witnesses to the fact that our conversation is without the Bible's intended conversation. The new covenant will is ordained for the purpose of having the living God's commandments engraved upon the conversation's conscience, for when it says, "I will put my law in their inward parts, and write it in their hearts,[2404] it is that there is a confession of a certain creative work, even like as it says, "I will put my fear in their hearts, that they shall not depart from me."[2405] For this cause it says, "Thou desirest truth in the inward parts."[2406]

2. Seeing as how it says, "Thy word is truth,"[2407] "the law of truth"[2408] is what the living God hopes to engrave within our faith's inward parts, to the end it is become a new *creature* that is "holy and without blame before him

---

2404 Jeremiah 31:33
2405 Jeremiah 32:40
2406 Psalm 51:6
2407 John 17:17
2408 Malachi 2:6

in love,"[2409] "and this is love, that we walk after his commandments."[2410] The Bible's desire, through this new covenant, is the same desire of the old, even the keeping of every one of the living God's ten laws, and as the former *host* sought loyalty to them by imposing handwritten laws, the new *host* forwards harmony with the Creator's *voice* by the impression of a kind law upon the spirit of the mind. Therefore, concerning "the law of the Spirit of life,"[2411] it says, "A law shall proceed from me, and I will make my judgment to rest for a light of the people."[2412]

3. Now, "the commandment is a lamp; and the law is light";[2413] and by doing salvation's law and commandment, the heart is to find itself returning to the Mind that gave that judgment, fulfilling the vision, "Therefore are they before the throne of God, and serve him day and night in his temple: and he that sitteth on the throne shall dwell among them."[2414] Seeing as how "the Word was with God, and the Word was God,"[2415] and that the Word is still today "God," and that "God is a Spirit,"[2416] it is that the *throne* of *God* is the throne of the Spirit, and seeing as how this is that "Spirit of truth, which proceedeth from the Father,"[2417] the throne that we are to find our mind before is the throne of the Mind of that ascended Wisdom and Conversation.

4. There is only one *Royal Throne* in the *heavenly* Temple, and "the LORD sitteth King for ever."[2418] It is therefore well to know that "there is one God, and one mediator between God and men, the man Christ Jesus,"[2419] for this man's conversation, who is that intercessor, fulfills the saying, "Blessed is the King of Israel that cometh in the name of the Lord."[2420] This man figuratively stands before the living God's host as one specifically appointed to minister in the Creator's *name*, being one who "was separated...to burn incense before the

---

2409 Ephesians 1:4
2410 2 John 1:6
2411 Romans 8:2
2412 Isaiah 51:4
2413 Proverbs 6:23
2414 Revelation 7:15
2415 John 1:1
2416 John 4:24
2417 John 15:26
2418 Psalm 29:10
2419 1 Timothy 2:5
2420 John 12:13

LORD, to minister unto him, and to bless in his name for ever."[2421] Today, it is the conversation of the living God's chief apostle that is given this office.[2422]

5. Herein we may understand why, if not willing to observe that conversation once on the tree now within the heavenly Temple, the vision of only *one* on a tree is an incomplete doctrine. Because didn't this same man say, "My kingdom is not of this world"?[2423] Wherefore when servant to *one* upon a tree and found within the religious world, especially when he says, "I leave the world, and go to the Father,"[2424] must we believe that we honor salvation's new will and doctrine? It is necessary that this *King* over creation's science appears before the *King* of *heaven* and *earth*, for if of old the priesthood was not blessed without Aaron, must we take the new covenant's intercession to be complete without a high priest?

6. Aaron was a minister for the ignorance and the failure of the conversation. If the conversation failed in any way to do and to keep the *LORD's* commandments, it was the responsibility of that conversation to find itself before *Aaron* for correction. Likewise, because devotional perfection is no longer by the conversation, but "that which is born of the Spirit is spirit,"[2425] it is the Creator's will to "purge your conscience from dead works to serve the living God,"[2426] the conversation of the ascended and consecrated conversation of the living God's chief apostle, to the end the mind may receive correction on salvation's *voice*, becoming that intercessor for conversations. Like as the former host stood under *Aaron's* order,[2427] so the second covenant, which is the present will, has a heavenly Sanctuary "with all spiritual blessings in heavenly places."[2428]

7. Without vision of "one like unto the Son of man, clothed with a garment down to the foot, and girt about the paps with a golden girdle,"[2429] we will own an erroneous conversation. The living God's man on the tree represents a devotional sacrifice; was any sacrifice of old without a priest? How incomplete is a sacrifice without one sanctified to perfect that offering? How strange would

---

2421 1 Chronicles 23:13
2422 Hebrews 5:4,5
2423 John 18:36
2424 John 16:28
2425 John 3:6
2426 Hebrews 9:14
2427 Hebrews 9:1
2428 Ephesians 1:3
2429 Revelation 1:13

it be for the people to take the sacrifice to be the end of the act? To help the people understand that no sacrifice should find itself slain and reverenced without the priest, the *LORD* counseled, "In the court of the tabernacle of the congregation they shall eat it."[2430]

8. All service to the living God is to find itself conducted "in the place which the LORD thy God hath chosen to place his name there,"[2431] and since it was said to Moses, "Make me a sanctuary; that I may dwell among them,"[2432] so too the same direction is given to that consecrated conversation.[2433] If it is that we will to rightly honor the living God's new testament, it is that we must find our faith and spirit "above, where Christ sitteth on the right hand of God."[2434] This renders all *things* on *earth* as passed away and abominable, for with that conversation before the living God, when "he saith, A new covenant, he hath made the first old."[2435]

9. Herein we are made to understand that an idolatrous celebration of *one* upon a tree is blatant heresy "in blasphemy against God, to blaspheme his name, and his tabernacle, and them that dwell in heaven."[2436] For, "whatsoever God doeth, it shall be for ever,"[2437] wherefore when observing that Prophet upon a tree, it is that the annihilation of a conversation bound to handwritten charges can never be undone. It is an eternal fact that the handwritten religious code is cursed by the philosophy within the scriptures, and not only cursed, but it is also absolutely forgotten, for when "he saith, A new covenant, he hath made the first old."[2438]

10. The living God's chief apostle upon that tree represents a lifeless form of worship and service that is become categorized as "sin" by the new covenant's philosophy, wherefore are we not become erroneous by advocating for that form of devotion the living God has put to rest? An inordinate celebration of that tree, because whatsoever is nailed to it is accursed of the Word, is but an expression of devotion to an empty conversation, which devotion is only apparent due to a failure to accept the right revelation of that man crucified.

2430 Leviticus 6:16
2431 Deuteronomy 6:11
2432 Exodus 25:8
2433 Zechariah 6:13
2434 Colossians 3:1
2435 Hebrews 8:13
2436 Revelation 13:5
2437 Ecclesiastes 3:14
2438 Hebrews 8:13

We may understand our conversation is without *heaven's* will by the government regulating our conversation, for if by handwritten commandments and doctrines we are servants to *righteousness*, then this man's conversation is not become that Deliverer of our confidence. This man on the tree represents deliverance from the old testament's will, and "through knowledge shall the just be delivered."[2439] For this cause, we understand our faith is vain when it openly displays a lacking of knowledge on just what the mediation of this man's wisdom rescues from.

11. The former will involved no knowledge for *righteousness*; simply hear, do, and keep what is handwritten for *righteousness*. This is a flawed manner of devotion because instead of possessing self by the commandment, there is a greater possibility that the commandment will possess self, which is why the *LORD* said of this people, "This people draw near me with their mouth, and with their lips do honour me, but have removed their heart far from me, and their fear toward me is taught by the precept of men."[2440]

12. With faith's confession through the activity of the conversation, there is no real need for sanctity, for I, by doing the commandment, am pure. So long as I hear and do the commandment, it doesn't matter whether or not I care for the commandment, or for the end of the commandment, because the goal is *righteousness* and *favor* with *God*. If I, then, by simply doing through my body, am *blessed* of *God*, then my route for *righteousness* is finished, for I have done, and routinely keep on doing, the commandment. This covenant is therefore an inevitable stumblingblock, because by chasing righteousness through deeds and acts, through deeds and acts the conversation fails to achieve it.[2441] Trying to attain *rightness* by a bodily labor will not procure blessing to the mind, but if the Jews had spent brainpower on Moses' law, they would have obtained knowledge of the commandment within their person.

13. Adherence to this old devotional approach will move the heart to embrace teaching and following legal religious standards, which flesh-based conception the living God has forever blotted out of his devotional character. If it is that the sacrifice of his chief witness is valued, we too will find our conversation without a handwritten traditional and superstitious influence to personally know the philosophy within the scriptures; this is the only reason why he found himself upon the tree.

2439 Proverbs 11:9
2440 Isaiah 29:13
2441 Romans 9:31,32

14. "He that is hanged is accursed of God,"[2442] and what is accursed by the living God is forever excommunicated. The *LORD* admitted this former religious manner to help educate the people on the service to appear after it.[2443] Therefore if we are still today found under the rule of the former practice, it is that a working faith has not come to us, meaning that, because we openly reject the rightly consecrated conversation, no living conversation is within us, and the living intercession of that Prophet's conversation is not known to us. The hanging of this body upon a tree means an accursed and judged religious philosophy. It means the recognition of an abhorred form of devotion. To find self lauding what is abominable is to find the mind frozen within a prison, and it is imprisoned, for it says of the *dragon's* religion, "That opened not the house of his prisoners."[2444]

15. Why does our conversation, as Paul says, no longer need a schoolmaster? It says, "Faith came."[2445] The dawning of faith upon the personal devotional conversation removes every reason to follow a handcrafted religious script. Faith's appearance means an opportunity for knowledge, which means the strengthening of the mind, which strengthening is the engraving of precepts upon the heart for the conscience of the conversation to both know and do. Faith was secondary under the first will, for it took faith to believe that a physical act should benefit the inward parts, even while understanding that such ordinances "could not make him that did the service perfect, as pertaining to the conscience."[2446] It took no faith to do a commandment for *righteousness*, for if righteousness is by the law, and if I am a doer of that charge, then I am righteous and need not strain my self any further. Nevertheless, it took faith to believe that, by the act, *His* righteousness should bless my conversation, and that by those actions, my heart should learn the end of that commandment.

16. The primary concern for the first will was in doing a commandment not by faith on the inward benefit, but by faith on the nominal and temporal blessing, making the act of doing the commandment a key component for enduring the charge. This, in and of itself, is a lame devotional manner, which is why these things were "a figure for the time then present."[2447]

2442 Deuteronomy 21:23
2443 Galatians 3:23-25
2444 Isaiah 14:17
2445 Galatians 3:23
2446 Hebrews 9:9
2447 Hebrews 9:9

17. Being a figure for what should afterwards appear, Moses sought to educate the people on the new will that they should adhere to. If "the invisible things of him from the creation of the world are clearly seen, being understood by the things that are made,"[2448] then what is visibly sanctioned is made to expound upon the things that are invisible. The physical routine of the first will was ordained to explain the discipline to replace that covenant, for what they physically did, they, under the rule of the second will, were to do within the spirit of the mind. The first covenant was forwarded by acts of the conversation to reap *righteousness*, but the second is blessed to activate the conversation's mind for reaping the benefit of mental activity: seeing as how "God is a Spirit,"[2449] only the spirit of the mind can rightly obtain "God's" righteousness.

18. Therefore, when doing this physical routine, it took faith to believe that a *LORD* who was not flesh should accept and bless flesh, for in all actuality, "the law having a shadow of good things to come, and not the very image of the things, can never with those sacrifices which they offered year by year continually make the comers thereunto perfect."[2450] Moses' first intention was, on the surface, heavily flawed, for flesh, and a fleshly priesthood, cannot please what is Spirit, but if they had rightly examined the intention behind the routine, they would have found warmth in it by the intention to appear after it. Because this first will put no ultimate rule over the flesh, but made the flesh ruler of a spiritual plane, religious error removing knowledge from sight, causing it to be said of them, "Thou hast rejected knowledge."[2451]

19. The living God never gives any *thing* for us to follow without the opportunity to bring our issues, complaints, or questions to his Wisdom. A useless religion is a thoughtless religion, and a thoughtless religion is a tradition without cleansing "by the spirit of judgment, and by the spirit of burning."[2452] All *things* given by the living God are for our mental examination; if that Wisdom is that God, and if God is Spirit, then it is a fact that we cannot rightly know the living God's words by any tangible or physical routine, for "they are spiritually discerned."[2453]

2448　Romans 1:20
2449　John 4:24
2450　Hebrews 10:1
2451　Hosea 4:6
2452　Isaiah 4:4
2453　1 Corinthians 2:14

20. "A spirit hath not flesh and bones,"[2454] wherefore must we believe that what is produced by flesh and bones may suffice for a right conversation? The old will may have sanctioned flesh and bones to lead the practice, but this people, understanding that *He* is "the LORD, the God of the spirits of all flesh,"[2455] should have taken better care of what *He* had moved Moses' hand to write, for those laws spoke of a break from the *flesh* for a spiritual communion with the Creator. When we observe the living God's chief apostle on that tree, we are observing the handwriting of every religious elder on that tree, that every law and charge of such an elder is become not only dead to the mind operating within that conversation, but is also become accursed of the living God. What is accursed upon the tree is every religious law of every *Moses* that should walk the *earth* claiming to be *the LORD's lawgiver* and *messenger*, but the sacrifice of that Prophet blatantly rejects the pen of any elder forwarding a handwritten bill, which is why it says, "Christ hath redeemed us from the curse of the law."[2456]

21. When we find figures after the likeness of Moses prescribing hand-written religious ethics, and professing that they know the *LORD* and are in service to *His High Priest*, we may understand that these ministers have no knowledge of salvation's science and are but liars fulfilling the saying, "Of your own selves shall men arise, speaking perverse things, to draw away disciples after them."[2457] Religious error did not mainly occur outside of the Christian church, but from within it; the apostles understood how ministers mocked the living God's philosophy by admitting into it "Jewish fables, and commandments of men, that turn from the truth."[2458]

22. "The truth" has a definition. When it says, "Thy law is the truth,"[2459] and, "Thy word is truth,"[2460] we may understand that the living God's truth, because we are "to be strengthened with might by his Spirit in the inner man,"[2461] is a counsel to "purge your conscience from dead works to serve the living God."[2462] The first will could not do this, for what physical act can *wash* the mind? The second will is superior to this first testament due to the fact that it, by the words

---

2454 Luke 24:39
2455 Numbers 27:16
2456 Galatians 3:13
2457 Acts 20:30
2458 Titus 1:14
2459 Psalm 119:142
2460 John 17:17
2461 Ephesians 3:16
2462 Hebrews 9:14

of the scripture's wisdom, will personally claim the mind, to the end "he might sanctify and cleanse it with the washing of water by the word."[2463] This was not promised under the first will, which was regulated by the purifying of the conversation by a handwritten code, yet the promise of the second covenant is blessed to edify the organs of the conversation, and this promise met when "comparing spiritual things with spiritual."[2464]

23. The physical routine endorsed of old is now become a mental education for our faith's higher learning. The living God, by the sacrifice of that Prophet's conversation, blotted out of his wisdom's conversation all government of the personal religion by a handwritten religious script. For us, therefore, to endorse commandments and doctrines not founded by the living God's *right hand*, and to do so professing *God's man*, is to show forth skepticism in the new will for the conversation, evincing that we are not honoring the new covenant philosophy within the Bible.

24. A great misunderstanding is forwarded when wrongly honoring the body of the Bible's knowledge.[2465] There is absolutely no reason for any mind to find itself ignorant on any *thing* within the Bible; seeing as how "where the Spirit of the Lord is, there is liberty,"[2466] perpetual liberty for our faith's intellect by the passing and the regeneration of that Prophet's conversation is today unsealed to us. If we are not where this conversation is, we cannot, and will never know the liberty ordained by its *voice*, which is why it is well to hear and examine the saying, "I leave the world, and go to the Father."[2467]

25. The conversation that said this says, "I go and prepare a place for you."[2468] This man's conversation, after passing away from the religious world, found itself gone "into heaven itself, now to appear in the presence of God for us."[2469] The *Place* that it has prepared for us is even as "the high place that was at Gibeon; for there was the tabernacle of the congregation of God, which Moses the servant of the LORD had made in the wilderness."[2470] The Place of our learning is a heavenly Sanctuary, for this conversation, after ascending into this Building and becoming that "merciful and faithful high priest in things

---

2463　Ephesians 5:26
2464　1 Corinthians 2:13
2465　1 Corinthians 11:27-29
2466　2 Corinthians 3:17
2467　John 16:28
2468　John 14:3
2469　Hebrews 9:24
2470　2 Chronicles 1:3

pertaining to God,"[2471] opened up this Place to our conversation's conscience. Our conversation is to be where the *name* of this ministry is.

26. And we will be with it.[2472] Seeing as how this man's wisdom today holds an office of intercession between the conversation's spirit and the philosophy at the core of the scriptures, our reception of it, or its *appearing* to us, is not physical. The new covenant is according to the saying, "A new heart also will I give you, and a new spirit will I put within you,"[2473] making this covenant one where sanctification is inward, which is why it says, "Sanctify them through thy truth: thy word is truth,"[2474] and, "Be ye transformed by the renewing of your mind."[2475] Thus, because "that which is born of the Spirit is spirit,"[2476] and because birth is through the new covenant's philosophy,[2477] it is not that the man will physically appear to us, but rather a revelation of his *name* will dawn upon our mind, encouraging us to be members of "the general assembly and church of the firstborn, which are written in heaven."[2478]

27. By the training of the new covenant's discipline, the living God will have a people sealed to his devotional character. With faith's exercise now become the subject of conversion, and with knowledge as the means whereby faith is created, with the mind consistently examining his *voice*, it will be fulfilled, "They shall teach no more every man his neighbour, and every man his brother, saying, Know the LORD: for they shall all know me."[2479] Truly, then, if we fail to do salvation's will, it is inevitable that our conversation will confess that we do not know the *name* of the living God's chief apostle, "and hereby we do know that we know him, if we keep his commandments."[2480]

28. This living God has forwarded a commandment through the illustration of his chief apostle suffering the tree, which commandment states the perpetual end of *circumcision* by priests and elders after the manner of Moses. We understand that we adhere to a counterfeit devotional practice when observing a rule of sects and factions in direct conflict with this commandment. We should know that the violation of any one of the Bible's commandments means an imminent

---

2471 Hebrews 2:17
2472 John 14:3
2473 Ezekiel 36:26
2474 John 17:17
2475 Romans 12:2
2476 John 3:6
2477 James 1:18
2478 Hebrews 12:23
2479 Jeremiah 31:34
2480 1 John 2:3

violation and molestation of them all, for by regarding what is accursed while professing the body of the Bible's knowledge, it is an eternal fact that "God shall send them strong delusion, that they should believe a lie."[2481] This delusional lie is without the knowledge of the living God's "truth," for the *serpent* "was a murderer from the beginning, and abode not in the truth, because there is no truth in him."[2482] Thus, for every mind existing where that consecrated conversation is not, they are become a victim of the *dragon's* mind and conversation.

29. With the living God separating salvation's science and its conversation from the religious world, and with that contrary *wisdom* finally judged and sentenced to death, the religious world is come under the *dragon's* sway, and that serpent upon a pole is become the *King* of the *Jews*. There is then no greater *thing* without "truth" than that *body* upon the tree, yet the serpent would convince his host otherwise, even when it says, "He that is hanged is accursed of God."[2483] Herein we are faced with Adam's former challenge: will we take the *serpent's* speech to be credible, or will we examine the living God's words? There is no salvation blessed to any conversation by that body upon the tree, therefore if it says, "He that is hanged is accursed of God,"[2484] yet the human pen says, "When he looketh upon it, shall live,"[2485] will we consent to the tradition of *Moses*, or will we hear and take knowledge of the living God's *voice*?

30. We should not let the serpent's tongue confuse us. What is on that tree is accursed of the living God: there is no life in it; there is no value in it; it is become trash. Yet the *serpent* says to eat it, for it is a tree good for *food*, and full of *wisdom*, and is pleasant to the *eyes*, when the living God's *eyes* have burned it to ashes, making it void of counsel and detrimental to the stomach.

31. The *name* and doctrine of the living God's chief apostle is not on a tree. That conversation, along with the *body* of its knowledge, is passed away from the *earth* and "is gone into heaven, and is on the right hand of God."[2486] If we are not where this conversation is, we will find ourselves beguiled by that contrary devotional character and lauding a lie that does not exist.[2487]

2481   2 Thessalonians 2:11
2482   John 8:44
2483   Deuteronomy 21:23;
2484   Deuteronomy 21:23
2485   Numbers 21:8
2486   1 Peter 3:22
2487   John 16:11

30

Transgression's Emblem

1. It is only fitting that the emblem depicting the *serpent's* tradition is a tree. A right representation of salvation's science is of "one like unto the Son of man, clothed with a garment down to the foot, and girt about the paps with a golden girdle."[2488] *Creation's* present illustration provokes a sentiment for revival and reform, for with this philosophy "being come an high priest of good things to come, by a greater and more perfect tabernacle, not made with hands,"[2489] this wisdom's mediation is become one of creation through "circumcision made without hands, in putting off the body of the sins of the flesh by the circumcision of Christ."[2490]

2. Where is there a full blessing when observing that *wisdom* and *conversation* found upon the tree? Where is right circumcision manifested by that *philosophy* passed away upon the tree? What *priest* exists by what is accursed? That *body* of knowledge upon the tree is without the Bible's philosophy, "for he

---

2488 Revelation 1:12
2489 Hebrews 9:11
2490 Colossians 2:11

that is hanged is accursed of God."[2491] There is no revival or reform in what is accursed of *God*, for if the blessing given to what is accursed is condemnation and abomination, then "he hath blessed; and I cannot reverse it."[2492] But there is a *wisdom* that has "changed the truth of God into a lie."[2493] The *serpent* will redirect the living God's *speech* to the conversation without right knowledge of its *name*. To such as are willing to neglect their own individual accountability, "Satan himself is transformed into an angel of light."[2494]

3. When we find the preaching of a tree, or a cross, to be an emblem of salvation, we may understand that the one on that tree is none other than the serpent, and that the *light* about *his* figure is a bright "cloke of maliciousness."[2495] The living God cannot keep his doctrine tied to a tree because "he that is hanged is accursed of God."[2496] If this man; whose conversation is now creation's high priest; kept his doctrine idolatrously upon that tree, he would be forwarding devotional degeneration. On that tree he, by his fleshly body, represents "in his flesh the enmity, even the law of commandments contained in ordinances."[2497]

4. With him suspended between heaven and earth on that tree, and with his devotional conversation passed away in this body on that tree, he represents the fact that every handwritten commandment, both then and now, is passed away from salvation's science.[2498] Now, this man is dead, but the body of his conversation's spiritual understanding is yet alive, being figuratively brought up in to the Creator's *heavenly* Sanctuary. In reality, only a tree remains, and nailed to that tree is that body wherein rests the philosophy of the religious law. This tree therefore represents a conversation that is accursed due to it having within its heart the philosophy of *righteousness* by what is handwritten. To celebrate this tree is to celebrate a condemned conversation.

5. We cannot ignore the fact that the living God's chief apostle did not resurrect his own *self*, for it was "God the Father, who raised him from the dead."[2499] What resurrection must we then expect from what does not have power to

---

2491   Deuteronomy 21:23
2492   Numbers 23:20
2493   Romans 1:25
2494   2 Corinthians 11:14
2495   1 Peter 2:16
2496   Deuteronomy 21:23
2497   Ephesians 2:15
2498   Colossians 2:14
2499   Galatians 1:1

resurrect? What transformation must we expect from *one* whom, in and of their self, cannot transform themselves? The living God brought up this man's conversation to its throne, so when found lauding a tree *blessed* of the living God to be accursed, in what are we really celebrating? This tree, due to that *body* on it, has nailed to it the accusation and the sentence of, "Condemned," and, "Heinous," and, "Cursed," and, "Odious," and, "Disgusting." This tree represents a manner of worship and service that is contrary to the Bible's intention, wherefore any *house* holding up this tree reveals the spirit of the *serpent* to be its *head*.

6. Isn't it written, "The head of Christ is God"?[2500] Should not our head also be "God"? Seeing as how the "Word" is "God," it is that our conversation should find itself governed by the Word. Such a conversation; because "the Word of life"[2501] is "the Spirit of life";[2502] involves the mind mentally digesting the living God's *voice*, which is why it says, "Be renewed in the spirit of your mind,"[2503] and, "That which is born of the Spirit is spirit."[2504] "God" as our head is the Bible's Wisdom as our confidence, and if it is that the sacrificed conversation of the living God's chief apostle means anything to us, it is that we are passed away from former religious error to rightly honor the Bible's character by the impression of his Prophet's wisdom and conversation.

7. Paul, understanding the spiritual mischief entertained within the Christian camp, once wrote, "I determined not to know any thing among you, save Jesus Christ, and him crucified."[2505] Paul's main concern was in rightly understanding and teaching the depth behind the illustration of that man sacrificed. Paul then pronounces two great subjects of discourse: the first, "Jesus Christ"; the second, "him" crucified. Herein it is well for us to remember that, concerning "Jesus Christ," that this is not a term referencing a man, but rather a philosophy.[2506]

8. When hearing the phrase "Jesus Christ," it is well to understand that Paul speaks of no man. His language, in all actuality, because the result of "Jesus Christ" is a discipline pointing to devotional wellbeing, reveals "the Lord

---

2500 1 Corinthians 11:3
2501 1 John 1:1
2502 Revelation 11:11
2503 Ephesians 4:23
2504 John 3:6
2505 1 Corinthians 2:2
2506 2 Corinthians 5:16

Jesus Christ our Saviour"[2507] to be "the commandment of God our Saviour."[2508] Paul's first concern is over comprehending salvation's commandment, which commandment is "the doctrine of God our Saviour,"[2509] or rather, is "the law of the Spirit of life."[2510] Such a law is that commandment the spirit of the mind must embrace in order to experience "the kindness and love of God our Saviour toward man,"[2511] which "kindness" is "the faith of Christ, the righteousness which is of God by faith."[2512] Such a righteousness is the fulfillment of the prayer, "Create in me a clean heart, O God; and renew a right spirit within me,"[2513] and it cannot be correctly understood without examining the aim behind the sacrificed conversation of the living God's chief apostle.

9. Whatever subjects did not counsel on salvation's will and the newness promised to the conversation by the *offering* of that man, Paul wanted no part of it. Examining the philosophy of that crucified priest is not the same as lauding a crucified body, for where one embraces "those things which are above, where Christ sitteth on the right hand of God,"[2514] the other forwards what "descendeth not from above, but is earthly, sensual, devilish."[2515] Our examination of the man's crucified body informs the mind of an abolished will, even the will of a blessing procured to the doer of a handwritten religion.

10. This crucified body represents traditional and superstitious commandments and doctrines professedly leading the doer of them to *God's righteousness*, yet the crucifixion of this flesh means the complete end; in the generation of this crucifixion and every generation hereafter; of "philosophy and vain deceit, after the tradition of men, after the rudiments of the world,"[2516] from the living God's devotional character. The hanging of this man's body upon the tree means that every commandment and prescription of Moses in that time, and of every *Moses* until the world's complete end, is judged and taken out of the way of *heaven's* intended and accepted conversation. Life and time has done this so that the mind may intimately know it's Savior and Creator, which is why

---

2507 Titus 1:4
2508 Titus 1:3
2509 Titus 2:10
2510 Romans 8:2
2511 Titus 3:4
2512 Philippians 3:9
2513 Psalm 51:10
2514 Colossians 3:1
2515 James 3:15
2516 Colossians 2:8

that Prophet, who kept and dressed his conversation with "Jesus Christ," says, "I know him, and keep his saying."[2517]

11. This man crucified and passed away, his body representing that accursed religious routine, means the passing away of such a routine from the living God's will and wisdom, but the resurrection of this man, being figuratively illustrated to represent the resurrection of his conversation, witnesses to the living God's counsel for our conversation, which is why it says, "If the Spirit of him that raised up Jesus from the dead dwell in you, he that raised up Christ from the dead shall also quicken your mortal bodies by his Spirit that dwelleth in you."[2518]

12. The passing away of his body, the quickening of his body by the living God, and the bringing of that body in to the *heavenly* Sanctuary, figuratively illustrates the exodus of our conversation's conscience from the religious world into the *Place* of our conversation's wellbeing, which is why we are to "have escaped the pollutions of the world through the knowledge of the Lord and Saviour Jesus Christ."[2519] Above the prescriptions of *Moses* rests the Bible's *Mind*, even our faith's higher learning engrafting that *Mind's* saying upon the heart of our conversation for the reception of the intended righteousness. This man's crucified body means the release of the conversation's rule from hand-written religious craft to own personal knowledge of the living God.

13. The living God's righteousness is experienced when reviewing the illustration drawn by that man's crucified body, that is, through examining just what the body of this man represents for the mind and character of our conversation. The living God's righteousness is within this illustration's philosophy, and this righteousness is only for the spirit of the mind, seeing as how "that which is born of the Spirit is spirit."[2520] This philosophy's righteousness is "the kingdom of God," and "flesh and blood cannot inherit the kingdom of God,"[2521] wherefore a better *body* than that *body* forwarding what is handwritten is blessed to receive salvation's praise, which is why "that which is born of the Spirit is spirit."[2522]

14. A sole demonstration of faith through the body is no longer acceptable; that would retard the entire purpose of this man's *offering*. It was necessary that this man's body find itself crucified and accursed for illustrating the complete removal of a flesh-based experience from the living God's doctrine. With legal

---

2517 John 8:55
2518 Romans 8:11
2519 2 Peter 2:20
2520 John 3:6
2521 1 Corinthians 15:50
2522 John 3:6

religious acts removed from *heaven's* discipline, the organs of the mind become the subject of *heaven's* will. Therefore this man, having figuratively blotted out handwritten ethics for all ages from salvation's commandment through his body, and being put to death with that commandment existing within the members of his mind, him, being raised from the dead, is set forth as an example of the newness to appear within the conversation liberated from the handwritten religious rule. This is why it says, "In that he died, he died unto sin once: but in that he liveth, he liveth unto God."[2523]

15. One perpetually upon a tree represents a continually accursed religious error before the living God, but the illustration of his death, and of his resurrection and high priestly ordination, leaves his conversation as the symbol of an the eternal link to *heaven's* kind will, opening up the doors of the *heavenly* Sanctuary to the mind for the service of that will.[2524] This Priest of the living God's intention is the interceding conversation of that dead Prophet where that tree, and that former *confidence* nailed to it, is not. This man, through death, left that tree behind and within the religious world. How fitting, then, that the *serpent* should claim it as its own.

16. This man's sacrifice did no thing against the spirit of the serpent within the religious age. The mission of the living God's chief apostle was to purge the serpent's philosophy from the living God's doctrine, to build a *temple* for this philosophy, to establish and govern a heavenly ministry within that *temple*, and to seal to the character of conversations the regeneration hidden within the living God's new will. This minister fulfilled his mission, and when that labor finished, the living God figuratively brought up his wisdom and conversation to his throne to oversee creation's science within his *heavenly* Temple. Hereafter every right and sincere conversation should never know the *death* associated to the serpent or the tree, but the conversation not in the *Place* where that conversation officiates will find its mind under the *dragon's* rule.

17. This man's conversation was *taken up* to administer, by its intercession, the living God's will, but on *earth*, this man, through death, left that accursed tree behind. Therefore, at a certain time, elders not blessed by salvation's knowledge, and stubbornly ignorant of its will, who falsely professed the mind within the scriptures, found their conversation's persuaded by the *serpent's* philosophy, and like that man of old, hid the accursed *thing* in their *tent*. Hereafter the saying was fulfilled, "For this cause God shall send them strong delusion, that

---

2523 Romans 6:10
2524 Hebrews 7:25

they should believe a lie: that they all might be damned who believed not the truth, but had pleasure in unrighteousness."[2525]

18. To be "damned" is to be accursed, therefore we may understand that the tree accursed of the living God had made it in to the camp of individuals who "profess that they know God; but in works they deny him, being abominable, and disobedient, and unto every good work reprobate."[2526] Thus, being accursed by what is accursed, it is only that these ministers should keep up those accursed religious practices nailed to the tree, which is why we find that "there rose up certain of the sect of the Pharisees which believed, saying, That it was needful to circumcise them, and to command them to keep the law of Moses."[2527] What these *Pharisees* believed in was not *Jesus Christ* and the philosophy behind that crucified man, but rather the tree and the image upon it. By re-establishing what was abolished, they evince service to a contrary *mind*.

19. Herein we may understand why this sect of *believers* departed from what was originally taught.[2528] There is only one frame of mind born for subverting, and Paul, understanding that the Christian tribe was coming under attack by that disposition, wrote to their elders, "I fear, lest by any means, as the serpent beguiled Eve through his subtilty, so your minds should be corrupted from the simplicity that is in Christ."[2529] When we observe priests and elders advocating handwritten religious laws and traditions, we may understand that they have, within their camp, that accused and condemned tree; "they should believe a lie: that they all might be damned who believed not the truth, but had pleasure in unrighteousness."[2530]

20. Herein we are made to understand that what is "damned" or accursed is "unrighteous," and that "unrighteousness" is in mishandling and misinterpreting the living God's *voice* through what is accursed. This is easily understood from how it says, "All unrighteousness is sin,"[2531] that "sin" of "unrighteousness" being defined according to how it says, "The strength of sin is the law."[2532] It is then impossible that what is accursed should bless the conversation's mind, and we understand that it does not from how them that professed belief on the

---

2525 2 Thessalonians 2:11,12
2526 Titus 1:16
2527 Acts 15:5
2528 Acts 15:24
2529 2 Corinthians 11:3
2530 2 Thessalonians 2:11,12
2531 1 John 5:17
2532 1 Corinthians15:56

name of *God's Man* absolutely conducted their conversation by what that man's body has figuratively abolished. The mind attached to that accursed tree will develop spiritual plague within it, moving it to put a religious burden on it and on them around it.

21. What good is that tree to the conversation professing deliverance by the body of that Prophet? There are herein two different doctrines of deliverance given us: the first, that "Christ hath redeemed us from the curse of the law, being made a curse for us";[2533] the second being that "brasen serpent that Moses had made."[2534] This man's crucified body preaches the doing away of handwritten commandments and doctrines from the living God's doctrine. The man's crucified flesh, because it means the annihilation of a handwritten conversation, means the hope of a regeneration conversation, or the birth of a new conversation to the living God, which is why this man did not figuratively remain dead, but was brought up to the living God.

22. If this man's conversation stayed asleep, we would have no fit example of salvation's new will, and if his conversation had not passed away to find itself regenerated, we would not know the liberty secured to us by his wisdom's resurrection and priestly mediation. By this man is preached deliverance from the spiritual errors within the religious world to own a living devotional experience under the instruction of his conversation, but that other manner of *deliverance* through the tree is lame, involving no right thing for the mind or for the devotional character, encouraging the conversation in what avoids *heaven's* manner of righteousness.

23. This other *deliverance* preaches that "righteousness come by the law,"[2535] for the serpent has turned salvation's doctrine upside down. If the religious law is accursed,[2536] and yet *righteousness* is preached as coming from handwritten charges and ordinances, then blatant transgression occurs. There is only one that seeks to pervert the living God's commandment, and when we observe *houses* bearing that tree as an emblem, we may know that the character of the *serpent* rules their conversation.

24. There is therefore no better image for this spirit of error to use than that tree, for it makes open mockery of the *Mind* at the core of the scriptures.[2537] Herein we may understand just what our repentance towards the living God

---

2533 Galatians 3:13
2534 2 Kings 18:4
2535 Galatians 2:21
2536 Galatians 3:13
2537 Hebrews 6:6

should be, even repentance from false manners of worship and service. The only way for us to understand our wrong is to consent to the education of the new covenant, which is the sanctification of our conversation through discerning the intention of that present promise. The mind, by the reign of that Prophet's wisdom and conversation within it, is to be personally handled, convincing its heart of its need to reform.

25. We today face the same predicament that the *garden's* pair faced: will we take of life's right *tree* and eat, or will we eat from that *tree* of contrary *wisdom*? This tree of life owns such a title because it was once accursed, but upon its regeneration, it can never know *death* any more, being "made unto us wisdom, and righteousness, and sanctification, and redemption."[2538] *Life's* tree is in service to "the law of the Spirit of life,"[2539] wherefore by consuming of its fruit, devotional newness and resurrection is perpetually imparted.

26. But that *tree* of *good and evil* devotional knowledge is contrary to *life's tree*, for within it is a mind that, although framed after the living God, is yet accursed of the living God. This *tree* is corrupt, and "having a form of godliness, but denying the power thereof,"[2540] it, when it only imparts perpetual *death* to "the eyes of your understanding,"[2541] deceives its adherent to trust in its *saving* ability. Herein we are made to understand that the ministers of the *serpent* are indeed contrary to *heaven's* philosophy, for by owning a conversation wholly condemned of the living God, it is that they forward a religion of no real and living benefit.

27. Must a blessing come from what is accursed? Must *righteousness* come from unrighteousness? What conversation can reverse what the living God has accursed? All that the *serpent* can do is beguile the mind, and he did and continues to do so, working through them "who changed the truth of God into a lie, and worshipped and served the creature more than the Creator."[2542]

2538 1 Corinthians 1:30
2539 Romans 8:2
2540 2 Timothy 3:5
2541 Ephesians 1:18
2542 Romans 1:25

31

That Life To Now Live By

1. By the high priestly mediation of that Prophet's conversation, our conversation has a very real hope to know. By the passing away and the regeneration of his conversation, the example of a benevolent conversation devoted the living God's will and wisdom, to self, and to other minds, is clearly revealed. There is no clearer revelation of the intention behind this consecrated conversation's ministry than how it says, "The Word was made flesh,"[2543] for by passing through faith's higher education, every conversation is to confess, "The life which I now live in the flesh I live by the faith of the Son of God."[2544]

2. To hear of the Word being made flesh is to hear that "the life was manifested,"[2545] and for that *Life* to find itself manifested in and by *flesh*, it is that the conversation openly reflects the Wisdom and the Philosophy of the consecrated conversation. The Word made flesh is the living God's philosophy operating within the heart of the personal devotional conversation, leaving the conscience

---

2543   John 1:14
2544   Galatians 2:20
2545   1 John 1:2

of the conversation free to "live by the faith of the Son of God,"[2546] or free to find its self governed by "the knowledge of the Son of God."[2547]

3. Paul's counsel and confession is very plain. If the conversation is to find its self owning the philosophy and the conversation of the living God's chief apostle, then it is that the conversation is to find its self intelligently operated. Such an intelligent confidence is obtained by mentally discerning just what that Prophet's philosophy is. The conversation's constitution must find its self conformed to this man's devotional understanding, and because "that which is born of the Spirit is spirit,"[2548] his *voice* is strictly "spiritually discerned."[2549]

4. It would make no sense for an entirely mental and inward experience to find itself forwarded by a flesh-based religious tradition, yet the living God, for a limited time, sanctioned such an order under the old covenant. The former manner was ordained to provoke temporal blessing by devoutly adhering to commandments and ordinances. Under the old manner, the conversation hoping to obtain the promised blessing must faithfully do every handwritten prescription, which is why they were told, upon their compliance, "The LORD shall command the blessing upon thee in thy storehouses, and in all that thou settest thine hand unto; and he shall bless thee in the land which the LORD thy God giveth thee."[2550] This league between the *LORD* and ancient Israel was simple: "Do my requisite commandments and you will only know blessing." Not only should their temporal welfare find itself perpetually secure, but by applying to the commandment, they would comprehend the power of faith, that it was not their physical labor that procured blessing, but that it was their active confidence on the blessing to appear that gave them *God's smile*.

5. It took faith to believe that a physical act should bless not just the temporal world, but also the spiritual. It took faith to believe that their *God*; seeing as how "God is a Spirit";[2551] should return spiritual and secular blessings from physical acts. Through the old will, the people were to learn of faith's cleansing, that "he taketh not pleasure in the legs of a man,"[2552] but that "without faith it is impossible to please him."[2553] So then why not simply ratify faith's

---

2546   Galatians 2:20
2547   Ephesians 4:13
2548   John 3:6
2549   1 Corinthians 2:14
2550   Deuteronomy 28:8
2551   John 4:24
2552   Psalm 147:10
2553   Hebrews 11:6

course instead of counseling, by a faithless routine, on the faith to come? Why implement laws and judgments to burden faith's revelation instead of simply pronouncing a right conversation to this people? "Wherefore then serveth the law? It was added because of transgressions."[2554]

6. This people, after four hundred years under Egyptian lore, had lost the ancient faith of their *fathers*, which faith was established upon "the righteousness of faith."[2555] Having mingled the ancient *garden's* philosophy with Egypt's pagan religious tradition, this people, instead of faith, turned to idols and superstitious traditions. The law of Moses was implemented to correct religious error against the *LORD's* character, which character *His* finger engraved onto two tables of stones. Because the human being is slow to learn, is afraid of change, and is naturally ignorant of self and of the living God's *voice*, a carnal service was imposed on them for the purpose of blessing their understanding and returning them to the sober conversation of their fathers.

7. Abram's conversation knew no handwritten religious tradition. This man's conversation was simple; if the *LORD* spoke, he took the commandment, mentally examined it, and then carried it out, which is why the *LORD* says, "Abraham obeyed my voice, and kept my charge, my commandments, my statutes, and my laws."[2556] For, what superstitious tradition could this man subscribe to when told, "Get thee out of thy country, and from thy kindred, and from thy father's house"?[2557] This man's father did subscribe to the popular form of devotion. After the flood, the formerly popular religion resurrected, and in Abraham's day, although many of Noah's line professed Shem's conversation, there were many among Shem's assembly that honored that false religion of "the flood in old time, even Te'rah, the father of Abraham, and the father of Na'chor."[2558]

8. The *LORD* called this man out of his *family's* religious tradition in to a land unfamiliar to his conversation and for the reward of a promise not yet evident.[2559] The *LORD* spoke the commandment and this *man* obeyed, relying on no *thing* or no one to fulfill that commandment for him, keeping the commandment with its promise in his mind and simply moving forward. Herein

---

2554 Galatians 3:19
2555 Romans 4:13
2556 Genesis 26:5
2557 Genesis 12:1
2558 Joshua 24:2
2559 Hebrews 11:8

is the reason why the *LORD* promised him, "I will bless thee, and make thy name great; and thou shalt be a blessing."[2560]

9. For Abraham's obedience, the living God blessed his name, that through his *name*, every one sincerely desirous to honor his *name* would find themselves blessed by the same blessing that kept his conversation's character safe. For this cause, it is well to know how the living God blesses, and to where this blessing is sent, and it says, "I will pour my spirit upon thy seed, and my blessing upon thine offspring,"[2561] and, "I will pour out my spirit unto you, I will make known my words unto you."[2562]

10. Because of his faith on the *LORD's* promise, the *LORD* not only blessed his conversation's mind, but also his conversation's *name*, for before the new covenant found itself ratified, the living God opened up its ministry to Abraham's understanding. Because "God is a Spirit,"[2563] only the inward parts can ultimately find themselves cared for by the living God, for whether it is today or in Abraham's day, we are "to be strengthened with might by his Spirit in the inner man."[2564] Abraham had the only conversation in his age that rightly honored the ancient *garden's* philosophy, and for his obedience, he was given a sign of faith signifying the baptism of his mind, even the act of circumcision.

11. Circumcision appeared after faith and not before faith. Circumcision didn't mean that he was blessed of the *LORD*, but that he had been already blessed of the LORD. His circumcision, then, because obedience is mental, was within the spirit of his mind before it took place in his flesh. Thus, for mentally keeping and dressing his conversation with a spiritual promise, Abraham was blessed "with the knowledge of his will in all wisdom and spiritual understanding,"[2565] and if we today keep his *name*, we too will share in the same refreshing. This is why it says, "Christ hath redeemed us from the curse of the law...that the blessing of Abraham might come."[2566]

12. It is herein well to remember, with this man's *name* coming under a blessing, how it is written, "Thou blessest, O LORD, and it shall be blessed for

---

2560 Genesis 12:2
2561 Isaiah 44:3
2562 Proverbs 1:23
2563 John 4:24
2564 Ephesians 3:16
2565 Colossians 1:9
2566 Galatians 3:13,14

ever,"[2567] and, "He hath blessed; and I cannot reverse it."[2568] No matter what should afterwards appear from *men*, the living God's commandment stands, for, although he sanctioned Moses' handwritten laws, these commandments and judgments should not disrupt the blessing already existing on Abraham's *name*. "That faith of our father Abraham"[2569] continued alongside the old covenant, for even though this people received a religious bill to follow, it was still their responsibility, that they may act it out by faith, to mentally discern the commandment.

13. Abraham's *name* is defined as an educational course by an experimental faith; the *name* of Abraham is the exercising of faith for knowledge of the living God's manner of righteousness. So long as this people took what Moses gave them and mentally discerned that charge, the blessing fallen upon Abraham would find itself fallen upon them; like Abraham, they would have heard, by rightly examining *God's* voice, how it was told them, "My doctrine shall drop as the rain."[2570] Spirit can only commune with spirit, wherefore this people, to keep their conversations subject to his will, should have spiritually comprehended the living God's words. It is then no surprise that they not only failed to subject self to the former will, but also that they perverted it by defining it with sayings of their own. Because they would not learn faith, they did not continue in that covenant and were removed from their *LORD's* presence.

14. Thus, for the conversation to confess, "The life which I now live in the flesh I live by the faith of the Son of God,"[2571] it is a very great confession to make. There is a reason why the living God's chief apostle "took on him the seed of Abraham"[2572] and passed away with a conversation under that government: if he did not, then our conversation would find its conscience unlawfully bound to handwritten sayings and ordinances. For, circumcision, after Abraham's age, represented the standard of a tradition, but when was he blessed, "in circumcision, or in uncircumcision? Not in circumcision, but in uncircumcision."[2573] The Bible did this to educate us on how unnecessary a scripted tradition is to the intention of salvation's science.

2567   1 Chronicles 16:27
2568   Numbers 23:20
2569   Romans 4:12
2570   Deuteronomy 32:2
2571   Colossians 2:20
2572   Hebrews 2:16
2573   Romans 4:10

15. To find the flesh circumcised is to find the person within the *LORD's* assembly by circumcision. The person, through circumcision, is automatically become *blessed* of *God*, for by this act, they are fallen into the line of a tradition supposedly *blessed* by *God*. But Abraham received the effect of righteousness when uncircumcised, when without the religious tradition, confirming to us the saying, "This is the will of God, even your sanctification."[2574] Whether circumcised or uncircumcised; whether baptized into a religious tradition or not; nothing matters to the living God but our diligent obedience to *voice* at the core of the scriptures. Faith's right learning is without handwritten religious tradition, being held entirely to the mind, which is why his faithful say, "With the mind I myself serve the law of God."[2575]

16. Herein we may understand why the living God's chief apostle told this people, "If ye were Abraham's children, ye would do the works of Abraham."[2576] This people did not properly digest the Creator's devotional philosophy, but instead added on to that *voice* a legal ethic for honoring that *voice*, which is why he told them, "Full well ye reject the commandment of God, that ye may keep your own tradition."[2577] Rejecting God's commandment; because "God is a Spirit";[2578] requires mental and spiritual negligence, doing contrary to the counsel, "Be ye transformed by the renewing of your mind,"[2579] and, "Be renewed in the spirit of your mind."[2580] Because a commandment is not physical or tangible, all rejection first appears within the mental faculties before the limbs and members of the body are activated. By failing to investigate the living God's voice, this people failed to receive the promised blessing to appear by dressing the conversation with Abraham's *name*, which blessing is knowledge of the Creator's philosophical will and wisdom for the inward person.

17. Had this people honored Abraham's course of learning, they would not have only recognized the living God's chief apostle, but they would have accepted his conversation. But for their spiritual negligence, this man said of them, "Had ye believed Moses, ye would have believed me: for he wrote of me. But if ye believe not his writings, how shall ye believe my words?"[2581] Herein we

2574 1 Thessalonians 4:3
2575 Romans 7:25
2576 John 8:39
2577 Mark 7:9
2578 John 4:24
2579 Romans 12:2
2580 Ephesians 4:23
2581 John 5:46

are made to understand that "belief" appears by spending brainpower on the living God's sayings. If we are not personally acquainting our heart with the philosophy within those sayings, then in what can we have faith in?

18. The answer is found in the serpent, and there is a reason why the living God moved John to note the serpent as being "that old serpent."[2582] The use of the word "old" connotes a former or old manner of worship and service, for, when the living God "saith, A new covenant, he hath made the first old."[2583] It is then no surprise to see the serpent acknowledged as "old," for his brand of religion follows after the old or former covenant, which testament has, by the passing and regenerating conversation of the living God's chief apostle, become accursed.

19. The serpent's religion will deceive its adherent to regulate their conversation by formerly abolished religious manners. The serpent's religion is without faith's exercise, wherefore it is well to know that "whatsoever is not of faith is sin,"[2584] and that "the law is not of faith."[2585] With that Prophet on that tree "blotting out the handwriting of ordinances"[2586] not only for his age, but for every age thereafter, and "nailing it to his cross,"[2587] every law of a religious tradition fashioned by any *Moses* hereafter becomes abominable to salvation's discipline. This man on the tree is an illustration of what "sin" today is categorized as, and because every the handwritten law is without faith, and because "sin" is found in what is without faith, it is plain that "the strength of sin is the law."[2588] By subscribing to "philosophy and vain deceit, after the tradition of men, after the rudiments of the world,"[2589] we corrupt and belittle this man's act, making a mockery of the new covenant will.

20. The serpent is that old serpent because its religion must do contrary to the living God's *name*; according to the serpent, when the scriptures "saith, A new covenant,"[2590] they are lying. It is the mission of the serpent's philosophy to convince its adherent that "death" will not appear by what the living God has accursed, and seeing as how it says, "He that is hanged is accursed of God,"[2591]

2582 Revelation 12:9
2583 Hebrews 8:13
2584 Romans 14:23
2585 Galatians 3:12
2586 Colossians 2:14
2587 Colossians 2:14
2588 1 Corinthians 15:56
2589 Colossians 2:8
2590 Hebrews 8:13
2591 Deuteronomy 21:23

that tree, having nailed to it a condemned devotional character, according to the serpent, has not found itself accursed. This is absolutely foolish logic, for isn't it written, "He whom thou blessest is blessed, and he whom thou cursest is cursed"?[2592] And isn't it written, "Christ hath redeemed us from the curse of the law, being made a curse for us: for it is written, Cursed is every one that hangeth on a tree"?[2593]

21. Can we see the subtle craft of this contrary philosophy? The living God plainly curses that will and conversation on the tree. That *body* on the tree is absolutely accursed: there is no blessing in any *thing* nailed to it. To honor this tree and that *body* on it is to unquestionably honor "sin" and religious error. This *figure*, as *it* hangs on the tree, represents a conversation bound to handwritten religious laws, and being dead on this tree, and having given up the *ghost* on this tree, represents a conversation that is eternally passed away from the living God's discipline. What hangs on this tree is accursed because it lacks faith's right service for righteousness' effect, wherefore because "whatsoever is not of faith is sin,"[2594] if our conversation would honor what is today acknowledged as "sin," it too is become just as accursed as what it is subject to.

22. The curse that the body of the living God's chief apostle figuratively inherited cannot be reversed, which is why it is was necessary to not only bring his conversation up from *death*, but to also appointed it over salvation's science. Today, this conversation is not on a tree, but is rather "a merciful and faithful high priest in things pertaining to God"[2595] "that died, yea rather, that is risen again, who is even at the right hand of God, who also maketh intercession for us."[2596] This man is no longer figuratively nailed to that tree, and this symbolizing that what that tree has nailed to it is without the living God's will and wisdom. Thus, we understand that the Word is not made flesh within our conversation, and that the life of that ascended and consecrated conversation does not keep and dress our conversation's conscience, by our subjection to that old serpent's philosophy, which tradition we know we care for when a *tree* is become the sign of our *circumcision*.

23. This tree has nailed to it an accursed religious standard. With that Prophet's conversation no longer on it, but alive and holding office before the living God; as it says, "An high priest, who is set on the right hand of the throne

---

2592 Numbers 22:6
2593 Galatians 3:13
2594 Romans 14:23
2595 Hebrews 2:17
2596 Romans 8:34

of the Majesty";[2597] what this tree has nailed to it is today become irrelevant: the tree and its philosophy is cursed, but the blessing on Abraham's *name* yet remains. If Abraham's *name* is passed away, the living God need not bring up that conversation to himself, for then faith's exercise is become acceptable by sensual practices. But since this man "took on him the seed of Abraham,"[2598] his conversation removed from the tree and brought up to the living God speaks to reveal that mental discernment for spiritual wisdom rules the living God's present philosophical dominion, cancelling every other manner to *bless* the conversation.

24. The aim of the reign of the living God's wisdom by his chief apostle's conversation is for the doer of that commandment to experience mental and inward revival and reform. The Word, or the new covenant's philosophy, is to find itself swallowing up the conversation's constitution to create within it a mind liberated from dead religious works, which lame service this man figuratively abolished by his passing. This intention is halted by subscribing to that old serpent, for what blessing can appear by what is accused? It is the serpent's intention to pervert the new covenant will and promise, and it is no marvel that his *philosophy* should magnify what the living God has accursed.

25. This tree, this cross, it is no symbol of salvation, but its illustration is captured in the saying, "God forbid that I should glory, save in the cross of our Lord Jesus Christ, by whom the world is crucified unto me, and I unto the world."[2599] How odd, then, is it to observe the symbol of a conversation passing away from the religious world's spiritual ethics, made to ultimately draw the person back in to that vanity? Crucifixion from legal religious tradition is the end of the vision of the living God's chief apostle suffering that tree, so then how is it that a handwritten religion is formed around such a vision? The serpent's religion is a combination of good and evil, for, while representing resurrection from the religious world, his religion bounds the conversation to the religious world, omitting the *Place* every resurrected conversation should ascend to, which is why it says of this contrary *wisdom*, "That opened not the house of his prisoners".[2600]

26. By focusing his religion on the tree; even as he did of old in Eden; the serpent's conversation keeps the heart on *earth*, never comprehending that, by

---

2597   Hebrews 8:1
2598   Hebrews 2:16
2599   Galatians 6:14
2600   Isaiah 14:17

the living God not only bringing up that man's conversation from *death*, but also consecrating it as that Governor over his will, they are to "have escaped the pollutions of the world through the knowledge of the Lord and Saviour Jesus Christ."[2601] The *serpent's* dwelling is within the religious world, for this superstition is the religious world's illness. The living God condemned this craft by nailing it to that tree, which is why it says of that man's passing, "Through death he might destroy him that had the power of death, that is, the devil; and deliver them who through fear of death were all their lifetime subject to bondage."[2602]

27. This man's sacrificed conversation represents a wound to "death" and to *death's* "bondage" or service, and since this *death* is to "the eyes of your understanding,"[2603] by this sacrifice, it is purposed that the Bible's present wisdom "purge your conscience from dead works to serve the living God."[2604] Fear or respect for all "bondage under the elements of the world"[2605] comes to an end by the refreshing of the spirit of the mind, which is why "that which is born of the Spirit is spirit,"[2606] and why "of his own will begat he us with the word of truth."[2607] If it is that we soberly accept the revelation of this man's sacrifice, it is that our mind, to quit religious error against *heaven's* discipline, is become subject to that new will and wisdom. We therefore understand that we fail to do salvation's will and wisdom when our conversation honors an old and accursed manner of devotion.

28. Today, the present righteousness is experienced by mentally and spiritually learning of the living God's intention, to live it. Of old, *righteousness* existed only in name and by handwritten religious commandments and ordinances, which labor "could not make him that did the service perfect, as pertaining to the conscience."[2608] Because "God" is Spirit, it is the living God's intention to beautify the spirit of our faith's mind by its service to the new covenant law of creation. The mind is to honor the *Wisdom* at the core of the scriptures, even as Abraham did.[2609] If our conversation is without faith's higher learning for

---

2601 2 Peter 2:20
2602 Hebrews 2:14,15
2603 Ephesians 1:18
2604 Hebrews 9:14
2605 Galatians 4:3
2606 John 3:6
2607 James 1:18
2608 Hebrews 9:9
2609 Romans 7:25; Romans 1:9

the development of our conversation's organs, then it is that we honor what that tree has nailed to it, which is a flesh-based religious conversation existing without faith's exercise for knowledge of the Creator's *name*, and "whatsoever is not of faith is sin."[2610]

29. Because "the law is not of faith,"[2611] it had to go. If they had honored Abraham's mind, and if we today are continuing in Abraham's *name*, it will be understood that such carnal ordinances were "added because of transgressions, till the seed should come to whom the promise was made."[2612] Thus, by honoring what is accursed, and by hailing that tree as a *blessing* to the conversation, we actually confess that we still look for a *Savior*, and indeed have found him, being beguiled, even as of old Israel worshipped "the brasen serpent that Moses had made."[2613]

30. The living God's Word is to exist within our *flesh's* constitution, or within our conversation's conscience; not that lore of the *serpent*. By acting out a conversation entirely *blessed* by the serpent's curse, do we honor the Word? In the beginning "the Word was with God, and the Word was God";[2614] the Word is still "God." "The Word of life"[2615] is "the Spirit of life from God,"[2616] and to hear that the Word was made flesh, it is to hear one confessing, "The law of the Spirit of life in Christ Jesus hath made me free from the law of sin and death,"[2617] which is why Paul writes, "The life which I now live in the flesh I live by the faith of the Son of God."[2618] If it is that this Word, who is the living God's Philosophy, is the "God" of our conversation, which "God" is also the law of devotional creation, is manifest and continues within the spirit of our conversation, it is that our conversation is passed away from relying on what is scripted and handwritten to own a conversation free from religious error.

31. This is why our right offering to the living God, that "he might sanctify and cleanse it with the washing of water by the word, that he might present it to himself a glorious church, not having spot, or wrinkle, or any such thing; but that it should be holy and without blemish,"[2619] is the spirit of our faith's

---

2610 Romans 14:23
2611 Galatians 3:12
2612 Galatians 3:19
2613 2 Kings 18:4
2614 John 1:1
2615 1 John 1:1
2616 Revelation 11:11
2617 Romans 8:2
2618 Galatians 2:20
2619 Ephesians 5:26,27

mind. We evince our confidence on the *name* of the living God's chief apostle by advancing in his conversation's mediating law of creation, but we express our unbelief and spiritual negligence by upholding a conversation through what his sacrifice perpetually denounces, "even the law of commandments contained in ordinances."[2620] This is why it says, "The strength of sin is the law."[2621]

2620 Ephesians 2:15
2621 1 Corinthians 15:56

32

He Will Forgive And Cleanse

1. Truly "the blood of Jesus Christ his Son cleanseth us from all sin."[2622] Now, that "sin," due to the illustration of that Prophet suffering the tree, is clearly defined as a continuance in "the handwriting of ordinances,"[2623] "even the law of commandments contained in ordinances."[2624]

2. A right acceptance of reconciliation's *blood* therefore means our conversation removing from a false manner of worship and service. "Whatsoever is not of faith is sin,"[2625] and because "the law is not of faith,"[2626] right reverence towards the living God's chief apostle is witnessed by our conversation passing away from the ignorance of the religious law to "seek those things which are above, where Christ sitteth on the right hand of God."[2627] We understand that we possess a *risen* conversation when found with a heart and mind removed from religious error against the Bible's present will and knowledge.[2628]

2622 1 John 1:7
2623 Colossians 2:14
2624 Ephesians 2:15
2625 Romans 14:23
2626 Galatians 3:12
2627 Colossians 3:1
2628 2 Peter 2:20

3. Today, we have a discipline apart from our former religious understanding opened up to our conversation, wherefore it is necessary to drink reconciliation's *blood* to receive perpetual entrance into creation's science. When hearing of "blood," it is well to remember that, before his ordeal, "his sweat was as it were great drops of blood."[2629] His "blood" is his "sweat," and to drink his "sweat" is to bear the cross or trial of his conversation. It is to say, "I may know him, and the power of his resurrection, and the fellowship of his sufferings, being made conformable unto his death."[2630]

4. Because our human and our devotional illness is mental; as it says, "Alienated and enemies in your mind";[2631] we must understand that our redemption or deliverance is inward. It is this man's "sweat" that removes our mind from sacrificing the *eyes* of our conversation to an accursed religious practice. From how he conducted himself during the hour of his hardship, his actions are our example "that we, being dead to sins, should live unto righteousness."[2632]

5. We who care to pass through the course of his sweat, to own the same righteousness by an exercised faith on the intention of that righteousness, are instructed, "Through the Spirit wait for the hope of righteousness by faith."[2633] In his hour of trial, he beat back the impulse to please himself by the Wisdom that lived within his mind. Instead of honoring his natural will, he consecrated himself to the will of the Creator at the expense of his self. The lesson preached is a lesson pointing to the possession of self for right service to the living God's will. The fact that he, by passing through faith's higher learning, possessed self to the praise of the Creator's character, witnesses to the fact that we who also pass through the same experience will abandon natural religious impulse to our conversation's constitution in subjection to that mind conceived by that same Wisdom. This is why it says, "That which is born of the Spirit is spirit."[2634]

6. The living God's Prophet, in this scene of distress, perfectly displays the new covenant's will. If he did not say, "I know him, and keep his saying,"[2635] then he would have performed a contrary will. Herein is witnessed Adam's curse come under the instruction of a benevolent law, for by him rejecting the temptation to quit the *LORD's* commandment, he reveals *creation's* ultimate intention, which

---

2629 Luke 22:44
2630 Philippians 3:10
2631 Colossians 1:21
2632 1 Peter 2:24
2633 Galatians 5:5
2634 John 3:6
2635 John 8:55

intention is the redemption of the inward parts to wholeheartedly love the living God's *voice*, "and this is love, that we walk after his commandments."[2636]

7. This man expresses love to the living God by the fact that he fully honored his will, and this he did by no accident, and also by no spiritual concoction, for he only kept salvation's saying. Seeing as how "of his own will begat he us with the word of truth,"[2637] it is that this man learned and executed the living God's wisdom to experience the intended righteousness, which righteousness is according to the prayer, "Create in me a clean heart, O God; and renew a right spirit within me."[2638] Thus, to "know him, and the power of his resurrection, and the fellowship of his sufferings, being made conformable unto his death,"[2639] is to "live according to God in the spirit,"[2640] examining his *voice* to obtain right principles to keep and dress the conversation with. Therefore, the minister may say that his "blood" purifies, but in reality it is that "through knowledge shall the just be delivered."[2641]

8. That accursed tree today represents "sin" and "death." "Having abolished in his flesh the enmity, even the law of commandments contained in ordinances,"[2642] "blotting out the handwriting of ordinances"[2643] "after the tradition of men, after the rudiments of the world,"[2644] it is that *heaven's* discipline is ordained to purify the mind from a false religious ideology, namely the saying, "It shall be our righteousness, if we observe to do all these commandments."[2645] The former covenant pronounced *righteousness* by doing a handwritten tradition, wherefore it was believed that *blessing* and *favor* appeared by simply doing a charge, when such a charge is naturally without faith, and "whatsoever is not of faith is sin."[2646]

9. "Sin," according to the scriptures, is primarily the handwritten religious ordinance. The illustration of this Prophet on that tree; because "he that is hanged is accursed of God";[2647] teaches that "Christ hath redeemed us from the

---

2636 2 John 1:6
2637 James 1:18
2638 Psalm 51:10
2639 Philippians 3:10
2640 1 Peter 4:6
2641 Proverbs 11:9
2642 Ephesians 2:15
2643 Colossians 2:14
2644 Colossians 2:8
2645 Deuteronomy 6:25
2646 Romans 14:23
2647 Deuteronomy 21:23

curse of the law, being made a curse for us: for it is written, Cursed is every one that hangeth on a tree."[2648] Through this man's suffering, so that we may have our understanding regenerated and reformed from former manners of worship and service, a course encouraging devotional recovery is freely opened up to us. To receive this promise, it is that his "blood" or his "sweat," or the knowledge of his faith's training and learning, must be experienced.

10. Should we take right faith on his sacrifice to accept his conversation's wisdom, we are promised, "Whosoever believeth in him should not perish, but have everlasting life."[2649] It is crucial to the development of our faith's character that we comprehend just what this means. To "perish" is not to literally fade away, but it says, "That which decayeth and waxeth old is ready to vanish away."[2650] The conversation subscribing to what is "old" in manner will perish and pass away, and because the psalmist prays, "Lighten mine eyes, lest I sleep the sleep of death,"[2651] we may know that this perishing is within the *eyes*, even "the eyes of your understanding."[2652]

11. Because it is our spiritual understanding that should perish by practicing old religious standards, we must understand that the "eternal life" that is promised is for the *eyes* of our understanding. Belief on the *name* of the living God's chief apostle procures "eternal life" to the "eyes," and seeing as how the psalmist prays for light to his eyes that he may escape "death," it is well to understand that "the law is light."[2653] Our understanding must examine and prove "the law of the Spirit of life,"[2654] "rightly dividing the word of truth"[2655] for wisdom to act out. By handling the Bible's *voice*, knowledge of its intention will sanctify the mind for the good of the conversation's conscience. Belief is not born without knowledge verified to the mind, which is why we are counseled, "Handle me, and see."[2656]

12. Our mind needs help if it should do contrary to its natural inclination. There is a promise of "everlasting life" for eating and drinking the doctrine and the experience of the Bible's knowledge because it is "the grace of God

2648 Galatians 3:13
2649 John 3:16
2650 Hebrews 8:13
2651 Psalm 13:3
2652 Ephesians 1:18
2653 Proverbs 6:23
2654 Romans 8:2
2655 2 Timothy 2:15
2656 Luke 24:39

that bringeth salvation."[2657] "The Spirit is life"[2658] because it gives "the grace of life,"[2659] and because this is that "eternal Spirit,"[2660] through the offered conversation of that Prophet, "that eternal life, which was with the Father,"[2661] is shared with our conversation.

13. Grace is the living God's creative power. It is this creative substance entered in to our mind that encourages our thoughts to "press toward the mark for the prize of the high calling of God in Christ Jesus,"[2662] "forgetting those things which are behind, and reaching forth unto those things which are before."[2663] What is behind us are handwritten religious standards and requirements, but what is before us is the creation of a new mind of devotion, "therefore if any man be in Christ, he is a new creature: old things are passed away; behold, all things are become new."[2664] Again, what is passed away are old religious manners concerning devotional rightness. The new *creature*, by honoring salvation's Wisdom by the spirit of the mind, understands that "the darkness is past."[2665] What is become "past" are those practices that did "serve unto the example and shadow of heavenly things,"[2666] "which stood only in meats and drinks, and divers washings, and carnal ordinances, imposed on them until the time of reformation."[2667]

14. We today live in the time of our conversation's reformation, where that former approach to *God* was but "a figure for the time then present, in which were offered both gifts and sacrifices, that could not make him that did the service perfect, as pertaining to the conscience."[2668] Yet today the living God has provided a better sacrifice for a better consolation with better promises for a better purification under a better covenant. At this time, "the darkness is past, and the true light now shineth,"[2669] for the passing away of this man's body means the blotting out a theory of *righteousness* to ratify the fact of righteous-

---

2657 Titus 2:11
2658 Romans 8:10
2659 1 Peter 3:7
2660 Hebrews 9:14
2661 1 John 1:2
2662 Philippians 3:14
2663 Philippians 3:13
2664 2 Corinthians 5:17
2665 1 John 2:8
2666 Hebrews 8:5
2667 Hebrews 9:9
2668 Hebrews 9:9; Hebrews 10L1,2
2669 1 John 2:8

ness, that "by the deeds of the law there shall no flesh be justified in his sight,[2670] and that "the Spirit is life because of righteousness."[2671] With the sin and error of what is handwritten abolished, the deeds of legal religious ethics are taken out of the way of *heaven's* will. Acts of the human body by any law of a religious tradition are accursed by this man's dead body; "now the righteousness of God without the law is manifested."[2672]

15. That which stood as a representative of the course of learning to appear is to be put away, for "before faith came, we were kept under the law, shut up unto the faith which should afterwards be revealed."[2673] Now, if the living God's will is today not only revealed, but is also forwarded by the wisdom and conversation of that Prophet, this means that no conversation rightly honoring the living God is bound to any handwritten ordinance. With that Prophet's conversation manifested, there is a change in order, which is why we are counseled, "The true worshippers shall worship the Father in spirit and in truth."[2674]

16. Seeing how it says, "Thy word is truth,"[2675] and, "Thy law is the truth,"[2676] and, "Sanctify them through thy truth,"[2677] the prayer of the living God's chief apostle is for the condition of our conversation. By allowing salvation's law to purify the spirit of our understanding, "The law of the Spirit of life in Christ Jesus hath made me free from the law of sin and death,"[2678] we will confess. By diligently bringing the full "law of Christ"[2679] in to our conversation's conscience; which law is "the word of righteousness";[2680] our spiritual understanding is to find itself so matured that we need no prescription to maintain our confidence, which is why creation's law is also known as "the doctrine which is according to godliness."[2681]

17. Herein we are, according to the Bible, made to understand the definition of "godliness," that "godliness" is a conversation without sin and religious error against the new covenant philosophy. By learning of and doing this philosophy's

---

2670   Romans 3:20
2671   Romans 8:10
2672   Romans 3:21
2673   Galatians 3:23
2674   John 4:23
2675   John 17:17
2676   Psalm 119:142
2677   John 17:17
2678   Romans 8:2
2679   Galatians 6:2
2680   Hebrews 5:13
2681   1 Timothy 6:3

will, the conversation is to find itself wholly consecrated to its Word or Wisdom. Godliness is maintaining a benevolent conversation to self and to the mind in sight of that Wisdom without entertaining that old religious standard. It is now our righteousness to do and to experience this philosophy's intention within our inward person. This is why it says, "Every one that doeth righteousness is born of him."[2682]

18. Now, if "of his own will begat he us with the word of truth,"[2683] and if "every one that doeth righteousness is born of him,"[2684] and if "he that doeth the will of God abideth for ever,"[2685] then it is evident that the living God's righteousness is without handwritten religious ordinances. Righteousness must be experienced in order for one to know it, and this *birth*, because it is by the living God's saying, is only for the spirit of the mind, seeing as how "that which is born of the Spirit is spirit."[2686]

19. The flesh does not rule in the spirit's realm. No act accomplished by the body can procure the knowledge or the grace to the mind that diligent mental examination can bless the conversation with; by handling the living God's *name*, the heart has material to prove, and grace is blessed to it for every experiment conducted by faith. We need grace's substance to forward creation, and grace is not given without knowledge, and knowledge is not acquired without exercising faith on the new covenant's commandment. We therefore find handwritten religious tradition canceled out "by the law of faith."[2687]

20. If we are doers of reconciliation's experience, we will understand why our "acknowledging of the truth which is after godliness"[2688] is so important. It is the knowledge of the wisdom contained within the conversation of the living God's chief apostle that recovers our understanding from sin, or rather, from all confidence on the spirit of every *Moses*. If we are doers salvation's law, it is that our understanding will find itself put to death for a resurrection, for it is written, "By his knowledge shall my righteous servant justify many."[2689]

2682   1 John 2:29
2683   James 1:18
2684   1 John 2:29
2685   1 John 2:17
2686   John 3:6
2687   Romans 3:26
2688   Titus 1:1
2689   Isaiah 53:11

21. The knowledge of this Prophet working within the inward parts is "the doctrine which is according to godliness."[2690] It is then evident that the Bible would have the conversation honor the living God by the law of this new covenant understanding, which is why it says, "Unto me every knee shall bow, every tongue shall swear."[2691] This labor was prophesied to occur through words, even like as it says, "The isles shall wait for his law,"[2692] which is why the present season of devotional reformation demands that we are "strengthened with might by his Spirit in the inner man."[2693] Thus, seeing as how a law is not physical, salvation's law exists within the person by the spending of brainpower on its wisdom, which is why it says of the faithful, "In his law doth he meditate day and night."[2694] Today, it is the reformer's primary responsibility to learn of and do this wisdom above a handwritten bill, for by taking knowledge of its will, right love will swallow up the conversation's conscience, "and this is love, that we walk after his commandments."[2695]

22. "We have received a commandment from the Father"[2696] for godliness through the offered conversation of his chief apostle. We understand we keep the living God's commandments by our involvement with this man's doctrine, for "he that saith, I know him, and keepeth not his commandments, is a liar, and the truth is not in him."[2697] We fail to honor creation's covenant because we fail to allow the goodness of salvation's law to work within our inward parts.[2698] That which is become filthy and excessively disobedient is what is nailed to that tree, which is why the apostle says to lay such a mind apart from the conversation, becoming doers of the Word's righteousness.

23. We understand our discipline has been by the living God's will by our moving away from that former mind existing under the first covenant to honor the counsel, "Worship God in the spirit."[2699] Our failure to not only forget such an accursed routine, but to maintain confidence in it, witnesses to the fact that our conversation is a sinning conversation; the conversation nailed to and remaining on that tree is categorized as "sin." The sinning conversation, then,

---

2690 1 Timothy 6:3
2691 Isaiah 45:23
2692 Isaiah 42:4
2693 Ephesians 3:16
2694 Psalm 1:2
2695 John 1:6
2696 2 John 1:4
2697 1 John 2:4
2698 James 1:21,22
2699 Philippians 3:3

is one that will not bring salvation's saying in to the mind for "knowledge of his will in all wisdom and spiritual understanding."[2700] The sinning conversation will not hear the counsel, "Make you a new heart and a new spirit."[2701]

24. If it is that we are today upholding a conversation by the handwritten religious bill, and if it is that we today care to learn of and receive the living God's righteousness, all is well, for "whatsoever God doeth, it shall be for ever: nothing can be put to it, nor any thing taken from it."[2702] Because we are naturally wrong, and will always be innately erroneous devotionally, the offering of this man's conversation is sure for every age; it is an everlasting consolation. The passing and the regeneration of the spirit of this man's conversation preaches repentance from adhering to handwritten religious policies and pardon from having entertained such a conversation. The heavenly ministry of his conversation is for the purification of our understanding so that we might come to rightly honor the living God. A right and sober acceptance of this conversation's ministry is one confessing to the conscience the conversation's error in obtaining righteousness, for by upholding a personal religion "exceedingly zealous of the traditions"[2703] "after the commandments and doctrines of men,"[2704] and finding self properly before him on the tree, it is that the conscience will wound the heart, calling the spirit of the mind into a conference to right the wrong committed against salvation's Wisdom.

25. Herein the heart is made sorry for its ignorance, and this sorrow is good for the mind. This type of disappointment moves the person to quit the performance of wrong, causing the mind to carefully examine the Bible's *voice* for alleviation. This experience can never find itself accomplished by what is nailed to that tree, which is why it is right to "live according to God in the spirit."[2705]

26. The conversation of the living God's Prophet was sacrificed for every conversation, and because this is the work of the living God's mind, the sanctification promised by that conversation's mediation is open for ever. This man sacrificed his own conversation so that we may know what sin is, and that same conversation was revived so that we might know what course of learning remains for our devotional confidence. Every conversation, when conceived within the religious world, is therefore naturally sinning against salvation's

---

2700   Colossians 1:9
2701   Ezekiel 18:31
2702   Ecclesiastes 3:14
2703   Galatians 1:14
2704   Colossians 2:22
2705   1 Peter 4:6

higher learning, for by adhering to manners accursed of *heaven's* will, our practice is contrary to what is right.

27. The aim of salvation's commandment is not to unlawfully criticize or to cruelly demean us for our innocent misunderstanding, but to heal our conversation. His chief apostle may have opened up creation's higher education to us, but it is our responsibility to learn of that discipline, to do it. The illustration of his suffering teaches us that sanctification's right course of learning is open to every conversation,[2706] yet if we adhere to what is now an old devotional approach, it is that we do not acknowledge his contribution to salvation's discipline and are therefore become violators of the new covenant's doctrine.

2706 Hebrews 9:17

33

Our Purging From Thorns

1. The illustration of the living God's chief apostle on the tree and then in the living God's direct presence preaches repentance and newness from an accursed devotional character. This illustration, also forwarding a lesson of perpetual forgiveness for upholding a conversation by that accursed devotional mind to learn right reform through the instruction of this same man's philosophy, further shows how we may understand that it is not of the living God to sanction or encourage any religious bill written by elders and ministers. By "blotting out the handwriting of ordinances"[2707] from every *Moses* for ever, and "nailing it to his cross,"[2708] "having abolished in his flesh the enmity, even the law of commandments contained in ordinances,"[2709] it is that every right conversation of *creation's* science should confess, "With me it is a very small thing that I should be judged of you, or of man's judgment: yea, I judge not mine own self."[2710]

2707 Colossians 2:14
2708 Colossians 2:14
2709 Ephesians 2:15
2710 1 Corinthians 4:3

2. Paul denounced the judgments and commandments of elders over his conversation, warning them to quit such a desire and habit because this form of religion had passed away through the slain body of the living God's chief apostle. This is why it says, "Why is my liberty judged of another man's conscience?"[2711] Him on that tree, according to the scriptures, symbolizes the crucifixion of handwritten religious laws and judgments. This is why Paul, when observing certain elders performing what had been abolished, counseled, "If I build again the things which I destroyed, I make myself a transgressor."[2712]

3. By picking up what the scriptures have condemned and blotted out, we admit that we are not wrong and that it is the liar. This man on that tree is a symbol of what *sin* and *death* is. His flesh represents the handwritten law of a religious tradition, and the passing away of that flesh is the passing away the conversation from relying on such a devotional practice. If it were not wrong to honor salvation's course by such flesh-based craft, then he need not find himself upon a tree,[2713] but since "God is a Spirit,"[2714] and since "a spirit hath not flesh and bones,"[2715] because "flesh and blood cannot inherit the kingdom of God,"[2716] the living God must bless that other *body*.[2717]

4. Because "that which is born of the Spirit is spirit,"[2718] and because the living God's righteousness is wholly ordained for the spirit of the mind, handwritten ordinances and commandments cannot now, nor could they ever, suffice for learning of and experiencing "the kindness and love of God our Saviour toward man."[2719] Even though ancient Israel was given a legal religious standard to follow, they were still required to do Abraham's labor, which was an active practice initiated by the conversion of the mind by exercising faith on the commandment. Israel never learned that an intelligent faith procures blessing. Thus, by relying upon the flesh, they perverted salvation's first intention.

2711 1 Corinthians 10:29
2712 Galatians 2:18
2713 Galatians 3:21
2714 John 4:24
2715 Luke 24:39
2716 1 Corinthians 15:50
2717 1 Corinthians 15:44
2718 John 3:6
2719 Titus 3:4

5. The *LORD's* manner of righteousness never appeared by handwritten statutes and judgments; such laws cannot, of themselves, reach into the inward parts to heal the conscience. The doer's conversation oddly found itself content and satisfied by simply keeping and acting out a handwritten tradition, but not the mind. The conversation; by the handwritten ordinance; found itself to be *righteous* due to the stimulus given to it by the religious routine, but not the mind. And even while these things existed and were permitted, they encroached upon the liberty of the mind to think and to do for itself, the religious law burdening the blessing secured to Abraham's *name*.

6. The blessing of this man's *name* is righteousness appropriated to the mind by searching after and living by knowledge found when meditating on the Creator's voice, but if by simply doing what is handwritten I am *righteous* and am performing *righteousness*, then I need not exert my mind, for the written ordinance has disturbed the *LORD's right intention*, overtaking that intention. This is why Paul says, "Sin, taking occasion by the commandment, wrought in me all manner of concupiscence."[2720] "Sin" is in taking the traditional commandment to be a sign of *righteousness* for the living God's blessing, and in so doing, leads the person away from salvation's inward intention to bind its *voice* by routine and unnecessary obligations with expectations, increasing religious error against its will, which in turn injures the inward person.

7. Righteousness is an inward work of creation only forwarded by an experimental faith on the new covenant's commandment.[2721] To devotionally maintain what is presently accursed is to confess that we are not spiritually erroneous, even though by this man's offered and regenerated conversation we are proven to be wrong in thought and in feeling. Salvation's righteousness is a course of learning whereby *Adam's* inward parts are made to accept subjection to its creative law, and this is truly a great and mysterious work, seeing as how "the carnal mind is enmity against God: for it is not subject to the law of God, neither indeed can be."[2722]

8. What holds enmity against the Word's righteousness is that condemned "enmity, even the law of commandments contained in ordinances."[2723]

2720 Romans 7:8
2721 2 John 1:4
2722 Romans 8:7
2723 Ephesians 2:14

Instead of bringing "the law of the Spirit of life"[2724] into the organs of the mind, a handwritten religious bill is forwarded to obtain a theoretical end of that course without passing through that course, and such a carnal mind and conversation is what is nailed to the tree. The living God's chief apostle removed every bill from every professed *Moses* from out of the way of salvation's science, wherefore it is well to understand that "whatsoever God doeth, it shall be for ever: nothing can be put to it, nor any thing taken from it."[2725] There is no resurrection for what is nailed to that tree, but the resurrection of the conversation found on that tree is a witness that "if ye through the Spirit do mortify the deeds of the body, ye shall live."[2726]

9. With the mind subject to salvation's law, death to such former practices will occur to assist in understanding *creation's* present intention. What halts the living God's righteousness is any *thing* that does not encourage the mind and body to intelligently exercise and experiment with faith; "whatsoever is not of faith is sin,"[2727] and "the law is not of faith."[2728] Therefore, by subscribing to the handwritten religious law, we are in fact become spiritually negligent violators of the new covenant science at the heart of the scriptures.

10. The handwritten religious law strips the mind from the conversation by making the creator of that law the conscience of the conversation, when in reality we are to "live according to God in the spirit."[2729] Understanding that the Word is God, and that God is Spirit, the mind is to find itself completely regulated by the law of the Word.[2730] The mind, free from scripted religious chains, is to find its conversation conceived to a new and more benevolent estate to honor the Creator by that wisdom within his chief apostle's conversation. With the mind rightly examining that Word or Wisdom, with the heart entirely consecrated to its *voice*, the person will find their conversation's conscience fellowshipping with its knowledge to learn *heaven's* right manner. Having nailed former religious ignorance to that tree, it is that every conversation risen with his mind, when doing his wisdom, will kill those religious deeds by the knowledge obtained.

2724 Romans 8:2
2725 Ecclesiastes 3:14
2726 Romans 8:13
2727 Romans 14:23
2728 Galatians 3:12
2729 1 Peter 4:6
2730 James 1:18

11. The deeds of the faith's *body* are represented by him upon that tree, and when it says, "He said, It is finished: and he bowed his head, and gave up the ghost,"[2731] it is an indicator that those deeds have passed away from that *body* of the religious conversation so that *body* can know a new mind of understanding. This is why it says, "When we were in the flesh, the motions of sins, which were by the law, did work in our members to bring forth fruit unto death. But now we are delivered from the law, that being dead wherein we were held; that we should serve in newness of spirit, and not in the oldness of the letter."[2732]

12. The "letter," or the handwritten religious bill of a tradition, is a motion of sin and religious error to the Bible's mind, doing no right thing for the conversation but only sensually pleasing it. Hereafter, by this man's offered and regenerated conversation, it is now advised, "Put off concerning the former conversation the old man...and be renewed in the spirit of your mind; and that ye put on the new man, which after God is created."[2733]

13. The living God's new will is for the regeneration of the human and the devotional mind, but that former will, peddled through a handwritten religious tradition, deceives the person to believe that they are a creature of the Spirit by doing scripted commandments. Being an instrument of flesh created for and ordained by flesh, there is no life-giving power within the decree that is handwritten by flesh. Such ordinances removed the mind from the living God's intention, deceiving the heart to fear the handwritten order above faith's right course.

14. For this cause it is written, "As the children are partakers of flesh and blood, he also himself likewise took part of the same; that through death he might destroy him that had the power of death, that is, the devil; and deliver them who through fear of death were all their lifetime subject to bondage."[2734]

15. This man could not find himself partaking of any other *fleshly* order, for if "a testament is of force after men are dead,"[2735] then this man, if owning a carnal or sensual fashion within his flesh, could not enforce the living God's new will. Because Adam's conversation found itself compromised by a certain *confusion* working within it, it is necessary that this man's conversation find itself alleviated from the *confusion* working within it, and not only alleviated,

---

2731   John 19:30
2732   Romans 7:5,6
2733   Ephesians 4:22-24
2734   Hebrews 2:14,15
2735   Hebrews 9:17

but sacrificed in that alleviated condition so that like "as by one man sin entered into the world, and death by sin,"[2736] and like "as by the offence of one judgment came upon all men to condemnation; even so by the righteousness of one the free gift came upon all men unto justification of life."[2737]

16. This man's passing on the tree represents a passing away from an old mind of devotion, but the illustration of this same man resurrected witnesses to the fact of a religious conversation entirely devoted to the Mind at the core of the scriptures without any flesh-based chain upon the conversation. This man, being offered with a conversation owning creation's new covenant will, it is that the mind of our devotion should pass away from the rule of religious ministers to accept the rule of the living God's wisdom. This is fair to conclude because before he passed away on that tree, he said, "Father, into thy hands I commend my spirit: and having said thus, he gave up the ghost."[2738]

17. Blessed revelation! The ghost of dead legal commandments and ordinances is passed away, but what remains without corruption in the Creator's hands is the character of that man's mind. The flesh of the man; which is an illustration of the religious deeds of his conversation and the *ghost* within that practice; may have perished, but he found *himself* quickened by the spirit of his mind. Herein we are made to understand just what sin and religious error is, for by adhering to what has no ghost, we too are become ones owning a conversation without life, "but if ye through the Spirit do mortify the deeds of the body, ye shall live. For as many as are led by the Spirit of God, they are the sons of God."[2739]

18. We may clearly understand the steward of salvation's science by their resurrection from "philosophy and vain deceit, after the tradition of men, after the rudiments of the world,"[2740] to own the saying, "The law of the Spirit of life in Christ Jesus hath made me free from the law of sin and death."[2741] Such a mind honors salvation's sure philosophy by the spirit of their mind through the course of that philosophy's law and judgment, saying, "God is my witness, whom I serve with my spirit in the gospel of his Son."[2742] Because the Word was and still is "God," the living God's Word or Wisdom is become the God of the

---

2736 Romans 5:12
2737 Romans 5:18
2738 Luke 23:46
2739 Romans 8:13,14
2740 Colossians 2:8
2741 Romans 8:2
2742 Romans 1:9

conversation, which is why "the Spirit itself beareth witness with our spirit, that we are the children of God."[2743]

19. As student-patients of this Wisdom, our conversation is therefore without the error and practice of handwritten laws and doctrines, for like as how it says, "In that he died, he died unto sin once: but in that he liveth, he liveth unto God,"[2744] so too we who are doers of salvation's law are sanctified by it to receive a new heart and mind solely devoted to its truth. Now, as it says, "Thy word is truth,"[2745] and, "Thy law is the truth,"[2746] creation's science cannot commence unless "through sanctification of the Spirit and belief of the truth."[2747] This allows us to understand that no handwritten commandment can bless the conversation with *heaven's* intended refreshing, for if we are to believe truth, and if it says, concerning belief's right work, "If ye believe not his writings, how shall ye believe my words?"[2748] it is an indisputable fact that right belief takes place by mentally examining the Bible's words.

20. These former priests confronting the living God's chief apostle clearly failed to faithfully investigate the scriptures; they couldn't understand that before Abraham's *name* existed, the *name* of "I am" only existed."[2749] Taking the handwritten tradition of elders to be the *LORD's* righteousness, they passed over faith's knowledgeable learning, moving the living God's chief witness to say of them, "Ye tithe mint and rue and all manner of herbs, and pass over judgment and the love of God: these ought ye to have done, and not to leave the other undone."[2750] The Word's judgment is the Word's love, which benevolence is the living God's righteousness, which righteousness cannot commence if not firstly brought into the organs of the mind.

21. Truth must be done, and because this truth is not physical, no fleshly charge can admit its benefit within the inward parts. For, "he that doeth truth cometh to the light, that his deeds may be made manifest,"[2751] seeing as how "all things that are reproved are made manifest by the light: for whatsoever

---

2743 Romans 8:16
2744 Romans 6:10
2745 John 17:17
2746 Psalm 119:142
2747 2 Thessalonians 2:13
2748 John 5:47
2749 John 8:58
2750 Luke 11:42
2751 John 3:21

doth make manifest is light."[2752] Because "God is light"[2753] and "the law is light,"[2754] and because "the Word of life"[2755] is "the Spirit of life,"[2756] the *Spirit's* law is that light correcting our personal devotional conversation on right devotional, educational, and dietary manners. The end of salvation's law is the manifestation of and correction from erroneous deeds concerning worship and service, which deeds are hidden by a subjected routine under the handwritten commandment.

22. The Creator's promise to our conversation is, "From all your filthiness, and from all your idols, will I cleanse you. A new heart also will I give you, and a new spirit will I put within you,"[2757] and, "I will put my spirit within you, and cause you to walk in my statutes, and ye shall keep my judgments, and do them."[2758] This *Mind* within the character of our conversation is defined as, "I have filled him with the spirit of God, in wisdom, and in understanding, and in knowledge,"[2759] and, "I will pour out my spirit unto you, I will make known my words unto you."[2760] This new covenant will is for filling our mind "with the knowledge of his will in all wisdom and spiritual understanding,"[2761] and this cannot occur if the mind is resisting faith's higher learning. We therefore show forth our rejection of the new covenant's promise and intention by our adhering to former religious manners.

23. The spirit of our mind, if we should ever think to receive the living God's will, must "be strengthened with might by his Spirit in the inner man."[2762] Concerning what the inner man must have within it, it says, "I am full of power by the spirit of the LORD, and of judgment, and of might,"[2763] and, "My spirit that is upon thee, and my words which I have put in thy mouth."[2764]

2752 Ephesians 5:13
2753 1 John 1:5
2754 Proverbs 6:23
2755 1 John 1:1
2756 Revelation 11:11
2757 Ezekiel 36:25,26
2758 Ezekiel 36:27
2759 Exodus 31:3
2760 Proverbs 1:23
2761 Colossians 1:9
2762 Ephesians 3:16
2763 Micah 3:8
2764 Isaiah 59:21

24. The inward parts must have within them the words of the new covenant's judgment. The living God's chief apostle informs us of what that judgment is by saying, prior to passing away, "Father, into thy hands I commend my spirit."[2765]

25. The offering of his conversation did not put salvation's commandment within any conversation. His offering only bound the conversation's constitution, the organs of the mind, and the member of the heart, to *heaven's* course of learning to receive the end of that discipline. By the death, resurrection, and high priestly consecration of his conversation, the opening up of the *heavenly* Sanctuary for the revival and the reform of our conversation is preached; whether or not the person allows their conversation to pass into this *Building* rests entirely on the person.

26. If the conversation's faith and character should find itself passed away from the religious world and into salvation's Temple, isn't it that to us "Christ our passover is sacrificed for us"?[2766] This man's mind, by his conversation's death, resurrection, and priestly appointment, ratified to our conversation a discipline for passing over in to creation's *heavenly* Building, and if "Christ" is come in to our flesh's mind, or is come into our conversation's character to deliver the deeds of that *body* from an accursed practice, it is well to remember that "though we have known Christ after the flesh, yet now henceforth know we him no more."[2767]

27. What passes our thoughts in to *heaven's* Sanctuary to care for *heaven's* will is "the Lord Jesus Christ our Saviour,"[2768] which Savior is, in reality, because this passage is mental and occurs inwardly, "the commandment of God our Saviour."[2769] Because man's error is inward, we cannot expect deliverance to occur in any other place than our mental, moral, and devotional faculties. This is why it says, "If the Spirit of him that raised up Jesus from the dead dwell in you, he that raised up Christ from the dead shall also quicken your mortal bodies by his Spirit that dwelleth in you."[2770]

28. What must be quickened are those *elements* within the conversation influencing the limbs of the human being. The only right way to recover the human being from emptiness is to reform the mind of that human being's devotional conversation. That reformation cannot commence if not through the

---

2765 Luke 23:46
2766 1 Corinthians 5:7
2767 2 Corinthians 5:16
2768 Titus 1:4
2769 Titus 1:3
2770 Romans 8:11

spirit of the mind,[2771] which is why it says, "Through knowledge shall the just be delivered."[2772]

29. To adhere to handwritten policies is to do contrary to creation's new will, for, if the heart is blessed through understanding, yet I, through a religious bill am *blessed*, then through the bill I am *delivered* from human *violence*. As a result of obtaining a blessing by this means, because no handwritten religious charge can alleviate the flesh's mind, the injurious condition of the flesh is further magnified within the person, thwarting salvation's intention due to the pride and the liberty found in that handwritten commandment. This is why it says of the Bible's words, "They are life unto those that find them, and health to all their flesh."[2773]

30. If the *name* of the living God's chief apostle is become our sacrifice for quitting old religious manners to inherit a new and benevolent conversation, it is that the *voice* of his conversation's intercession must purify our understanding, which is why he said, "Now ye are clean through the word which I have spoken unto you."[2774] This counsel allows us to comprehend that since cleanliness is now from words, and that words are not physical, a right conversation receives right learning "not in the words which man's wisdom teacheth, but which the Holy Ghost teacheth; comparing spiritual things with spiritual."[2775]

31. This man on the tree represents human religious wisdom and judgment over the living God's law or commandment of righteousness, and with him on that tree and passed away, we learn why it says, "By the deeds of the law there shall no flesh be justified in his sight: for by the law is the knowledge of sin. But now the righteousness of God without the law is manifested."[2776] He is figuratively set forth as an example for passing away from the accursed manners of the religious world in to the manners found within *heaven's* Sanctuary, and if the commandment of his conversation's mediation is become the God of our conversation, we too will pass away from traditional religious dominion, saying, "He that judgeth me is the Lord."[2777] Blessed revelation! By keeping the mind on salvation's commandment, patiently and temperately examining its *voice*,

2771 Ephesians 4:23; Colossians 3:10
2772 Proverbs 11:9
2773 Proverbs 4:22
2774 John 15:3
2775 1 Corinthians 2:12
2776 Romans 3:20,21
2777 1 Corinthians 4:4

"the Lord Jesus Christ our Saviour";[2778] which Savior is "the doctrine of God our Saviour";[2779] will govern our faith's conscience to the praise of the Bible's *Mind*, and of that Wisdom's Creator.

32. If the Bible, by its Word and Wisdom, has accursed that *body* on the tree to death; because "Christ hath redeemed us from the curse of the law, being made a curse for us";[2780] when hearing a doctrine contrary to its speech, it is well to understand that "this wisdom descendeth not from above, but is earthly, sensual, devilish."[2781] A doctrine forwarding justness through what is handwritten is encouraged by the Bible's ultimate enemy mentality.[2782] This we understand from how it says, "The soldiers platted a crown of thorns, and put it on his head."[2783]

33. The "thorn" here mentioned should not be thought of literally. When describing pagan people, it was anciently said, "They shall be snares and traps unto you, and scourges in your sides, and thorns in your eyes,"[2784] and, "They shall be as thorns in your sides, and their gods shall be a snare unto you."[2785] When we observe a crown of thorns upon the man's head, because "the head of Christ is God,"[2786] and because "God" is the Word, it is that we are made to observe the fact that the Word, or the living God's Wisdom, should find itself surrounded by priests that "profess that they know God; but in works they deny him, being abominable, and disobedient, and unto every good work reprobate."[2787]

34. The "thorns" of the crown are as the *stars* of the crown of that woman John beheld in vision, and concerning the definition of a "star," it says, "The seven stars are the angels of the seven churches."[2788] An "angel" is a teacher of *heaven's* will and science, and to find a crown of thorns placed upon the man's head, it is to have prophesied to us a vision of *teachers* owning a contrary mind and mocking the living God's Wisdom. Thus, when observing this man on that tree wearing a crown of thorns, the illustration is but of a revelation concerning

---

2778 Tutus 1:4
2779 Titus 2:10
2780 Galatians 3:13
2781 James 3:15
2782 Philippians 3:18,19
2783 John 19:2
2784 Joshua 23:13
2785 Judges 2:3
2786 1 Corinthians 11:3
2787 Titus 1:16
2788 Revelation 1:20

a religion forwarded by unsanctified priests honoring a contrary religious philosophy by what is accursed on that tree. Therefore when writing in "Greek, and Latin, and Hebrew, THIS IS THE KING OF THE JEWS,"[2789] a foreshadowing of an erroneous religious world and denomination is preached to us.

35. The denomination of these *elders* professedly honoring *the Word* while bound to Greek and Roman paganism will find its understanding articulated by *thorns*. These *thorns*, because "that which beareth thorns and briers is rejected, and is nigh unto cursing,"[2790] are those elders cast out of the living God's assembly because they admit an accursed religious philosophy into their fellowship.[2791] Thus, being removed from the *heavenly* Sanctuary's culture and doctrine, these ministers are confined to *earth*, wherein it is fulfilled, "The great dragon was cast out, that old serpent, called the Devil, and Satan, which deceiveth the whole world: he was cast out into the earth, and his angels were cast out with him."[2792]

36. It is then no marvel why this host should honor that accursed tree, for being confined to that *tree* of good and evil, their kingdom or denomination should find itself preaching "the brasen serpent that Moses had made,"[2793] "and the superscription of his accusation was written over, THE KING OF THE JEWS."[2794] Herein is portrayed to us a very wrong religious tradition forwarded by the instruction of *thorns*, which dominion by priests and elders witnesses to the fact that they have rejected the living God's right intention. Thorns surrounding the living God's philosophy speak to reveal a handwritten religious tradition "ordained by angels in the hand of a mediator,"[2795] which acts are outlawed and abolished by that *ghost* passing away from the man when crucified.

37. Thus, the serpent would beguile the conversation to handle what is nailed to the tree, convincing it that what is crucified is for *salvation* and *righteousness*, but the sight of thorns upon this man's head is a warning for our conversation to handle its self with care.[2796] These *thorns* are lewd ministers endorsing an accursed religious standard as no accursed *thing*. The religion of

---

2789   Luke 23:38
2790   Hebrews 6:8
2791   Colossians 2:14
2792   Revelation 12:9
2793   2 Kings 18:4
2794   Mark 15:26
2795   Galatians 3:19
2796   Proverbs 4:14-16

these elders is not that understanding taught by the initial apostles, but is the invention of ministers that walked away from the living God.[2797]

38. The vision of this crown of thorns upon the head of the living God's chief apostle reveals a religion in direct conflict with that promise within the *heavenly* Sanctuary, which is why it says, "Let us keep the feast, not with old leaven, neither with the leaven of malice and wickedness; but with the unleavened bread of sincerity and truth."[2798] By forwarding a religion with old manners now acknowledged as sinful to the living God's intention, these *elders* reveal their intercourse with a contrary *wisdom*. There is no right *thing* on that accursed tree, and by forming a handwritten religious tradition around what is nailed to that *tree*, it is evident that such priests, and adherents to their persuasion, are "subverted, and sinneth, being condemned."[2799]

2797 1 John 2:19
2798 1 Corinthians 5:8
2799 Titus 3:11